The Politics of Smallness in Modern Europe

The Politics of Smallness in Modern Europe

Size, Identity and International Relations since 1800

Edited by
Samuël Kruizinga

BLOOMSBURY ACADEMIC
LONDON • NEW YORK • OXFORD • NEW DELHI • SYDNEY

BLOOMSBURY ACADEMIC
Bloomsbury Publishing Plc
50 Bedford Square, London, WC1B 3DP, UK
1385 Broadway, New York, NY 10018, USA
29 Earlsfort Terrace, Dublin 2, Ireland

BLOOMSBURY, BLOOMSBURY ACADEMIC and the Diana logo
are trademarks of Bloomsbury Publishing Plc

First published in Great Britain 2022
Paperback edition first published 2024

Copyright © Samuël Kruizinga, 2022

Samuël Kruizinga has asserted their right under the Copyright, Designs
and Patents Act, 1988, to be identified as Editor of this work.

For legal purposes the Acknowledgements on p. x constitute an
extension of this copyright page.

Cover image: The Divine Creator endowed all the animals with their
own ways of defending themselves: giant tusks, a mighty beak, piercing
claws. But the small fox terrier was not satisfied with what was given,
and armed himself as the larger creatures did.
Cartoon by Johan Braakensiek in De Amsterdammer, 7 April 1912.

All rights reserved. No part of this publication may be reproduced or transmitted
in any form or by any means, electronic or mechanical, including photocopying,
recording, or any information storage or retrieval system, without prior
permission in writing from the publishers.

Bloomsbury Publishing Plc does not have any control over, or responsibility for,
any third-party websites referred to or in this book. All internet addresses given
in this book were correct at the time of going to press. The author and publisher
regret any inconvenience caused if addresses have changed or sites have
ceased to exist, but can accept no responsibility for any such changes.

Every effort has been made to trace copyright holders and to obtain their
permissions for the use of copyright material. The publisher apologizes for any
errors or omissions and would be grateful if notified of any corrections that
should be incorporated in future reprints or editions of this book.

A catalogue record for this book is available from the British Library.

A catalog record for this book is available from the Library of Congress.

ISBN: HB: 978-1-3501-6888-6
PB: 978-1-3502-9991-7
ePDF: 978-1-3501-6889-3
eBook: 978-1-3501-6890-9

Typeset by Integra Software Services Pvt. Ltd.

To find out more about our authors and books visit www.bloomsbury.com
and sign up for our newsletters.

Contents

List of Illustrations	vi
Notes on Contributors	vii
Acknowledgements	x
Acronyms and Abbreviations	xi
Introduction *Samuël Kruizinga*	1
1 Belittling Spain. Hispanophobia and the mirror of greatness *Yolanda Rodríguez Pérez*	15
2 Dealing with smallness in Habsburg Bohemia, Ottoman Albania and Tsarist Georgia in the late nineteenth and early twentieth centuries *Adrian Brisku*	35
3 Smallness and the East-West binary in nationalism studies. Belgium and Romania in the long nineteenth century *Raul Carstocea and Maarten Van Ginderachter*	55
4 'Poor Little Belgium'. Food aid and the image of Belgian victimhood in the United States *Marjet Brolsma and Samuël Kruizinga*	73
5 Science, health and American money. Small state strategies in interwar Czechoslovakia and Denmark *Elisabeth Van Meer, Casper Andersen and Ludvig Goldschmidt Pedersen*	97
6 Neutral news. Forging a small states' transnational media network, 1914–40 *Vincent Kuitenbrouwer*	115
7 'Whoever says that Serbia is small is lying!' Serbia, ontological (in)security and the unbearable smallness of being *Christian Axboe Nielsen*	133
8 Iceland's smallness. Acceptance or denial? *Baldur Thorhallsson and Guðmundur Hálfdanarson*	151
9 Great Britain and Little Ireland. Reimagining British and Irish relations in BIPA, Brexit and beyond *Sara Dybris McQuaid*	167
10 From David to Goliath? The question of size in Israel's identity politics *Alexei Tsinovoi*	185
Conclusions *Samuël Kruizinga and Karen Gram-Skjoldager*	205
Bibliography	214
Index	240

Illustrations

1.1	Victorious America teaching Spain a lesson in the ways of civilization following the end of the Spanish-American War, 1898	16
1.2	Spain as crown of Europe and Christianity, 1570	21
2.1	Naughty Boys in School, or the Sacrificing of the Empire, 1899	38
2.2	Alimony, 1914	45
2.3	Facing a Strange Judgement	47
3.1	Country Scene	66
4.1	Food ship for Belgium, 1915–16	79
4.2	Have you done your bit for Belgium?	84
4.3	Belgium: The Kingdom of Grief	89
5.1	Small, but our own, 1938–39	102
5.2	European Scientists Honours Copenhagen Jubilee University, 1929	107
6.1	Radio Kootwijk	119
6.2	The ANP telex office in 1949	127
7.1	Die Weltwoche, 2001	143
8.1	A real puzzle?	155
8.2	A view from the centre of Reykjavík, 1900	157
9.1	UK's flag removed from the European Council building in Brussels on Brexit Day, 2020	174
9.2	A 'hard border' down the Irish sea	180
10.1	An Israeli soldier on the cover of *Life* magazine, 1967	189
10.2	A Palestinian protester faces an Israeli tank, 2000	198

Contributors

Casper Andersen is Associate Professor of Philosophy and History of Ideas at Aarhus University. His research focuses on the history of ideas, science and technology in imperial and global contexts, with particular emphases on decolonization-era Africa and Denmark. His English-language work has appeared in leading journals such as *Technology & Culture, Isis, Canadian Journal of African Studies, History & Anthropology, Transactions of the Institute of British Geographers*, amongst others.

Adrian Brisku is Associate Professor at the Institute of International Studies at Charles University, Prague, and Senior Post-Doctoral Fellow (Grantee of the Austrian Science Fund, FWF) at the University of Vienna. His research interests include modern European identity, politico-economic thought, reform and empire in the Balkans, the South Caucasus and nineteenth-century Ottoman and Russian political history. His latest publications include *Political Reform in the Ottoman and Russian Empires: A Comparative Approach*.

Marjet Brolsma is Lecturer of European Cultural History at the Institute for European Studies of the University of Amsterdam. She specializes in the cultural history of the First World War and the Interwar period. Her English-language work has been published, inter alia, in *Journal of European Periodical Studies*.

Raul Carstocea is Lecturer in Modern European History at the University of Leicester. He has previously held research positions at the European Centre for Minority Issues in Flensburg and at the Imre Kértesz Kolleg of the Friedrich Schiller University in Jena. His research interests focus on the intellectual, cultural and conceptual history of Central and Eastern Europe in the nineteenth and twentieth centuries. His latest publications include *Modern Antisemitisms in the Peripheries: Europe and Its Colonies, 1880–1945*, co-edited with Éva Kovács.

Sara Dybris McQuaid is Associate professor in British and Irish History, Society and Culture and Director for the Centre for Irish Studies at Aarhus University. Her research focuses on the role of collective memory in conflict and peace processes, with a particular focus on Northern Ireland since the 1990s. Her most recent book project is *Ireland and the North* (co-edited with Fionna Barber and Heidi Hansson).

Maarten Van Ginderachter is Professor of World and Contemporary History at Antwerp University. He has also held visiting positions at Harvard University (as a Fulbright scholar), at the University of California at Berkeley (Peter Paul Rubens Chair for the History and Culture of the Low Countries) and at the University of North

Carolina at Chapel Hill. His latest publications include *The Everyday Nationalism of Workers: A Social History of Modern Belgium*.

Karen Gram-Skjoldager is Associate Professor of International History at Aarhus University. Her research interests cover Scandinavian foreign policy, interwar international organizations and diplomacy. Her most recent publications include *Organizing the World. The Emergence of International Public Administration 1920–1960* (with Haakon A. Ikonomou and Torsten Kahlert).

Guðmundur Hálfdanarson is Professor of History and Jón Sigurðsson Chair at the University of Iceland. He has published extensively on social history, the history of political ideas, the history of nationalism and the history of Iceland. His English-language work has appeared in leading journals, including *Scandinavian Journal of History*, *History of European Ideas* and *History & Memory*.

Samuël Kruizinga is Senior Lecturer and Researcher in Modern History at the University of Amsterdam. His research focuses on the entangled histories of conflict, war and international systems in nineteenth- and twentieth-century Europe. His English-language work has appeared in leading journals such as *European Review of History*, *War in History* and the *Journal of Modern European History*.

Vincent Kuitenbrouwer is Senior Lecturer History of International Relations at the University of Amsterdam. He specializes in nineteenth- and twentieth-century imperial history, and has a special interest in colonial media, particularly radio broadcasting. In recent years he published numerous articles on Dutch transnational media networks in the late colonial era and the era of decolonization.

Elisabeth Van Meer is Adjunct Professor at the College of Charleston. Her research involves the international technological, cultural and political history of East Central Europe, particularly interwar Czechoslovakia. She is completing a book manuscript on *Expertise, Internationalism, and the Construction of Czechoslovakia, 1900–1948*.

Christian Axboe Nielsen is Associate Professor of History and Human Security at Aarhus University, Denmark. He has worked as an analyst at the International Criminal Tribunal for the Former Yugoslavia, and has appeared as an expert witness in international and domestic criminal and civil cases. His latest book is *Yugoslavia and Political Assassinations. The History and Legacy of Tito's Campaign against the Emigrés*.

Ludvig Goldschmidt Pedersen is a PhD student at the University of Aarhus. He is currently finishing his dissertation about the role and development of economics at the Danish civil service as evidenced by the role of statistics, models and new ideas of bureaucratic expertise.

Yolanda Rodríguez Pérez is Associate Professor in European Studies at the University of Amsterdam. She specializes in Spanish-Dutch-Anglo relations and cultural exchanges in the early modern period and beyond, with a focus on the intersection between literature and ideology, nation-building processes, imagology and translation studies. Her most recent publications include *Literary Hispanophobia and Hispanophilia in Britain and the Low Countries (1550–1850)*.

Baldur Thorhallsson is Professor in Political Science, Jean Monnet Chair in European Studies and Research Director of the Centre for Small State Studies at the University of Iceland. His research areas are primarily small state studies, European integration, Icelandic politics and Iceland's foreign policy. He has written numerous books and articles on small states, most recently *Iceland's Shelter-Seeking Behavior: From Settlement to Republic*.

Alexei Tsinovoi is a Postdoctoral researcher at the Department of Political Science of the University of Copenhagen. His research focuses on the role of communication technologies in international relations and his postdoctoral research project, funded by the Carlsberg Foundation, examines the role of new media technologies in the remediation of the Israeli-Palestinian conflict. His work has appeared in leading journals such as *European Journal and International Relations, Journal of International Relations and Development, First Monday,* amongst others.

Acknowledgements

This book project, naturally, started out small. In 2015, I was asked to contribute to a class on the history of international relations (IR). I originally set out to teach on various ways in which the Netherlands' international politics had been framed as either the result of long-standing cultural predispositions or of quasi-unmovable geological and geopolitical constraints. Looking for an 'angle' that might make the class a bit more exciting, I happened – more by chance than by design – on 'smallness'. I taught the class, and ended up writing an article connecting the history of international politics to political science literature on small states. Pushed by the editors of the journal to develop my argument further, I ended up writing a critique of small state literature, and argued for a re-focusing on smallness not as something essentialist, but as an attribute, connected to wider ideas of identity and belonging. After discussing these ideas with my colleagues at the University of Amsterdam, we were lucky enough to receive a grant from the Netherlands Organisation for Scientific Research (NWO) to further develop these ideas in a series of consecutive and interconnected workshops.[1] Thanks to additional funding from the Universities of Amsterdam, Aarhus and Iceland, we were able to meet several times to collectively ponder how 'smallness' (the *notion* or *belief* that a certain country is small) affects policy and identity on various levels. This not only helped us produce the individual chapters that make up this book, but also hone in on how we could most effectively apply 'smallness' as a prism to help us see and understand new things about how 'size' gave, and continues to give, shape to our world. These discussions and the collective sense of focus and mission it produced helped immeasurably in making the project a true collaboration and this book, I hope, a coherent whole. Therefore, its authors and editor owe a debt of gratitude to the NWO; the universities of Aarhus, Amsterdam and Iceland; Bloomsbury Press; and to the following colleagues who contributed in various but important ways to the workshops and/or the book: Paul Reef, Diana Panke, Anna Starkmann, Julia Guro, Pia Hansson, Tómas Joensen, Susanna Erlandsson, Rimko van der Maar, Ruud van Dijk, Karin van Leeuwen, James Gibbons, Laura Reeves, Maddie Holder, Rhodri Mogford and Suriya Rajasekar.

Note

1. Project 'Getting the Big Picture on Small States. Towards a New Research Agenda for Small State Studies, 1814–present day', NWO Internationalisation in the Humanities Grant, file no. 2017/GW/00274572.

Acronyms and Abbreviations

ANP	Algemeen Nederlands Persbureau (General Dutch Press Agency)
ANTEA	Algemeen Nieuws- en Telegraaf-Agentschap (General News and Telegraphy Agency)
AVČR	Akademie věd České republiky (Czech Academy of Sciences)
BBC	British Broadcasting Corporation
BCR	Business Cycle Research
BIPA	British Irish Parliamentary Assembly
CNN	Cable News Network
CPI	Committee on Public Information
CRB	Commission for Relief in Belgium
DNB	Deutsches Nachrichtenbüro (German Press Agency)
EEA	European Economic Area
EFTA	European Free Trade Area
EU	European Union
EU27	European Union member states minus the UK
HoL	House of Lords
ICTY	International Criminal Tribunal for the Former Yugoslavia
IDF	Tsva ha-Hagana le-Yisraʼel (Israeli Defence Force)
IHB	International Health Board
IHS	Institut for Historie og Samfundøkonomi (Institute for Economics and History)
ILO	International Labour Office
IMF	International Monetary Fund
INTERREG	Interregional Community Initiative
IR	International Relations
ISC	International Studies Conference

JNA	Jugoslovenska Narodna Armija (Yugoslav People's Army)
KITLV	Koninklijk Instituut voor Taal-, Land- en Volkenkunde (Royal Netherlands Institute of Southeast Asian and Caribbean Studies)
LEPL	Legal Entities under Public Law (Georgia)
LGBTQ	Lesbian, Gay, Bi, Trans, Queer
MLA	Member of the Legislative Assembly of Northern Ireland
MP	Member of Parliament
MSP	Member of the Scottish Parliament
NACR	Národní Archiv České Republiky (National Archives of the Czech Republic)
NATO	North Atlantic Treaty Organisation
NBDN	Nationaal Bureau voor Documentatie Nederland (Dutch National Information Service)
NDP	De Nederlandse Dagbladpers (Association of Dutch Newspapers)
NGO	Non-Government Organisation
NL-HaNA	Nationaal Archief Den Haag (Dutch National Archives, The Hague)
NSDAP	Nationalsozialistische Deutsche Arbeiterpartei (National Socialist German Workers Party)
NSF	Nederlandse Seintoestellen Fabriek (Dutch Transmitter Factory)
NWO	Nederlandse Organisatie voor Wetenschappelijk Onderzoek (Netherlands Organisation for Scientific Research)
OEEC	Organisation for European Economic Co-operation
PEACE I-IV	United Kingdom-Northern Ireland Peace Programme
PR	Public Relations
PTT	Posterijen, Telegrafie en Telefonie (Postage, Telegraphy and Telephony)
RAC	Rockefeller Archive Centre
RD	Rikarkivet (Danish National Archive)
RF	Rockefeller Foundation
RPD	Rijkspersdienst (State Press Service)
SNP	Scottish National Party
SNS	Srpska Napredna Stranka (Serbian Progressive Party)
SRS	Srpska Radikalna Stranka (Serbian Radical Party)

Acronyms and Abbreviations xiii

SSD	Social Science Division (of the RF)
SSR	Socialist Soviet Republic
SSRIP	Sociologický Ústav Akademie věd České republiky (Social Science Research Institute of the Czech Republic)
SÚ	Sociální Ústav Československé Republiky pro Studium Sociálních věd (Social Science Research Institute of Czechoslovakia)
SZÚ	Státni Zdravotní Ústav (Institute for Public Health)
TD	Teachta Dála (Member of Parliament)
U-boat	Unterseeboot (submarine)
UN	United Nations
UNSC	United Nations Security Council
US	United States (of America)
UK	United Kingdom

Introduction

Samuël Kruizinga

Size and state behaviour

Are all states equal? Theoretically, the answer is yes. Since the Peace of Westphalia (1648) formally decreed that states possessed absolute autonomy over their territory, states have increasingly been understood as sovereign entities, meaning that they allow one another the fullest degree of independence when it comes to dealing with whatever and whomever resided within their boundaries. The notion that all states deal with one another on the basis of non-interference in their internal affairs found its ultimate expression in the United Nations charter (paragraph 1, article 2), which proceeds from the principle of sovereign equality and argues that in principle, and in spite of asymmetries and inequalities in areas such as military power, geographical and population size, and levels of industrialization and economic development, states have the same international rights and duties.

But as one legal scholar perceptively noted in a 1944 article, in practice 'equality does not mean equality of duties and rights, but rather equality of capacity for duties and rights'.[1] Only under the same conditions do states have the same duties and the same rights. Of course, conditions are never the same, so in reality inequality is and always has been the general, if often unspoken, rule, simply because states are not considered equal.[2] The clearest example of this acknowledged asymmetry, perhaps, is the habitual division of states into a multitude of different categories. Developed states, for example, are commonly understood as economic and institutional success stories and thus models for developing states. In the nineteenth and early twentieth centuries, 'civilized' states were deemed to be essentially different from their 'non-civilized' counterparts – a distinction that lives on today whenever a Western and a non-Western state are juxtaposed.

Other distinctions – made by historians, political scientists, politicians and diplomats, activists and commentators – include those between strong and weak states, successful and failing or even failed states, and those amongst allies, neutrals and enemies. These labels, applied by a variety of actors for a wide array of reasons, often result in real consequences affecting the behaviour of state representatives – either because they themselves believe such labels to express an essential truth about the country they represent or because others with whom they interact do.[3]

This book is about one of the key and most common means of differentiation between states, one which has had an enormous impact on the framing of the possibilities and limitations of states' foreign policies throughout history and up through the present: size. A state's size is often seen as a predictor for its foreign policy behaviour, and therefore essential differences are often imagined to exist between 'big' and 'small' states. 'Big' suggests a 'great' power, or even a 'superpower' whose foreign policy spans continents or even the entire globe, but it also smacks of domination, overreach, even the abuse of power. 'Small', by contrast, evokes a state that is a rule-taker rather than a rule-maker, and therefore indicates a lack of power or influence in the international affairs that really matter. But it might also suggest 'nimble' or 'flexible'.

This book is about 'smallness'. It is not about whether a state *is* or *was* small but about what people thought or think a small state was or is. Even more specifically, it focuses on the effects of such an attribution, which is to say it asks what smallness does. What should a small state do or not do? What is its proper place, its appropriate behaviour? What rights and duties come with its diminutive size? To explain how we analyse 'smallness', this book will first detail how size and smallness have been understood since the late eighteenth century, and how an enduring interest in size and specifically in smallness gave birth to a specific field of scholarly activity: small state studies.

Small states in the nineteenth and twentieth centuries

Size as a key means of differentiating states entered the general European idiom in the eighteenth century. In particular, the Seven Years' War (1756–63) – arguably both the first global war and the first international conflict to spawn, almost immediately, a host of narrative commentaries and histories across Europe – was a critical moment in the separation of small from great: great powers were the active participants in the war, small powers those nations on the sidelines. These great powers – Britain, France, Russia, Prussia and Austria – were seen as superior in resources and therefore able to make war and peace, and on the basis of their strength to offer other ('lesser', 'minor') powers guarantees against attack by others.[4] During the Congress of Vienna (1814–15) following the French Revolutionary and Napoleonic Wars, the distinction between great and small powers was formalized.[5] Questions of continental and global importance were now 'le droit exclusif' of the 'Big Five'.[6] Only occasionally were representatives of certain smaller states invited to join the Great Power deliberations, and then only to discuss specific issues; others were deemed too small and summarily ignored.[7]

The Congress of Vienna also initiated another trend. As a result, chiefly, of decisions made by the Big Five, certain small states were enlarged to such a size that they became viable (junior) partners in the combined efforts to combat threats to European peace and stability. In Vienna the German kingdom of Prussia was nearly doubled in size, while a United Kingdom of the Netherlands was cobbled together from the old Dutch Republic, the Austrian Netherlands (present-day Belgium) and Luxembourg.[8] The notion that states needed to be of a certain physical size to be able to play an important role in affairs reinforced what some political commentators of the day saw as a historical trend: states either became greater or fell into obscurity, both physically and morally. Under the influence of the Social Darwinist application of biological concepts related to natural selection and survival of the fittest to international politics, in the second half of the nineteenth century German political thinkers began to protest the fragmentation of Germany into smaller political units as signposts of its decline.[9] The political commentator Ludwig August von Rochau, for example, wrote in his *Grundsätze der Realpolitik* that these small German states, impediments to the dream of a single great and united Germany, were 'the source of our historic misfortunes, our lack of power […] the maiming of our national spirit and our political irrelevance'.[10] The noted geographer and ethnographer Friedrich Ratzel, meanwhile, warned that 'small residual states form an exception to the rule that states need to grow and develop'; instead, so he believed, they had become 'fossilized'.[11] Even more famously, the historian Heinrich von Treitschke argued that small states lacked the capacity to develop a successful culture and that their disappearance would be 'an act of historical necessity'.[12] He also warned that a united Germany should not fall prey to *Kleinstaaterei*, or the inward-looking particularisms Treitschke felt were innate to smaller states.[13] This type of reasoning became increasingly popular both within and outside Germany at the close of the nineteenth century.

However, not everyone agreed that small states bred small-minded men; some even felt that small was preferable to great. These advocates grounded this view on an intellectual lineage traceable to classical Greek republican thought via writers such as Machiavelli, Rousseau, Milton and Montesquieu, a tradition concerned with civic virtue and political participation within a polity and with dangers to that polity, such as corruption, emanating from within.[14] Montesquieu, for example, argued in his *De l'esprit des lois* (1748) that an ideal republic – a state belonging to its citizens rather than being the private property of hereditary rulers – would be small rather than large.[15] Large states and their citizens would have many global interests, he opined, meaning that they would be inclined to pursue these private, global interests above the common good. Moreover, a large state was less likely to be homogenous than a small state and thus its citizens would be so diverse as not to have anything in common with one another. Finally, argued Montesquieu, a large state must have a sufficiently large army to attain its many foreign policy objectives. These massive military machines quickly outgrew the possibility of civilian control, especially when soldiers operated in territories far outside the borders of their own state. To control these armies, larger states would therefore gravitate towards governments possessing strong executive powers concentrated at a single point, or else these armies would in turn overthrow their governments and establish such a strong executive.[16] So Montesquieu essentially agreed with Treitschke that a state's size would fundamentally predict its behaviour – and that of its rulers and of its inhabitants more generally – but he was much more optimistic about the sort of global citizens bred by smallness than the conservative German historian was to be.

Montesquieu's notion that small was beautiful precisely because of an institutional lack of interest in power and conquest came to prominence once again during the First World War, in which the Allies proclaimed to be fighting for the rights of small nations against the naked aggression of an unchecked Great Power in the form of Germany. Nine months after the United States (US) had joined the Allied war effort, President Woodrow Wilson stressed in his 'Fourteen Points' speech that the American war aims included the goal of a postwar peace settlement instituting a supranational body to afford 'mutual guarantees of political independence and territorial integrity to great and small states alike'.[17] When that body, as the League of Nations, was created through the negotiations of the Paris Peace Conference in the wake of the Allies' November 1918 victory (though without the United States as a member, despite Wilson's prior advocacy), all its member states were indeed theoretically equal, but the traditional 'great powers' dominated its decision-making apparatus, fuelled in part by apprehensions that newer European 'small' states such as Czechoslovakia and Hungary were inherently unstable, and also by lingering suspicion that small states were acting in their own interests as neutral war profiteers. Nonetheless, to many observers the notion that small states occupied an integral part of the global system – a position advocated in Scandinavia, Switzerland and the Netherlands even before 1914 – was in ascendance.[18] The supposed innate impartiality and active interest in global peace and security on the part of European small states were seen as key boosts to the League's organizational capacity and its efforts to promote international law, arbitration and disarmament. Their Latin American and Asian counterparts, however, supposedly lacked these qualities and were therefore in a sense considered not to be 'true' small states.[19]

Small state studies

After another world war, the post-1918 enthusiasm for small state internationalism came to seem short-lived and, in retrospect, even painfully naïve. The doyen of the study of international relations, E. H. Carr, for example, echoed Treitschke in the second edition of his *The Twenty Years' Crisis*, published a year after the end of the Second World War: '[t]he conclusion now seems to impose itself on any unbiased observer that the small independent nation-state is obsolete or obsolescent'.[20] The onset of the Cold War seemed further evidence that independent small states were becoming a global curiosity: standing alone, they could never hope to survive a conflict with great powers, whose nuclear arsenal now elevated them to the status of superpowers, so why did they continue – or why were they allowed – to exist? This question animated Anette Baker Fox's 1959 book *The Power of Small States*. Focusing not on the Cold War but on the recent global conflict, in which some small states had managed to survive unscathed while others had fallen prey to either Nazi conquest or Allied domination, Baker Fox concluded that small states were able to exploit conflict between great powers to retain 'genuine choice of action', as long as they were able to 'convince the great-power belligerents that the costs of using coercion against them would more than offset the gains'. Despite enormous asymmetries between the Axis and Allied powers on the one hand and the small(er) states of Spain, Turkey and Sweden on the other, the latter nations managed, through skilful diplomacy and/or the exploitation of their favourable geostrategic location vis-à-vis the battle lines, to remain neutral and independent.[21]

Following Anette Baker Fox's work, a new strand of political science research began to focus on small states' 'security dilemmas', which were created by size-induced strictures in the military, economic and governance spheres which small states somehow needed to overcome in order to survive. Small state studies, as the burgeoning field began to be called, moved into the limelight after waves of decolonization created a host of new 'small states' in the 1950s and 1960s, prompting questions about their long-term viability; the creation of the Non-Aligned Movement in the early 1960s spurred debate as well about how its small state members might survive without superpower protection.[22] Seizing upon the topicality of 'small state studies', political scientists and international relations scholars theorized that these and other small states might solve their security dilemma either through 'balance' – playing larger countries, notably the superpowers, against one another – or by 'bandwagoning' – joining with one of the powerful nations in an alliance, in which they traded some measure of independence of action for protection. Moreover, economists also began studying small states, arguing that these nations not only shared a security dilemma but were similarly also subject to a macroeconomic development pattern caused by the small size of their domestic markets, the low diversification of their economies and the scarcity of natural resources. These factors resulted in higher costs of production and lower economies of scale, a lack of competition, and low research and development expenditure, which in turn caused, these economists argued, dependency on external trade, the tendency to run trade deficits, overreliance on a single export commodity and the lack of an exportable surplus of industrial goods.[23]

Thus, a consensus slowly emerged amongst political scientists and economists who held that states of similar size tended to act in similar ways and were distinguishable from other 'types' of states. It would follow that the decision-making processes by actors within small states would qualitatively differ from those of great powers.[24] However, empirical studies could not verify the hypotheses generated by small state scholars on the behaviour of such states.[25] In a landmark 1975 article, the political scientist Peter Baehr, in an analysis of recent foreign policy decisions made by the governments of several small states, found that such decisions differed wildly both from those made by other small states and from those of larger states. Therefore, he concluded that the notion of a 'sharp dichotomy between large and small states' had no explanatory power.[26] Other comparative efforts to find commonalities amongst small states, however defined, were similarly fruitless. This empirical impasse, in turn, fragmented the field of small state studies, resulting in a lack of cumulative insights and a dearth of coherent debates. By the 1980s, scholarly interest in small states had pretty much waned.[27]

However, after the end of the Cold War, small state studies saw something of a resurgence as, once again, newly (politically) independent states entered the international scene, this time not in Africa but in Europe, as a result of the collapse of the Soviet Bloc and the dissolution of Yugoslavia.[28] Work on small states continued to emphasize their innate constraints and limitations in the face of new types of external threats, such as the global financial crisis of 2007–8 and climate change.[29] But a new strain of research did not focus on small states' supposed limits as compared to larger states but rather set out to discover the unique qualities that allowed small states to survive and, especially in Europe, to thrive. This new emphasis was indicative not only of an unspoken assumption that since the end of the Cold War and of great power rivalry in Europe the international environment had become much friendlier to small states than it had been.[30] Even more importantly, it reflected key methodological changes within the study of international relations. 'Power', a core concept within the field, was understood no longer in terms only of (potential) coercion but also as involving the ability to influence through attraction and co-option, thereby 'getting others to want the outcomes that you want'.[31] Wielding 'soft power', several researchers have hinted, is something that small states are 'naturally' very good at.[32]

This new small state literature has generated a number of fascinating case studies showing 'small states' navigating the possibilities and limitations of regional and global systems in various time periods and contexts. Perhaps most importantly, their work continues to provide sorely needed antidotes to the overt theoretical, methodological and empirical biases towards 'hard power' and 'Great Powers' in the study of international relations, historically and in the present alike.[33] However, even the new 'small state studies' has produced little in the way of generalization. The chief cause of this lack is an enduring disagreement over the *subject* of small state studies. In essence, the new small states literature, although methodologically innovative and capable of generating rich empirical materials, is dogged by an age-old problem that has hounded the study of small states since the field's very inception: What exactly *is* a small state? In other words, what are the criteria for being deemed 'small'? The search for such criteria, independent of time and place, has resulted in a plethora of suggestions for metrics, with population size, land mass and GDP being the most popular candidates. However, every suggestion offered has been met with endless, and ultimately fruitless, debate about where to locate the border separating large from small states – a discussion further muddled by the introduction of additional size categories such as micro and medium states.[34] In the end, it has proved simply impossible to find universal characteristics inherent to all small states, and therefore universal indicators of small state behaviour. 'Small state studies' thus continues to be a field without a subject, and the category 'small state' still generates more confusion than insight.[35]

Being, feeling and acting small

The central argument of this book flows from both our critique of the current state of small state studies and from the premise that its authors strongly believe that the concept still holds. That argument, simply stated, is that rather than continuing the fruitless search for timeless definitions of state size, or contenting ourselves with analyses of the politics of countries lumped together in an undefined category (i.e. 'small'), we should recognize that size in international politics is not rigid and static but perceptual and subjective. The essays in this book are therefore not about small states per se, in the sense that they do not delineate a discrete category of states that 'are' small. Rather, they are about *smallness*, which we understand as an attribute that actors can recognize either in their own polity or in another. Therefore, we would argue that a category like 'small state' (or, indeed, 'great power') has real meaning if, and only if, a polity is recognized as such either internally or externally, or both, and if people act on the basis of beliefs resulting from this recognition. Therefore, the essays take up not only the attribution of the label 'small' but also what is produced by such an attribution. Specifically, they connect smallness to discourses about the identity of states and to concrete policy actions where smallness is performed on the domestic or the international stage. Finally, this book's chapters emphasize change and relationality: the self-perceived attributes of states, or the attitudes taken towards them, can and do evolve over time, and issues related to size are almost always seen in contrast or in some other relation to the size of others.[36]

In connecting 'smallness' to identity and policy, this book builds upon two interrelated developments in the study of international politics. The first is concerned with the construction and development of the state system or the formal and informal structures that govern the relationships amongst states. Political scientists and theorists of international relations have long assumed that this system functions essentially like a game of billiards, the balls constantly clashing against one another and differing only in their force and speed of impact. Recent decades have seen the emergence of trends in international history that no longer cast the international system as a mass of empty air for the billiard balls to roll around in but rather regard it as an environment filled with norms and rules which help guide, and which is simultaneously shaped by, the behaviours and ideas of state and non-state actors alike.[37]

Ayşe Zarakol has argued persuasively that both the formal and informal organization of states into regional and global systems takes the shape of a series of changing and overlapping hierarchies. Within these 'deep structures of organized inequality' states are either institutionally or informally super- or subordinated to others. The 'distinctions' made between groups of states mentioned at the beginning of this introductory chapter – between developing and developed states, Western and non-Western, great and small – can be understood as positions within these hierarchies. Relations between metropoles and their former colonies, between Security Council members and other actors within the United Nations, and between 'civilized' states and 'dangerous' failing states or non-state actors can then be reframed, and better understood, as organized inequalities.[38]

Following Zarakol, we propose a new understanding of size in international relations as a hierarchy of 'organized inequality', with 'smallness' given a historically contingent status. This conception allows us to analyse the construction and evolution of the 'size hierarchy' along with the (changing) conditions and meanings of small state status. It also allows us to question who the reference group is: Who or what do states feel they have to measure up to in order to either confirm or defend their status, or to ascend to a higher position within the hierarchy?

Crucially, we posit that there is a direct connection between a state's status in a size hierarchy on the one hand, and the worldview of historical actors identifying with that state on the other. Specifically, building upon Barry Buzan and Ole Waever's investigations into the nexus connecting foreign policy with identity, this book argues that debates about size are enmeshed within fundamental societal debates about a state's 'we' in comparison to an 'other' – either another state or group of states, or some (imagined) past version of 'us' or 'them'.[39] Debates about size in the late nineteenth and early twentieth centuries in and concerning the Netherlands were, I have argued previously, inextricably linked to discussions about the country's 'natural' role in Europe and the world, where it had a supposedly historical duty as an 'exemplar nation' leading not by force but by example. Moreover, these debates were bound up with implicit and explicit comparisons either to other countries deemed to be part of the same (European) reference group – its colonial possessions, for example, supposedly elevated it 'above the rank of Denmark' – or, due to its early twentieth-century economic and scientific booms, to the country's seventeenth-century 'Golden Age'.[40]

The key takeaway here is that hierarchies of size are not just academic constructs: they have real-world effects. However, the essays in this book do not posit an *automatic* connection, as both Montesquieu and Treitschke suggested in respectively the eighteenth and nineteenth centuries, that would link 'being small' with 'feeling' and 'acting small'. If a nation's politically relevant majority considers the country small, this perception will exert an influence on policy: it will affect beliefs about how the state should be treated, what it is entitled to and what it has no place doing. Obviously, it is possible to propose policies that radically differ from what most people would consider appropriate, given their idea of their country's size and the implications of that size. But, as Lene Hansen has shown, advocating for such policies is a daunting task, especially when one's political opposition can point out the obvious imbalance between identity and policy. Daunting, but not impossible, since constructed identities are hardly timeless; they can and do move from being (near-)hegemonic to being politically contested over time, allowing established policy boundaries to be contested along with them.[41] Moreover, 'smallness' not only forms an integral part of debates about the identity of one's own state identity but can also be attributed to another state. This descriptor can then be accepted by relevant actors within that state, either happily or begrudgingly, but such an attribution, if felt to be unfair, can be seen as 'belittling'. These attributions, too, produce real-world ramifications: if another state is seen as small, certain expectations will rise while others recede; accorded particular roles, a state will be denied others.

Discourse and image

To study size, we look first and foremost to sites where size – either of one's own state or of another – is the subject of discussion and debate. To analyse these sites, we look to discourse analysis. Made famous by Foucault and Derrida, discourse analysis concerns itself (inter alia) with how language, along with the ideas, concepts and categories that language seeks to put into words, is used to construct meaning and identity. What specifically interests us here is that in building meaning and identity, language functions as a referential system, in which things and people are identified through differentiation and linking.[42] Put very simply, differentiation holds that something *is* something or has a certain *meaning* because it is not something else. Switzerland, for example, might be construed as a small state because it is small when compared to relevant others – it is smaller than great and medium-sized states such as the United States, China and Brazil, but greater than microstates such as Liechtenstein. Through linking, concepts such as smallness are then connected to sets of ideas and values, either positively or negatively. Switzerland's smallness, for example, might be analysed as being intimately connected to values held to be positive, such as being peace-loving, internationalist or neutral. Such differentiations and linkages, being complex and multifaceted, are inherently unstable. Size comparisons between states are subject to interpretation and debate: what is obvious to one might not be so apparent to another. And connections between smallness and a certain value (or values) might change if the perception of a particular value changes. For example, the connection between smallness and neutrality was generally and highly valued in Denmark in the decades prior to the Second World War but was not so prized after the Nazi occupation, when this linkage became associated not with high-minded idealism and safety but with negative values such as cowardice and helplessness.[43]

Of course, a huge number of actors have used referential language, in an equally wide variety of circumstances, forms, fora and media, to express their notions of how their state's size compares to others' and what positive or negative ideas and values it is linked to. We suggest, however, that a select number of common themes, reproduced in media and repeated back through policy, were prevalent in public debate. Not that everyone shared them or agreed with them, but we suggest, following Lene Hansen, that these common themes do provide 'a lens through which a multitude of different representations and policies can be seen as systematically connected', even in opposition or as foci for discussions. Moreover, smallness, and indeed size in general, is also something that can be ignored or simply go unmentioned. Such passing over might be unconscious – when, for whatever reason, thinking in terms of smallness or size plays no role in discourses related to state identity or policy – or deliberate, as when smallness is considered a taboo subject. Accordingly, the essays in this book focus not only on smallness when it is made explicit in policy or within identity-related discourses but also on smallness in action, where smallness is 'performed'. Even when it goes unmentioned, smallness can still serve to legitimize actions and can thus be read back from these actions, often through either differentiation – an action is justified because it is not another type of action which we cannot or should not undertake – or through linkage, often through terms such as neutrality or peripherality that are associated (positively or negatively) with smallness. Thus, the essays in this book treat the relationship between the *politics of smallness* and *discourses on smallness* as mutually constitutive: 'small' politics rely upon representations of 'small' identity, which is in turn produced and reproduced through political action. Both, meanwhile, form important elements within processes of identity formation.[44]

To aid comparisons across time and space when discussing these discourses on smallness – and their attendant processes of linking and differentiation – in their complicated, reciprocal relationships with policy and identity formation, this volume's essays refer to common themes therein as *images* – a shorthand, often given the French rather than the English pronunciation, derived from *imagology*. Originally a method devised to analyse, compare and contrast the discursive articulations of national characterizations or *ethnotypes* ('all Frenchmen love wine, wear berets, and refuse to speak English'), imagology nowadays has a much wider purview: it assists in analysing those discourses of representation that invoke images of the national Self in contrast to the Other by prescribing particular characters to them.[45] Like discourse analysis, with which it shares a linguistic background, imagology focuses on relationality and the use of differentiation (Self vs. Other) and linkages (characteristics associated with both Self and Other). Following Joep Leerssen and Manfred Beller, we differentiate the three terms *auto-images*, *hetero-images* and *meta-images*. The first term applies to those discourses that refer to one's own polity or to another form of collective Self; the second to discourses related to another state, group of states or (collective of) Other(s); and *meta-images*, meanwhile, are about projections: how we think, hope or fear the Other thinks of Us, or what We imagine the Other thinks, hopes or fears We think of Them.[46]

Chapter breakdown

The essays presented here discuss the politics of smallness, *images* related to smallness, and wider but related issues of identity formation as they intersect with often conflicting notions of size. Their temporal focus is mostly on the nineteenth and twentieth centuries, beginning with the period after the difference between great powers and small(er) states was formalized at the Treaty of Vienna. Two essays, however, connect the historical (re)construction of size to current events, underscoring the continued relevance of size hierarchies in our world today, while one essay casts its gaze further back into history, questioning the established chronology of the history of 'smallness'. Geographically, the essays in our book focus primarily but not exclusively on Europe. Europe's preponderance here is not because smallness or size-based hierarchies play no role in discourses on policy and status in areas outside of Europe but because in domestic and international debates, actors from European states – or states that define themselves partly or wholly as 'European' – have tended, until the late twentieth century, to focus nearly exclusively on references to other European states. In other words, for European debates about 'smallness', the reference group in debate status within size-based hierarchies was almost exclusively other European states. A singular focus on Europe helps to bring this emphasis to the fore. However, within these spatial and geographical constraints, the chapters feature a wide range of approaches, collectively designed to highlight the utility of the focus on 'smallness' and the methodology outlined in this introduction across a variety of empirical settings.

The first chapter, 'Belittling Spain. Hispanophobia and the mirror of greatness' by Yolanda Rodríguez Pérez, focuses, for example, on analysing literary history and its key role in forging canons, featuring explicit auto- and meta-images on the 'size' of states' literary and cultural achievements. Rodríguez Pérez shows how, in developing British and Dutch literary canons, Spain was 'belittled' by being given the taint of a set of negative stereotypes that impacted its place and stature within Europe and the world in the arts as well as in politics.

Adrian Brisku's chapter, 'Dealing with smallness in Habsburg Bohemia, Ottoman Albania and Tsarist Georgia in the late nineteenth and early twentieth centuries', meanwhile, deals with the intellectual vanguard of nascent national movements within multinational empires. The collective self-images they promoted of their nations as small within 'great' imperial states deeply influenced how they viewed relations with the imperial centre and their advocacy for specific constitutional, political-economic and geopolitical strategies oriented towards national survival and growth. The third chapter,

'Smallness and the East-West binary in nationalism studies. Belgium and Romania in the long nineteenth century', by Raul Cârstocea and Maarten Van Ginderachter, uses smallness to probe existing schemas of classifying different varieties of nationalism. It focuses on Romanian elites' conscious adoption of Belgium as a developmental model, a choice closely related to their mutually recognized smallness but linked as well to ideas and values that the Belgians and the Romanians alike attached to it: peripherality, (political and constitutional) liberalism and the ability to bridge different cultures.

In Chapter 4, '"Poor Little Belgium". Food aid and the image of Belgian victimhood in the United States', by Samuël Kruizinga and Marjet Brolsma, smallness is an essential part of the campaign waged on behalf of the Commission for the Relief of Belgium to solicit money, goods and political capital on behalf of beleaguered Belgium during the First World War. Belgium's hetero-image in the United States, though bearing echoes of the modern small state that had been so attractive to the Romanians, was mostly concerned with suffering: Belgium was mostly known as the Great War's primary, tragic victim. This hetero-image developed in tandem with that of Germany as the instigator of Belgium's woes and to an auto-image of America as a moral great power, a conception profoundly affecting the cultural mobilization that surrounded the entry of the United States into the war in 1917.

Our analysis moves to the interwar period with Chapter 5, 'Science, health and American money: Small-state strategies in interwar Czechoslovakia and Denmark', co-written by Elisabeth Van Meer, Casper Andersen and Ludvig Goldschmidt Pedersen. Scientists and bureaucrats in the new Czechoslovak Republic and in Denmark both followed internationalist agendas that were quite similar in their alignment with a self-image in which smallness was innately linked with scientific internationalism. In pursuing such aims, they sought subsidies from the American Rockefeller Foundation (RF), which had emerged from the First World War as a leading philanthropic entity on the global stage. The RF, meanwhile, regarded both countries as attractive candidates for the advancement of its own scientific agenda, precisely because they were small enough either to be built from the ground up (Czechoslovakia) or to be used as a pre-mapped and charted miniature testbed for international scientific collaborations and new research methodologies. Chapter 6, 'Neutral news. Forging a small states' transnational media network, 1920–40', by Vincent Kuitenbrouwer, is likewise interested in the connection between smallness and 'truth', albeit not in a scientific sense. His chapter details the creation of a network of small state news agencies intended to collectively parry the propaganda efforts of those states that threatened to monopolize the physical means of transmitting news as well as the news' contents. Their auto-images as small and neutral played key roles in their joint efforts to safeguard their independence on the eve of the Second World War and to deliver 'neutral' or 'true' news to further the cause of peace.

Chapters 7 and 8 both take longer views of the development of auto-images of smallness and their relation to international and domestic politics and to national identity narratives. In '"Whoever says that Serbia is small is lying!" Serbia, ontological (in)security and the unbearable smallness of being', Christian Axboe Nielsen details the emergence of two conflicting auto-images in nineteenth-century Serbia: one where it reconciled itself with its size and focused on internal development, and one advocating a push for a Greater Serbia, traces of which are still detectable in the country today. The latter conception quickly lost out, but the auto-image of Serbian political elites remained, and remains, characterized by a fear of smallness – defined territorially, but also (geo-)politically and demographically. Chapter 8, 'Iceland's smallness. Acceptance or denial?' by Baldur Thorhallsson and Guðmundur Hálfdanarson, tracks the connection between Icelandic auto-images as they developed in the late nineteenth and early twentieth centuries and its foreign policy throughout the twentieth and the early twenty-first centuries. The authors conclude that Icelandic policymakers generally consider smallness a taboo subject, as it undermines a widely circulated and oft-repeated claim that the country has a natural right to self-determination and is beholden to no one. At the same time, Icelandic governments have sought forms of economic, military and geopolitical protection, which has amounted to an unspoken admission that small Iceland needed to find shelter to weather storms such as the Cold War and the financial crisis of 2008–11.

Chapters 9 and 10 move closer and closer towards the present. Sara Dybris McQuaid argues in 'Great Britain and Little Ireland. Reimagining British and Irish relations in BIPA, Brexit and beyond' that smallness functions as a lens through which to understand the relationships amongst various territorial, national and political communities across the British Isles as they negotiate Brexit and its impact on the Republic of Ireland and Northern Ireland and on the constitutional makeup of the UK. She shows, by analysing the British-Irish Parliamentary Assembly, that political actors across the UK and Ireland use size in shifting and multiple ways in order to question, (re)frame and (re)position the constituent parts of the UK in relation to one another, to the two parts of Ireland and to the European Union (EU). In the final chapter before the book's conclusion, 'From David to Goliath? The question of size in Israel's identity politics', Alexei Tsinovoi argues that Israel's dominant auto-image rests on three pillars: its Jewishness, its status as a security provider and its democratic values in an otherwise autocratic region. Through these identity narratives, Israel emerged as an embattled small state. However, the narratives proved unstable and began to clash, causing fissures in both Israel's auto-image and its hetero-image in other parts of the world, exerting a severe impact on ongoing attempts to end the Israeli–Palestinian conflict. The book's final chapter, by Samuël Kruizinga and Karen Gram-Skjoldager, summarizes the various essays' findings and reflects on the utility of our understanding of smallness and of size more generally.

Notes

1 Kelsen, 'The Principle of Sovereign Equality of States as a Basis for International Organization', 209.
2 Wright, 'The Equality of States'.
3 Tucker, *The Inequality of Nations*; Clark, *The Hierarchy of States: Reform and Resistance in the International Order*.
4 Scott, 'The Seven Years War and Europe's Ancien Régime', 429; Scott, *The Birth of a Great Power System 1740–1815*, 117–42; Neumann, 'Status Is Cultural', 103.

5   Schulz, *Normen Und Praxis*, 35–71.
6   Meisel, *Cours de Style Diplomatique, Volume II*, 133–4.
7   Peterson, 'Political Inequality at the Congress of Vienna', 539–42; Graaf, 'The Allied Machine. The Conference of Ministers in Paris and the Management of Security, 1815–18', 140; Graaf, 'The Legacy of the Wars for the International System'.
8   Schulz, 'Cultures of Peace and Security from the Vienna Congress to the Twenty-First Century. Characteristics and Dilemmas', 24–5, 28–9.
9   Holdar, 'The Ideal State and the Power of Geography the Life-Work of Rudolf Kjellén'.
10 '[D]as Erb- und Grundübel, an dem unsere Nation seit Jahrhunderten elend darniederliegt, die Quelle alles unseres historischen Unglücks, unserer Ohnmacht, unserer inneren Zerwürfnisse, unserer Niederlagen und unserer Bürgerkriege, der Verkrüppelung unseres Nationalgeistes und unserer politischen Unmündigkeit'. Rochau, *Grundsätze Der Realpolitik, Angewendet Auf Die Staatlichen Zustände Deutschlands, Volume 1*, 117.
11 'Die kleinen Reststaaten machen eine Ausnahme van den Wachstumsgesetzen der Staaten; sie sind wie versteinert'. Ratzel, *Politische Geographie, Oder Die Geographie Der Staaten Des Verkehres Und Des Krieges*, 184.
12 '[E]inen Akt der historischen Notwendigkeit'. Treitschke, *Die Zukunft Der Norddeutschen Mittelstaaten*, 24.
13 Original citations from Amstrup, 'Perennial Problem', 163–4. I have re-translated them from the original texts.
14 Pocock, *The Machiavellian Moment*.
15 See Montesquieu, *The Spirit of the Laws*.
16 Levy, 'Beyond Publius', 50–2. See also Alexis de Tocqueville's description of the United States as 'free and happy as a small nation', and 'glorious and strong as a great one'. Tocqueville, *Democracy in America: And Two Essays on America*, 191.
17 Wilson, 'An Address to a Joint Session of Congress, 8 January 1918'.
18 MacGinty, 'War Cause and Peace Aim?' 47–50, 55; Schulz, 'La Société Des Nations et La Résolution Pacifique Des Différends: Règles, Normes et Pratiques'.
19 Gram-Skjoldager, Ikonomou and Kahlert, 'Scandinavians and the League of Nations Secretariat, 1919-1946', 11–12.
20 Carr and Cox, *The Twenty Years' Crisis*, cvi. Cynicism regarding the long-term viability of smaller states in the face of renewed European conflict had become a feature of political writing as early as the 1930s. See e.g. Rappard, 'Small States in the League of Nations', 544–75.
21 Baker Fox, *The Power of Small States*, 8–9.
22 Sens, 'The Newly Independent States, the United Nations, and Some Thoughts on the Nature of the Development Process'.
23 Neumann and Gstöhl, 'Introduction: Lilliputians in Gulliver's World?' 11; Jesse and Dreyer, *Small States in the International System. At Peace and at War*, 12–48.
24 Barston, 'Introduction'.
25 Thorhallsson, 'Studying Small States: A Review', 23–5; Neumann and Gstöhl, 'Introduction: Lilliputians in Gulliver's World?' 10–15; Steinmetz and Wivel, 'Introduction', 9–10.
26 Baehr, 'Small States: A Tool for Analysis', 466. See also East, 'Size and Foreign Policy Behavior', 566–76; Amstrup, 'Perennial Problem', 178–9. Cf. Carlsnaes, 'Foreign Policies', 13.
27 Neumann and Gstöhl, 'Introduction: Lilliputians in Gulliver's World?' 12.
28 Thorhallsson, 'Studying Small States: A Review', 19–21.

29 Bailes, Rickli and Thorhallsson, 'Small States, Survival and Strategy', 26, 32; Benwell, 'The Canaries in the Coalmine: Small States as Climate Change Champions', 199–200; Streeten, 'The Special Problems of Small Countries', 197–8.
30 Thorhallsson and Steinsson, 'Small State Foreign Policy'.
31 Nye, Jr., *Soft Power. The Means to Success in World Politics*, x, 1–21.
32 Crump et al., 'Introduction. Smaller Powers in Cold War Europe'; Long, 'Small States, Great Power?' 194–201; Panke, 'Small States in EU Negotiations: Political Dwarfs or Power-Brokers?' 124; Cooper and Shaw, 'The Diplomacies of Small States at the Start of the Twenty-First Century: How Vulnerable? How Resilient?' 3; Browning, 'Small, Smart and Salient?' 670; Chong, 'Small State Soft Power Strategies: Virtual Enlargement in the Cases of the Vatican City State and Singapore', 385–402.
33 Hey, 'Introducing Small State Foreign Policy', 2; Case, *Between States*, 2.
34 Crowards, 'Defining'; Thorhallsson and Wivel, 'Small States in the European Union: What Do We Know and What Would We Like to Know?' For debates about 'middle' states, see e.g. Chapnick, 'Middle Power No More? Canada in World Affairs Since 2006'; Ravenhill, 'Entrepreneurial States'.
35 Some even go so far as to advocate simply ignoring the issue altogether. 'After all, quibbling over definitions has not prevented the small state from becoming a fact of international political life'. Baldacchino, 'Mainstreaming the Study of Small States and Territories', 7. Others have argued that small is, in essence, equal to 'weak', but this observation only shifts, rather than solves, issues of definition. Alford, 'Security Dilemmas', 365; Elman, 'Foreign Policies of Small States', 172–5.
36 See Kruizinga, 'A Small State? The Size of the Netherlands as a Focal Point in Foreign Policy Debates, 1900–1940'; Dijk et al., 'Conclusions and Outlook. Small States on the Global Scene'. Such an approach was also championed by Smith, Pace and Lee, 'Size Matters'.
37 For an overview of recent developments, see Manela, 'International Society as a Historical Subject', 184–99.
38 Zarakol, 'Theorising Hierarchies'; Lake, 'Laws and Norms', 3–13, 28–9; Renshon, *Fighting for Status. Hierarchy and Conflict in World Politics*, 2–11, 21–44; Welch Larson, Paul, and Wohlforth, 'Status and World Order', 7–10.
39 Buzan and Wæver, *Regions and Powers*, 20–1, 33–5.
40 Baudet, 'Nederland En de Rang van Denemarken'; Kruizinga, 'A Small State? The Size of the Netherlands as a Focal Point in Foreign Policy Debates, 1900–1940'. Referring to the seventeenth century as the Netherlands' 'Golden Age' has come under increasing scrutiny, rightly I believe. I use it here because early-twentieth-century elites employed the term specifically to mirror their own advances, albeit in different fields of endeavour.
41 Hansen, *Security as Practice*, 18–53.
42 For a very readable introduction to these themes, see Hall, Evans and Nixon, *Representation*.
43 See Gram-Skjoldager, 'The Other End of Neutrality. Denmark, The First World War and The League of Nations'.
44 Hansen, *Security as Practice*, 1.
45 See Sierp and Karner, 'National Stereotypes in the Context of the European Crisis'; III, 'What's in a National Stereotype?'
46 Beller, 'Perception, Image, Imagology'; Leerssen, 'Imagology. History and Method'; Leerssen, 'Imagology'.

1

Belittling Spain. Hispanophobia and the mirror of greatness

Yolanda Rodríguez Pérez

The year 1898 is known as one of the most ominous years in Spanish history. Popularly known at the time as 'The Disaster', the year saw Spain lose its last imperial remnants in the Caribbean and the Pacific as a result of its war with the United States. The consequences of the 'splendid little war', as the US ambassador in London, John Hay, called it, were enormous.[1] The United States won its first overseas possessions, driving Spain out of the Western Hemisphere and establishing a new identity for itself on the world stage as a Great Power. Spain, by contrast, emerged diminished. In the late nineteenth century, becoming 'smaller' was widely understood to have ramifications extending well beyond the mere loss of territory. Conservative British Prime Minister Lord Salisbury, for example, remarked in a speech to his party on 4 May 1898 that the international system consisted of 'dying' and 'living' nations. According to this neo-Darwinian approach to international relations, 'the living nations will gradually encroach on the territory of the dying, and the seeds and causes of conflict amongst civilized nations will speedily appear'. Living nations were 'great countries of enormous power, growing in power every year, growing in wealth, growing in dominion, growing in the perfection of their organization'.[2] Dying nations, by contrast, were weak states that, having failed in the international competition for resources and prestige, were doomed to irrelevancy. Although he did not mention Spain by name, Spanish intellectuals and politicians largely took Salisbury's address to be referring to The Disaster: the United States was the vital, growing nation, the declining Spain its moribund foil.[3]

The vehemence of the Spanish reaction to a British political speech can be explained by the long history of 'belittling' visions of the country. At its zenith in the early modern period, the Spanish Empire was a composite or polycentric monarchy that other nations viewed with varying degrees of distrust, envy and admiration. Its international reputation was marked by an alleged thirst for world dominance, or *Monarchia Universalis*, which became a recurring *topos* in contemporary political discourse. This

---

Research for this article was financially supported by the Dutch Research Council (NWO) within the project 'Mixed Feelings. Literary Hispanophilia and Hispanophobia in England and the Netherlands in the Early Modern period and the nineteenth century' (Vidi-276-30-011).

Figure 1.1 A cartoon (from the Kinsley Graphic, 2 September 1898) shows victorious Great America teaching defeated Small Spain a painful lesson in the ways of civilization following the end of the Spanish-American War. © Out of copyright.

negative image should be understood against the backdrop of a strong anti-Hispanism that materialized in the so-called Black Legend of Spanish Tyranny, a complex of negative qualities supposedly inherent to the Spanish national character.[4] Anti-Hispanism is even considered to be central to the process of European proto-national identity formation,[5] since it helped shaped the political and cultural self-definition of nations like England and the Netherlands, two nations with a shared sense of historical connectedness. Once Imperial Spain started to crumble, it would be reframed internationally as the anti-example for all prosperous and modern nations, symbolizing decadence and decline. Once a political exemplar of greatness worth emulating, Spain was certainly no longer regarded this way after the seventeenth century.

The present volume aims to reflect on the different meanings of 'smallness' in international relations in a transnational and diachronic manner through its focus on political discourses that expose and question (pre)conceptions of smallness and the ways they are constructed. This chapter will address Spain, which has not fit in well with the existing literature on small states. Neither its territory nor its relevance for the history of imperial and international politics qualifies it to be studied alongside countries such as Denmark or Luxembourg. However, this chapter's focus on Spain makes it possible to highlight how states can be perceived as or 'made small' by other states via a display of 'belittling' rhetoric. This mechanism can be accepted by relevant actors within a certain state or nation – happily or begrudgingly – but it can also be contested.[6] Furthermore, it is my contention here that to fully understand the discursive stretch of the notions of 'small' vis-à-vis 'great' requires transnational historical contextualization and engagement with the cultural field alike. Although considerable research on size has been undertaken from the perspective of international politics, an approach from cultural history can be highly fruitful, too, since it exposes the undeniable early modern conflation of political and cultural hegemony with regard to Spain.

The lens of the Spanish case allows us to explore an additional dimension of the concept of 'smallness'. This concept possesses two sides. First, Spain offers an example of how 'big' or 'great' can be transformed into 'small' or 'irrelevant' over time. The decline of Spain's visible role in the international arena gave rise to a steady process whereby Spain's 'greatness' was reduced or 'belittled'. Second, this process was strongly manifest within the cultural context. From the Enlightenment onwards, Spain's prior cultural hegemony and legacy within Europe were contested and downplayed, so that Spain was demoted to a 'small' nation having no international significance, politically or culturally. Literature, and in particular claims to a literary canon of significance and relevance, was of paramount importance for a nation, since such collective literary achievement also illustrated a country's greatness. Focusing on the discipline of literary history as a key agent in the forging of narratives of nationhood and national canons in the nineteenth century, this chapter analyses the belittling of Spain via the development of discourses on cultural hegemony and cultural legacies in Dutch and British national literary canons. The genre of literary histories might at first seem a rather rarefied and restricted field of study, but it is important to understand that in the nineteenth century, literary history was perceived to be a discipline in the service of national unity, possessing the potential to effect political change.[7] Literary histories were also instrumental in current debates on the production and circulation of knowledge. From our perspective, analysis of this particular genre is pertinent and timely since 'national traditions of "doing" literary history still remain to be charted comparatively'.[8]

Cast as a traditional enemy, Spain exerted considerable influence on the emerging respective origin stories of the nation-states in Britain and the Netherlands, and in a process of continual renegotiation its influence was downplayed, occluded or silenced on many occasions. The reconstruction here of the tropes and images employed in this 'belittling process', following the approach adumbrated in this volume's introductory chapter, concentrates on the tracing of overt or latent discourses and self-images and hetero-images regarding Spanishness, Spain and the country's role in the political and cultural arenas of the time. As Joep Leerssen states, images and prejudices function as dormant or latent frames that can be submerged and then can re-emerge over time.[9] Beginning with a historicization of the Black Legend narrative as an overpowering 'default' vision of Spain and Spanishness, this chapter will explore examples of the rhetorical dynamics at work in this process.

Transnational historical contextualization: The Black Legend as a negative mirror of Spanish greatness

Although it has generally been assumed that Julián Juderías coined 'Black Legend' (*Leyenda Negra*) in his famous 1914 essay of that title, the writer Emilia Pardo Bazán had already used the term at a conference in Paris in 1899. One year after the disaster of 1898, Pardo Bazán, like many other Spanish intellectuals, found herself dwelling on Spanish decline and the possibilities of regenerating the nation. Without specifying what is precisely entailed by this critical Black Legend of Spain, she blames the current situation on the existence, in the country, of a myth that exalted a great and glorious Spain. This 'golden legend', or glittering 'self-image' of Spain and its historical past, fed in her eyes on certain key moments such as the 'discovery' of the New World or the cultural zenith represented by the illustrious Spanish Golden Age. The 'counter-narrative' of this 'golden legend' would be, she writes, a Black Legend.[10] For his part, Juderías, the term's alleged 'father', explained the concept as a European conspiracy aimed at tarnishing the reputation of Spain, its people and the nation's overall cultural and artistic achievements.[11] This Black Legend projected an image of the Spaniards as a cruel and tyrannical people, thirsty for gold and world dominance, an untrustworthy nationality given over to religious zealots. Moreover, the barbaric Spanish character reflected the Spaniards' impure blood, which was an unholy mixture of Moor and Jew.[12] This interpretation of the Spanish national past was paired with an attitude of victimization that many Spaniards would interiorize.[13] Some Spaniards, ruminating on their past imperial greatness, felt belittled by the surrounding nations. Years before The Disaster, the writer Juan Valera used these very words:

> Spain has been the nation most belittled and denigrated in general histories and in the histories of civilization that are now being written. The contempt has been so contagious that foreigners have succeeded in implanting it in the mind of many Spaniards.[14]

Despite this conspiratorial and victimist approach, Juderías flawlessly detected how the Black Legend had resurfaced at crucial moments in Spanish history at the hands of Spain's opponents, such as during the colonial wars of independence in Latin America or during the 1898 war with the United States.[15]

The prejudicial image of Spain and its people, put forth since the sixteenth century as anti-Spanish propaganda, gradually became ingrained in Europe and established itself as the mainstream foreign image of the Spaniard in the early modern period. This disparaging collective portrait was most strongly propagated by the Dutch and the English. Obviously, ethnotypes often involve apprehension towards powerful great nations and an appreciation of harmless small nations.[16] Such apprehension, sometimes expressed as open aversion and unbridled hate, was to be directed at Spain. The particular cases of England and the Dutch Republic were marked by a process of self-definition achieved via the flourishing of enmity that was strongly connected to the Hispanophobic Black Legend. In the Low Countries, this development has to be understood against the backdrop of the Dutch Revolt and its continuation in the Eighty Years' War (1568–1648) against Philip II of Spain and his successors, the legitimate overlords of those territories. In England, Elizabeth I eventually came to support the revolt in the Low Countries, a decision that linked the destinies of England and the Dutch Republic during a key period in both their histories. The famous Armada victory of 1588 against Spain, resounding through the centuries up to the present day, became a defining historical episode for the development of English identity. Both northern nations also felt connected through their self-branding as 'Protestant' nations against Catholic/Papist Spain. As John Elliott has phrased it, the Black Legend 'etched itself into the English national consciousness', with a primacy that is even greater in the corresponding narrative of Dutch national identity, in which anti-Hispanism constitutes 'the backbone of the Dutch Revolt canon'.[17] To legitimate their struggle against their lawful overlords, the rebel Netherlandish faction deployed a highly effective propaganda machine directed against a Spanish 'Other' that embodied the image of a 'common' enemy. This hetero-image of the Spaniard would become deeply intertwined with the Dutch people's own national *Gründungmythos* and become inseparable from their self-image as heroic fighters for liberty (civic and religious). Furthermore, within this theatre of war, the Low Countries managed to become a major creative and intermediary hub in the making and circulation of published political propaganda in Europe, combining the power of strong words with the impact of striking images. Pamphlets produced in the Low Countries enjoyed a rich and influential life throughout Europe, whether in their original form or in translation. Many of these publications contributed especially to the development of a very negative reputation of the Spaniards as a nation in general, and of their soldiers in particular.[18]

This rhetoric of vilification directed towards the Spanish enemy often repeated the allegation that, in line with the idea of *Monarchia Universalis*, the Spanish thirst for expansion was unquenchable. Vigorously propagated within the Dutch context as the revolt raged was the idea that the Spanish monarchy cunningly intended to dominate Europe.[19] The Dutch rebel leader William of Orange and his partisans stressed this narrative in an attempt to promote some sort of 'balance of power' with other European nations. Spain, in their eyes, posed a danger sufficiently immanent for weaker states to band together in self-interest against this menacing giant. In the Dutch discourse one frequently encounters size-related tropes: the Dutch Republic was likened to the diminutive David who, despite the mismatch against his foe, would eventually defeat the Spanish Goliath.[20] *Monarchia Universalis*, though it may seem primarily a political concept, possessed an undeniable religious dimension. The Spanish monarchy's self-representation as *the* defender of the *Universitas Christiana* helps explain the tinge of anxiety or threat it elicited from neighbouring nations. Modern nations have been forged and have acquired a great deal of their characteristics through their relationship with biblical tradition.[21] Along these lines, the Spanish monarchy defined itself not only by its struggle against infidels but also by the way it underscored its undeniable messianic mission and its exceptionalism.[22] This idea of a 'chosen nation' aligned with a discourse that enabled Spain – through Emperor Charles V – to cast itself as a successor to the four great preceding monarchies: the Assyrian, Persian, Greek and Roman. Following the tradition of the *translatio imperii*, and seeing themselves as a 'Fifth Monarchy or Fifth Kingdom', they linked their imperium to the Old Testament and to Daniel's prophecy of a new and final kingdom on earth, the most powerful and magnificent in human history.[23] This privileged position could only be fulfilled by a monarchy chosen by God.

Given this context, many leading European intellectuals of the time committed themselves to contributing to a discourse on the 'universal' character of the Spanish Monarchy. Amongst these writers was the Italian Dominican Tommaso Campanella (1568–1639), a radical and innovative thinker who was imprisoned in Naples in 1599 on charges of heresy and of plotting against Spanish rule.[24] Although this anti-Spanish side of Campanella seems to be what is now most remembered about him, the fervent pro-Hispanic character of his career's first phase makes him an intriguing figure. He provided the Spanish monarchy with a solid line of argumentation to support its self-understanding as a 'Universal monarchy'. In his *Monarquía Hispánica*, written in the 1590s, Campanella states that the Spanish monarchy has been entrusted by divine will with the *Universitas Christiana*, the defence of Catholicism on earth. But he takes the idea a step further by arguing that only divine determinism can allow a given nation to aspire to become a Universal monarchy. It is God who grants that a certain monarchy will rule universally and, most importantly, it is He who will withdraw his favour and condemn this monarchy to its downfall if He deems it fit to do so.[25] To stress his point, the Dominican praises the virtues and excellencies of the Spanish nation from time immemorial in the tradition of the 'laus Hispaniae', praise of Spain. Interestingly, parts of his *Monarquia Hispánica* were translated and published in the Dutch Republic in 1618, during the Truce with Spain (1609–21), a time marked by a strong political debate on whether the war should continue. One of the Dutch editions was even commissioned by the States of Friesland, one of the constituent seven provinces of the Dutch Republic. The work's translators selected those passages that could unmistakably display the ominous threat posed by Spain, stressing its intention to achieve universal monarchy. What had originally been written to illustrate the chosen character of Spain in its universal Christian endeavours was renegotiated and integrated into the Dutch discourse as a tangible example of their evil efforts.[26] Illustrated pamphlets like the well-known *Het Spaens Europa* ('The Spanish Europe'), published in 1598 (the year of Philip II's demise), had already broadcast this menacing narrative. Here Spain is presented topographically as the head of Europe, brandishing a sword and thus ensuring it will not be taken as a peaceful entity. In any case, we see here how the very notion of greatness can be used variously by two distinct parties possessing different agendas. One envisions 'greatness' as something worth achieving, to be deserved almost naturally; the other regards it as something to be wary of, which needs to be thwarted. Amongst other political theorists of the time, Gregorio López Madera in his *Excelencia de las Monarquías* (1597) mentions in his dedication to Philips II his desire to show in his book 'the greatness of the Empire that God has reserved for him'.[27] The propagandistic discourse of Spanish greatness and supremacy and the undeniable Spanish hegemony over the European theatre notwithstanding, scholars still do not agree whether Philip II, or his predecessors, had formulated a master plan for a universal empire. Some stress that Spain's policy towards foreign powers was actually more defensive than offensive, whereas others speak of a 'great strategy' that points to imperialistic designs.[28]

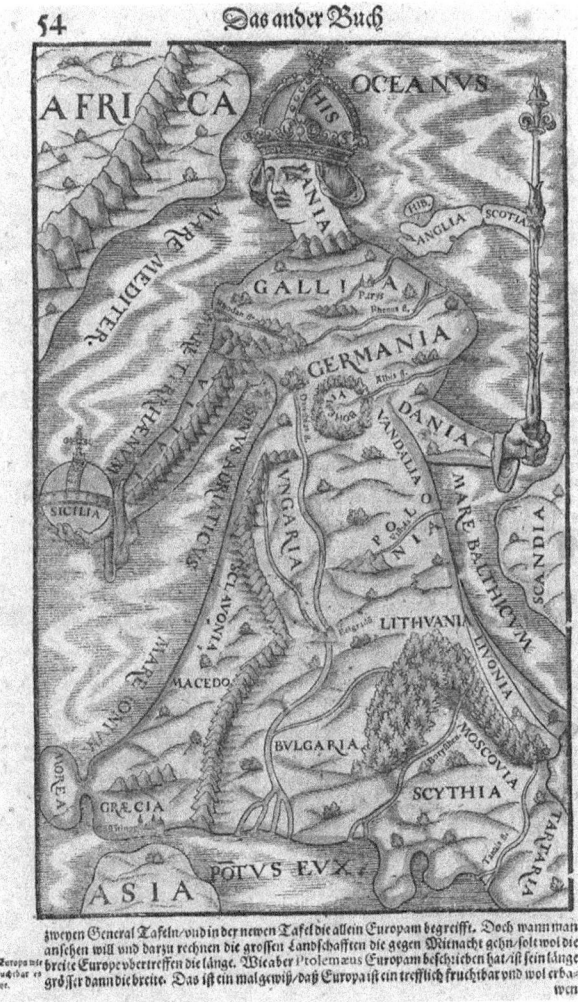

Figure 1.2 This map, adapted from a 1537 original cartographer Johannes Putsch, was printed in *Cosmographia* by Sebastian Münster (1488–1552) in 1570. A similar version was used in *Het Spaens Europa*. They both depict Spain as a true universal monarchy: the "crown" of both Europe and Christianity. © Wikimedia Commons (public domain).

Decline and cultural belittling

Spain's political hegemony did not stand on its own but rather coincided with a period of cultural hegemony that would be later baptized the *Siglo de Oro*, the Golden Age, starring canonical authors such as Miguel de Cervantes (1547–1616) and playwrights such as Félix Lope de Vega (1562-1635) and Pedro Calderón de la Barca (1600–81), both of whom would exert an enormous impact on early modern European drama. Over time, Spain's role as the 'historical enemy' of many a European nation was to be decisive in the development of a bias within the cultural sphere that occluded or downplayed Spanish influence.[29] An obvious case in point is the Dutch Republic, whose national founding myth was forged in complete opposition to the 'Spanish Other', framed as a resilient historical enemy. Against this oppositional backdrop, it was difficult to envision Spain and its legacy in cultural interaction with the Low Countries.[30] The occlusion, silencing or downplaying of Spanish influence had already been set in motion during the early modern period, but not until its incorporation into nineteenth-century historiography would it become a full-fledged discourse, as we will see.

Understanding of the cultural hegemony and legacy of Spain in the early modern period likely received its most pervasive framing from the French encyclopaedists. In the eighteenth century many French Enlightened intellectuals were extremely critical of Spain, which they regarded to be a primitive and fanatical nation. Their prejudices fed on the Black Legend narrative that had been abundantly exploited in France during the previous century.[31] In 1782, Nicolas Masson de Morvilliers published a famous entry on Spain in the *Encyclopédie méthodique*. His text unleashed an acrid international polemic on Spain's contributions to European civilization, to which Spaniards reacted with indignation. He wondered: 'What do we owe Spain? And what has she done for Europe in the last, two, four, six centuries?'[32] Morvilliers's answer was unequivocal: nothing at all. Spain resembled 'those weak and miserable colonies that constantly need the metropolis's protective arm'. Given that Spain, at the end of the eighteenth century, was regarded as both colony and empire, the Spanish Empire would understandably elicit contradictory emotions, as Krauel has pointed out.[33] One could add that there is an interplay between notions of greatness and smallness in Morvilliers's argumentation. Spain is defined by Morvilliers as a passive nation that suffers from incurable lethargy and, strikingly, as a 'nation of pygmies'.[34] In light of the terminological context of size that informs this volume, this reduction of Spain to 'pygmy' scale is revealing. Although recent scholarship has contested the entrenched vision of eighteenth-century intellectual France as exclusively a bulwark of anti-Hispanic prejudices,[35] the anti-Hispanic French discourse became dominant amongst discourses on modernity and within Enlightenment historiography addressing Spain. Particularly telling as well is the denial of Spanish literary influence amongst eighteenth-century Italian critics, who instead stressed the claim that Spanish literature had contaminated good taste in Europe and that in the Italian case the influence was inevitably, and negatively, linked to military occupation.[36] These French and Italian lines of argument are relevant because they thus downplay not only Spain's international political international role but also its contributions to European culture.

This sort of discourse belittles the nation's 'great' character and its influential cultural heritage, rendering them 'small' and therefore irrelevant in comparison to what other nations had achieved.

Figurations and perceptions of Spain did not remain exclusively negative over the following centuries. Just as a distinct hispanophobic discourse was prevalent during the early modern period, the watershed of the nineteenth century brought a more widespread and positive acknowledgement of Spain: a hispanophilic 'Romantic Spain'. The Peninsular War or 'Guerra de Independencia' (1807–14) cast the Spanish people in a new light as courageous and persistent opponents of the occupying French, the aggressors of the era's political landscape. Although the image of Spain had now shifted to the positive side of the spectrum, there was no full suppression of lingering or latent negative stereotypes. Furthermore, some elements evident in this newly laudatory appreciation, such as Spain's 'authenticity' or its exoticism, are so tinged with a patronizing view of the country that we might even define it, too, as belittling. Indeed, the Romantic appreciation of a purported Spanish authenticity is in fact related to Black Legend ideas of Spain's primitivism or its anti-modern character, analogous to the way visions of exoticism are enmeshed with perceptions that the country is Oriental and therefore 'non-European'.[37]

Over the course of the nineteenth century, Spain had to accustom itself to its new status as a downgraded nation forced to contend with British and then US imperial ambitions in the process of colonial expansion.[38] In line with Hegel's perception that France, Germany and England made up the 'centre of Europe', an idea of 'imperial difference' started gradually to take shape. Within this new vision of an international balance of power, Spain was to be placed in a secondary, indeed peripheral position. The Black Legend narrative proved essential in the shaping of this 'imperial difference' since European powers instrumentalized certain elements of this narrative (such as Spain's cruelty overseas) to legitimize their own imperial projects and to present themselves as enlightened and modern, as opposed to the old world order of 'tyrants, priests and hypocrites'.[39] With their modern imperial templates, the northern nations cast themselves as the opposite of Spain's colonial model, which was seen as pre-commercial and pre-rationalist, religious and barbaric. These prejudices resonated in historiographical interpretations of Spanish history. Indeed, for instance 'Prescott's paradigm', named after the American historian William Hickling Prescott (1796–1859), would prove pervasive and resilient in the appraisal of Spanish history (and literature). According to Prescott, Spanish history was to be understood as a consequence of Spanish absolutist and monarchical decadence and of the tyrannical nature of Spanish Catholicism.[40] This interpretation can be considered a latter-day version of the Black Legend. Negative images and representations of Spain were so entrenched from the early modern period onwards that once Spain's threat as a 'great' power had disappeared, the criticism and vilification directed towards it seemed to shift and extend into the cultural sphere. Once 'a country that had been one of the privileged sites for the enunciation of European history in the early modern era', Spain had become, by the eighteenth century, increasingly 'an object of representation – and symbolic subordination – for a newly dominant northern Europe', as Michael Iarocci points out. He speaks of a 'symbolic amputation' of Spain from 'modernity', 'Europe' and the 'West'.[41] This bodily metaphor of exclusion or rejection can also be interpreted from the perspective of (lessened) size and conscious reduction, enabling Spain's great and continually relevant contributions to European culture and history to thus be belittled.

The Spanish Golden Age's legacy in Dutch and English literary historiographies

When reconstructing perceptions of Spain and its cultural legacy through the prism of literary histories, we see, despite the novel figurations of a 'Romantic Spain', the persistence and strong influence of the Black Legend narrative. Foreign authors, even when attempting to value Spanish literature and the 'greatness' of its cultural relevance, fell prey to a rhetorical tension between appreciation and rejection, influenced as they were by those longstanding and prejudiced hetero-images. In this way, English and Dutch authors writing at different moments in the nineteenth century reflect the belittling process endured by Spain within the cultural sphere.

The narratives employed in these two national contexts are obviously distinct, since their respective historical circumstances and particular interaction with Spain differed. Writings as reflective of cultural attitudes in both nations reflect, nonetheless, this process of belittlement. Since Golden Age dramas collectively form one of the centrepieces of the Spanish literary canon (the second being Cervantes's *Don Quixote*), the present analysis will focus on how literary histories engage with Spain's theatrical legacy. Drama was intimately related to the reputation of a nation since its artistic form was conceived to be represented in front of the eyes of the people.[42] Two English examples serve to illustrate this trend. Charles Dibdin (1745–1814) was the author of *A Complete History of the English Stage, Introduced by a Comparative Review of a Wide Range of Theatres* (London 1800), a comparative review of drama from Asian examples through the ancient Greeks and covering a wide range of European examples.[43] The second author is George Henry Lewes (1817–78), who occupies quite another position on the spectrum of literary criticism. Dibdin was an author of plays, sea songs and operas, a theatrical manager and an actor, not to mention his voluminous *A Complete History* and an extensive autobiography. For his part, Lewes was one of 'the most interesting and engaging men of letters of his time'. A polyglot writer, philosopher, scientist, editor and gifted literary critic,[44] Lewes was the author of what is considered to be the first in-depth study of Spanish theatre in English: *The Spanish Drama: Lope de Vega and Calderón* (1846).

Regarding the Dutch context, the two authors under scrutiny here will be William De Clercq (1795–1844) and Petrus van Limburg Brouwer (1795–1847). De Clercq was the director of the Dutch Society of Commerce, a foreman of the Dutch section of the Protestant movement the *Réveil* and a literary scholar whose diaries (1831–44) offer a wealth of information about the political and cultural developments of the period.[45] Although literature was not his primary field of endeavour, he was a well-known writer with close connections to the most important scholars and intellectuals of his time. In 1821 De Clercq entered an essay prize competition with his *Treatise in response* to the question: *What influence has foreign literature, in particular, Italian, Spanish, French and German, had on Dutch language and literature, from the beginning of the fifteenth century up to today?*⁴⁶ His ambitious endeavour is considered to be one of the first European comparative literary studies.⁴⁷ Van Limburg Brouwer was a professor of Philosophy and Literature at the University of Liège.⁴⁸ Beginning his professional career as a doctor, he later devoted himself to literature, competing in 1822 for a prize by addressing the question whether Dutch national drama could boast of a tragic tradition: *Do the Dutch possess a national drama regarding tragedy?*⁴⁹ This question was relevant, as we will see, since tragedy was considered to be one of the most distinctive ancient genres, a well-known basis for high literary prestige.

All these literary-historical works reveal the role that notions of nationality (Englishness and Dutchness) play within the discourse of literary histories, since they determine acts of inclusion and exclusion and the invention of traditions through canon formation, etc., and not only within one's own national canon but also with regard to the works of other nations.⁵⁰ Furthermore, the belief in a *Volksgeist* that transcended all spheres and therefore permeated the literary further stressed the close link between the literary and the national. These authors, except Dibdin, are to be understood against the backdrop of literary historians like the brothers Schlegel, Sismonde de Sismondi and Madame de Staël, who first dwelt on Spanish literature and its characteristics and indulged prejudices connected to anti-Hispanic stereotypes.

In his *Comparative History*, Charles Dibdin attempts to chart a panorama of the evolution of dramatic art from its very beginnings to his present time. When reaching the sixteenth and seventeenth centuries, the period when Spanish drama was at its zenith, Dibdin acknowledges clearly that Spanish plays 'have served like a rich mine for the French, and, indeed, the English at second hand to dig in'; they 'have furnished some very rich material which the French and English theatrical chemists have ingeniously extracted to ornament their own productions'.⁵¹ Nonetheless, he later downplays the real value and relevance of these Spanish materials: 'Their wit, however, like their hard dollars, can never be considered as staple, but a useless mass of no intrinsic value till manufactured into literary merchandize by the ingenuity and labour of other countries.' With these words, Dibdin diminishes Spain's influence on the development of European drama. There is nothing great about those Spanish raw materials; the merit belongs to the English, the French and others who reworked them and made them great and superior.⁵² Or as Lewes phrased it in a comparable way: the literary 'skeletons' the Spaniards provided needed to be imbued with flesh and blood in order to function.⁵³ And in his autobiography, *The Professional Life of Mr. Dibdin, written by himself*, Dibdin characterizes the essence of Spanish drama in a similar way:

> I went over the strange and irregular conduct of the Spanish theatre; the inexhaustible wit and extraordinary singularity of Lopez de Vega, Cervantes, and all that string of poets, that gave birth to their monstrous and heterogenous mass of dramatic entertainments, without character of uniformity, but which, nevertheless, have furnished a large fund of materials for the imitation of the French and English theatres.⁵⁴

Again, Spanish plays are presented as a raw source of inspiration, brought forth in a negative light as an empty vessel or amorphous mass of chaotic material, ripe for plundering.[55]

However, even more important in his appraisal of Spanish theatre is an actual dismissal of Spanish drama's very essence, as he stresses in his *Comparative History*: 'As the theatre in Spain, even to this moment, has never had to boast of anything regularly dramatic, it would be difficult, if not impossible, to give a methodical account of it.'[56] Without denying the wit and humour that 'lavishly pervade' Spanish works, he regards these literary efforts as 'crude and irregular' and therefore needing to be reworked and 'merchandized' by others if any degree of literary quality is to be achieved. The problem, it seems, is that Spanish plays cannot be deemed genuinely 'dramatic'. He does not beat about the bush when he concisely asserts: 'As for Melpomene [the Muse of tragedy] she never even to this hour resided in Spain.'[57] Spain is presented as having a national literature in which tragedy, rhetorically the highest form of drama, never took hold. Interestingly enough, Dibdin felt it very important to contest the assertion made by writers from other countries that 'the dramatic art arrived to no perfection in England till it had been perfected by all its neighbours'.[58] His own agenda, aimed at stressing and evincing the relevance and superiority of English drama above all, steers his appraisal of Spanish drama.[59]

Lewes, despite his positive appreciation of Spanish drama in general and especially of the star dramatist Lope de Vega,[60] coincides with Dibdin in denying Spain its tragic dimension and reducing its essence, its status, and the very character of its dramatic influence. As a literary critic, Lewes, child of his time, draws from the Schlegels' and Madame de Staël's intellectual legacy with respect to North-South national and literary polarities and differences: 'The Spanish Drama, inasmuch as it is national, is distinguished from that of other nations by certain characteristics which I will here endeavour to bring into view.'[61] He builds his inherent opposition between English and Spanish drama on a pairing of the unrivalled Shakespeare and the problematic Calderón de la Barca: 'Calderon was not only a Spaniard and eminently religious; he was also a member of the Holy Inquisition, and was not one to tamper with its dogmas.'[62] Lewes follows here the judgemental view of the Swiss literary critic Simonde de Sismondi, who considered Calderón to be 'the poet of the Inquisition'.[63] The influence of the Black Legend narrative here is crystal clear. The word 'Inquisitor' appears six times in Lewes's work, with four occurrences linked to Calderón. This connection is conclusive when denying Calderón the status of 'philosophical poet', and with this literary denial comes a refusal to grant his capacity to produce real tragedy. The Spaniard is, in his eyes, a splendid *playwright* rather than a great *dramatist*,[64] a manifestation of an essential distinction dictating the main difference between English and Spanish drama: the *theatrical* vs. the *dramatic*. He offers as proof of his point a comparison between an original play by Calderón (not his favourite) and its adaptation by the Elizabethan playwrights Beaumont and Fletcher. Bottom line: 'With Calderón it is little more than an *imbroglio*; with Beaumont and Fletcher it is tragedy.'[65] This remark, made in passing, encapsulates and anticipates what would become a longstanding literary prejudice against Spain: Spanish drama is without the tragic dimension and, when compared to English drama, lacks universality. Over centuries, and up through the present, we come across this misconception in comparative transnational literary histories.

In *The Spirit of Baroque Tragedy* (1956), Joseph Herbert Muller stated a clear difference between Elizabethan England and Spain: 'For Spain remained orthodox, Catholic, hierarchical; and Spain wrote no tragedy.'[66] His opinion, clearly tinted by nineteenth-century ideas such as Dibdin's and Lewes's, seems to have exercised a wide influence on many scholars, including Hispanists. In this way a sort of 'Baroque taboo on tragedy' with regard to Spain's theatrical production found its way into literary history.[67] Dibdin and Lewes reflect the tension in English literary historiography about Spain that acknowledges and stresses the literary luxuriance and abundance of Spanish literature even while vilifying its alleged lack of regularity in form and plot, such features recalling an exotic 'Oriental prodigality'.[68]

Dutch authors, for their part, were not particularly receptive to the possibility of a Spanish literary legacy when reflecting on the period when Dutch national literature was forged, the era of their own Golden Age or *Gouden Eeuw*. In fact, only very recently has there been historiographical acknowledgement of Spain's role as a leading cultural nation in the early modern period and an influence on Dutch literature (especially drama).[69] The troubled historical past shared with Spain complicated Dutch-Spanish relations. The undeniable close interaction with Spain proved difficult, in the nineteenth century, to situate within an appropriate cultural framework. Interestingly enough, Spanish influence ended up being explained as a sort of 'catalyst' or 'facilitator' of Dutch cultural grandeur. Along these lines, the struggle against Spain had helped elevate Dutch spirits and led them to produce remarkable literary works.[70] The connection between nations' greatness and their cultural production was very clear in the eyes of nineteenth-century scholars, as Limburg Brouwer attests. At the beginning of his *Treaty on the question: Do the Dutch possess a national drama regarding tragedy?* (1823) he states that one of the most relevant illustrative elements of national greatness is a country's possession of its own literature, so that grandeur encompasses 'not only the fame of weapons, the wide extension of its possessions, the weight of commerce'. Moreover, within literature a hierarchy can be distinguished, with drama at the top since it is the genre most evidently interwoven with a nation's reputation.[71]

Van Limburg Brouwer's question posed in his title – 'Do the Dutch possess a national drama regarding tragedy?' – was relevant since from a rhetorical perspective tragedy was considered to be the highest form of drama. He levels the criticism that the Dutch do not have a national drama, which one finds only amongst the Greeks in antiquity, as well as amongst the Spaniards and the English.[72] While pondering whether Dutch literature can in fact achieve a national drama and how this should happen, he reflects on the characteristics of those other European national dramas. In this way, he acknowledges the national character of Spanish drama and therefore its position at the highest levels of literary achievement and of its greatness as a nation. Calderón de la Barca is mentioned a couple of times as exemplifying Spanish tragic production, Lope de Vega once. However, stereotypical prejudices rear their heads in Van Limburg Brouwer's argument. The Spanish and the English each had a national drama, but these dramas differed, just as the Spanish and English differ with regard to character and mentality. The Spanish works display no unity of action, time or place; they mix the tragic with the comic and are irregular in plot and expression.[73] Not so the English. Van Limburg Brouwer stresses further the chivalric and religious character of Spanish literature and its Oriental essence due to Spain's interaction with the Moors. Here he echoes Sismondi's belief that Spain's literature was different from other literatures and therefore 'Un-European', an example of an Oriental and barbaric Other in the midst of Europe. Madame de Staël's idea of two opposing literatures (one modern, from the North, one pre-modern, from the South) also filters in here.[74] An obvious reduction or belittling of Spanish literary production is present in the above argumentation. Furthermore, several passages in Van Limburg Brouwer's treatise express a certain 'northward' preference. When referring to great and inspiring dramatists he mentions Shakespeare, Corneille, Racine and Schiller – but not a single Spanish author.[75]

Like Van Limburg Brouwer, William De Clercq had to cope with certain prejudices when dealing with Spain. His biased perspective is in line with the conviction, entrenched from the early modern period onwards, that the respective natures and characters of the Spanish and the Dutch were diametrically opposed.[76] He even uses the word 'aversion' (*afkeer*) to describe the impossible religious and political interaction between these two nations.[77] As a logical consequence, De Clercq unambiguously rejects that there might be a Spanish cultural legacy and downplays any manifestation of Spanish influence. From the start, he points to the 'faint impressions that Spanish literature has left on ours'.[78] The possible influences that Spanish drama exerted on Dutch authors are minimized, as when he argues that despite a certain undeniable resemblance to Spanish drama it is difficult to determine whether the imitation did not actually come *through* the French drama that had been inspired by Spanish and Italian theatre.[79] Although he cannot help acknowledge the production of canonical Dutch dramatist Bredero's plays to be in line with 'the Spanish school', he muffles the influence of or interest in Spanish letters at the time. He argues that the present, with its readers of Herder's *Cid* or Schlegel's *Calderón*, represents an utterly different situation. Knowledge of the Spanish language in the Low Countries is yet another aspect soft-pedalled by De Clercq. And when considering authors who mention Spanish writers or works, de Clercq asserts that such references do not imply any sort of influence, adding that in some cases, like that of the learned politician and literary man Constantijn Huygens, author of a well-known book on Spanish sayings (*Spaansche Wijsheid*), the reader may well be disappointed by the lack of references to Spanish authors.[80]

De Clercq cannot possibly value the most influential Spanish dramatists, like the star author Lope de Vega, since their religious background is incompatible with his: 'A Lopez de Vega, familiar of the Inquisition, could never be a loved Poet for the Reformed/Protestant Dutch.'[81] His connection to the Inquisition makes Lope de Vega a 'questionable' playwright who could never have appealed to a Dutch non-Catholic public. Obviously, the Inquisition projects a dark shadow on Spanish cultural production in its widest sense.[82] De Clercq possesses a distinctive view of Dutch national character that seems incompatible with its Spanish counterpart since one of its main features is the 'light inflammable feeling for religious elevation, moral greatness and true love for the fatherland'.[83] Therefore, religion endows the Dutch with a superior dimension, since there is no other nation where religion has so deeply influenced products of the spirit.[84] The other great Spanish playwright, Calderón de la Barca, another example of 'Roomsgezinde Dichters', Catholic poets, was treated with a certain degree of greater neutrality, since German authors had discovered and appreciated him due to his metaphorical and mystical dimension.[85]

Conclusion

Spain, the first global empire to lose its scant political radiance at the end of the nineteenth century, offers a revealing case study to elucidate the variegated possibilities in the (re)construction and negotiation of conceptions of size. The study of Spain is particularly fruitful because it highlights the intersection of international politics with cultural history and with the field of knowledge production, leaning on an imagological framework. Not only in international politics can states be submitted to 'belittling' processes that question their role, relevance and significance in the future or the past. This process can also persistently take shape, over centuries, within the cultural context. Moreover, these two processes are intertwined, shaping and strengthening each other. The Spanish case is especially telling because it shows how a nation of such onetime political weight endured a gradual process of cultural belittling once it began its political decline. From the early modern period onwards, Spain's international reputation was to be tainted by a set of negative and stereotypical images that stressed its urge for universal dominance and posited a purportedly inherent tyrannical disposition and an intolerant and fanatical mentality at the heart of the Spanish character. These latent images of the Spanish 'Other' remained pervasive and filtered into a biased perception of Spanish cultural influence and achievements within Europe. Literary histories engaged in the construction of national canons by asserting literary 'greatness' and superiority; by contrast, the downplaying, occlusion or silencing of the Spanish cultural legacy and its relevance provided a counterexample of a nation defined by its diminishment and its inability to achieve the heights of other nations. The English and Dutch authors under scrutiny reveal how, under the influence of latent hetero-images of the Spaniards, categories regarding 'great' and influential status, as well as small and irrelevant status, could be renegotiated in the cultural field, framing Spain as a nation that had not significantly contributed to European literature in general, nor had ever produced any work that could genuinely be deemed tragedy (the highest literary form and the expression of the highest national pride). Spain became, over time, a culturally pygmy nation, moribund, a failed and declining state. Splendid or not, the 'little war' of 1898 merely confirmed what most cultural commentators already believed they knew.

Notes

1   Smith, 'Splendid Little War'.
2   *New York Times*, 4 May 1898, 6: 'Living and Dying Nations. From Lord Salisbury's Speech to The Primrose League, May 4'.
3   de la Torre del Río, 'La Prensa Madrileña y El Discurso de Lord Salisbury Sobre "Las Naciones Moribundas" (Londres, Albert Hall, 4 Mayo 1898), VI, (1985) 163–80'.

4   For the Black Legend see: Maltby, *The Black Legend in England: The Development of Anti-Spanish Sentiment, 1558–1660*; Swart, 'The Black Legend during the Eighty Years War'; García Cárcel and Ruiz Ibáñez, 'Reflexiones sobre la Leyenda Negra'; Greer, Mignolo, and Quilligan, *Rereading the Black Legend: The Discourses of Religious and Racial Difference in the Renaissance Empires*; Rodríguez Pérez, Sánchez Jiménez, and Boer, *España ante sus críticos: Claves de la Leyenda Negra*.
5   Schmidt, *Spanische Universalmonarchie oder 'Teutsche Libertet'. Das Spanische Imperium in der Propaganda des dreissigjahrigen Krieges*, 446.
6   See the introduction to this volume.
7   London, *Literary History Writing: 1770–1820*, 6, 11. Literary histories could even offer alternatives to national decadence: Johannes and Leemans, *Worm en Donder, Geschiedenis van de Nederlandse Literatuur 1700–1800: De Republiek*, 42.
8   Nünning, 'On the Englishness of English Literary Histories as a Challenge to Transcultural Literary History', 167.
9   Leerssen, 'Imagology', 25.
10 Sánchez Jiménez, *Leyenda Negra: La Batalla Sobre La Imagen de España En Tiempos de Lope de Vega*, 91–4.
11 Juderías, *La Leyenda Negra*, 13–14.
12 Over time, the actions of the Spaniards were to be qualified not from the point of view of *ethos* but of *ethnos*; that is, the evil actions of the Spaniards were determined by their *nature*, by their intrinsic, unchangeable character. Griffin, *English Renaissance Drama and the Scepter of Spain: Ethnopoetics and Empire*, 47.
13 Iglesias, 'España Desde Fuera'.
14 Cited in Kamen, *Imagining Spain. Historical Myth and National Identity*, 189.
15 During the twentieth century (and until now) this Black Legend narrative continued to be instrumentalized in different forms, depending on the historical circumstances: Villanueva, *Leyenda Negra. Una Polémica Nacionalista En La España Del Siglo XX*.
16 Leerssen, 'Imagology', 18.
17 Elliott, *Spain, Europe and the Wider World, 1500–1800*, 27; Lenarduzzi, '"De Oude Geusen Teghen de Nieuwe Geusen." De Dynamiek van Het Oorlogsverleden Ten Tijde van Het Twaalfjarig Bestand, Special Issue of Holland, Historisch Tijdschrift 43.2 (2011) 65–80, 68', 68.
18 Harline, *Pamphlets, Printing, and Political Culture in the Early Dutch Republic*; Horst, *De Opstand in Zwart-Wit: Propagandaprenten Uit de Nederlandse Opstand (1566–1584)*; Rodríguez Pérez, '"The Spanish Seignor" or the Transnational Peregrinations of an Anti-Hispanic Dutch Broadsheet'.
19 Swart, 'The Black Legend during the Eighty Years War', 44–5. See, for the development of the term *Monarchia Universalis* since the medieval period, and for its imperial and papal variants: Bosbach, *Monarchia Universalis: Ein politischer Leitbegriff der frühen Neuzeit*.
20 Rodríguez Pérez, *The Dutch Revolt through Spanish Eyes. Self and Other in Historical and Literary Texts of Golden Age Spain (ca. 1548–1673)*, 195.
21 Hastings, *The Construction of Nationhood: Ethnicity, Religion and Nationalism*, 1.
22 Rodríguez-Salgado, 'Patriotismo y Política Exterior'.
23 Rodríguez-Salgado, 105.
24 Martínez Luna, 'Las Monarquías de Campanella: Una Propuesta de Enfoque Imagológico'.
25 Martínez Luna, 195.

26 Martínez Luna, 203–4.
27 López Madera, *Excelencias de La Monarchia y Reyno de España*.
28 Swart, 'The Black Legend during the Eighty Years War', 44–5; Parker, *The Grand Strategy of Philip II*.
29 See Fuchs's pioneering work on the occlusion of Spanish influence on English drama during the early modern period. Fuchs, *The Poetics of Piracy: Emulating Spain in English Literature*.
30 For the way this anti-Hispanic cultural narrative, mainly forged in the nineteenth century, became dominant, see Rodríguez Pérez, 'Covering the Skeletons'.
31 Marín Pina and Infantes, *Poesía y Prosa contra España: Emblemas del perfecto Español y rodomuntadas Españolas*.
32 Masson de Morvilliers, 'Espagne', 565.
33 Krauel, *Imperial Emotions: Cultural Responses to Myths of Empire in Fin-de-Siecle Spain*, 20–1.
34 Masson de Morvilliers, 'Espagne', 565.
35 Many instances of curious and even positive evaluations are to be found in a variety of French sources, see: Checa Beltrán, 'Leyenda Negra y Leyenda Rosa'; Étienvre, 'Montesquieu y Voltaire: Sus Visiones de España'; Checa Beltrán, 'Lecturas Sobre La Cultura Española En El Siglo XVIII Francés'.
36 Grazia Profetti, 'Para La Fortuna de Lope En El Siglo XVIII'.
37 See Rodríguez Pérez, 'On Hispanophobia and Hispanophilia across Time and Space'; Torrecilla, *España Exótica. La Formación de La Imagen Española Moderna*.
38 Hobsbawm, *The Age of Empire: 1875–1914*, 57.
39 Pagden, *Lords of All the World: Ideologies of Empire in Spain, Britain and France c.1500–c.1800*, 10.
40 Burguera and Schmidt-Nowara, 'Introduction: Backwardness and Its Discontents', 279.
41 Iarocci, *Properties of Modernity: Romantic Spain, Modern Europe, and the Legacies of Empire*, ix. As Iarocci illustrates, the effects of eighteenth- and nineteenth-century northern European cultural imperialism continue to reverberate within the field of 'European literature' today. Iarocci, 8, 28.
42 Limburg Brouwer, *Verhandeling*, 4.
43 Dibdin, *Complete History*.
44 Ashton, 'Lewes, George Henry (1817–1878)'. Accessed 13-01-2020. https://doi.org/10.1093/ref:odnb/16562.
45 https://www.historici.nl/de-koopman-en-de-dominee-dagboekjaren-1831-1844-van-willem-de-clercq-online/. Last accessed 13-01-2020.
46 Clercq, *Verhandeling*.
47 Schenkeveld, *Willem de Clercq En de Literatuur*, 75.
48 Aa, 'Petrus van Limburg Brouwer'.
49 Limburg Brouwer, *Verhandeling*. The treatise was published in 1824 with an epilogue; a second edition followed in 1826. Schenkeveld, *Willem de Clercq En de Literatuur*, 75. See also Jensen, 'In verzet tegen "Duitschlands Klatergoud". Pleidooien voor een nationaal toneel, 1800–1840'.
50 Nünning has remarked on this regarding the English case, but it is equally applicable to the Dutch. Nünning, 'On the Englishness of English Literary Histories as a Challenge to Transcultural Literary History', 163.
51 Dibdin, *Complete History*, vol. I, 131, 145.
52 Dibdin, vol. I 131, 139.
53 Rodríguez Pérez, 'Covering the Skeletons'.

54 Dibdin, *The Professional Life of Mr. Dibdin, Written by Himself. Together with the Words of Six Hundred Songs Selected from His Works and Sixty Small Prints Taken from the Subjects of the Songs, and Invented, Etched, and Prepared for the Aqua Tint by Miss Dibdin*, 112.
55 Dibdin, *Complete History*, vol. I 139. Fuchs sees a connection in the metaphorical way that Spanish plays are plundered according to Dibdin and the exploitive extraction of precious metals in the New World: Fuchs, 'The Black Legend and the Golden Age Dramatic Canon', 233.
56 Dibdin, *Complete History*, vol. I 131. 1.
57 Dibdin, vol. I 132.
58 Dibdin, vol. II 221–2.
59 Dibdin, vol. II, 220. 'The English reader will now see that I have so long kept him at a distance from his native country only that it may be the more dear to him on his return. […] I have done this to prove, upon a comparative review, the superiority of our theatre at home.'
60 Lewes, *The Spanish Drama. Lope de Vega and Calderon*, 7–8. 'Any one desirous of throwing light on the old English Drama should read extensively the less known works of the Spaniards'. Lewes's admiration for Lope de Vega is obvious: he believes that the playwright has been 'written down' in foreign literary histories. Lewes, 88, see also 92, 93, 96, 124.
61 Lewes, *The Spanish Drama. Lope de Vega and Calderon*, 99.
62 Lewes, 111.
63 Lewes, 179.
64 Lewes, 177, 184.
65 Lewes, 9. *Imbroglio*: an extremely confused situation.
66 Muller, *The Spirit of Tragedy*, 149.
67 Kluge, 'Ambiguous Allegories: What the Mythological Comedia Reveals about Baroque Tragedy'.
68 See for the themes of literary luxuriance as an aspect of Anglo-Spanish national difference: Rodríguez Pérez, 'Covering the Skeletons', 323–9.
69 Blom and Marion, 'Lope de Vega and the Conquest of Spanish Theater in the Netherlands'; Blom, 'Enemy Treasures: The Making and Marketing of Spanish Comedia in the Amsterdam Schouwburg'.
70 Jeronimo De Vries posited in his 1810 literary history the connection between freedom from Spanish oppression and the elevation of the arts, especially poetry. Vries, *Proeve Eener Geschiedenis Der Nederduitsche Dichtkunde*, 389.
71 Limburg Brouwer, *Verhandeling*, 3.
72 Limburg Brouwer, 4, 151–2.
73 Limburg Brouwer, 151.
74 Limburg Brouwer, 156; Dainotto, *Europe (in Theory)*, 114.
75 Limburg Brouwer, *Verhandeling*, 156.
76 Rodríguez Pérez, 'Covering the Skeletons', 333.
77 Limburg Brouwer, *Verhandeling*, 180.
78 Limburg Brouwer, 13, 179.
79 Limburg Brouwer, 122.
80 Limburg Brouwer, 119, 179, 181.
81 Limburg Brouwer, 180. 'Een Lopez de Vega, *de familiaar der Inkwisitie*, kon nimmer een geliefd Dichter voor den *hervormden* Nederlander worden'.

82 This also holds for the canonical *History of the Spanish Literature* by the American writer George Ticknor (1844–55, 3 vols.), which became very influential on other literary histories. This multivolume work transmits Ticknor's biased and reductive vision of Spain. Vélez Sainz, 'La Hispanofobia en el Hispanismo: Ticknor, de Gayangos y De Vedia entre la Leyenda Negra y el Siglo de Oro', 207.
83 Clercq, *Verhandeling*, 49.
84 Clercq, 41.
85 Clercq, 180. As mentioned above, Lewes considered Calderón to be 'the poet of the Inquisition'.

2

Dealing with smallness in Habsburg Bohemia, Ottoman Albania and Tsarist Georgia in the late nineteenth and early twentieth centuries

Adrian Brisku

Smallness within Empire

The borderlands of the Habsburg, Ottoman and Tsarist Empires, stretching from the Baltics to the Balkans, have long been understood by historians of the region as zones of conflict between imperial despotism on the one hand and emerging cultural and ethno-national societies on the other. These conflicts supposedly reached their zenith in the late nineteenth and early twentieth centuries, eventually resulting in the destruction of either the empires themselves or, in the case of the Soviet Union, the fall of the old regime and their replacement by an unprecedented socio-political experiment. But, following Jürgen Osterhammel historians have more recently begun to study the remarkably peaceful co-existence of nations and empires up until the First World War.[1] This chapter helps explain why, by focusing on and comparing the role played by smallness in political discourse amongst elites in three different imperial settings: in Habsburg Bohemia, Ottoman Albania and Tsarist Georgia.

It focuses, firstly, on the writings of Czech philosopher, and first president of Czechoslovakia, Thomas G. Masaryk (1850–1937), who, together with the leader of Czech National-Liberal Party and the first Czechoslovakian Prime Minister Karel Kramař (1860–1937),[2] reflected on the 'problem of the small nation that [...] was resolved through the task of the small state' in his book *The Czech Question* (1895).[3] Within Ottoman Albania, the question of smallness within Empire was pondered by the imperial bureaucrat and head of the first Albanian government Ismail Qemali (1844–1919), the Enlightenment figure Sami Frashëri (1850–1904) and the Albanian Prime Minister Fan Noli (1882–1965). Frashëri, for instance, wrote about an Albania that was 'becoming smaller' in his book *Albania: Past, Present and Future* (1899).[4] In the Tsarist Georgian context we examine writings by Georgian Enlightenment figures such as Ilia Chavchavadze (1837–1907), Niko Nikoladze (1843–1928) and the head of the first Georgian government Noe Zhordania (1869–1953).[5] Zhordania, for example, described the newly independent

Georgia of 1918 as a 'small nation' uncomfortably sandwiched between two larger entities: Soviet Russia and the Ottoman states.[6]

Critically, a focus on the discourses of smallness allows us to compare and contrast not only chronologically but diachronically as well. The three case studies betray the effects of similar processes of imperial reform and national development (albeit with difference in interactions, speed and intensity) as entities within Austro-Hungary, the Ottoman empire and Tsarist Russia, respectively. These states also became independent at roughly the same time, which is to say just before and just after the First World War: Albania became a state in 1912, and Georgia and Czechoslovakia followed suit in 1918. During the Cold War each was part of the Soviet bloc (with Georgia part of the Soviet Union itself). We should also note that synchronically, during the postsocialist period, Albania, Czechia and Georgia – as independent republics – have sought or aim to become incorporated into larger politico-economic (the EU) and political-military (the North Atlantic Treaty Organization (NATO)) structures.[7] Moreover, Albanian and Georgian historiographies have constructed similar sorts of historical narratives about their respective nations being 'ancient small nations surviving great empires'.[8] And while this kind of narrative is absent from Czech historiography,[9] the prominent Czech political theorist Miroslav Hroch, in his book *Social Preconditions of National Revival in Europe* (1986)[10] used 'smaller' as a descriptive term to analyse nineteenth- and early twentieth-century Bohemian nationalism in relation to other European states of comparable size. In other academic disciplines as well, such as international relations (IR) and European Studies, we find Czech scholars, in their assessment of the country's behaviour and influence in the EU's decision-making, categorize it as a 'small country'.[11] In public discourse, too, 'small nation'[12] and 'small state'[13] are used interchangeably. Georgian scholars in IR and European Studies also describe the country as 'a small state' in international relations,[14] whereas the governmental discourse conceives it as a 'small but active state'.[15] In the Albanian context smallness appears – in addition to within the historiographical narrative – in governmental discourse. Speaking at the annual NATO Military Committee Conference held in 2017 in Tirana, Prime Minister Edi Rama described Albania as a 'small member' of the NATO Alliance devoted to carrying out 'small tasks'.[16]

It is important here to demonstrate the historical continuity of the smallness discourse up through the contemporary period for the countries considered here. But understanding what smallness *meant* for the selected protagonists matters, too, especially given the lack of a conceptual historical study on this question, either as individual cases or comparatively. This chapter, then, maintains that the three cases exhibit similar discourses on smallness: namely, these discourses all share the premise that to be a small nation within an empire entailed the recognition that it was in a state of national weakness primarily in relation to its imperial centre, though even an empire could be regarded this way in relation to other empires. But this type of situation also necessitated the invention of strategies (constitutional, political-economic, geopolitical) to cope with such a predicament, and even of ways to thrive as a result of power imbalances within and outside it.

Habsburg Bohemians: Within a 'union of small nations'

In the case of Habsburg Bohemia, Masaryk and Kramář are arguably two of the most pertinent examples of the late nineteenth- and early twentieth-century intellectual and political milieu who discussed the smallness of the Bohemian nation(-state). Hailing from different social backgrounds, trained in distinct areas of education (doctoral studies in sociology for Masaryk and jurisprudence for Kramář) and having been exposed to varying sorts of political ideas, the political views of these two men converge briefly in the early 1890s when they participate in the national and imperial elections of 1891 as members of a small new political group, the Realists. Winning seats as Realists – a group affiliated with the National-Liberal Party – in both the Bohemian and the imperial Diets, they sought to implement their group's 1890 'Návrh programu lidového' (Outline of a People's Programme)[17] calling for political, economic and social rights for Bohemians within a federalized Austro-Hungary.

In one of the speeches he delivered in 1891 at the imperial Diet discussing the merits of Austro-Hungary's membership in the Triple Alliance (a military alliance with Germany and Italy established in 1882), Masaryk referred to Bohemia as a 'small nation', a part of the Austro-Hungarian empire, while describing the empire as a 'union of small nations'. He made these characterizations while criticizing the alliance on financial grounds for being disproportionately unfair to Bohemia. Moreover, aside from being against wars per se, Masaryk considered Austro-Hungary's decision to join the alliance a strategic error: it would increase militarization in Europe and trap Austro-Hungary into becoming involved in unwanted wars. Here the discourse of smallness encompasses more than Bohemia's weakness as a nation within the empire unable to alter the terms of an unwise alliance. In recognizing Bohemia's smallness and by extension through the term (the auto-image) 'union of small nations' highlighting the smallness of Austro-Hungary as a whole vis-à-vis (the hetero-image) other European powers, Masaryk projected a morality onto being or becoming a small nation. Smallness entailed disengagement from power politics defined by war and military alliances; smaller political entities were thus not warmongering by definition. Austro-Hungary, and Bohemia within it, need not give up on power per se, but influence in Europe was to be exerted through its cultural and economic strengths.[18] In this light, smallness as a foreign policy orientation for a small nation or for a 'union of small nations' meant opposition to military alliances and war – a sense shared by some within the Tsarist Georgian context, to be discussed below.

The views of Kramář, in his own criticism of the Triple Alliance, converged with Masaryk's positions on heightened militarization and Austro-Hungary's war projects. His concern, however, was directed not towards the unfair financial burden endured by the empire but rather the fear that in pursuing its foreign policy in accordance with the alliance, the empire would put its internal integrity at stake. As he wrote in his memoirs (published in the 1930s), recalling the Habsburg and Bohemian politics of the 1890s, 'Austria in its make-up [was] not cut out for expansive foreign policy' because there was little consensus amongst the empire's nationalities.

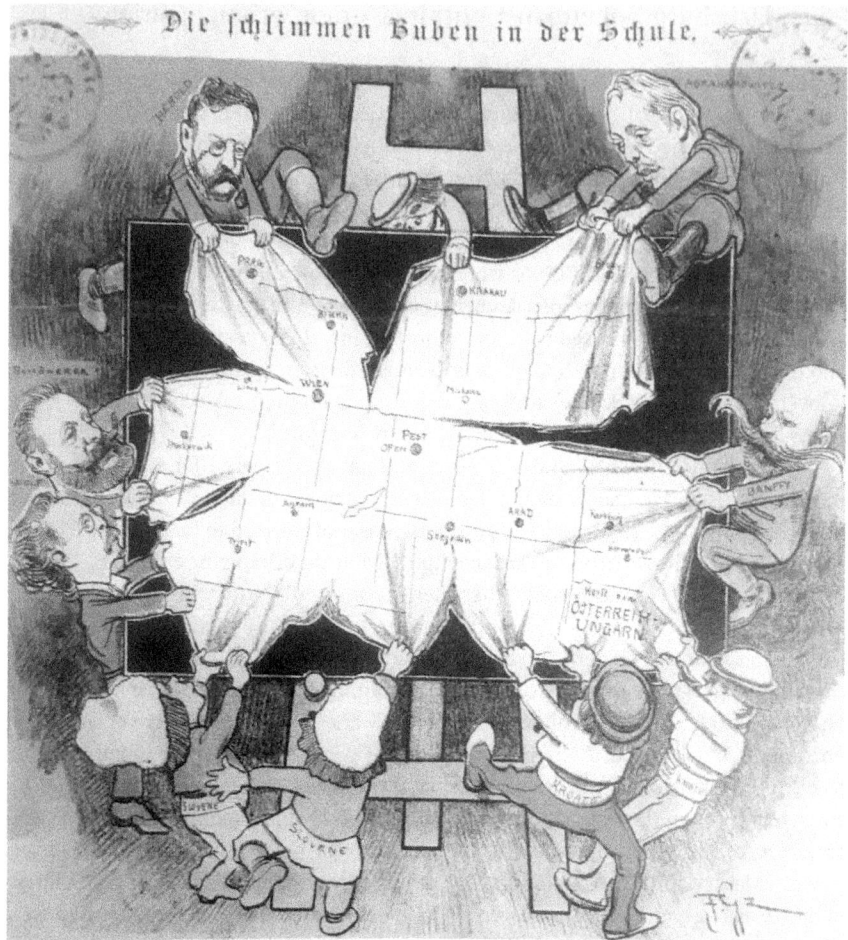

Figure 2.1 'Naughty Boys in School/or the Sacrificing of the Empire'. This cartoon, printed in *Neue Glühlichter*, 19 January 1899, highlights the increasing disunity amongst the small nationalities of Austria-Hungary. © Out of copyright.

Accordingly, this lack of unanimity was a sign of the empire's smallness, because it made it a smaller player vis-à-vis other European states such as Germany. Thus, being small meant external weakness and internal disunity. To overcome this condition, Kramář, like Masaryk, advocated the strengthening of the empire's economic power via a foreign policy oriented towards trade, specifically with the Balkans and with Russia.[19]

From a Bohemian/Czech perspective, thus, as Masaryk and Kramář both saw it, Austro-Hungary in relation to other European powers and Bohemia in relation particularly to German Austrians and Hungarians within the empire were or had become smaller, hence weaker. To deal with this relative decline, they argued, the empire's foreign policy should project cultural and economic strength rather than be entangled in military alliances and war. This policy shift would bode well for Bohemia, which had become one of the most industrialized nations in Europe and was keen to export its industrial surplus. However, to change the empire's orientation, Bohemia would have to share the prerogative of decision-making in imperial foreign trade. However, thanks to the Dual Monarchy's constitutional arrangement of 1867, together with its military policy, foreign trade remained in the hands of Habsburg Austrians and Hungarians.

In response, Masaryk and Kramář employed the language of federalism. They were not the first to do so, though. The mid-nineteenth-century politician and the 'father of the nation' František Palacký (1798–1876) – who famously refused to participate in the 1848 all-German Diet in Frankfurt because it was a pan-German rather than a Czech affair; that same year he became the leader of the first Czech party, the National Party – was amongst the first to demand that the political rights of the Bohemian state/kingdom (with its regions of Bohemia, Moravia and Silesia) be restored via a federalized Austrian empire.[20] As framed in his book *The Idea of the Austrian State* (1865), Palacký had been hopeful about such a reorganization in the wake of the 1861 imperial constitutional reforms that had established the imperial Diet. In this book, he foresaw an intensification of ethno-cultural differences between the large and small nations of the empire. His solution for small nations such as Bohemia was federalism: Bohemia as a state with the empire. More generally, his idea entailed a federalized Austria based on the principle, on the one hand, of 'historical rights' for the medieval Austrian, Bohemian and Hungarian kingdoms/states and, on the other, of 'nationality rights' for those new entities that were to be established on imperial territories that were linguistically distinct and compact, such as those of the south Slavic groups (the Slovenes and the Croats).[21] Like many other Bohemians, he saw his hopes dashed by the constitutional *dualism* of the Dual Monarchy of 1867 between German Austrians and Hungarians. And as a matter of political protest, his National Party and the new National-Liberal Party established in 1874 – which Kramář led from 1897 – rejected this dualism and occasionally boycotted the imperial Diet.[22]

For Masaryk and Kramář, however, participation in imperial politics and the federalization of the empire were crucial means of strengthening Bohemia's position within the imperial space. To recall, in their 1890 Realists project, they rejected the boycott and declared that 'a federal Austria [was] our ultimate goal'.[23] In an essay entitled 'On the Czech State Right' (1888), Masaryk argued for a federalist project similar to what Palacký had adumbrated, a vision based on both the 'historical' and 'nationality rights' principles, with stress on the importance of ethno-linguistic affinities between Czechs and Slovaks added to the latter.[24] Kramář, however, in his book *The Czech State Right* (1896) favoured a form of federalization based only on 'the historical rights' principle, that is, the recovery of Bohemia's political rights, similar to what Hungary had restored in 1867.[25] Thus the existing *dualism* would yield to the *trinity* of Austria, Hungary and Bohemia. Bohemia, then, would no longer be burdened by the problem of having no political say on trade policy, which since 1867 had served the interests of Habsburg German bureaucrats and Hungarian landowners.[26] Bohemia would thus be on an equal footing with Austria and Hungary in status and influence.

Tied to federalization and the reorientation of imperial foreign policy – both generating a Bohemian discourse of smallness vis-à-vis Austro-Hungary – was their understanding of what the Bohemian-Czech nation(-state) was and what it meant to them. Masaryk discussed the matter extensively in his book *The Czech Question* (1895), linking this question in the preface to Palacký's federalist project, 'the task of the small state', which he considered to be the resolution of an earlier discourse initiated by the Pan-Slavism ideologue Ján Kollár (1793–1852) as 'the problem of the small nation'. Masaryk regarded Kollár – whose discourse of smallness emerged within the early nineteenth-century context of the rise of pan-Germanism (the idea of a political unity of all German-speaking peoples) – to have framed the problem of Slavic nationalities within Austria in terms of their small size, individually, vis-à-vis the German-speaking peoples. 'The education of small nations – tiny and tiniest of nations [synonymic variations of the small]', Kollár had maintained, was 'not enough, for they exist but do not live fully. Their humanity is dimly and restrictedly manifested.'[27] Together with education, a unification of Slavic nations that would increase their collective presence – what Kollár conceptualized as the Slavic Reciprocity, or latter referred to as pan-Slavism – would enable Bohemian Czechs and other Slavic nations to handle the rise of pan-Germanism and overcome, for each, the problem of being a small nation. Masaryk, in turn, acknowledged Kollár's discourse of smallness; in fact, one of the virtues he assigned to his definition of the Bohemian-Czech nation, as Kollár did, was its humanity. But Masaryk thought that 'the vexation [that Kollár had] about the smallness of our national life [was] only temporary and to be ended'. Accordingly, Czech national life had to be seen from the perspective of it being 'reborn' on the material basis of the now rather than the historical view of what it had been, though Masaryk acknowledged that the historical perspective could not be dismissed entirely.[28] As such, his understanding of the Czech nation combined a consideration of its past and of its present ethno-cultural traits with an assertion of a universalizing quality, that is, humanity, meaning individual responsibility, solidarity and sociability.[29]

Going beyond an ethno-cultural definition of the nation allowed Masaryk to overcome the discourse of smallness, as he did in the book *The Social Question* (1898), whereby a Bohemian nation defined by its humanity and sociability – from a political-economic perspective – meant that it encompassed not only Bohemian-Czech labour and capital but also the labour and capital of their Bohemian-German compatriots.[30] Accordingly, 'we [Czechs] and our German compatriots' had been and continued to be part of a developing, industrializing Bohemia.[31] Kramář, however, conceptualized the nation purely in ethno-linguistic and historical terms. Thus, when it came to how he viewed strengthening the nation from a political-economic perspective, he favoured the rights of ethnic Czechs (capitalist and workers) versus those of their Bohemian-German counterparts. And to compensate for this narrower definition, he placed the nation within the pan-Slavic space in which the Czech worker was not only 'our national vanguard' but also the 'Slavic colonist, advancing not aggressively but peacefully in the imperial space'.[32]

By the turn of the century, despite the efforts of Masaryk and Kramář, the smallness of the nation remained something to be reckoned with in political and intellectual considerations about national and imperial life. Being small in the political power relations within the empire and of the empire vis-à-vis other European states had more downsides than advantages. Simultaneously, smallness was something to be handled through federalization and the expansion of the Bohemian nation's cultural and economic reach beyond its historical confines. But while agreeing that this could be achieved via cultural and political-economic means, they kept disagreeing about who could be included in the nation and which other nations these means could be extended to.

Indeed, since 1893 there had been more disagreement than agreement amongst the two men, since they had politically parted ways, though they corresponded until the late 1930s. Kramář, as mentioned, became leader of the National-Liberal Party in 1897. Masaryk – having returned to academia from 1893 to 1907 – re-entered parliamentary politics in 1907 with his left-leaning liberal Realist Party. They disagreed on Czech and Slovak unity, with Masaryk in favour[33] and Kramář opposed, and did not see eye to eye about the position of the Bohemian-Czech nation within the pan-Slavism discourse of the late nineteenth century. The debate on pan-Slavism, framed back in Palacký's time in terms of an orientation towards Austro-Slavism, a defence of Czech/Slav rights within the empire and Kollár's Slavic Reciprocity, had been rehashed in the late 1890s in Kramář's party,[34] with Kramář clearly positioning himself with the latter. In fact, in 1908 Kramář became one of the main proponents of neo-Slavism, which saw Czech national and economic interests better served via a constitutional arrangement – a Slavic federation – that grouped all Slavic nations under the political authority of the Russian Romanov dynasty.[35] This situation, for Kramář, aligned well with a Czech national economic policy, which he subscribed to, framed as 'one to oneself', whereby the nation's expanding industrial and financial 'muscle' – which had overpowered their Bohemian-Germans counterparts on 'an unprecedented scale even in Europe'[36] – would extend into other Slavic regions of the empire, the Balkans and Tsarist Russia. This economic expansion, in turn, was articulated in a language of 'mutual Slavonic interests' and 'Slavic brotherhood'.[37] For his part, Masaryk positioned the nation within the Austro-Slavism discourse, meaning that Czechs – as he put it during a rally of his Realist Party (a party that embraced reform, democracy, universal suffrage and gender equality) in 1907 on the eve of imperial and national elections – were better off defending their rights in the Austrian state. Wider global political and economic trends, as he saw them in 1907, convinced him of the viability of 'larger political and economic units', which meant that the nation was better served within this larger imperial space despite the latter's encroaching centralization, bureaucratization and Germanization. Federalism for him[38] and for Kramář had been the strategy to deal with the underrepresentation of the Bohemian voice at the imperial level.

This federalist strategy gained little traction or support amongst other Bohemian parties at the turn of the century, however. Thus Masaryk – after the universal vote was applied in the imperial elections of 1907 – adopted democracy as a new blueprint. As he put it in a speech to the Bohemian Diet in 1907 entitled 'Democracy and the Nationality Question in Austria', democracy was better equipped to transform imperial power structures. In this light, a democratized rather than a federalized empire allowed the voices of the empire's nationalities and of the common people to be heard in the venue of the imperial Diet. Here these voices could overrule those of the nobility and of the capitalists who, up to then, had decided on military and trade policies. In this way, Masaryk was convinced that the Bohemian nation would become an influential member of 'Austria [as] a Great Power, *a cultural Great Power*' [italics in original] with which he could identify.³⁹

Ottoman Albanians: 'Becoming smaller'

As in the Habsburg-Bohemian case, a sense of the nation's smallness became part of the late nineteenth-century Ottoman-Albanian political and intellectual discourse. Similarly, the aspects that influenced its articulations were considerations about the empire's standing in European politics and about an emerging Albanian nation's place and development vis-à-vis the imperial centre and the neighbouring states. But unlike Masaryk and Kramář, who worried that their empire would become embroiled in European wars, the discourse of Ottoman-Albanians such as Ismail Qemali, Sami Frashëri and the Ottoman/American-Albanian Fan Noli was more directly and acutely influenced by the wars their empire was fighting (and mostly losing): the Russo-Turkish War of 1877–8, the Italian-Turkish War of 1911 and the First Balkan War of 1912–13.

Even before articulating directly – in written form – the smallness of the Albanian nation, there was the term 'Great Powers' within the political vocabulary of politically active Ottoman-Albanians. This term referred to Britain, Austro-Hungary, France, Russia, Germany and Italy, the large and powerful states whose concerted actions exercised a large impact on the future of the empire and, by extension, of the Ottoman-Albanians. The Great Powers' presence became keenly felt particularly around the time of the Congress of Berlin (1878) – following the Ottoman defeat in the Russo-Turkish War. These states were about to recognize the independence of Romania, Serbia and Montenegro from the Ottoman Empire but would not consider the demands made by some Ottoman-Albanians (amongst them those who in 1878 had founded the League of Prizren, a political and military league) for self-rule under Ottoman supervision.⁴⁰ In fact, the German chancellor, Otto von Bismarck, saw Albania merely as a 'geographical expression'.⁴¹ As it happened, the Great Powers recognized the independence of the three states and forced the sultan's hand to grant autonomy to the principality of Bulgaria.⁴² Meanwhile, the League of Prizren, which sought from the Ottoman Bulgarians the same sort of arrangement granted by the Great Powers, were not successful in this regard.

Ismail Qemali, though he had nothing to do with the League, was an influential insider in Ottoman politics, holding high positions in the imperial administration – including governorships in several Ottoman provinces⁴³ – and granted direct communication with the Ottoman sultan Abdülhamid II (r. 1876–1908). In his writings – two memoranda he wrote in 1892 and 1897 – Qemali engaged with the discourse of smallness, articulating the auto-image of small nation(-state) versus the hetero-image of the Great Powers. He did so within the context of his pursuit of imperial reform and realignment with the Great Powers, especially with Britain – but initially did not address the Albanian nation in this regard. This latter concern would emerge only from 1900 onwards, after he fell out politically with the sultan and, from his exile in Western Europe, he began to work with the Ottoman opposition (the Young Turks) to institute reform and federalization and with Albanian patriots on Albanian political rights within the empire.[44]

The two memoranda aimed to sway the sultan into restoring the constitution and parliament (active between 1876 and 1878) that he had suspended (measures that would return the empire to the path of Western-oriented reforms). It also sought to convince him to re-orient the empire towards relations with the Great Powers – in the aftermath of 1878 Berlin Congress the sultan had pursued an isolationist policy[45] – and especially with Britain (which earlier had served as the guarantor of empire's security and territorial integrity) so as to reverse its decline in power and hence return as a honourable actor amongst the other European powers. More specifically, Qemali advised the sultan to pursue a 'realistic' (interest-based) approach in foreign affairs; he proposed a 'world policy' towards the Great Powers and especially Great Britain and Russia (which would seek out common interests amongst them and act on them), joined by a 'special policy' for small and newly independent Balkan states.[46] In the latter policy, the discourse of smallness prevailed. Certainly, while recognizing their formal independence, he viewed these states (Romania, Serbia and Montenegro) as militarily and economically weak and unviable. Accordingly, it was their smallness, which made them dependent on Russia's military might and Austro-Hungary's economic prowess, 'which scared them with its capacity to absorb their economic resources'. He believed that they could not do much about their small and weak state of being. But he saw an opportunity for the empire to transform itself into a 'Grand Oriental State' and to offer to these small and weak states a 'defensive alliance' and 'economic accord' – seemingly better than what Austro-Hungary and Russia could do for them – which in turn would contribute to the 'economic development of the empire'.[47]

It was doubtless not appealing to be a small state in the sphere of international relations, if the situation was regarded, as it was by Qemali in these memoranda, from the viewpoint only of imperial interests and not that of the Albanian nation. To be small here meant a perpetual condition of weakness and dependency on other larger states/empires. The writings of the Ottoman-Albanian Enlightenment figure Sami Frashëri, however, presented a different framing of smallness.[48] Frashëri interacted with Qemali and other Albanian patriots in Istanbul when he served as the chairman of the cultural society of Albanians in Istanbul established in 1872. In his book *Albania: What It Was, What It Is and What It Will Be* (1899) – considered a national political manifesto in Albanian historical discourse[49] – he placed Albania within the discourse of smallness as an entity that was 'becoming smaller'. This conception emerged in his account of its history: out of its ancient past as the oldest nation in Europe, and a large one, Albania had over time been diminished and, especially during his era, was in terms of territorial size 'becoming a small country'.[50] Echoing fears expressed by the League of Prizren – whose leader was his elder brother, Abdyl – that the new Balkan states were eager to possess Albanian lands, he reiterated that 'since then [the ancient past] Albania has become smaller'.[51]

Yet even though the nation's territorial size was diminishing, Frashëri's view of its future remained hopeful. 'Albania, despite being small, has all kinds of climates, soils and could become prosperous and feed four times more people than it can feed today.'⁵² He was convinced that its prosperity and strength would come from its 'human resources' (a population of some 2 million) and its people's national character: a smart, brave people who worked hard at any kind of labour and a nation that was capable of raising an army of 300,000 soldiers.⁵³ Reflecting on the weak geopolitical state of the Ottoman empire – and taking into account the pressures on the Albanian-inhabited lands from Greek, Serbian and Montenegrin nationalist projects – he called on Albanians to establish their own government to defend the rights of Albanians. Accordingly, this government would first be placed under Ottoman rule. But if 'Turkey fell […] it will be on its own [i.e., an independent state]'.⁵⁴

As mentioned, after having failed to convince the sultan of his views on imperial reform as well as the re-orientation of its foreign policy and having gone into exile in 1900, Qemali began to collaborate with the Young Turks on the issues of parliamentarism and federalism – the latter he saw, as Masaryk and Kramář did, as the means to deal with the nation's smallness within the empire – and with Albanian patriotic groups on securing language rights, self-rule and unity under the sultan for the four predominantly Albanian-speaking Ottoman provinces (Kosovo, Scutari, Janina and Monastir). These efforts occasioned a brief collaboration in Brussels in 1900 with another prominent Ottoman-Albanian intellectual, Faik Konica (1875–1942), whose periodical, *Albania* – in print between 1896 and 1909⁵⁵ and interestingly in 1899–1900 was entitled *Little Albania* – included his contributions. For instance, in 'The Call of Ismail Qemal bey Vlora to Albanians after Leaving Istanbul', published 15 October 1900, Qemali stated his reasons for leaving Istanbul. In addition, he offered an ethno-linguistic and historical conceptualization of Albania as 'ancient nation' and called for unity amongst Albanian patriots in defending their national rights within the empire. He also urged them to work on securing the support of the Great Powers so as to preserve the territorial integrity of their empire.⁵⁶ Thus, not only for Qemali – who already had expressed his view on the political and economic viability of small states in the international order – but also for many Albanian political activists of the early 1900s, such as the Ottoman/American-Albanian Fan Noli, the question whether the small nation Albania could viably become independent was made conditional on the empire's survival in the Balkans. As the editor-in-chief of the newspaper *Vatra* – the mouthpiece of the Albanian diaspora in the United States – Noli, in the publication's inaugural 15 January 1909 issue entitled 'Albania for Albanians', also called for self-rule with the sultan as the 'governor of Albania'.⁵⁷

The answer to this question was positively confirmed following a series of political and military events that engulfed a militarily weakening empire: first the 1908 Young Turk Revolution, which restored constitutional monarchy and parliamentarism but did not institute federalism and did not allow for self-rule for an all-Albanian united province,⁵⁸ then the military defeats at the hands of Italy (1911), in the Albanian uprisings (1911) and from the Balkan states in the First Balkan War (1912–13). But to Qemali and many other Albanian patriots, the independence of a little Albania – promulgated on 28 October 1912 – could not be fully realized without the backing of the Great Powers, more precisely Austro-Hungary and Italy. The discord between these two Great Powers in supporting this little Albania was insightfully depicted in a political caricature published in *Wiener Caricaturen*, 1 February 1914, as illustrated in Figure 3.2, showing a 'baby Albania' in the hands of a nurse talking to the foreign minister of Austro-Hungary about the baby's absent father, Italy.

So, at this point, the question became not whether a small nation like Albania would be viable – which Qemali had doubts about, based on his views of other small

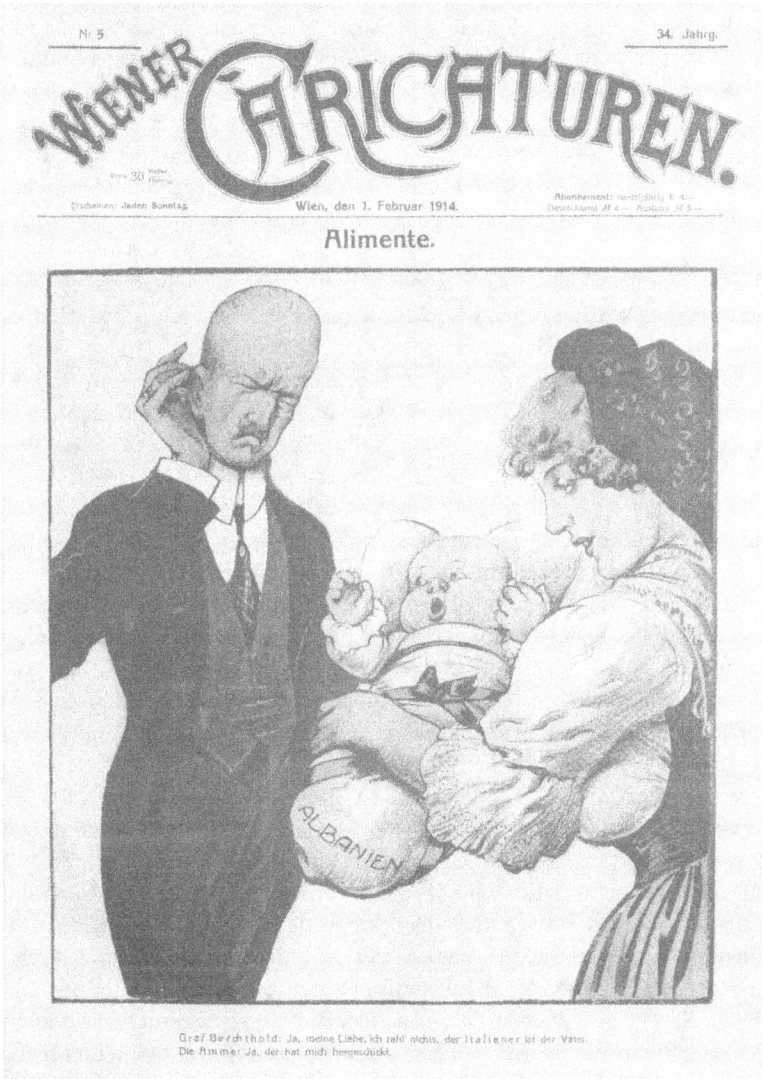

Figure 2.2 'Alimony'. The caption has Leopold Count von Berchtold, the Austro-Hungarian Foreign Minister, say: 'Yes, my dear, but I do not pay, the Italian [i.e. the Italian State] is your father.' The nurse replies: 'Yes, he sent me here.' From *Wiener Caricaturen*, 1 February 1914. © Out of copyright.

Balkan states – but whether it should exist on its own given the collapse of Ottoman rule in the Balkans. Considering the latter, he was certain that it should.

Tsarist Georgians: 'A small nation... seeking its own comfort'

Unlike the two previous cases, where the discourse of smallness contains direct articulations of the term itself, that is, the small nation/state, in the Tsarist Georgian instance overt considerations of 'smallness' would not become as evident until 1918. The Georgian political and intellectual elite began to articulate the notion more conspicuously when the country became independent on 26 May 1918, though this short-lived era of independence ended when Georgia became part of Soviet Russia on 25 February 1921. Indeed, the auto-image of a small, independent and self-declared neutral Georgia vis-à-vis the hetero-images of the Great Powers fearing the actions of neighbouring Soviet Russia and the Ottoman empire was articulated by the Georgian head of government Zhordania, who wrote that 'it was incomprehensible that they [Russia and the Ottoman empire] would hate such a small nation [...] which does not disturb anybody but is seeking its own comfort'.[59] The size differential was also visualized in a contemporary Georgian satirical magazine, *Devil's Whip* (see Figure 3.3), which depicted the small, fictionalized representatives of the Georgian government – seeking recognition of its independence at the Versailles Peace Conference in 1919 – stunned by a gigantic sphinx symbolizing the Great Powers.

The discourse of smallness did, however, exist in the Tsarist Georgian context examined here, during a period which, as in the Habsburg-Bohemian and Ottoman-Albanian cases, imperial reform and national cultural and economic development processes were exerting their impact. In fact, three intellectual and cultural groups – recognized in Georgian historiography as the first, second and third groups, a differentiation based largely on their varying cultural orientations and political ideologies – came to discuss the nation's past, present and future in cultural-economic and political terms in relation to the changes within and outside of the imperial centre.

For one of the most prominent figures of the first group, Ilia Chavchavadze – recognized in the late 1980s by the Soviet Georgian Republic as 'the father of the Georgian nation' – the Georgian nation consisted above all of its ancient history, its language and Georgian Orthodox Christianity. He saw its future resting on its cultural development, on the education of its people and on the preservation of a strong alliance with the Russian state.[60] But rather than discussing Georgia directly in terms of its smallness, he addressed Georgia conceptually as an 'old nation'. For Chavchavadze, the venerable Georgian nation – 'two millennia of historical continuity based on language and religion' – entailed, as in the Ottoman-Albanian case, as sense of autochthony and, as in the Habsburg-Bohemian instance, a sense of a historical right. That historical right derived from the medieval Georgian kingdom, which fragmented in 1466 into several small kingdoms that after 1555 had fallen under Persian control to the east and Ottoman rule to the west, and then was annexed as the kingdom of Kartli-Kakheti (then under Persian control) in 1801 by the Russian Empire. The latter, in the first half of the nineteenth century, had 'gathered the Georgian lands'[61] and then, in the

Figure 2.3 A political cartoon printed in the Georgian satirical magazine ეშმაკის მათრახი (Devil's Whip), 7 December 1919, featuring two Georgian politicians at the Versailles Peace Conference with the Great Powers symbolized by a great sphinx. The illustration was captioned 'Facing a Strange Judgement'. © Out of copyright.

second half of the century up through 1917, had ruled the Georgian people in the two administrative provinces of Tbilisi and Kutaisi. Georgia was not 'old' in the sense of a spent force, as a Russian author had suggested in 'A Letter on Georgia', published in 1889 in the Russian journal *Severnyy Vestnik*. Indeed, to this author's statement that 'Georgian nation is really old [...] it is empty of its power for it has not showed it now [...] and it would not in the future',[62] Chavchavadze retorted with fourteen letters that rejected the Russian author's description of the nation as 'nonsensical'. Even so,

Chavchavadze admitted that Georgians needed to be more active in spurring their country's cultural and societal development.[63]

'Old' signifying a spent and thus weak force entailed a diminished entity but, as he underscored in his 1889 article 'Hundred Years Ago' – marking the centenary of when the Russian army came to the assistance of the Kartli-Kakheti kingdom fighting against Persian control – Georgia would have remained spent only if Russia had not 'opened the doors of Enlightenment… [and] Georgia found peace. The patronage of our fellow believers [thus, Russian Orthodox] quelled our fear of the enemy […]. The exhausted country became tranquil […] and rested from war and struggle.'[64] Chavchavadze was convinced that without Russia's patronage Georgia's political existence in the Caucasus and within the European order would be difficult. His mental geopolitical map of Europe – where the discourse of smallness featured strongly – in his other writings published from 1882 to 1898 was governed by an order comprising 'first', 'second' and 'third-rate' countries. Size, military prowess and the focus of their interests on either external or internal affairs, or both, determined where countries were situated. The 'first-rate' countries were Britain, France, Germany, Russia, Italy and Austro-Hungary, characterized as 'competing colonial powers', warmongering entities keen to advance their interests via military rather than diplomatic means. As for the 'second' and 'third-rate' categories, he cobbled together under these rubrics Sweden, Norway, Denmark, Switzerland, Belgium, Holland and Portugal, describing them – though some were colonial powers, too – as peaceful and as focused on their own internal affairs.[65] In this ranking, of course, he could not envisage that Georgia even be listed with the third-rate countries because he was certain that Russia would not allow its independence. He made this latter point clear in 1897 to a group of Georgian students who were studying in St Petersburg. Was it, they asked, 'the time when Europe will take the right position and recognize the self-determination of nations'[66] as the Great Powers had done for Cretan Greeks in their 1897 war of independence against the Ottoman state? He responded that Europe would not support Georgia's self-determination and advised them to concentrate their efforts on the nation's internal development.[67]

To some extent, the focus on the nation's internal rather than its external affairs was an element of the Georgian nation's discourse of smallness. Chavchavadze seemed convinced that only large states could engage properly in both internal and external spheres. Niko Nikoladze – a prominent figure of the second group – pursued this way of thinking, too. He thought that Georgia had to focus on its internal development, especially its economic process.[68] And given that modern capitalist economic development, as he saw it, extended beyond national and imperial political confines, he argued in his 1894 article 'The Necessary Power' that Georgians could use Russia's geopolitical power to enter and compete in international markets. Ultimately, it was up to Georgians to establish their economic independence by strengthening their national capital and industry. Accordingly, the nation could be strengthened if Georgians worked, as quickly as possible, towards economic independence, for 'the more time passes, and the more foreign countries advance, the more difficult it becomes to establish our production and industry'.[69] In another article from 1894 entitled 'On French Affairs', he made an even stronger case for economic independence; that is, for more industrialization, arguing that smaller and poorer nations had to industrialize just like the richer and larger nations had, otherwise 'soon [people] become slaves of richer neighbours and regardless of how smart and energetic its members are, they would not be able to rid themselves of their common [economic] slavery'.[70]

For Nikoladze, thus, internal economic development was a dynamic process and, especially for smaller nations, society's actors (industrialists, merchants, researchers) must be committed to achieving national economic independence. He also viewed Georgia's political relations with Russia in a dynamic and rather evolutionary way, seeking ultimately greater Georgian autonomy from Russia. In his 1873 'Life in Russia: A Survey', he saw 'our country's fate and future [to be] strongly entangled with the Russian condition, and Russian social and political life has influence on our country's destiny'.[71] But in an article entitled 'Kossuth and Deak' published in 1897, he contemplated whether the 1867 Austro-Hungarian Dual Monarchy was a viable option for Georgia to emulate in its relations with Russia. Like Hungary, Georgia could have its national parliament, its own finances, laws and army[72] and thus it could share power with Russia even on matters of foreign policy.

Within the Tsarist Empire, however, Georgia never was able to obtain a status comparable to that of Hungary within the Habsburg Empire. However, a more evolutionary path championed by Nikoladze, involving the renegotiation of better relations between small Georgia and large Tsarist Russia, along with the cultivation of stronger links he advocated to Russian 'progressive forces', that is, liberal and constitutional politics, did manage to yield results. The 1905 Russian Revolution (triggered by the Russian military defeat at the hands of Japan in 1905 and workers' strikes in St Petersburg) led to the establishment in 1906 of a constitutional monarchy, the imperial Duma and self-government for nations in the Empire including the two Tsarist Georgian provinces of Tbilisi and Kutaisi. Seven years later, in his brief article 'Father to Son Advice' (1913), Nikoladze continued to wax enthusiastic about the political changes that had transpired: 'the flag of self-government [...] convinces our country [the Russian Empire] and all its nations of liberty, equality and fraternity'.[73]

Meanwhile, as for Noe Zhordania, one of the main figures of the third group – which would actually become a political party in 1900, the Georgian Social-Democrats, initially a Georgian branch of Lenin's Russian Social Democratic Workers' Party (established in 1898), which split in 1903 between Bolsheviks and Mensheviks, the Georgians siding with the latter – the small Georgian nation and the Russian Empire alike would have to be transformed through revolutionary means into a social-democratic state.[74] For Georgia, being small and isolated, politically economically and geopolitically, was not an option for its survival and development. Zhordania, like Chavchavadze and Nikoladze, placed the auto-image of the nation under protection of the hetero-image of Russia against that of the Ottoman Empire. Born in a frontier zone within that empire, he recalled in his political memoir that people of his region 'did not want Russian administration, Russian internal rules, but they wanted and respected the Russian army'.[75] And when it came to national economic development, thanks to his embrace of a Marxist reading which saw capital accumulation as constant and expansionary, Georgia's viability – as he explained in an article in 1898 – depended on it being part of a 'large economic unit'.[76] In his 1913 article 'Our National Question', he reiterated that a large economic unit was more viable than a small nation.[77] And while he agreed with Nikoladze on the dangers for small nations in the world market, asserting in a seminal 1894 piece entitled 'Economic Development and Nationality' that 'economically weak nations are often subdued in the world market', the two men disagreed on what to do about the problem. For Zhordania, not only the empire's geopolitical clout and an embrace of industrialization were required; the rights of the 'working people' needed to be strengthened and their cooperation with national capital ensured if the Georgian nation were to be adequately developed.[78]

To Zhordania, again in his 1913 article 'Our National Question', the Georgian nation could become stronger and more prosperous through a social-democratic political platform – the programme, in fact, his Georgian Social-Democratic Party (which he led) pursued in the first two decades of the twentieth century. Subscribing to a conceptualization of the Georgian nation beyond its ethno-cultural traits, this platform – he maintained – ensured national economic and cultural development beyond the confines of the nation-state. Accordingly, the model of nation-state, 'one nation, one state [did] not exist' in reality and were it applied to Georgian the nation would be made smaller. Taking, like Nikoladze, the example of the Dual Monarchy but using it to illustrate a different point, he asserted that 'contemporary larger states [were] not national states. The predominant nation [was] the minority among the majority that [was] comprised of different subordinate nations.'[79] In this light, such a state, given Georgia's ethnic diversity, would undermine the rights of non-Georgians. Thus the Georgian nation's smallness of the Georgian was not a concern since, accordingly, he saw Georgians as those who 'blended with other nations and vice versa. Georgia does not cover Georgians and Georgians do not cover Georgia'.[80]

Smallness without empire

Wars, and especially the First World War, with their impact on and reactions from their respective empires and nations, changed the calculations of the protagonists examined in this chapter whereby the option of the nation becoming an independent state was seriously considered and ultimately embraced. For Ottoman Albanians this calculation had been weighed even earlier given the empire's continued decline and its numerous military defeats; perhaps this was also why its declaration of independence happened earlier (1912) than Bohemia's and Georgia's (both in 1918). Thus, what had been regarded as strategies or ways of coping (politically, economically and constitutionally) with the power imbalances of the respective nation's smallness within empire no longer seemed appealing or even viable during and after the war, especially when the victorious Allied Powers (Britain, France and the United States) agreed to a postwar European order based on the principle of self-determination.

But as they embraced the strategy and the project of national independence, the auto-image of the small nation(-state) received greater articulation and became more direct. Indeed, as the war began and once Masaryk set his mind on Bohemia and Slovakia abandoning the Dual Monarchy – because it failed to federalize and the German minority ruled over a Slav majority[81] – and promoting their independence as one country, the phrase 'the problem of small nations' reappeared in his writing. Quite tellingly, his inaugural lecture in 1915 at the University of London, King's College was entitled 'The Problem of Small Nations in the European Crisis'. Here he argued that not only in political-economic terms did Bohemia, a small 'nation of workers', deserve to become independent, but in geopolitical terms as well, because, together with other small Eastern European nations, it would serve as a barrier against the large and imperialist German state.[82] Two years later, in his book *The New Europe*, he acknowledged the geopolitical weakness of small nations in the postwar European inter-state order and the difficulty of standing alone without the backing of larger powers. In response he outlined a strategy in which Bohemia was part of a 'federation of smaller states [...] freely founded, created on real needs of nations'.[83]

In Qemali's vocabulary, too, the discourse of smallness, referring directly to Albania as small, manifested itself. Heading the first Albanian government in the autumn of 1912 – recognizing that his government controlled only a 'small extent of the country' – he frantically sought to demonstrate to the Great Powers, while seeking their recognition, that Albania could rule itself[84] and to prove to a cynical Ottoman government that 'Little Turkey (Albania) in the Balkans was [not] submitting to new patrons of Austro-Hungary and Italy'.[85] And yet, he and many other Albanians were to be greatly disappointed when, though receiving the greatly sought-after recognition of independence by the Great Powers at the London Conference of Ambassadors (1913), their nation-state was recognized within smaller borders. His reaction to such a recognition was to regard it as a bittersweet development: thankful for it, he nonetheless lamented the new fact that 'the most flourishing towns and most productive parts of the country hav[e] been taken away',[86] rendering Albania perpetually economically weak and constantly dependent on the will, decisions and appetites of the Great Powers. On the latter point, Noli – who on behalf of the American-Albanian diaspora had lobbied for the Great Powers' recognition in 1912–13 – also bemoaned the independence of small Albania, which the Great Powers had agreed to guarantee, in these terms. The security guarantee was especially salient in the midst of the First World War when Britain, in its attempt to sway Italy to leave the Central Powers and join the Entente Powers, signed the London Secret Treaty of 1915 with Italy, ceding parts of already recognized Albanian territory to the latter in exchange for its shift of alliances. Noli called this act a betrayal of 'this little country'.[87]

In Zhordania's discourse, too, the emergence of the modern Georgian state on 26 May 1918 – following the implosion of Tsarist Russia (due to the 1917 February and October Revolutions) and the retreat of its military from the Caucasus – was accompanied by the articulation of the auto-image of the small nation. He feared for the survival of his 'small nation' given the threats of total annexation by Bolshevik Russia and the snatching of its territory by the Ottoman Empire.[88]

Clearly, the late-nineteenth- and early-twentieth-century discourse of smallness in these three cases pointed to a recognition that a nation's condition as small, meaning weak, within and in relation to the empire was nonetheless a manageable situation. In fact, the small nation could be strengthened provided that rightful changes for the nation were made if they were within an empire. Not so, however, when such nations were outside an empire. Arguably, the more directly this discourse of smallness was articulated, the more it became a sign of a nation(-state) in distress.

Notes

1. Osterhammel, *The Transformation of the World*, 392–468.
2. Winklerová, *Karel Kramář*.
3. Masaryk, *Česka Otázka*, 4.
4. Frashëri, *Shqipëria*, 3.
5. Khundadze, *Kartuli Inteligentsiis Evronuli Profili Metskhramete Saukuneshi*.
6. Zhordania, *Chemi Tsarsuli*, 105.
7. The Czech Republic became a NATO country in 1999 and an EU member state in 2004; Albania became a NATO country in 2008 and began EU accession negotiations in 2020; Georgia has since 2004 sought membership in both the EU and NATO, but no clear path to incorporation in either supranational organization has yet emerged.
8. Brisku, *Bittersweet Europe*, 15.
9. See Pánek and Túma, *A History of Czech Lands*.
10. Hroch, *Social Preconditions of National Revival in Europe: A Comparative Analysis of the Social Composition of Patriotic Groups among Smaller European Nations*.
11. See Weiss, *Promoting National Priorities in EU Foreign Policies: The Czech Republic's Foreign Policy in the EU*; Kaniok and Majer, 'Small Countries in the EU: The Czech Republic Case'.
12. See Sedláček, 'Politici Tvrdí, Že Jsme Malý Národ, Který Potřebuje Uchránit Před Neexistující Hrozbou'. https://www.irozhlas.cz/zivotni-styl/spolecnost/tomas-sedlacek-demokracie-politika-rozhovor-sametova-revolucehistorie_1905081600_lac. Last accessed 9 May 2019.
13. Lizcova, 'USA Ani Čína Se Nechtějí o Pozici Supervelmoci Dělit, to Je Hlavni Problém Světové Politiky, Říká Německý Expert'. https://zahranicni.ihned.cz/c1-66586200-usa-ani-cina-se-nechteji-o-pozici-supervelmocidelit-to-je-hlavni-problem-svetove-politiky-rika-nemecky-expert?fbclid=IwAR3yHr9pJUqiBjiPDUfzvI KQIv6gnqthcJMizBg_76ocKdFtGaIUMy6gD0. Last accessed 13 June 2019.
14. Kakachia and Minesashvili, 'Identity Politics: Exploring Georgia's Foreign Policy Behaviour', 171.
15. Janelidze, 'Address', 7. http://infocenter.gov.ge/uploads/files/2018-05/1525259726_n14_a4_web.pdf. Last accessed 10 June 2019.
16. 'Speech by the Prime Minister of Albania, Edi Rama at the Annual NATO Military Committee Conference Attended by the Chiefs of Staff of Alliance Member Countries, Tirana, Albania'. https://www.nato.int/cps/en/natohq/opinions_146877.htm?selectedLocale=en. Last accessed 10 June 2019.
17. Winklerová, *Karel Kramář*, 63.
18. Masaryk, *Parliamentní Projevy, 1891–1893*, 370.
19. In Kramář, *Paměti Dr. Karla Kramáře*, 306.
20. Cibulka, Hájek, and Kučera, 'Definition'.
21. Plaschka, 'The Political Significance of František Palacký', 52.
22. Cibulka, Hájek, and Kučera, 'Definition'.
23. Marholeva, 'Kramářův a Masarykův', 323.
24. Masaryk, 'O Českém Státním Právu', 274.
25. Bažantová, 'Karel Kramář a Jeho Zájem o Národohospodářskou a Finační Vědu', 68.
26. Kořalka, *Tschechen Im Habsburgerreich Und in Europa, 1815–1914: Sozialgeschichtliche Zusammenhänge Der Neuzeitlichen Nationsbildung Und Der Nationalitätenfrage in Den Böhmischen Ländern*.
27. Masaryk, *Česka Otázka*, 4.

28 Masaryk, 4.
29 Masaryk, 8.
30 Masaryk, *Otázka Sociální: Základy Marxismu Filozofické a Sociologické.*
31 Masaryk, *Parliamentní Projevy, 1891–1893*, 88.
32 'Návrh Programu Lidového'.
33 Masaryk, *Parliamentní Projevy, 1907–1913*, 156–7.
34 Doubek, *T. G. Masaryk: A Česka Slovanska Politika, 1882–1910*, 75.
35 Marholeva, 'Kramářův a Masarykův', 330.
36 Cibulka, Hájek, and Kučera, 'Definition', 352.
37 Teichova, 'Continuity and Discontinuity: Banking and Industry in Twentieth-Century Central Europe', 68.
38 Masaryk, *Student a Politika*, 12–14.
39 Masaryk, *O Democracii*, 34.
40 Brisku, *Bittersweet Europe*, 28–31.
41 Brisku, 2.
42 Initially there were two principalities, Bulgaria in the north and Eastern Rumelia in its south, that were given autonomy in 1878. They were united in 1885 as the principality of Bulgaria, which declared its independence in 1908.
43 Puto, 'The Idea of Nation during the Albanian National Movement, 1878–1912', 189–90.
44 Taglia, 'The Feasibility of Ottomanism as a Nationalist Project: The View of Albanian Young Turk Ismail Kemal', 340–6.
45 Brisku, *Political Reform in the Ottoman and the Russian Empires: A Comparative Approach.*
46 Kemal, *Memoirs*, 209–13.
47 Kemal, 217.
48 Frashëri is recognized by both Albanian and Turkish historiographies for his contributions to Albanian and to Turkish nationalisms.
49 Frashëri, *Shqipëria*, 3.
50 Frashëri, 11.
51 Frashëri, 22.
52 Frashëri, 24.
53 Frashëri, 26–7.
54 Frashëri, 53.
55 Konitza, *Selected Correspondence, 1896–1942.*
56 'Thirrje e Ismail Qemali Be Vlores Mi Shqiptaret Kur Iku Nga Stambolli'.
57 Duka, *Shekujt Osmanë Në Hapsirën Shqiptare*, 46–7.
58 Duka, 47.
59 Zhordania, *Chemi Tsarsuli*, 105.
60 Jones, *Socialism in Georgian Colours*, 37–8; Brisku, *Bittersweet Europe*, 37–8.
61 Suny, *The Making of the Georgian Nation*, 64.
62 Chavchavadze, *Publitsisturi Tserilebi*, 12–13.
63 Chavchavadze, 148–9.
64 Chavchavadze, 186.
65 Chavchavadze, *Tserilebi Literaturisa Da Khelovnebaze*, 55–95.
66 Bakradze, *Ilia Chavchavadze*, 33.
67 Bakradze, 35.
68 Jones, *Socialism in Georgian Colours*, 30–48; Brisku, *Bittersweet Europe*, 37–8.
69 Nikoladze, 'Sachiro-Dzala', 133.

70　Nikoladze, 'Safrangetis Sakmeebzed', 154.
71　Nikoladze, *Tkhzulebani, 1872–1873*, 3:358.
72　Nikoladze, *Kartuli Mtserloba*, 14:186–213.
73　Nikoladze, 'Mamashviluri Rcheva', 4–5.
74　Jones, *Socialism in Georgian Colours*, 30–48; Brisku, *Bittersweet Europe*, 37–8.
75　Zhordania, *Chemi Tsarsuli*, 15.
76　Zhordania, 'Dghevandeli Sakhitkhebi', 1.
77　Zhordania, *Erovnuli Kitkha*, 201–3.
78　Zhordania, 2–9.
79　Zhordania, 172.
80　Zhordania, 173.
81　Masaryk, *Nová Evropa*, 101–2.
82　Masaryk, *The Voice of An Oppressed People*, 19–23.
83　Masaryk, *Nová Evropa*, 102.
84　Kemal, *Memoirs*, 373.
85　Milo, *Politika e Jashtme e Shqipërisë*, 62.
86　Kemal, *Memoirs*, 377.
87　Noli, *Faqe Të Panjohura Te Nolit*, 29.
88　Zhordania, *Chemi Tsarsuli*, 105.

3

Smallness and the East-West binary in nationalism studies. Belgium and Romania in the long nineteenth century

Raul Carstocea and Maarten Van Ginderachter

Smallness and the varieties of nationalism

This chapter investigates whether the concepts of smallness, (relative or metaphorical) size and the attendant images of superiority or inferiority are perhaps better suited to capture the different varieties of nationalism than the framework setting eastern, ethnic nations in opposition to their Western, civic counterparts. A comparison of Belgium and Romania, focusing on the representations of governing elites and their nations' respective positions within the international system, helps to subvert East-West dichotomies. By exploring perceptions of 'smallness', its relation to 'peripherality' and the entanglements that made Belgium a model for Romania, this essay draws attention to the ways in which nationalist projects were consistently shaped with a view to the international order and the respective nations' positions within it. Or, put differently and in the terms of this volume's introduction, nationalists' auto- and hetero-images were intimately linked to the status of individual nations within a larger community of states.

Throughout the nineteenth century, Belgian and Romanian governing elites imagined their countries in similar ways: as small, peripheral nations bridging the divides between larger 'civilizations' and as vanguard battleground areas where larger empires fought their wars. Challenging essentialist and reified binaries of 'Eastern' and 'Western' nationalism and adopting a more nuanced view, our analysis argues instead that we read nineteenth-century nationalisms as local variants of a profoundly transnational phenomenon. By examining similarities and parallels between two cases associated with the 'West' and the 'East' and looking at the constitutive relationship between them, this essay reveals the relative synchronicity of these imaginings, which were based on 'smallness' rather than an opposition of West and East during the nineteenth century.

The relational concept of smallness indeed helps us to overcome East-West binaries. First, the similarities in actors' self-perceptions point to the salience of 'smallness' as a category, even given significant differences ranging from socioeconomic conditions through demographic aspects to geographic location. Second, these similarities in auto-images are complemented by the choice of Belgium as a model by Romanian nineteenth-century state-building elites, which in turn points to several other important aspects. On the one hand, this orientation highlights the actors' self-awareness of such elective affinities and their attendant hetero-images, once more indicating the relevance of 'smallness'. On the other, it shows that 'Eastern' nationalists were far more liberal than established binaries would have us believe. Finally, nuancing the 'botanical metaphors' of Western models being 'transplanted on alien soil',[1] the adoption of such models is revealed to be much less indiscriminate and much more selective (of some features and not others) than has been assumed, including by contemporary critics of such 'imports'.[2]

East-West binaries

Hans Kohn's distinction between 'Western' and 'Eastern' types of nationalism has exerted remarkable staying power as *the* binary structure underlying nationalism studies.[3] According to this dichotomy, nationalism emerged earlier in Western Europe and the United States, where nationalism 'was primarily a political occurrence', whereas 'in Central and Eastern Europe and in Asia nationalism arose not only later' but 'found its expression predominantly in the cultural field'.[4] As a result Western nationalism was rational, cosmopolitan, progressive and grounded in notions of citizenship, while the Eastern type was emotional, particular, backward and rooted in the 'infinitely vaguer concept of "folk"'.[5] Despite certain variations in the conception in which, for example, German and Italian nationalisms were 'Eastern' for Kohn[6] but 'Western' for another prominent scholar of nationalism, John Plamenatz,[7] all of its proponents would firmly place Belgium in the Western and Romania in the Eastern categories, respectively.

Informed as well by the Cold War split, which helped reify essentialist notions of a 'totalitarian' East squared off against a liberal West,[8] the binary acquired normative implications that ultimately associated 'civic' with 'good' and 'ethnic' with 'bad' nationalism. The conflicts in the former Yugoslavia in the 1990s brought such distinctions to the fore, so that despite intense academic criticism,[9] the East-West binary 'persists not only in political and journalistic parlance, but also in academic writings', as 'most of the classical texts on nationalism have perpetuated this dichotomy'.[10] A corollary of the binary, no less important both to its internal structure and political implications, is the notion of 'lateness', whereby nationalism was transmitted or transferred from West to East, with an associated temporal lag.[11] In such a reading, the West constitutes the 'normal' (and implicitly benign) course of development, with the East as its belated, incomplete, and therefore 'deviant' counterpart, the type of nationalism whose essence explains its eventual excesses.

Adopting a Koselleckian interpretive framework,[12] we can read the East-West binary along the lines of asymmetric counterconcepts, where the West is the main point of reference and the East, a derivative opposite, is meant mostly to confirm the normative status of the 'West'. Such a reading actually aligns with Kohn's original use of the concepts: the 'Eastern' type was much more vaguely defined, with 'Western nationalism' being contrasted instead with 'nationalism outside the Western world'[13] in a formulation reminiscent of Stuart Hall's 'the West and the Rest'.[14] Moreover, this approach seems applicable to the case study under consideration because 'ethnotypes' are also constructed as counterconcepts: Kohn also invokes the Hellene-Barbarian dyad at the basis of Reinhart Koselleck's analysis in his interpretation of the respective hetero-images of Germans and Slavs.[15]

Small nations on the brink

'Europe' was the permanent reference point in the discourse of Belgian and Romanian state-building and governing elites alike during the nineteenth century. On the one hand, this 'Europe' was an elastic concept without clear geographical limits that pointed in the vague direction of France and Britain, an example of what Dipesh Chakrabarty calls 'hyperreal terms' which refer to 'certain figures of imagination whose geographical referents remain somewhat indeterminate'.[16] On the other hand, 'Europe' entailed the very practical, at times grudging, appeal to the favour of European powers amongst the aspiring governing elites.

Before gaining independence in 1830 as Belgium, the country's territory had been known for centuries as the Southern Netherlands or the Southern Low Countries, a series of distinct principalities governed by the same crown. Although the Northern Netherlands gained their independence with the Dutch Revolt (1566–1648), the Southern Netherlands remained a part of the Spanish and later the Austrian Habsburg Empire. Subsequently it was incorporated into the French Republic (1794–1814) and the UK of the Netherlands (1815–30). Belgium's secession from the latter in 1830 surprised many contemporaries and has sometimes been described as a Brussels riot gone awry due to the Dutch king William I's ham-fisted reaction. The country's independence was recognized internationally only on the condition that it would always be neutral in conflicts.[17]

Because of Belgium's position between France, the Netherlands, Germany and, across the Channel, Britain, Belgian governing elites never felt geographically peripheral to Europe. But this hardly assuaged their sense of metaphorical marginalization, which stemmed from the country's small territory coupled with its peculiar international position as a mandated neutral state and the unflattering hetero-images of Belgium as an upstart, artificial nation.[18]

Belgium's second-tier role in the *concert des nations* hamstrung the diplomatic ambitions of the country's governing elites, not to mention its king. Not to be outdone, they rhetorically turned smallness from a liability into a boon. The pervasive discourse of *la petite Belgique* (in relationship to *les grandes nations* or *les grandes puissances*), a country deemed the epitome of Western modernity as an industrially precocious, highly urbanized and politically liberal nation, turned a negative hetero-image into a positive auto-image, a conception that foreigners, to a certain extent, reproduced in their contacts with Belgians. When the Belgian princess Stéphanie and archduke Rudolf of Austria-Hungary were engaged in 1880, Belgian newspapers proudly quoted the accolades for '*cette petite Belgique* which, according to the flattering expression of baron de Haymerlé, [the Austrian] minister of Foreign Affairs, [...] is "the model of constitutional states"'.[19]

The age-old, peaceful cohabitation of Dutch- and French-speaking Belgians within one nation was presented as an example to the whole continent (linguistic strife became a real challenge to the country's unity only after the First World War).[20] It made the small country particularly suited to mediate between the large European rivals.[21] In this strand of cultural nationalism, readily enhanced by the country's governing elites, Belgium's unique position derived from its assimilating/appropriating what was foreign to its own purposes and from the bridgehead function it served between the Germanic and Romance cultures.[22]

Although Belgium differed substantially from Romania demographically (as a heavily urbanized region) and economically (as the first industrialized country on the Continent), the similarities in nationalist representations are remarkable. The history of the two Romanian principalities Wallachia and Moldova was to some extent distinct from that of their 'Balkan' neighbours in that they were client states of the Ottoman Empire, tributary to but not formally incorporated within its territory. Though the extent of this autonomy had varied significantly over time, the Russian occupation of the Principalities (1828) and the formal establishment of a protectorate following the Treaty of Adrianople (1829) significantly limited Ottoman influence and endowed Wallachia and Moldova with their first proto-constitutional arrangements, known as the 'Organic Regulations'. Despite their modernizing provisions, their imposition had prompted a reaction from the local *boyars* (noblemen) and a sharp turn away from their prior Russophilia (based on their ties to the Christian Orthodox world) and towards an orientation towards the 'West', particularly France, due to perceptions of a shared 'Latin' heritage. The Latinity claim (harking back to the Roman conquest of 106 CE and mostly based on the Romanian language being a Romance language, uniquely amongst the languages of South-Eastern Europe) was 'proof' that they belonged to 'Europe'[23] despite being acutely aware of the country's peripherality, both geographically and symbolically (i.e. to European modernity). In this context it is important to mention 'nesting'[24] or 'lateral' Orientalisms.[25] All national elites in South-Eastern Europe tended to imagine the boundary of 'Europe' – and consequently of 'civilization' – as lying either south or east of their borders. The Romanians' Latinity claim indeed performed this function, in order to 'prove' not only the country's belonging to Europe but also its resultant 'superiority' to its Slavic neighbours.[26]

Furthermore, the Romanian Principalities' semi-autonomous status had allowed them to support the holy places of Christian Orthodoxy and offer refuge to clergy, mainly Greek, who were fleeing Ottoman territories; later they 'served as a territorial base for the Greek national struggle, sheltered as they were from direct Ottoman interference'.[27] Thus governing elites could portray Romania as a Christian vanguard nation, a bulwark of Christianity against the Ottoman Empire, further emphasizing their claim to 'Europeanness'.[28] This vanguard position was, however, imperilled, located as the country was at the crossroads of three competing empires, who in the course of their frequent conflicts often occupied Romanian territory.

Similarly, in Belgium, Catholic opinion-makers saw themselves manning the ramparts against the Protestant Netherlands and atheist France. This self-conception, too, was a variation on a common nationalist trope. Imagining Belgium as the eternal battlefield of Europe, both Catholic and Liberal governing elites saw the country's history as a long struggle pitting freedom-loving Belgians against foreign (Spanish, Austrian, French and Dutch) tyranny. Belgium's eventual and successful independence, grudgingly accepted by the Great Powers, served as a model for other aspiring small nations, particularly in South-Eastern Europe.[29]

Given the opposition of all three bordering empires (Habsburg, Ottoman and Russian) to the Romanians' national ideals, the country's elites turned to the 'Western' Great Powers in their international diplomatic outreach, especially in moments of crisis. Hetero- and auto-images of 'smallness' were extremely important for the Romanians' international activity within an international state system structured by a hierarchy of 'organized inequality'.[30] The first project of the Romanian elites, the union of the Principalities, was motivated as much by ideal notions of 'national unity' (given that the overwhelming majority in both principalities spoke Romanian and prayed in the Orthodox Church) as by pragmatic considerations of size: a larger country was seen as preferable to two smaller ones. That pragmatism was indeed the more important of these considerations can be inferred from the self-imposed limits of 'national unity', which, even amidst the turmoil of 1848, did not extend to the Romanian speakers in Transylvania, then part of the Habsburg Empire and engaged in their own separate revolution, but whose autonomy was only contemplated within Transylvania.[31] Representatives of all the neighbouring empires, in their opposition to the union, also invoked considerations of relative size; from their standpoint, two smaller principalities appeared more manageable than an enlarged Romanian state.[32]

The 1848 Revolution was only briefly successful in Wallachia and was fully suppressed in Moldova, but the exiled revolutionaries managed to acquire increased international recognition for the 'Romanian question' and for themselves as legitimate 'national' elites. As such, the subsequent crisis, engendered by the Crimean War, provided them the opportunity to place their claims on the agenda of the Congress of Paris. In accordance with the 1848ers' wishes, the protectorate of the defeated Russian empire was replaced with collective international protection and the Romanians were allowed to convene legislative and consultative assemblies known as 'ad hoc divans' that would have a say in the future organization of the principalities. Convening from 1857 to 1859, these gatherings produced, unsurprisingly, very similar documents that called for the union of the principalities under a foreign prince, as well as their neutrality.[33] The call for neutrality was extremely important for the Romanian state-building elites given the contested nature of their territory, part of the 'Eastern Question' looming over nineteenth-century European politics. Although all the Great Powers, except for France, opposed the union at the 1859 Convention of Paris, the unionists in the principalities made recourse to a subterfuge and elected the same man, Alexandru Ioan Cuza, as prince in Wallachia and Moldova, thus fulfilling their aspirations through a personal union.[34] The administrative union of the two principalities under Prince Cuza was established through the enactment of unitary legislation that, indeed, was inspired by the Belgian model.[35]

Belgo-Romanian relations

In fact, from the moment Belgium became an independent state in 1830, with its constitution and its Great Power guarantee of neutrality, Romanian state-building elites looked up to it as a model, seeing, as Silvia Marton neatly summarizes, 'two main similarities between Belgium and Romania [...]: the comparable territorial dimensions of the two states; and their relatively identical constitutional destinies, 1830 for Belgium and 1866 for Romania'.[36] As such, relative size was a very prominent factor prompting the comparison, whereas the similar notion of 'constitutional destiny', as shown in what follows, was largely of the Romanians' own making, due to their conscious and highly discriminate adoption of the Belgian constitution as a model for their own.

Not merely a sense of 'small nation' affinity directed the Romanian governing elites' collective gaze towards the Low Countries by the North Sea. There were, indeed, important structural relations between Belgium and Romania. First, because of publishing piracy, Brussels held a pivotal global position in the francophone world during the first half of the nineteenth century. Books cheaply reprinted in the Belgian capital enabled the world to encounter Romantic literature and liberal ideas hailing from France. Reading rooms in Bucharest and across the Danube principalities were stocked with materials printed in Brussels.[37]

After the European revolutions of 1848, a great many Romanian revolutionaries – including Constantin Alexandru Rosetti (1816–85) and Cezar Bolliac (1813–81) – fled, first to France, then, after the proclamation of the Second Empire, to Brussels. The turn away from the earlier French model towards the Belgian template, as well as these revolutionaries' move from Paris to Brussels in 1851, was partly spurred by Napoleon III's seizure of power and the establishment of the Second Empire, which the Romanian emigrés read as a betrayal of the liberal principles of 1848.[38]

In the 1850s Romanian refugees in Brussels founded the freemason lodge *Steaua Dunării/Étoile du Danube*, which published an eponymous journal and would come to play a pivotal role in the eventual proclamation of Romanian independence, and established *Republica română*, an organization and accompanying journal propagating the Romanian cause.[39] Through these expatriate communities Belgium became a model to emulate, and thus we see Belgian influence in the writing of the Romanian constitution and in Romania's defence plans (the Belgian general Henri-Alexis Brialmont devised the plans for the fortifications of Bucharest).[40] The affinity between the two countries was also evident in the many Romanian students at Belgian universities, a population so large that in October 1920 General Iliesco, the former head of the Romanian army's general staff, quipped that the majority of Romanian intellectuals had graduated from Belgian universities.[41]

And then there were the important commercial and industrial relations between the two countries. Immediately after Belgian independence, representatives of the

Belgian Foreign Ministry in Constantinople and Vienna began to establish contacts with the Danube principalities to find market outlets for Belgian industry.[42] During the Belle Époque, the economic relations between Belgium and Romania became tighter. In 1888 Belgian exports of glass, iron, steel, firearms, chemical products and sugar to Romania amounted to almost 17 million Belgian francs.[43] In the favourable economic conditions after 1895, Belgian investment in Romania increased. Belgians accounted for 75 per cent of investments in sugar refining.[44] From 1886 to the outbreak of the First World War Belgium was the first or second largest importer of Romanian products, mainly cereals, vegetables and other agricultural commodities.[45] In 1912, an astonishing 94 per cent of all Romanian cereal exports were destined for Belgium (although most were meant for re-exportation through the port of Antwerp).[46] Not surprisingly, Romania was represented at the Belgian World Fairs of Antwerp (1894), Brussels (1897), Liège (1905) and Ghent (1913). In the commemorative *Golden Book* of the Liège Fair Romania was affectionately called the 'Belgique de l'Orient'.[47]

'Belgium of the East'

The epithet 'Belgique de l'Orient' (Belgium of the East) was coined by Romanian nationalists in the 1850s following the failed revolution of 1848 in the Danube principalities. It expressed their desire to establish a constitutional monarchy in the mould of Belgium, headed by a European prince and having its international neutrality guaranteed by the Great Powers. In addition to the progressive Belgian legal-political arrangement and a neutral position in the international system – particularly valuable for Moldova and Wallachia, with three large empires as neighbours with which they were often embroiled in competition – Belgium was an industrialized, urban nation, a model of (francophone) 'Western' modernity writ small. These ideas about Belgium as an exemplar for Romania were disseminated in brochures, pamphlets and journals published by Romanian exiles in the European capitals of London, Paris and Brussels. For instance, the first issue of *L'Étoile du Danube*, published in Brussels on 4 December 1856, offers testimony that 'the Romanians of the Danube are pleased to consider her [i.e., Belgium] as the model for their future organisation' and, in reference to the Danube principalities, uses the phrase 'la Belgique orientale'.[48]

At least until Romanian independence (1878), which gave rise to a discourse critical of the indiscriminate adoption of 'Western' modernization models, Romanian governing elites supported the import of the same 'Western' modernizing project: national, liberal and capitalist. One concrete example of this ideal was the parliamentary discussions about the concession of Romanian railways that took place from 1866 to 1871. To the Members of Parliament (MPs), liberal and conservative alike, railway construction provided a way to consolidate the nation and to lead Romania 'towards Europe', as had happened in Belgium. In 1868 the Liberal MP Anastase Stolojan quoted Michel Chevalier, the French politician and follower of Saint-Simon, at length about the Belgian government's intention to use railroads 'to create for Belgium a certain entrance ticket among the European states'.[49] Railroads also offered Romania a means of defending itself against larger neighbours and to fend off marginalization and isolation: to tackle, in other words, the two aforementioned ubiquitous concerns regarding smallness and peripherality. In May 1868 MP D. Ghica claimed: 'We are threatened by the railroads of Hungary and Bucovina that will encircle us from all sides, which will transport all riches there, while our country will be completely poor and isolated in Europe.'[50]

In the international arena, 'Romanian nation- and state-builders became scholars of international relations' by learning to argue their case for independence in the language of *jus publicum Europeaum*.[51] As such, rather than a picture of prostrate 'Eastern' elites in thrall to and indiscriminately adopting Western modernity, the careful and highly selective importation of certain models, always with a view to local conditions, demonstrates the agency and self-awareness of local actors in navigating highly asymmetrical relationships as part of their quest for international recognition. This perspective was clearly articulated by one of the architects of the Romanian nation-state, Mihail Kogălniceanu: 'Europe gives its sympathies to and supports only countries that aspire to align their institutions with those of the civilized world. [...] To show Europe our desire to Europeanize our country will be to attract the sympathies and support of the Great Powers and of foreign public opinion.'[52] Where auto-images revealed a country too small to stand on its own against its larger and more powerful neighbours, such smallness was to be mitigated by integration (also via the often-invoked Latin heritage) into a (Western) Europe that appeared to stand at the apex of the hierarchical international system, overshadowing even the anxiety-inducing neighbouring empires.

The stereotype of the 'Belgium of the East' was consecrated in 1866.[53] That year, Cuza was forced to abdicate and the provisional government sought to swiftly resolve the crisis that could have threatened the fragile union by seeking a foreign prince and promulgating a constitution. In both cases, the model was, again, small Belgium, demonstrating the appeal it exerted as a modern, industrial, urban country that was politically liberal and internationally neutral (all things that Romania was not but aspired to be), while also being perceived as a francophone country, which corresponded to the self-professed 'Latinity' of Romanian governing elites and the more practical fact that French was the most widely spoken language amongst them. Perceptions of 'small' Belgium as a success story in a space that was also subject to intense contestations amongst rival Great Powers, as well as its internationally guaranteed neutrality, made it the most suitable model for a small 'Balkan' country aspiring to flourish in an analogous way. But it is equally clear that Romanians also appropriated the Belgian model on their own terms: latching onto the Latin nature of Belgium, they neglected the bi-cultural strands within the Belgian auto-image.

Philip of Flanders, the brother of Leopold II, the king of the Belgians, declined the Romanian throne when approached. Ironically, it was precisely Belgium's neutral status that prevented Philip from accepting.[54] The eventual accession to the throne by the Prussian Charles of Hohenzollern-Sigmaringen, at the behest of Otto von Bismarck and as part of the latter's attempts to increase Prussian influence in the lower Danube,[55] further shows the realpolitik and the geopolitical considerations inflecting such contingent choices.

Both in form and substance, the Romanian Constitution of 1866 was modelled on the Belgian Constitution of 1831, arguably the most frequently imitated constitution in South-Eastern Europe and beyond.[56] Keen modernizers imagining their country as a 'Belgium of the East', the Romanian governing elites 'could think of no more suitable model for themselves than a constitution which had allowed a small nation to make such enormous progress in a little over three decades'.[57] Following previous legislation modelled on Belgian laws,[58] the extension of the vote in 1884 and the introduction of compulsory voting in 1918 also followed the Belgian example.[59]

It is, however, important to note that neither the Constitution of 1866 nor the other pieces of Belgian-inspired legislation were simple copies or translations from their models but were instead, from the outset, modulated to take stock of local conditions.[60] Of the many divergences noted by the Romanian jurist Andrei Rădulescu in his 1932 tract on the 'Belgian influence on Romanian law', two are especially worth noting, as they reflected particular anxieties besetting Romanian governing elites: Article 3, prohibiting 'colonization with populations of foreign stock [gintă]'; and the controversial Article 7, restricting naturalization to 'foreigners of Christian rites'[61] and thus effectively barring Jewish emancipation. Both measures reflected longstanding anxieties regarding underpopulation noted by local elites and foreign observers alike,[62] a demographic pattern that on the one hand represented yet another 'small' attribute of nineteenth-century Romania and on the other diverged significantly from what could be seen in Belgium, with its booming population.

Independence followed another international crisis, caused by the Russo-Turkish War of 1877, which saw Romanian participation despite initial Russian refusal of its support. Independence was made conditional on a territorial exchange that Romanian politicians did not want (a transfer of the province of Bessarabia to Russia in exchange for the Ottoman province of Dobrogea, whose multi-ethnic and multi-confessional makeup contrasted strikingly to the homogeneity of Romania proper) and on the emancipation of the Jews, which the 1866 Constitution had avoided.[63] Full Romanian independence was eventually unanimously accepted by 1881, despite the country's non-compliance with Jewish emancipation. This refusal came against a background of xenophobia and rising anti-Semitism in the country, prompted by anxieties related to the absence of a secure native middle class, whose slowly emerging exponents found themselves in economic competition with 'foreign' elites (Jews, Greeks and Bulgarians). As such, in Romania ethno-linguistic diversity, unlike in Belgium where it was seen as integral to Belgian auto-images, was perceived as a curse, associated with both the 'poisoned apple' that Dobrogea was perceived to be and a 'Jewish question', articulated at the intersection of the 'national' and 'peasant' 'questions' dominating political debate, that was also marked by concerns about underpopulation.[64] Interestingly, once independence was achieved, the relationship with the Great Powers changed significantly: having sought their favour in order to accomplish what a small nation could not manage on its own (as proved in 1848), Romanian governing elites, following the Congress of Berlin, sharply altered their discourse to express resistance against foreign interference in the affairs of an independent state, as evident in international pressure for Jewish emancipation.

From prescriptive auto-image to running joke. The end of the Belgian model

After Romanian independence, the earlier, quasi-unanimously accepted Western models came under attack from Conservative politicians who criticized them as 'forms without substance', a trope that eventually became omnipresent in South-Eastern Europe at the turn of the twentieth century.[65] This development marked the beginning of a potential second phase in the evolution of nationalism in Romania and in South-Eastern Europe more generally. Arguing that the indiscriminate imitation of Western models did not produce the desired results, Conservatives increasingly argued for a project of modernization more attuned to local realities, which were clearly diverging from those of the French or Belgian models. Liberals countered that only accelerated modernization based on Western models would allow Romania to leave behind its 'backwardness' and thus catch up and align itself with the 'civilized' West, although their discourse, initially rejecting anything 'Eastern' as a negative legacy, increasingly contained the metaphor of a 'bridge' between East and West, a figure becoming ubiquitous not only in Romania but in the region more broadly.[66] Now that the earlier political consensus on modernization and its inherent optimism had evaporated, anxieties about the country's smallness, peripherality and underdevelopment came to the fore. As is typical of societies grappling with 'backwardness' and 'catching up', divergences were interpreted as 'lacks' or 'failures', and the earlier reliance on international crises as moments of opportunity yielded to a fear of an internally generated crisis, a sense that 'time was running out'. As throughout the long nineteenth century, foreign intervention was the spectre invoked, and with it all the anxieties provoked by the possibility of social unrest and by a peasantry that continued to remain opaque to state-led nationalizing projects.[67]

As such, the consecration of the 'Belgium of the Orient' stereotype in 1866 can also be said to mark the beginning of its decline in popularity. Titu Maiorescu wrote his programmatic essay 'Against the Current Direction in Romanian Culture' in 1868,[68] and its criticism of 'forms without substance' signals the beginning of the turn away from Western cultural, legislative and institutional models and towards a quest for some kind of 'authenticity', a substantial though nonetheless elusive essence. This shift had less to do with auto-images of 'smallness' than with the content of the 'Western' model, with Belgium acting as its (small but modern) epitome. Consequently, the optimistic self-description, always evidence more of wishful thinking than reality, of 'Belgium of the Orient' was increasingly used ironically by Romanian governing elites to criticize various aspects of Romanian society and politics that they found lacking.

By 1903, when the first issue of the satirical newspaper *The Belgium of the Orient* was published in Bucharest, the notion had become a complete joke. The eponymous first editorial, 'The Belgium... of the Orient', spoke of a country thus called 'because it climbed the steps of civilization with the elevator, so that it gets dizzy whenever, bumping its head against the ceiling, it sees the floor below'.[69] What followed were scathing criticisms of corruption, superficiality, illiteracy, an incompetent political class and a disastrous economy in contemporary Romania, complete with an allusion to its small size (still four times larger than 'Occidental Belgium') and a mention of its 'neighbours who, out of love, would swallow it whole with a spoonful of water at any hour of the day or night'.[70] Of the commercial relations with 'the Belgium of the West', it noted ironically (yet not off the mark, as we have seen) that the Oriental variant 'exports cereals and imports [...] baccalaureate diplomas [...] and even those on credit' and that 'the national language is French', while a pun turned the model Belgian form of government into '*constitutional anarchy*' when applied to the 'Belgium of the Orient'.[71] The terms of the comparison – from (relative) size compared with its much larger neighbours to the constitutional model, Latinity, imitation of Western culture and modernization – were still there, still familiar from the period when the model had been taken seriously. At this point, however, they served to emphasize how Romanian realities diverged from the model, and how they had, perhaps inevitably, failed to successfully emulate it. Also stressed was the highly asymmetrical relationship between the two countries (evinced by their trade relations).

Two things are important to note here: first, the late nineteenth-century criticism regarding allegedly indiscriminate imports from Western Europe – which, as shown above, were anything but – did not yet entail their complete rejection, a stance which would become dominant in the discourse only during the interwar period, but rather demanded their adaptation to local realities. Far from what was envisioned in congratulatory self-representations as a 'Belgium of the Orient', these realities were revealed to be much more rural and agrarian than those prevalent in the Western model, and persistently so in the absence of the infrastructural capacity for turning 'peasants into Romanians'.[72] Second, the criticisms of the model were attuned to and synchronous with similar developments in the West itself, where narratives of decline and degeneration had challenged a positivist faith in progress, so that by the *fin de siècle* a pervasive sense of crisis and cultural despair[73] all but replaced the earlier narratives of open-ended societal advance.[74] However, a Koselleckian perspective is once again very useful here, warning as it does against neat periodizations that would clearly demarcate these two phases, the liberal era from its successor, marked by criticism of the liberal models. Such a frame allows instead for the coexistence of the two discourses and their corresponding temporal horizons, and the *gradual* replacement of one by the other, the latter moving out of its initially marginal location and into the hegemonic position over time. Most importantly for the present argument, the 'Belgian model' so enthusiastically embraced by Romanian governing elites was itself now subject to criticism in Belgium, joined by suspicions of foreign intervention.

In Belgium, the rise of socialist mass politics from the late 1870s onwards made the nation's Catholic and liberal governing elites increasingly wary about Great Power intervention and neutrality. Abroad and at home, growing labour unrest (and accompanying violence) was often interpreted as a sign of foreign intervention. In the 1880s Paris and Berlin suspected each other of inciting and using labour violence as a pretext to occupy Belgium pre-emptively because the country supposedly could no longer guarantee its internal order and its internationally imposed status of neutrality. There was speculation that Leopold II had been party to a secret agreement with Bismarck in exchange for German support for his imperialist ambitions in the Congo.[75] These developments challenged the Belgian self-image of smallness and neutrality.

Figure 3.1 'Country Scene' (in French) and 'A great foreign scholar fell into admiration when he heard them speak… French' (in Romanian). This cartoon, printed in *The Belgium of the Orient*, 8 March 1907, mocks Romania's francophonie and pretensions of being the 'Belgium of the Orient' by evoking the violence of the Romanian peasant revolt of 1907, out of place in a modern country and more reminiscent of pre-modern times. © Out of copyright.

A minority current within Belgian governing elites and amongst diplomats started to dream of a larger imperialist Belgium and viewed the mandated neutrality (which limited the country's geopolitical ambitions) as an emasculation of Belgium's potential greatness. For the colonialist faction it was clear that Leopold II's Congo meant that Belgium has been awarded a higher ranking within the international community. Or as the French senator Ribot put it upon Leopold II's death: the king had shaped 'a colonial empire […] which assures to *la petite Belgique* resources and outlets which are the envy of the *grandes puissances*.[76] These expansionist currents would come to a head during and after the First World War, when 'poor little Belgium', the victim of 'German barbarianism', sought redress in the form of territorial annexations. At the Versailles Conference Belgian diplomats tried to enlarge the country through the inclusion of parts of the Netherlands and the Grand Duchy of Luxemburg. The nation had become too small for the most ambitious nationalists.

Conclusion

The present essay has sought to undermine East-West binaries by using the concepts of 'smallness' and 'relative size' to compare how Belgian and Romanian governing elites imagined their nations within Europe and within the international system. Such a comparison, subverting a number of preconceptions that draw on normative readings of 'East' and 'West', ultimately helps reveal a European history far more transnational than previously imagined.

First, there are the numerous parallels in the auto- and hetero-images subscribed to by Belgian and Romanian governing elites over the long nineteenth century. These conceptions related not only to a pervasive (self-)perceived 'smallness' that acted as an important political factor in both countries. They also were linked to peripherality (either with respect to Europe or to more 'prominent' civilizations); to the metaphor of a 'bridge' (straddling either Germanic and Latin cultures in the case of Belgium, or East and West in the case of Romania); to notions of the respective territories as battlegrounds where larger empires fought their wars (and consequently constantly threatened to overrun these small countries); to ideas that both were religious 'rampart nations' (with Catholic Belgium manning the defences against Dutch Protestantism and French atheism, and Romania acting as a bulwark of Christianity against the Ottoman Empire); and to the tension between leaning on the Great Powers as a guarantee of statehood and the insistence on their non-interference in internal affairs, which was itself indebted to size-related auto-images. Moreover, in both cases we encounter numerous references to 'Europe' as both a guarantor of international order and a civilizational ideal. All these elements draw attention to the many commonalities traversing the East-West divide, despite significant differences in socioeconomic conditions, and to the imbrication of the national and the international across the nineteenth century. As a result, the picture of nationalism that emerges from this reading is less a dichotomous image – reliant on and in turn reinforcing stereotypes about ideal types of nationalism prevailing respectively in the East and West – and more of a transnational phenomenon articulated distinctly in different spaces. Power asymmetries, played out within the context of a hierarchical international state system indebted as much to relative size and the associated power capabilities as it was to geography, come to the fore.

Second, the importance of the Belgian model in Romania and its selection from a range of available 'Western' templates help debunk both the notions of an 'Eastern' type of nationalism and the idea that Western models were indiscriminately imported to Eastern Europe, whose nationalism would in consequence have been 'late' and derivative. The choice of 'small Belgium' rather than 'big sister' France (as it was affectionately called) as a developmental model reveals that Romanian elites were pragmatic actors aware of their country's smallness and position within the international order. In hopeful self-representations of their country as the 'Belgium of the Orient', Romanian governing elites proved themselves not only to be more liberal than binary understandings of nationalism would characterize them, but also to have availed themselves of a choice that, given the parallels enumerated above, appeared to be the most viable model. Ultimately, it does not matter much whether the respective representations hardly corresponded to reality and the notion eventually slid into irony and later ridicule. As Silvia Marton also acknowledges, at stake here is not the truth of such comparisons, but rather the reasons why nineteenth-century governing elites saw them as legitimate and legitimating for their political projects in their own terms.[77] Read along these lines, such choices reveal the agency of local actors in shaping the terms of their exposure to Western modernity, given that they themselves were unable to set these terms.[78]

Finally, tracing the evolution of such comparisons, the fate of the 'Belgium of the Orient' metaphor over the long nineteenth century does much to invalidate notions of a temporal lag in the eastward transmission of Western models. Viewed in a *longue durée* perspective, the zenith of the Belgian model, the increasing criticism directed towards it, and its eventual decline all appear rather synchronous in Belgium and Romania (as elsewhere in Eastern and Western Europe), with geopolitical considerations accounting for Romanian statehood's 'late start' to a far greater extent than conceptual lag would explain. With Romanian governing elites clearly attuned to Western modernity (in its various guises) and with their own modernizing project certainly not lacking in ambition – albeit one pragmatically tempered by 'smallness' – the alleged developmental lack and temporal lag appear much more as a matter of internal dynamics, of different infrastructural capacities shaped by the uneven deployment of capitalism and its attendant power asymmetries.

While Belgian neutrality was mandated as a precondition for the state's independence (and eventually came to be resented), Romania sought such neutrality for itself (as yet another facet of the Belgian model, based on the security dilemma ensuing from its self-perceived smallness) at the various international conferences where its recognition was discussed. These efforts were in vain. Here geographical location did matter, for the space of the 'Eastern Question' was both much more salient geopolitically in nineteenth-century Europe and much more volatile. It was also seen as more open to intervention by all the parties involved, due to a 'standard of civilization' that appeared much more problematic in the eyes of 'the West' than the indisputable civilizational attainment of 'Western' Belgium.[79] Consequently, where auto-images saw parallels, similarities and terms of comparison, the Western gaze saw indelible difference, arguably contributing to the (re)production of this difference in the process. To this day, analytical categories such as the East-West binary remain loaded with such normative, political connotations; undermining them, by drawing attention to the historically dialogical, constitutive relationship between the two terms and to the salience of other categories, such as 'smallness', for historical actors, thus has not only scholarly but also political implications.

Notes

1. Todorova, 'The Trap of Backwardness', 154.
2. Maiorescu, 'În Contra Direcției de Astăzi În Cultura Română'.
3. Kohn, *The Idea of Nationalism*; Kohn, 'Western and Eastern Nationalisms'.
4. Kohn, *The Idea of Nationalism*, 329, 4.
5. Kohn, 300.
6. Kohn, 4.
7. Plamenatz, 'Two Types of Nationalism', 22–36, 33.
8. See the essay collection Laczó and Lisjak Gabrijelčič, *The Legacy of Division: East and West after 1989*.
9. Shulman, 'Challenging the Civic/Ethnic and West/East Dichotomies in the Study of Nationalism', 555–62.
10. Todorova, 'Is There Weak Nationalism and Is It a Useful Category?' 682.
11. Kohn, *The Idea of Nationalism*, 329–34; Plamenatz, 'Two Types of Nationalism', 29–34.
12. Koselleck, 'The Historical-Political Semantics of Asymmetric Counterconcepts'.
13. Jaskułowski, 'Western (Civic) "versus" Eastern (Ethnic) Nationalism. The Origins and Critique of the Dichotomy'.
14. Hall, 'The West and the Rest: Discourse and Power'.
15. Koselleck, 'The Historical-Political Semantics of Asymmetric Counterconcepts', 157; Kohn, *The Idea of Nationalism*, 7.
16. Chakrabarty, *Provincializing Europe*, 27.
17. Witte, '1828–1847. De Constructie van België', 77–8.
18. Stengers, 'La Belgique de 1830, Une "Nationalité de Convention"?' 7; Hasquin, *Historiographie et politique en Belgique*, 33.
19. 'Les fiançailles', *L'Indépendance Belge* 14 March 1880, 1.
20. Ginderachter, *The Everyday Nationalism of Workers*.
21. Tollebeek, 'Het gevoelige punt van Europa. Huizinga, Pirenne en de plaats van het vaderland', 227, 233; Hasquin, *Historiographie et politique en Belgique*, 14.
22. Lem, 'Het Nationale Epos. Geschiedenis in Éen Greep', 186–7; Tollebeek, 'Enthousiasme en evidentie. De negentiende-eeuwse Belgisch-nationale geschiedschrijving', 72–3.
23. Hitchins, *Rumania, 1866–1947*, 2–10.
24. Bakić-Hayden, 'Nesting Orientalisms: The Case of Former Yugoslavia'.
25. Sorescu, 'National History as a History of Compacts'.
26. Georgescu, *Romanians*, 67, 119–21; Hitchins, *Rumania, 1866–1947*, 9.
27. Iordachi, 'From Imperial Entanglements to National Disentanglement: The "Greek Question" in Moldavia and Wallachia, 1611–1863'.
28. For the pervasiveness of such 'bulwark' notions in Eastern Europe, see Berezhnaya and Hein-Kircher, *Rampart Nations: Bulwark Myths of East European Multiconfessional Societies in the Age of Nationalism*.
29. Preda, 'L'influence Belge, Hier et Aujourd'hui'; Lagasse, 'Le Modèle Constitutionnel Belge'.
30. Zarakol, 'Theorising Hierarchies', 7.
31. The Risorgimento, by contrast, saw such pragmatism only after the failure of the 1848 revolution. See Romani, 'Political Thought in Action: The Moderates in 1859'.
32. Hitchins, *Rumania, 1866–1947*, 6.

33 Georgescu, *Romanians*, 148.
34 Georgescu, 148–50.
35 Niculescu, 'Andrei Rădulescu, La Belgique et Le Constitutionnalisme Roumain', 190.
36 Marton, 'Chemins de Fer', 28.
37 Hellemans, 'L'Imprimé Bruxellois dans la "Belgique de l'Orient" (1830–1865)'.
38 Rădulescu, 'L'influence Belge sur le Droit Roumain'.
39 Hellemans, 'La Belgique de l'Orient'. The links between freemason organizations in Wallachia and Moldova, and of both with European freemasonry, were crucial factors in the 1859 double election of Alexandru Ioan Cuza and thus to the union of the principalities. Georgescu, *Romanians*, 149.
40 Vlad, 'À La Recherche', 988.
41 Goddeeris, 'Les Relations', 48.
42 Vlad, 'Quelques Moments', 77.
43 Filimon, 'Quelques donnees concernant les Relations entre la Roumanie et la Belgique au 19e Siecle', 25–6.
44 Goddeeris, 'Les Relations', 49.
45 Vlad, 'Quelques Moments', 77.
46 Goddeeris, 'Les Relations', 48.
47 Vlad, 'Quelques Moments', 80.
48 Hellemans, 'La Belgique de l'Orient', 305.
49 Marton, 'Chemins de Fer', 32.
50 Marton, 42.
51 Sorescu, 'National History as a History of Compacts', 63.
52 Verdery, *National Identity under Socialism*, 35.
53 Vlad, 'À La Recherche', 986–8.
54 Duchesne, *Le Prince Philippe de Belgique, Comte de Flandre (1837–1905)*, 17–18.
55 Hitchins, *Rumania, 1866–1947*, 13.
56 Lagasse, 'Le Modèle Constitutionnel Belge', 13–14.
57 Hitchins, *Rumania, 1866–1947*, 19.
58 The law setting up the Court of Cassation (1861), the law regulating the press (1862), the legislation pertaining to the administrative divisions of the territory, the electoral law, the legislation regulating the functioning of the judiciary (1864), the law of expropriation, etc. Rădulescu, 'L'influence Belge Sur Le Droit Roumain', 195.
59 Vlad, 'À La Recherche', 986–8.
60 Rădulescu, 'L'influence Belge Sur Le Droit Roumain', 199–200.
61 *Constituțiunea din 1866* (The Constitution of 1866), available at: http://www.cdep.ro/pls/legis/legis_pck.htp_act_text?idt=37755. Last accessed 20 January 2020.
62 Sorescu, 'Visions of Agency', 82–8.
63 Hitchins, *Rumania, 1866–1947*, 50–3; Iordachi, 'Citizenship, Nation and State-Building: The Integration of Northern Dobrogea into Romania, 1878–1913'.
64 Cârstocea, 'Uneasy Twins?'; Sorescu, 'Visions of Agency', 167–85.
65 Mishkova and Daskalov, 'Forms without Substance'.
66 Todorova, *Imagining the Balkans*; Mishkova and Daskalov, 'Forms without Substance'.
67 Sorescu, 'Visions of Agency', 229–312.
68 Maiorescu, 'În Contra Direcției de Astăzi În Cultura Românā'.
69 Lafit, 'Belgia… Orientului'.
70 Lafit.
71 Lafit.
72 See Weber, *Peasants into Frenchmen: The Modernization of Rural France, 1870–1914*.

73 See Stern, *The Politics of Cultural Despair. A Study in the Rise of the Germanic Ideology*; Rider, *Modernity and Crises of Identity: Culture and Society in Fin-de-Siècle Vienna*.
74 While this sense of despair was not so pronounced in Belgium, due to the cultural dynamism of the art currents of *la jeune Belgique*, Belgium was by this point no longer a model in Romania, whose elites remained, however, attuned to cultural developments in Western Europe.
75 Guillen, 'La Crise Franco-Allemande de 1886–7 et Les Relations Franco-Belges', 88; Luykx and Platel, *Politieke Geschiedenis van België. Vol. 1: Van 1789 Tot 1944*, 158, 186–7; Puissant, *Sous La Loupe de La Police Française, Le Bassin Industriel Du Centre*, 11; Willequet, 'Belgique et Allemagne 1914–1945', 64; Mahieu-Hoyois, *L'évolution Du Mouvement Socialiste Borain (1885–1895)*, 42; De Vos, *Het effectief van de Belgische Krijgsmacht en de militiewetgeving, 1830–1914*, 230–46.
76 'Léopold II apprécié par le monde politique français', *L'Indépendance Belge* 18 December 1909, 2.
77 Marton, 'Chemins de Fer', 27, 32.
78 See Tipei, 'How to Make Friends and Influence People: Elementary Education, French "Influence," and the Balkans, 1815–1830s'.
79 Cârstocea, 'Historicising the Normative Boundaries of Diversity: The Minority Treaties of 1919 in a Longue Durée Perspective', Forthcoming.

4

'Poor Little Belgium'. Food aid and the image of Belgian victimhood in the United States

Marjet Brolsma and Samuël Kruizinga

Introduction

In early 1916, more than a year and a half after the outbreak of the Great War, the Belgian Finance Minister Aloys van de Vyvere returned to Le Havre in France, seat of his government-in-exile, from a diplomatic visit to the United States. His account of what Americans thought about Belgium revealed that two very different hetero-images of his country existed side by side in the United States. One was that of 'brave little Belgium', which, despite being almost completely overrun by German forces, continued fighting alongside its allies Britain and France. The other image, reported the minister, was much more pervasive. The country had assumed the role of 'poor little Belgium', the war's prime victim, inspiring pity and acts of charity.[1]

In this chapter, we investigate how the second of the two hetero-images of 'small Belgium' came to dominate American views of the country – and thereby heavily influenced American interpretations of the First World War. In its first section, we will highlight Belgium's important role in both Allied and German war propaganda and its impact on attitudes in the United States. The second section details the creation and evolution of war-specific hetero-images of Belgium and the ways that Belgium's smallness was instrumentalized and propagated by the Commission for Relief in Belgium (CRB), a charitable organization set up in October 1914 by future president Herbert Hoover to provide food aid to the Belgians – and, from 1915 onwards, the French – in German-occupied territory. The third section focuses on the complex relationship between 'great' America and 'small' Belgium that emerges from the CRB's unending campaign for funds and goods to keep its relief operations running – along with others' efforts supporting, in one way or another, the 'sufferers' of Belgium. The fourth section, finally, analyses the connection between hetero-images of Belgium and Allied propaganda, as well as the development of the hetero-image of Germany that developed, to a very large degree, in tandem with Belgium's. This section also highlights continuities in the CRB's and others' depiction of Belgium (and Germany) after the United States joined the Allies as 'co-belligerent' in their war against the Central Powers in April 1917. By way of conclusion, we will highlight the importance of the CRB's use of the image of 'poor little Belgium' in the cultural mobilization of the United States as first a neutral party and then a belligerent in the Great War, as well as the connections between 'smallness' and gender.

The chapter is nearly exclusively based on works published during the First World War in the United States about Belgium and/or the work of the Commission for Relief in Belgium. These sources include materials printed by or for the CRB (books, pamphlets, posters) and by or about its members (interviews, transcripts of meetings, books), materials used by other organizations engaged in some way in Belgian relief – not all of them formally or even informally associated with the CRB – propaganda materials printed in the United States both by or for the Allies and the Central Powers, and American newspaper clippings on the CRB and on occupied Belgium more generally. This chapter's authors had hoped to supplement this material with an analysis of archival materials related to the CRB, but the Covid-19 pandemic made trips to archives in the United States impossible. Despite having thus a more exploratory nature than originally envisioned, this chapter, its authors hope, will provide an impetus to debates about both Belgium and the United States during the First World War, the history of humanitarian aid and, most importantly, the political uses of 'smallness' therein.

'If the war has a hero, it is Belgium'

'I was reading the *New York Times*', wrote Leon van der Essen, a Belgian professor of history in 1916 from his British exile, 'when my eye was suddenly caught by one word, "Belgium," printed at the top of a column of recent book reviews':

> It was not without profound emotion and patriotic pride that I read the following passage: 'Why Belgium finds so scant a space in the war bibliographies is a question difficult to answer. Certainly, no country has aroused the popular sympathy and enthusiasm of the world to a like degree with this little kingdom, occupying a geographical area of about one-fourth the State of Pennsylvania, yet performing deeds of valour and enduring martyrdom that places it beyond all comparison in greatness. If the war has a hero, it is Belgium.'[2]

If Belgium was indeed the war's tragic hero, this was primarily because Allied propaganda made it so. After the German ultimatum of 2 August 1914, demanding free passage of its forces through Belgium into France, its refusal by the Belgian government and the German invasion of the country, the UK declared war on Germany, thereby turning a European conflict into a global war. As the British government cited Germany's violation of Belgium's neutrality, guaranteed by both Britain and Prussia in the 1839 Treaty of London, as its *casus belli*, Belgium quickly became a focal point in war propaganda designed to shore up support for belligerency at home and for Britain's cause abroad – in Allied and, crucially, in neutral countries.[3] At first, the propaganda campaign focussed on Britain as a protector of international treaty law, of order and stability, on behalf of a small state victimized by a much more powerful neighbour, and called upon its citizens and (potential) allies to share in their moral indignation on behalf of the victims of Germany's war of aggression.[4] See, for example, the novelist Coulson Kernahan's stirring poem to Britain's defence of the small state which was guilty only of the crime of upholding its treaty obligations:

Yet rather than our England cease to be
What England is Honour's own diadem
Rather than fail one single sword to them
(Our word, God's arm, their surest guarantee)
That "little," loyal race whom, near and far
A world acclaims for glorious, deathless deed
Rather than fail GREAT Belgium in her need
Rather than this, in God's own name, be war![5]

To the narrative articulated here, which also handily explained how a duplicitous Germany had forced Britain into war, new layers were soon added, as Allied propaganda seized upon news both of the resistance of the Belgian fortresses of Liège to German attack and of the invaders' atrocities. Belgian resistance to German might continued to be lionized long after the Liège fortresses had fallen, the Belgian army had been driven from the bulk of its soil, and the war's western front had stabilized into two opposed systems of trenches. By slowing down the German war machine, argued Charles Saroléa, another Belgian professor-in-exile in the employ of his government, Belgium had bought the Allies time to mobilize and to stage the counterattack at the Marne in September 1914 that prevented Paris, and France, from falling: '[i]n literal fact it is Belgium which saved Europe' from the spectre of German domination.[6] Even more importantly, the sufferings of the Belgian population during the invasion – the execution of civilians and the burning of the university town of Louvain as retribution for the real or imagined acts of *franc-tireurs* (irregular Belgian forces), looting, murder and rape – tinged the Belgian resistance to Germans as something forged with the heroism of self-sacrifice, made all the more tragic by 'small' Belgium having never stood a chance against 'great' Germany. In *King Albert's Book*, which collected essays in praise of Belgium and its king by 'representative men and women throughout the world' (and was printed in London and New York), celebrities such as the author Robert Hitchens provide ample evidence of the enormous propagandistic benefits of 'brave little Belgium':

When war began and the German army appeared before the forts of Liège, the world said, 'This will be the end of little Belgium.' There was deep pity in all hearts, but with it was mingled a certain sense of the impotence of the tiny nation confronted by the brutal might of Germany. I heard two men in a London street discussing the question of the opening war and the tragic situation of the Belgians. One of them, with a twist of his shoulders, said, 'What on earth can they do?' The other man replied, 'The right thing, and that's what they're going to do.' The little nation had decided. The guns of Liège opened fire. "The martyrdom of Belgium," as it has been called, began. Men, women, and even children were slain. Villages and cities were burned. Thousands were wounded; tens of thousands were rendered homeless. [...] When the first shot was fired from the forts of Liege a little nation died, but a nation that is great was born.[7]

The sufferings of little Belgium added the final elements to the hetero-image of Belgium that became the Allies' propagandistic trump card. Whereas the violation of Belgian neutrality was an affront to international treaty law, the violation of *Belgians*, and especially of Belgian women and children, allowed Allied propagandists to connect the intellectual case for war against Germany with a much more visceral argument. As Nicoletta Gullace has shown, images and tales of German crimes against the family, especially sexual violence against women, began to permeate the Allied public sphere. These accounts ranged from graphic images and sensationalistic stories in the British gutter press to the official *Report of the Committee on Alleged German Outrages*, headed by Lord James Bryce, the former British ambassador to the United States. The Germans were invariably lumbering brutes, shown by their crimes to be beyond the pale of morality; the Allies were defenders of the small and defenceless, the weak and womanly.[8] In short, for the Allies, 'Belgium' was key in creating a narrative of the Great War as a conflict of good versus evil.[9]

Of course, German propagandists could not ignore the good use Allied propagandists made of 'poor little Belgium', as Sophie de Schaepdrijver has shown. At first, German officials highlighted how they had been driven by military necessity to attack France through Belgium; Chancellor Theobald von Bethmann Hollweg even apologized for the infraction of international law during the Reichstag session of 4 August 1914, and Emperor William II sent a telegram to Woodrow Wilson that told the American president that his 'heart bleeds' for the Belgian civilians injured or killed during the invasion.[10] However, as the Allied propaganda machine gathered steam, the Central Powers were forced to change tack. Their propagandists disputed whether Belgian had 'really' been neutral, blamed any violence against civilians squarely on the Belgians themselves,[11] and even disputed Belgium's right to exist in the first place: as a state brought into being by legalities and treaties, it was nothing more than an outdated artificial construct and Germany had therefore been well within its natural rights to bring its existence to an end.[12]

The Allied and Central Powers voices alike reached – and were often even directed at – neutral America. But were they heard? Historians have long argued that, by and large, Americans wholeheartedly heeded Wilson's call for 'impartiality and fairness and friendliness to all concerned' by ignoring propaganda, that their primary reaction to the war was horror and revulsion, and that the political and business case to stay out of the war was generally accepted until early 1917, when the American leadership came to the conclusion that German policies made impossible the prospect of a general peace settlement acceptable to, ideally even mediated by, the United States. More recently, historians have been more sensitive to the enormous efforts undertaken by both Allied and German agents to bombard the American population with a wide variety of opinions on the war during the period of US neutrality, but as to the effects of these campaigns, much remains unclear. In particular, significant debate still rages over whether the American government needed to cajole an essentially unwilling 'neutral' population into war in 1917 or, conversely, whether government elites had to do their utmost to calm a population excited by Allied and German war propaganda from 1914 through the US entry into the conflict in 1917.[13]

Historians studying the (humanitarian) aid provided by US-based or -led organizations, such as the American Red Cross and the Commission for Relief in Belgium, are to be found in the first of these two camps. These organizations and the people supporting them are nearly universally portrayed as essentially neutral – at least up to the American declaration of war on Germany on 2 April 1917 – and their response has been cast as regarding the war as akin to a natural disaster, enabling them to make sense of the scale of the destruction without sympathizing with one belligerent side over another.[14] These historians also suggest that neutrality magnified the American sense of exceptionalism, which spurred Americans to give freely of their resources. In doing so, American largesse in support of Europe's victimized population could be contrasted to the wastefulness of Europe's degenerate and backward kings, counts and generals engaging overseas in a self-destructive orgy of violence.[15]

All of this inevitably raises the question of which images of Belgium spurred Americans to support the CRB, which, from 1 November 1914 to the summer of 1919 distributed over $927 million – equivalent in purchasing power to $13.8 billion in 2020! – worth of foodstuffs and clothing, including 120 million bushels of breadstuffs, nearly 550 million pounds of pork, 715 million pounds of rice and 113 million pounds of dairy products.[16] Was American generosity from 1914 to 1917 inspired by hetero-images of Belgium influenced by Allied propaganda? If so, was America's eventual armed participation in the conflict in 1917–18 also made on behalf of 'brave little Belgium', symbol of resistance against German oppression and brutality? We will attempt to answer these questions by analysing propaganda made by or on behalf of the CRB to find out whether it echoed that of the Allies and whether its direction shifted after the United States turned from neutral to belligerent in April 1917.

Small Belgium, great America

To mobilize American hearts, minds and pocketbooks, and to court business and political interests, it was of pivotal importance to the CRB to generate as much publicity as possible about poor little Belgium. The organization's press department in New York emphatically strove to keep the destitute Belgians at the forefront of the American public's mind by issuing daily press releases, organizing lecture tours and charity events, distributing posters, publishing first-hand accounts of American volunteers in occupied Belgium as well as advertisements, and producing and disseminating films – a novelty at the time.[17] The CRB believed that newspaper reports on its activities and the often emotionally charged advertisements placed by it or on its behalf were the most useful tools in its propagandistic arsenal, supposedly accounting for over three-quarters of the private donations made to the CBR's coffers.[18] Belgium's smallness, bearing affective connotations such as innocence, ingenuousness, youthfulness and noble-mindedness, was central to the CRB's publicity campaign.[19] Crucially, however, Belgium's smallness was also imagined in other ways and for other purposes.

First, the invocation of Belgium's smallness was instrumental in convincing Americans that the beleaguered country could be saved. It had to be crystal clear that Belgium was not a lost cause and that the money of the American donors was being well spent. Along these lines, the CRB continuously stressed that Belgium's need was grave but also localized: confined to a relatively small space and population, the dire problem could therefore be effectively addressed, provided Americans kept giving. The call for sustained expenditure was all the more important as the conflict continued past its opening phase since, in fact, the nature of Belgian relief changed quite early on in the war. In its opening stages, the CRB stressed the imminent peril of 'universal'[20] famine if Belgium, unable to feed itself, was not immediately supplied with emergency food aid. But after successful distribution of the first relief shipments, the spectre of immediate famine receded. Now, the organization engaged in what one might call pre-emptive relief: aid was provided to prevent Belgians from starving. The investment banker and philanthropist Frederick C. Walcott, for example, warned that 'even a momentary suspension of its activities would lead to terrible distress and misery within thirty days'.[21] And his colleague Alexander J. Hemphill, who had visited Belgium on behalf of the CRB, highlighted how the country had not devolved into 'chaos and unthinkable suffering' only because the CRB, in effect, had ensured its survival.

> It is only after being in Brussels for a little time, and after visiting Charleroi, Malines, Antwerp. Liege and other places that one realizes how misleading are first impressions of life in Belgium as it is today. The outward appearance of normality is sustained only by the fact that relief to the value of over $6,000,000 is, so to speak, injected into the country every month. The external calm is an amazing tribute to the efficiency of the system whereby the Relief organization provides and distributes to this whole nation the supplies without which there would be chaos and unthinkable suffering.[22]

Relief, then, was necessary, but why should Americans be the saviours of faraway Belgium? To answer that question, the CBR firstly emphasized that the Belgians were a people worth saving. The Woman's Section of the CRB suggested in a 1914 pamphlet that '[t]he highest aspirations and the finest achievements of the race are symbolized in this little country', which 'must be saved to the human family'.[23] Second, and even more importantly, the CRB sought to create an emotional connection between American (potential) donors and the Belgians under occupation by suggesting that Belgium and the United States were alike in certain important ways. This assertion of kinship lent a sense of familiarity, even of intimacy, to appeals for aid on behalf of a country a world away, on the far side of the Atlantic Ocean. In an early 1917 lecture on his experiences as a CRB 'delegate' overseeing the distribution of imported foodstuffs in the Belgian provinces of Antwerp and Limbourg, Robert Withington, for example, pointed out that America and Belgium were both youthful, modern states, suggesting that Belgium was more like the United States than like other European states, which were often portrayed as aged – venerable, yes, but old-fashioned.[24] And *The New York Times*, for instance, emphasized the innocence of the poor little Belgians, who 'like our own people, have sought to conquer only by the ways of peace, industry, and intellect'.[25]

But though related to the United States, Belgium was rarely its equal. Will Irwin, who had been one of the first American journalists in German-occupied Belgium and upon his return home had become the CRB's 'publicity manager in America',[26] for example, habitually referred to Belgium as the 'stricken little sister of the world'.[27] That Belgium's smallness was also, and often, explicitly gendered helped cast America in the role of a big 'brother' to the 'stricken little sister', entailing a noble duty that he come to her aid and shelter her from the horrors of war.[28]

Figure 4.1 'Food ship for Belgium'. CRB poster by Catharine Williams (Hoover Institution Library & Archives, XX343.26651), depicting a Belgian mother and her two children awaiting American aid. © Out of copyright.

But in CBR propaganda and the attendant newspaper coverage of the Commission's operations, a *second* hetero-image of small Belgium – one at odds with that of an advanced, modern people who were almost Americans-writ-small – came to the fore as well. This emergent hetero-image was constructed mostly to contrast the smallness of Belgium with an American auto-image of modernity, rationality and dynamism, exemplified by the CRB.[29] This auto-image, in turn, was created as a by-product of conscious efforts on behalf of the Commission to portray itself as no ordinary charity. Alexander Hemphill, the organization's treasurer, stressed that unlike most charitable institutions, the CRB was 'a marvel of efficiency and devotion', while CRB director Vernon Kellogg highlighted that the Commission used 'brains and heart in no less measure than commercial acumen and efficiency'.[30] The notion that the CRB was an endeavour halfway between a charity and a business was also exemplified, per Herbert Hoover, by its being 'perhaps the only philanthropic organization in the world which issues weekly balance sheets'.[31] The CRB, moreover, did everything in its power to suggest to American donors that it was not simply dumping food and other relief goods on Belgium but instead was engaged in a highly professional, targeted and scientific aid operation. It regularly issued press releases to update the media with an accounting of exactly how much money and how many shiploads of food had been sent to Belgium and how many daily meals had been provided to needy Belgians.[32] The New York head office heavily publicized the 'food boxes' created by its Woman's Department with the help of the chief chemist at the Department of Agriculture, Harvey Wiley, to ensure that they were tailored to the exact nutritional needs of various categories of Belgian 'destitutes' such as infants and the elderly.[33] Vernon Kellogg's wife Charlotte, who had toured Belgium in 1916 on behalf of the CRB, also stressed the CRB's 'ingenuity', and in her book *Women in Belgium* (1917) enthusiastically explained how the weekly menus distributed by the CRB in occupied Belgium were 'all based on scientific analysis of food values, and follow strictly physicians' instructions'.[34]

The CRB's depiction of itself as a uniquely rational, scientific and businesslike operation found favour with broad swathes of the American press. *The Sacramento Union*, for instance, praised the organization's 'expedition and thoroughness', while *The New York Times* celebrated its relief work as a 'giant business enterprise'.[35] Other newspapers, too, painted a picture of the CRB as an endeavour of experts and businessmen who, treating their highly complex relief operations like a business rather than a charity, had thereby kept administrative costs exceptionally low, were purchasing food supplies for the lowest obtainable price, and had cleverly negotiated reduced rates for ocean transportation, railroad tariffs and milling fees with American companies. *The New York Times* raved about the CRB's 'elaborate financial machinery' which ensured that bread was cheaper in Brussels than in London.[36] In sum, argued William C. Edgar, who had travelled through occupied Belgium, in the *Morning Press*, because of the 'efficiency, thoroughness and wisdom' of the relief operation, every penny donated to the CRB was well spent.[37]

These representations of the CRB as a highly effective, rationally organized, businesslike charity were often connected, by the Commission itself and by others, to the notion that it exemplified all the best qualities of America. *The Marin Journal* claimed that the great work of the CRB could never have been accomplished 'by any, but an American commission', as those reared in 'European universities, where rigid discipline is maintained and men are taught to do what they are told could not have met with the success attained by Mr. Hoover and his associates'.[38] In *The Need of Belgium*, the British novelist and playwright Anthony Hope sang the praises of America's admirable qualities, manifested, he believed, in its relief efforts. The Americans were 'emphatically a business people as well as a generous people' who, when Belgium needed help, had offered their assistance with their 'characteristically national clearness, promptitude, and confidence'. The CRB's relief operation was, according to Hope, a 'national work' destined to succeed, since America, 'with her splendid power of organization controlling and directing the impulse of her charity [...] will see that no failure attends on the enterprise which has had so magnificent an inception under the auspices of the Commission for Relief in Belgium'.[39] Herbert Hoover, the CRB's founder, was often presented as the incarnation of these admirable national characteristics.[40] Hemphill praised his 'genius for organization', while Irwin described Hoover as 'the Reliever of Belgium', 'the Friend of the Hungry' and 'the biggest human phenomenon brought out of America by this war'.[41] This image of Hoover as the epitome of America's greatest gifts also featured prominently in the press. In early 1917, *The New York Times*, for example, classified Hoover's coordination of Belgian relief as 'perhaps the most splendid American achievement of the last two years'.[42] And the socialite Aimee Ernesta Drinker, a keen reader of newspapers and periodicals and wife of a journalist, noted in her diary that her countrymen considered Hoover 'the greatest American alive to-day, and they fully expect him to go home and move to the White House when the war is over'.[43]

The CRB's efforts to present itself as the pinnacle of American efficiency, along with its overall business ethos – in sync with an American auto-image as an eminently modern country – left little space for Belgian agency. With increasing frequency, a particular sort of hetero-image of Belgium came to serve as the CRB's counter-image: Belgium emerged as an essentially un-modern country, peopled by simple agrarians who could do little but look on in awe and gratitude as their benefactors performed near-magical feats of logistical and financial ingenuity.[44] This hetero-image of a small, despondent and grateful Belgium, the counterpart to great, ingenious and generous America, was at odds with reality. Far from an agricultural society, Belgium, by the early twentieth century, was a thoroughly modern, heavily urbanized and industrialized country. And during the Great War, more than one hundred thousand Belgians worked as agents for the *Comité National de Secours et d'Alimentation* (National Relief and Food Committee), an aid organization founded and operated by Belgians which closely cooperated with the CRB to distribute aid.[45] But for the CRB, and for the American newspaper-reading public, they remained invisible. The one Belgian occasionally mentioned by name as playing an active role in the relief efforts in his country was Émile Francqui, the Comité National's director. A CRB official in Antwerp, Edward Eyre Hunt, recalled in his memoir *War Bread* (1916) that Francqui was 'a type familiar to Americans: a big-business man in the prime of life, self-made, brusque, bourgeois, sometimes intolerably rude, but always efficient'. In effect, Francqui was not *Belgian*, in the sense that he did not conform to the hetero-image of Belgians as dependent and grateful.[46] The other Belgians who were not simply (potential) victims were, interestingly enough, women. Charlotte Kellogg, writing about her experiences working for the CRB in her *Women of Belgium: Turning Tragedy to Triumph* (1917), describes how the business of relief was a strictly gendered affair. Business, diplomacy and finance may have collectively been, according to Herbert Hoover's foreword, 'a man's job' – specifically an *American* man's job – but the practical business of relief – running canteens for expectant mothers, babies and orphans, distributing clothes to the poor, holding workshops to provide employment – was 'woman's work'.[47] *The New York Times* also highlighted how American men had 'a great white army of women' working for them in Belgium.[48]

Apart from the contributions of Francqui and the CRB's 'army' of anonymous Belgian women, the Belgians' chief role in CRB propaganda was increasingly to be thankful. The CRB regularly updated the American public with messages sent via post by Belgians, preferably in simple French – 'Vive la bonne Amerique', 'Je prie Jesus pour vous'.[49] And American newspapers eagerly reported on the empty flour sacks that were embroidered with messages for the Belgians' American saviours that were sent back from the occupied land.[50] CRB official Hunt recalled in 1916:

> No one knows who first planned these gifts. They seemed to spring up spontaneously in all parts of Belgium as the simplest expression of the feelings of the people. To take the sacks, emptied of their precious flour, and turn them into souvenirs for the American donors was an inspiration, and some of the results have been very beautiful. Most of them are embroidered with designs in finest needlework, and lettered "Homage to America," "Thanks to America," "Out of Gratitude to America," "Grateful Belgium to Kind America," "To the Saviour of Belgium," or in simplest Flemish or French, "Thanks." One of them shows Lady Columbia with a Belgian baby in her lap and is inscribed, "The Protecting Mother of Belgium."[51]

Other newspapers lapped up the story of how Belgian peasants, caps in hand, had saluted CRB automobiles driving around their occupied country flying the Stars and Stripes, as '[t]o the Belgians the American flag is the outward symbol of their relief from possible starvation and they revere it accordingly'.[52] In *War Bread* Hunt emphasized how being thankful and looking up to America went hand in hand. He cited the Belgians' 'marvellous vision of America', which they 'believe in as they believe in God'. Their image of America 'was a vision of a new Atlantis, rich, kind, secure from the dangers of war; a land where there is no oppression, […] a mighty land which can afford to be generous to its neighbours, near and far'.[53]

As the image of Belgians as a kindred people was increasingly replaced by a conception of passive recipients at once at the mercy of America and in awe of its faraway benefactor, another aspect of the CRB's efforts on behalf of a small country increasingly came to the fore: its vision of America as a new type of Great Power. America came to Belgium's aid not only because it could but also because it *should* do so. In the words of a 1915 CRB brochure:

> Who is to help, then? Neighborly Holland is doing all and more than could be asked of her; herself a small country, she can do no more. Germany,

Austria-Hungary, France, and Great Britain are all belligerent Powers; that fact sternly limits both their means and their opportunities. [...] The answer came with all the characteristically national clearness, promptitude, and confidence—"Why, America, of course!"[54]

America was offering its help because it was not only a great but also a *humane* power.[55] In fact, argued CRB officials, America was a great power *because* it was humane, and through its aid to Belgium could become even more so and in this way lead the world, not through might but by example. Hoover, in early 1917, admonished his countrymen that 'Europe is looking at us',[56] and in one CRB brochure potential donors were told that '[t]he Belgian relief work has greatly influenced all thinking people of Europe in our favor' and would 'have a permanent value as an advertisement of the best sort, in winning us the respect and friendship of Europe'.[57] American newspapers, too, reported on how the CRB relief's work had given rise to 'a devotion and admiration for this country at large which many years will not be able to wipe out'.[58] British propagandists also extolled America's contributions through the CRB and praised the effects it surely would have on the country's reputation and 'soft power' – no doubt keen to ensure that the CRB kept supplying Belgium, preventing its government-in-exile from having to seek a separate peace with the Central Powers. American newspapers quoted the statement of the Under-Secretary of State for Foreign Affairs, Lord Robert Cecil, that Hoover and his colleagues 'would leave behind them in Europe a reputation which the United States could count on as a national possession in future years', and the novelist Alfred Mason added that 'no history of this great world war can ever be written which will not add a shining laurel to the fame of the United States'.[59]

But precisely because the aid to Belgium was so crucial to the ascendancy of the United States as a new, moral type of Great Power, it was doubly necessary that donations kept coming in. A curious shift in strategy thus emerged in the middle of 1915. Having effusively praised the American public for its generous giving, the ongoing fundraising efforts took on a decidedly darker tone after a year of war, probably to counter growing donor fatigue. The lynchpin of this negative campaign was the notion that Americans were uniquely responsible both for the Belgians' health and for America's reputation in Europe. Were Americans to stop giving, CRB delegate Robert Withington warned, Belgians would starve and America's reputation would suffer: 'Do we want the gratitude of the Belgians to fade? Do we want them to feel that they were mistaken in the meaning of the word America?'[60] In one campaign the CRB juxtaposed the amount of food consumed per day by the average inhabitant of greater New York City (42 ounces) with the amount available to the destitute Belgians (only 10 ounces).[61] Another made explicit comparisons between donations made by Allied countries to the CRB and those by Americans – often neglecting to mention that Allied contributions often took the form of government loans rather than private donations.[62] And in late 1915, the Committee asked shops selling boxed lunches to include the not-so-subtle message 'You are about to eat, and the Belgians are without food'. This admonitory reminder was in keeping with the CRB's instructions to its thousands of local chapters to ask potential donors to give at the 'psychological moment when the horrors of starvation are borne in upon them'.[63]

Figure 4.2 'Have you done your bit for Belgium?', this CRB poster (Hoover Institution Library & Archives, XX343.26691) asks of its audience. © Out of copyright.

These peremptory, even aggressive attempts to keep up donations and thereby bolster American prestige were picked up by others, often by tapping into feelings of guilt or shame. An op-ed in *The New York Times*, for instance, asked its readers: 'You surely don't want it on your conscience that for lack of a few dollars' worth of aid [...] an old man or a young girl [will] perish from want?'[64] And *The Auburn Daily* complained in May 1916 that the American populace had given just seven cents per capita to the CRB: 'That, surely, is nothing to brag of. [...] Certainly our prosperity would justify our giving more than that.'[65] Former president Theodore Roosevelt was even harsher, using a public rally to ask his countrymen: 'Are our souls rotten? Can we see only the dollar sign in the sky?'[66]

The road to belligerency

In their studies of American humanitarian relief during the First World War, Elisabeth Piller and Brandon Little have already pointed to the CRB's struggles to reconcile its identity as a neutral humanitarian organization with its advocacy for the cause of belligerent Belgium. Presenting itself as impartial was of pivotal importance since the CRB depended on the cooperation of the Allies and the Central Powers alike to carry out its overseas relief operation.[67] But while Hoover – who had to deal with German and British politicians and military leaders on a day-to-day basis – repeatedly emphasized the organization's neutrality, many Americans engaged in local CRB-related fundraising were much less careful not to combine their support for the Belgian civilian population with the expression of pro-Allied (and anti-German) sentiments. In 1916, for example, several Los Angeles–based women's organizations decided to raise money for the CRB by celebrating 'Belgian Flag Day' on the birthday of King Albert, the commander-in-chief of the Belgian army.[68] And even the CRB's New York headquarters occasionally skirted the line between neutral relief for civilians and partisanship on behalf of Belgium's wartime allies. Its Women's Section stood under the patronage of Belgium's Queen Elisabeth, whose foreword to an official history of its activities published in 1915 took the form of a message from Belgian Army headquarters: 'The food which your Country is daily providing to our women and children comes like a ray of sunshine in the darkest hour of Belgium's history. The Belgian women have fought a brave fight for the common cause of human liberty, so dear to every American woman's heart.'[69] And the CRB's collaboration with various organizations collecting money for wounded Russian, French, Italian and British soldiers in organizing 'Allied Bazaars' further muddled the notion that the CRB was strictly neutral.[70]

Although it was never the official line, it seems that the CRB even capitalized on pro-Allied feeling by portraying its activities as being in the interests of the Allies and its relief operations as analogous to active intervention on their side in the Great War.[71] 'We, as Americans', a pamphlet stated in 1915, 'are enlisted for the war to save seven million men, women and children'.[72] *The New York Times* even described the Commission's activities in Belgium in decidedly bellicose terms as 'the first really decisive victory of the war'.[73] This type of language also served to contrast negative views of American neutrality as a stance not befitting a great power – associated as it was with passivity and selfishness – with a much more positive interpretation of its role with regard to the war.[74]

As the conflict dragged on, the notion that America had intervened on the side of the Belgian population became increasingly entangled with the reality that it was not Americans alone working tirelessly in the cause of Belgian relief. The CRB frequently noted the large financial contributions made to its coffers by Allied governments, and even Hoover himself felt it no breach of neutrality to single out 'the English people' for their donations.[75] Unsurprisingly, the notion that Britain and the United States were 'Allies in relief' was also articulated by British voices, who recognized that highlighting the shared burdens shouldered by America and Britain was a boon to pro-Allied propaganda. The novelist May Sinclair, for example, wrote that the United States was saving Belgium 'more surely than the armies of the Allies'.[76]

In addition to creating a connection between relief and a type of pro-Allied, humanitarian intervention, official CRB publications and newspaper reports on its activities increasingly began to echo Allied propaganda. In the war's opening months, American newspapers picked up the British narrative of a 'brave little Belgium' saving civilization by delaying, at horrific cost, the German advance – a testament to the efficacy of Britain's War Propaganda Bureau, colloquially known as Wellington House. Reports on the German invasion of Belgium came to be painted as a face-off between 'might' and 'right', with the Belgians depicted as a noble people whose courageous struggle had a moral significance for Europe or even human civilization as a whole. The defence of Liège, in particular, was linked to the Battle of Thermopylae, with the Belgians cast as the heroic 'Western' Greeks waging a desperate fight against a vastly superior 'Eastern' force of Persians/Prussians.[77] Another frequent comparison set the Belgians against America's own belligerent past; the lawyer James M. Beck, for one, likened the courageous Belgian army to 'the Minute Men of the American Revolution who made their stand at Lexington' in *The New York Times*.[78] Such tropes were not confined merely to a section of the press. Even the CRB relief worker Frederic R. Coudert, at a March 1915 event at New York's Carnegie Hall, assured his audience that little Belgium fought for the same principles 'that lay at the very foundation of the [...] American Constitution'. Unsurprisingly, British propagandists attempted to play up this alleged kinship. The contribution of May Sinclair, for example, to *The Need of Belgium*, a 1915 CBR pamphlet, drew parallels connecting Belgium's bravery, America's vigour during its War of Independence and the 'splendor' of the CRB's relief operations.[79]

As the hetero-image of 'brave little Belgium' increasingly gave way to that of 'poor little Belgium', American news outlets and the CRB began echoing Allied propaganda equating the violation of Belgian neutrality and sovereignty with a literal violation of the sanctity of the home, and even more specifically of Belgian women and children. The CRB used imagery of women and (occasionally weeping) children to generate a sense of emotional proximity with the occupation and to elicit empathy from its potential donors.[80] It did so, partly, to appeal to the members of its large Woman's Division; by December 1914 six million American women were involved in relief work.[81]

The Committee also issued special brochures aimed at informing the American public about Belgian children in desperate need and organized campaigns – such as the introduction of subsidized school lunches for Belgian schoolchildren – specifically targeted to help them. Its advertisements indefatigably reminded Americans of these youngsters' destitution.[82] In *The Need of Belgium*, Will Irwin describes the misery of the Belgian children in such 'disaster-pornographic' detail that one can almost hear the incessant crying of toddlers in dirty, worn-out clothes and of babies in desperate need of milk. Similarly, the Irish playwright George Bernard Shaw wrote that in Flanders the only sound not drowned out by the 'thundering explosions' emanating from the Western Front was 'that curious, magical cry that penetrates everything – the cry of a hungry child'.[83]

The CRB also connected the dire situation of Belgian children and the country's decreasing birth rate to more general fears about the future health of the Belgian *nation* – as opposed to that of individual Belgians. CRB official William L. Honnold, for example, argued that without American food aid, young Belgians would not be able to grow to 'healthy maturity'.[84] Alexander Hemphill added that, even were they to survive the war without the CRB's support, the sorrows they endured would have tried 'the soul of any nation', while Edward Eyre Hunt argued that in order to save Belgium, 'a free and united people' had to rise from its 'crucified, dead, and buried' land.[85] Similar ideas about the inseparable connection between the survival of the Belgian children and the survival of the Belgian nation circulated in the American press. As the Santa Barbara, California, newspaper *The Morning Press* put it: 'The health of her children is being sapped; the future of her race imperilled.'[86]

Mothers, of course, also played a key role in the struggle for the survival of the Belgian 'race'. CRB officials drew public attention time and again to either the real or the potential threat of Belgian mothers not being able to nurse their children. In an effort to get the American public to donate more, Irwin expressed indignation at the meagre food ration the CRB could supply: 'One bun and one bowl of cabbage soup a day – for a nursing mother!' One of his most harrowing experiences in occupied Belgium, he continues, was the sight of Belgian women, all carrying their malnourished babies, scraping the rims of cans of condensed milk found on a trash heap behind a German camp, until they 'looked as bright as a new coin'.[87] In his introduction to Charlotte Kellogg's *Women of Belgium*, Herbert Hoover expressed the hope that thanks to the CRB, Belgian women would lead 'this stricken nation to greater strength and greater life'.[88]

Given the increasing attention paid to the miseries endured by Belgium's population and the cries of its mothers and children, it is unsurprising that these proved instrumental in conveying – implicitly and explicitly, intentionally and unintentionally – hetero-images of Germany to the American populace. Early in the war, there emerged a hetero-image of Germany as powerful but brutish, almost a counterpoint to the hetero-image of the country it had invaded. Here, once again, large sections of the American press echoed Allied propaganda casting the Germans as morally corrupt 'Huns' who, despite their impressive 'outward civilization' – evident in German advances in industry and science, along with their military strength and discipline – lacked true 'inner civilization', and therefore essentially human qualities such as humility, decency and love of others. But even though, within the CRB, neutrality and partisanship on behalf of the Allies were sometimes rather uncomfortably intertwined, the organization's officials were, at first, careful not to openly identify Germany as the culprit behind poor little Belgium's misery.[89] In an April 1915 *New York Times* interview, Herbert Hoover emphasized that the CRB was merely engaged in assisting the suffering Belgians and was not 'questioning the cause or the causes of this calamity'.[90] The CRB repeatedly stressed that although it worked for the Belgian civilian population, it maintained a friendly footing with their occupiers and occasionally even defended them in the court of public opinion, as in its public contradictions of the apparently persistent rumours that the German military had confiscated food shipments.[91]

The sinking of the ocean liner *Lusitania* by German submarines (U-boats) on 7 May 1915, resulting in 128 American deaths, and the (carefully timed) publication a few days later of the official British government report on German atrocities committed during their invasion of Belgium appear to have exerted a defining influence on public opinion, as Allied propaganda claiming that Germans cared little for civilian life or international law seemed to have been confirmed.[92] Along these lines, minor CRB officials began to openly critique Germany. In his memoirs, published in 1916, former CRB delegate Hunt suggested that Germans cared only 'for Deutschland über alles, over neutral ships and neutral nations, neutral thoughts and neutral silence'.[93] That same year, in the summer, CRB treasurer Hemphill warned that an 'influential German section' in occupied Belgium sought to steal the country's food supplies for its own uses.[94] This split between a 'good' and a 'bad' Germany – the latter comprising the governing elite – echoed, once again, Allied propaganda designed to make it easier for neutrals to denounce Germany's government or its army's practices out of supposed friendship with a hypothetical silent German majority who opposed the war.[95]

Anti-German sentiments within the CRB really came to the fore after the German occupational authorities decided, in October 1916, to deport Belgian civilians to work in German factories.[96] Hoover himself steadfastly refused to speak out against the German government – although in private he was livid[97] – and, when questioned by the press, simply replied that the deportations were 'too dangerous a subject to talk about'. CRB director Vernon Kellogg, however, did just that, highlighting that Belgians working for the CRB were amongst those detained, and warned Berlin in no uncertain terms of the 'resentment and antagonism' against Germany this policy had created. In wider circles, too, the deportations seem to have galvanized Americans into demanding that their government take decisive action against Germany. A Philadelphia Committee, which included the city's mayor, for example, urged President Wilson to strongly rebuke the Germans and even to threaten them with war if the measures were not rescinded. The main argument was that a people who through food aid and other relief measures had maintained the health of the small Belgian nation – even though it was the German occupier's duty to tend to those now under their control – could not stand by and watch that nation be destroyed through forcible deportation.[98] American public opinion was further enraged by the German decision to resume unrestricted U-boat warfare in February 1917 – which had been paused after the destruction of American ships in 1916 – leading soon to the sinking of eight CRB relief ships and the revelation of the 'Zimmermann Telegram' in March 1917 by British intelligence, which revealed to the American public the ill-thought-out German plans to incite a war between the United States and Mexico.[99]

Wilson gained congressional approval for war against Germany in April 1917, having painted an American entrance into the war in idealistic terms and Berlin as an enemy to American interests and the causes of international law and peace. Afterwards, the CRB continued to supply the Belgians with food and other much-needed supplies, and although American nationals in Belgium had to be replaced by neutral Spanish and Dutch personnel, Florence Wardwell of the CRB's New York chapter estimated that 'seven-eighths' of relief work was still being performed by Americans, including 'raising the money, planning expenditures, buying food and shipping it to Rotterdam'.[100] Moreover, Hoover, who in August 1917 would be named 'United States Food Administrator' and given absolute authority over the production, pricing and distribution of American food, managed to convince President Wilson to supply the CRB with monthly $12.5 million loans to buy food and other relief goods for occupied Belgium and northern France. These infusions diminished – but did not totally abolish – the CRB's need to publicly campaign for private funding.[101]

But as CRB officials lost their vocation as spokespersons for the commission, they gained a new calling as expert witnesses, employed in a campaign to further convince the American public of the need to go to war against the ruthless oppressors of 'poor little Belgium'. Hoover himself spoke up in early April, arguing that CRB officials, having kept their mouths shut to protect Belgian food supplies, could now freely express their opinions on Germany, 'born of our intimate experience and contact'.[102] Quickly thereafter, Will Irwin found employment at the Committee on Public Information (CPI), the war propaganda agency of the US government, which soon after the American entry into the war published *German War Practices*, a collection of German atrocity stories with prominent contributions from Kellogg and Hoover. Their reports of German misconduct and Belgian sufferings, which according to Hoover 'have heated my blood through the two and a half years that I have spent in work for the relief',[103] were presented as the reliable 'testimony of neutrals' that was 'based wholly on observations made before the United States entered the war'.[104]

Figure 4.3 Poster advertising the American Show Print Co. 'photo play' *Belgium: The Kingdom of Grief*, an assemblage of stills from the Western Front and occupied Belgium (Hoover Institution Library & Archives, XX343.33095). Photos and films lent additional weight to the statements of the CRB women and men who had witnessed the German occupation of Belgium first-hand. © Out of copyright.

Those CRB officials who had spent time in Europe eagerly sought to lend their first-hand observations of the sufferings of Belgian civilians and the conduct of German military and civilian authorities in Belgium in support of America's new cause. They were expert witnesses, telling the American public exactly why their country had been forced to declare war. Irwin made the case for the privileged role of the 'straight, coolheaded, reliable' American CRB delegates in his *A Reporter at Armageddon* (1918): they 'have been to the hospitals and talked with the victims; and they know'.[105] Next to Irwin, Vernon Kellogg might have been the most prodigious of the CRB-men-turned-war-propagandists. He went on speaking tours and published two books, *Headquarters Night* (1917) – an account of his experiences at the German army headquarters as the CRB's chief representative in Belgium – and *Fighting Starvation* (1918).[106] Like Irwin, he assured his readers that CRB men, after 'months of personal contact', knew 'what the German kind is'. What is more, he argued that the Commission officials who travelled to occupied Belgium did so intending to uphold the strictest impartiality, but 'came out no neutral'.[107] CRB delegate Arthur B. Maurice's *Bottled Up in Belgium* (1917) claimed that 'no American delegate of my time ever came out of Belgium pro-German'.[108] Critically, Maurice and the others who spoke, wrote or published memoirs of their time in Belgium after America entered the war cite the deportations of Belgians to German work camps ('a slavery of far more terrifying aspects than was ever imposed upon the American negro', per a hyperbolic Charlotte Kellogg)[109] as the straw that broke the camel's back. It provided the definitive, irrefutable proof that America's fight to save poor little Belgium, begun by the CRB in 1914, would now have to be waged on the battlefield.[110]

Conclusion

'How fortunate it was', remarked British Foreign Secretary A. J. Balfour after the war had ended, 'for the sake of our relations with America, that we had the outrage of Belgium'.[111] He was right. Hetero-images of 'poor little Belgium' were instrumental in galvanizing American support first for the provision of food aid to Belgium, and ultimately for a military campaign against its occupiers. In fact, 'poor little Belgium' not only played a crucial role in the cultural mobilization of America in support of war against the Central Powers but even inspired specific war aims, in particular those of Wilson's famous 'Fourteen Points' programme for peace related to Belgium's full restoration ('No other single act will serve as this will serve to restore confidence among the nations in the laws which they have themselves set and determined for the government of their relations with one another') and the rights of small states to 'mutual guarantees of political independence and territorial integrity' more generally.[112]

This essay, however, adds three important elements to this analysis of the significance of 'Belgium' to American understandings of and engagements with the Great War. First, it highlights how the Commission for Relief in Belgium was instrumental in keeping 'Belgium' at the forefront of American consciousness from the organization's inception in late October 1914 onwards. Its relentless publicity campaign, and the enormous amount of coverage of the CRB's activities and of Belgium in general in the

American press, drove home a variety of narratives on how Americans were supposed to feel and act towards Belgium. These narratives, true, were inconsistent, sometimes even contradictory. At first, they painted Belgians as brave Americans-writ-small and Belgium an island of modernity in an archaic and violent Europe, unfairly victimized by war. But this hetero-image of Belgium was soon mostly if not wholly supplanted by a conception casting defenceless and grateful 'poor little Belgium' as reliant on a new type of moral and modern great power: the United States. Second, this chapter has shown how hetero-image of Belgium also created its Other: that of Germany as a ruthless militaristic power waging war on mothers and children. The CRB, quite contrary to its stated mission to maintain strictly impartiality, was a critical agent in disseminating the notions that America was engaged in the war on the Belgians' side assisted by the Allies and that Germany did not share the values that had inspired great America to come to small Belgium's aid. Moreover, the CRB, and influential American news outlets along with it, increasingly echoed the tropes and images first introduced in Allied propaganda.[113] Finally, CRB delegates' roles as expert witnesses attesting to both the misery of poor little Belgium and the brutish perfidiousness of Germany were crucial in the portrayal of America's entry into the war not as a sudden break with its neutral past but as a continuation by other means of the fight for Belgium.

Smallness was key to all of this. This chapter has shown, however, that it was not merely smallness per se that inspired admiration for a small state that did great things, elicited pity in the way a great power treated a small people or prompted Americans to think about how their greatness related to Belgium's smallness. The smallness in play here was explicitly gendered. To highlight the hetero-image of 'poor little Belgium', the CRB highlighted the plight of desperate mothers and defenceless children. In an even more explicit gendering, it portrayed Belgians increasingly as a 'female' people without agency, in need of men (the CRB representing 'big brother' America) to come to its aid. Furthermore, images of violence against weak, 'female' Belgium by a brutish, male Germany slowly turned sympathy into outrage. Gendering small Belgium was therefore instrumental in mobilizing Americans, first for humanitarian assistance and then for military intervention.

Notes

1 Amara, 'La Propaganda Belge', 177–8.
2 Van der Essen, 'L'Opinion Publique', 126.
3 Bondallaz, 'Entre propagande et action humanitaire', 14.
4 On whether the violation of Belgian neutrality per se was the most important reason for Britain's declaration of war there is still a large measure of controversy. Mombauer, *The Origins of the First World War*, 197; Hull, *A Scrap of Paper*, 33–41.
5 Markland, *The Glory of Belgium*, 26.
6 Saroléa, *How Belgium Saved Europe*, 5.
7 Caine, *King Albert's Book*, 105–6.
8 Gullace, 'Sexual Violence and Family Honor: British Propaganda and International Law during the First World War', 714, 724–5. See also Green, 'Advertising War', 316–17.

9   Kunczik, 'Forgotten Roots of International Public Relations: Attempts of Germany, Great Britain, Czechoslovakia, and Poland to Influence the United States during World War I', 95.
10 De Schaepdrijver, *De Groote Oorlog. Het Koninkrijk België Tijdens de Eerste Wereldoorlog*, 96, 136.
11 *The Belgian People's War*, 6–8.
12 De Schaepdrijver, 'Champion or Stillbirth?' 65–8; De Schaepdrijver, 'Occupation', 267–9.
13 For an overview of debates, see O'Brien, 'The American Press, Public, and the Reaction to the Outbreak of the First World War', 449–51.
14 Little, 'Humanitarian Relief'; Irwin, 'The Disaster of War: American Understandings of Catastrophe, Conflict and Relief'; Nash, *The Life of Herbert Hoover. The Humanitarian, 1914–1917*, 362–5.
15 Piller, 'American War Relief', 621–2; Keene, 'Americans Respond', 266–8.
16 Ellerman, 'Starvation Blockade', 62.
17 Gay and Fisher, *Public Relations of the Commission for Relief in Belgium. Documents, Vol. II*, 246; Little, 'Humanitarian Mobilization', 135; Little, 'Band of Crusaders', 338.
18 *Los Angeles Herald* 31 March 1915, 'Belgian Relief Fund Exceeds Million Mark'
19 See e.g. Archer, *Belgian Relief Cook Book*, 10.
20 Bennett, 'Prodigious Problem', 9.
21 *New York Times* 22 January 1916, 'Belgian Food Shortage'.
22 Hemphill, *Belgium under the Surface*.
23 *New York Times* 13 November 1914, 'The Women's Section of the American Commission for Relief in Belgium'.
24 Withington, *That These May Eat*, 3.
25 *New York Times* 19 December 1914, 'Starving Rioters Killed in Belgium'.
26 Wagner, *America and the Great War*, 51.
27 *Colusa Sun* 13 January 1915, 'Uncle Sam Offers All Americans a Chance to Feed Starving Belgium'; *New York Times* 5 December 1914, 'Say Only America Can Save Belgians'.
28 Herbert Hoover used a related metaphor and proclaimed that the Belgian people had to be preserved, as they had been made 'wards of the world through the exigency of warfare' and were completely dependent on the benevolence of their appointed guardians. In: *New York Times* 18 April 1915, 'How Belgians Get Bread'.
29 *Morning Press* 12 January 1915, 'We're Ishmael of Europe, Says Belgian'.
30 Hemphill, *Belgium under the Surface*; Kellogg, *Fighting Starvation*, 179.
31 *The Morning Post* 3 January 1915, 'Belgian Relief Work Described By H.C. Hoover'.
32 See for example: *Colusa Daily Sun* 2 February 1915, 'Belgium Relief Must Continue until Summer'; *New York Times* 12 September 1915, '$80,000,000 Spent for Belgian Relief'; *New York Times* 18 September 1916, '$1,000,000 a Month Asked for War Aid'; *New York Times* 7 November 1914, '400,000 Meals a Day Given to Brussels'.
33 *Sacramento Union* 1 December 1914, 'Million Belgian Babies to Be Fed with Wiley Food'; *Madera Mercury* 14 May 1915, 'Dr. Wiley Prepares an Ideal Food Box for Starving Belgium'.
34 Kellogg, *Women of Belgium*, 35.
35 *New York Times* 13 January 1915, 'Belgian Relief Line Now Runs 31 Ships'.
36 *New York Times* 17 May 1915, 'Aiding Belgians on Business Basis'.
37 *Morning Press* 9 May 1915, 'Relief Effort for Belgians Approved'.
38 *Marin Journal* 11 March 1916, 'Preparedness and the European War'.

39 Hope, 'The Fleet of Mercy', 19, 21–2.
40 Nash, *The Life of Herbert Hoover. The Humanitarian, 1914–1917*, 366–7.
41 Hemphill, *Belgium under the Surface*; Irwin, *A Reporter at Armageddon*, 4.
42 *New York Times* 31 January 1917, 'Why Mr. Hoover Was Ashamed'.
43 Drinker Bullit, *Uncensored Diary*, 120–1.
44 For example: *Morning Press* 12 January 1915, 'We're Ishmael of Europe, Says Belgian'; *Morning Press* 9 May 1916, 'Germany Blights Belgium'.
45 See Van Bosstraeten, *Bezet maar beschermd*, 47–49; De Schaepdrijver, *De Groote Oorlog. Het Koninkrijk België Tijdens de Eerste Wereldoorlog*, 14, 115–18.
46 Eyre Hunt, *War Bread*, 272.
47 Kellogg, *Women of Belgium*, xiii. and xiv–xvi.
48 *New York Times* 14 January 1917, 'What the Women of Belgium Are Doing to Help'.
49 *New York Times* 28 March 1915, 'Belgian Children Cry Thanks, Thanks'.
50 For example: *New York Times* 17 October 1915, 'Belgians Decorate Empty Flour Bags'; *Stockton Independent* 5 August 1916, 'Flour Sack Sent As Gift'.
51 Eyre Hunt, *War Bread*, 229.
52 Cited in: *Sacramento Union* 28 February 1915, 'Belgian Peasants Glad to Salute Stars and Stripes'. See also *Los Angeles Herald* 27 February 1915, 'Belgians Moved to Cheers and Tears at American Philanthropy'.
53 Eyre Hunt, *War Bread*, 321.
54 Hope, 'The Fleet of Mercy', 19.
55 Galsworthy, 'To the Rescue - AMERICA!', 15.
56 *Morning Post* 14 March 1917, 'War or No War, America Must Feed Belgians, Says Hoover'.
57 *Belgium's Need*.
58 *New York Times* 8 April 1917, 'Last Man Out Tells of Belgian Relief'.
59 *Sacramento Union* 15 February 1917, 'Hoover Praised by Lord Cecil'; Mason, 'The Fleet of Mercy', 23.
60 *History of the Woman's Section*, 6.
61 Withington, *That These May Eat*, 7.
62 See for example: *The Children's Plight*; *Auburn Daily Journal* 8 January 1916, 'Embarrassing Gratitude'; *Belgium's Need*; Withington, *That These May Eat*, 3, 5; *Meeting to Protest against Deportation*, 23.
63 *History of the Woman's Section*, 16.
64 *New York Times* 17 January 1916, 'The Kingdom of Grief'; *New York Times* 30 July 1916, 'Is America Generous? A War Relief Analysis'.
65 *Auburn Daily Journal* 27 May 1916, 'Seven Cents for Belgium'. Other examples in: Withington, *That These May Eat*, 7; *New York Times* 10 September 1916, 'Belgium Needs More Funds'.
66 *New York Times* 15 March 1917, 'Roosevelt Appeals for the Hoover Fund'.
67 Piller, 'To Aid the Fatherland. German-Americans, Transatlantic Relief Work and American Neutrality, 1914–17', 198; Little, 'Band of Crusaders', 341.
68 *Sacramento Union* 4 April 1916, 'Next Saturday Is Belgian Flag Day'; *Los Angeles Herald* 7 April 1916, 'To Sell Flags for King'; *Los Angeles Herald* 8 April 1916, 'Sell Belgian Flags Despite Protest'.
69 *History of the Woman's Section*, 2.
70 *New York Times* 30 April 1916, 'Great Bazaar for Allies'; *New York Times* 31 May 1916, 'The Allied Bazaar'; *New York Times* 18 November 1916, 'Allied Bazaar Gave $477,475 for Relief'.

71 Piller, 'American War Relief', 621–2; Westerman, 'Rough and Ready Relief. American Identity, Humanitarian Experience, and the Commission for Relief in Belgium, 1914–1917', 4.
72 'An Appeal to Americans'.
73 *New York Times* 25 April 1915, 'America's Victory War's Greatest'.
74 Piller, 'American War Relief', 623.
75 *New York Times* 5 May 1916, 'Asquith Praises Our Belgian Relief'.
76 Sinclair, 'America's Part', 5.
77 De Schaepdrijver, 'Liège 1914 et l'opinion Publique Américaine'.
78 *New York Times* 18 March 1915, 'Restore Belgium, Choate Demands'.
79 Sinclair, 'America's Part', 5.
80 The same imagery was used by a number of other aid organizations focused primarily on Belgian children, such as the Belgian Baby Club, the Dollar Christmas Fund for Destitute Belgian Children and the Overseas Club to Aid Belgian Babies.
81 Little, *Band of Crusaders*, 332.
82 *The Children's Plight*; Kellogg, *Fighting Starvation*, 169. Madera Tribune 30 September 1916, 'Effort to Save Belgian Children'; Kellogg, *Fighting Starvation*, 169.
83 Irwin, 'Babes of Belgium', 10, 14; Shaw, 'The Case of Belgium', 27–8.
84 *The Children's Plight*. See also: San Diego Union and Daily Bee 25 September 1916, 'Belgian Children Must Have More Food, Ask Funds'.
85 Hemphill, *Belgium under the Surface*; Eyre Hunt, *War Bread*, 325.
86 *Morning Press* 23 December 1916, 'Christmas Offering of Overseas Club to Aid Belgian Babies'.
87 *The Children's Plight*; Kellogg, *Women of Belgium*, x–xi; Irwin, 'Babes of Belgium', 11–14.
88 Kellogg, *Women of Belgium*, xiv, 207.
89 Irwin, 'The Disaster of War: American Understandings of Catastrophe, Conflict and Relief', 22. Julia F. Irwin., 'The Disaster of War: American Understandings of Catastrophe, Conflict, and Relief', *First World War Studies* (2014), 22.
90 *New York Times* 18 April 1915, 'How Belgians Get Bread'.
91 *New York Times* 19 December 1914, 'Starving Rioters Killed in Belgium'; *The Morning Post* 3 January 1915, 'Belgian Relief Work Described By H.C. Hoover'; *Sacramento Union* 2 March 1915, 'Hoover Praises German Action'
92 Piller, 'To Aid the Fatherland. German-Americans, Transatlantic Relief Work and American Neutrality, 1914–17', 203; Flemming, *The Illusion of Victory. America in World War I*, 53–6; Trommler, 'The Lusitania Effect: America's Mobilization against Germany in World War I', 243–4.
93 Eyre Hunt, *War Bread*, 4, see also 3 and 166. In the CRB publication *The Need of Belgium* (1915), the British author Anthony Hope openly blamed the Germans for the starvation in occupied Belgium: Hope, 'The Fleet of Mercy', 23–4.
94 *New York Times* 10 July 1915, 'Report That Germans Block Belgian Relief'; *Sacramento Union* 10 July 1915, 'Food Withheld from Belgians'; *New York Times* 14 May 1916, 'Belgians Forced to Eat Dogs, London Hears: Famine Reported after Loss of Relief Ship'; *New York Times* 22 July 1916, 'Germans Put Down Belgian Food Riots'.
95 *Sacramento Union* 24 July 1916, 'Relief Work in Belgium Viewed'; *San Diego Union and Daily Bee* 27 August 1916, 'Germans Differ Regarding Plans to Aid Belgians'.
96 Thiel, *Menschenbassin Belgien*, 124–6, 159.
97 Nash, *The Life of Herbert Hoover. The Humanitarian, 1914–1917*, 309.

98 *Meeting to Protest Against Deportation.*
99 Kruizinga, 'Neutrality', 549–52.
100 *New York Times* 27 March 1917, 'Appeal to Keep Up Aid for Belgians'.
101 Nash, *The Life of Herbert Hoover. Master of Emergencies, 1917–1918*, 27–44.
102 *San Diego Union and Daily Bee* 4 April 1917, 'Hoover Applauds Wilson's Address'.
103 Munro, Sellery, and Krey, *German War Practices*, 81, 91–4.
104 Munro, Sellery, and Krey, 26.
105 Irwin, *A Reporter at Armageddon*, 59.
106 Kellogg, *Fighting Starvation*, 8, 168; Kellogg, *Headquarters Nights*, 22, 40, 84–5, 97, 102. Cf. *New York Times* 6 May 1917, 'Belgium's Need Is Growing'.
107 Kellogg, *Fighting Starvation*, 8; Kellogg, *Headquarters Nights*, 55.
108 Maurice, *Bottled Up in Belgium*, 132–3.
109 *Sacramento Union* 16 October 1917, 'Belgium's Woes Are Told Again'.
110 *San Diego Union and Daily Bee* 22 April 1917, 'German Atrocities in Belgium Exposed by Whitlock'; *New York Times* 9 April 1917, 'Belgium "Terror" As Official Saw It'; *New York Times* 19 April 1917, 'Whitlock Made Germans Yield'; *New York Times* 8 July 1917, 'Belgium Unbeaten by Boche Brutality'; *Sacramento Union* 16 July 1917, 'Pluck of Bleeding Belgium Vividly Depicted by Gray'.
111 Cited in Amara, 'La Propaganda Belge', 176.
112 Piller, 'American War Relief', 623; Little, 'Band of Crusaders', 359. Citations from Woodrow Wilson, 'An Address to a Joint Session of Congress', 8 January 1918, The Papers of Woodrow Wilson Digital Edition (Charlottesville: University of Virginia Press / Rotunda, 2017), https://rotunda.upress.virginia.edu/founders/WILS-01-45-02-0508. Last accessed 12 August 2020.
113 Obviously, not all American newspapers uniformly portrayed Belgium and the CRB in their press coverage, and certain sections of the American populace – German-Americans, for instance – were probably unmoved. See e.g. Wittke, *German-Americans and the World War*, 17–19; Horne and Kramer, *German Atrocities, 1914*, 249–55; Piller, 'To Aid the Fatherland. German-Americans, Transatlantic Relief Work and American Neutrality, 1914–17', 205.

5

Science, health and American money. Small state strategies in interwar Czechoslovakia and Denmark

Elisabeth Van Meer, Casper Andersen and
Ludvig Goldschmidt Pedersen

Variations of smallness

This chapter compares how auto- and hetero-images of *smallness* shaped interwar Danish and Czechoslovak approaches to scientific internationalism. Denmark and Czechoslovakia each persuaded the American Rockefeller Foundation (RF) to invest heavily in science and health infrastructure in the aftermath of the First World War. Denmark pursued RF-funded research as part of its longstanding doctrine of neutrality that sought to make the country a progressive, scientifically advanced 'great power' in the world of research. The newly established multinational Republic of Czechoslovakia, for its part, secured American RF funding to create its first independent public health and social science infrastructure. Because the nation won its independence from Austria-Hungary with Allied support in 1918, Czech smallness was not rooted in neutrality. But Czechoslovakia did share Denmark's longstanding commitment to scientific internationalism.

Our argument supports Samuël Kruizinga's observation that 'an identity as a small state is prescriptive' in the sense that it influences the actions that agents perform on the state's behalf.[1] In the cases we examine here, Danish and Czechoslovak agents, with their small-state identities, pursued internationalist agendas to promote specific scientific institutions as well as the normative adoption of scientific methods in their respective small states' external relations and within state administration.

As several scholars have demonstrated, the commitment to and the enactment of scientific internationalism in interwar Europe were particularly pronounced amongst the elites in the continent's smaller states. One important collective study rightly points out that in this volatile era, political neutrality and international scientific collaboration offered attractive positions for small states new and old alike to defend and define their raison d'être: 'As impartial middle grounds, mediating between the Great Powers, and preserving true internationalism, they claimed a special and vital role in the world.'[2] Furthering this line of analysis, we demonstrate how small state scientific internationalism in Denmark and in Czechoslovakia was not enacted exclusively through fundamental research and a politics of neutrality but also involved the fields of health and social science, where RF funding exerted important financial and ideological influence.

Although Denmark was and is mostly associated with Scandinavia, and Czechoslovakia's common reference group comprised the countries of Slavic east-central Europe, the two states recognized each other as small scientifically internationalist peers in the interwar era. When Czechoslovakia celebrated its tenyear anniversary as a republic (in 1928), a plaque was placed above the Danish grave of Dagmar of Bohemia. In both Danish and Czech, Dagmar was commemorated for having brought peace, freedom and love from Bohemia to Denmark when she became King Valdemar II's queen (1205–13).[3] These carefully chosen words highlighted Danish-Czechoslovak diplomatic ties by projecting their shared commitment to a peaceful international order all the way back to the Middle Ages.[4] The gesture was reciprocated when the RF-financed Danish Institute for Economics and History heralded Czechoslovakia as 'the last bastion of democracy' in Central Europe after Hitler's rise to power in the 1930s.[5]

Nevertheless, the political histories that gave rise to the respective Danish and Czechoslovak auto-images of smallness differed significantly.[6] When the philosopher and future Czechoslovak leader Tomáš Masaryk developed his political programme to 'emancipate the Czech nation' from Germanic culture and from Austria's political and economic rule in the 1890s, Danish nation-building was already well established; politically, economically and culturally, Denmark perceived itself to be as independent and homogenous as a small state could be. Masaryk's Bohemian Lands, meanwhile, consisted of nationally committed Germans and nationally committed Czechs sharing a territory with nationally indifferent citizens who identified first and foremost as either Austrian, Bohemian or Jewish. But like most Czech leaders of his generation, Masaryk wrongly equated all Bohemian history with Czech (and later Czechoslovak) history. Medieval Bohemians like the theologian Jan Hus, the pedagogue John Amos Comenius and Queen Dagmar of Bohemia were re-imagined as the inherently anticlerical, enlightened and internationalist embodiments of 'Czech smallness'.

Moreover, whereas independent Denmark fostered a positive self-image of successful democratic neutrality, Czech nationalists such as Masaryk saw their own smallness within Austria-Hungary as both a sign of inherent democratic potential *and* a 'problematic' reality. In *The Problem of a Small Nation* (1905), Masaryk drew inspiration from Denmark's success as an independent small state. But Bohemia's geographic and political reality was not the same as Denmark's: 'Danes [...] have sea on three sides and are joined to Germany [only] by a narrow strip of land [whereas we are] surrounded by an alien nation, and we are without a sea.'[7] When the First World War broke out, Masaryk went into exile to convince the Allies that it was in their interest to grant Czechoslovakia full political independence. Wilhelmine German and Habsburg Austrian 'imperialism and authoritarianism' had made Central Europe a perennial 'danger-zone', Masaryk told a British readership in *The Problem of Small Nations in the European Crisis* (1915). The peaceful reconstruction of Europe, Masaryk then stressed, required the independent democratic development of east-central Europe's small

Slavic nations. The Czechs, Slovaks, Poles and Serbo-Croats were 'continually striving and fighting for liberty and independence'; with Allied support, these small nations could fulfil their democratic destiny, block pan-Germanism and lead Central Europe into an era of scientific small state progressivism.[8]

In sum, when Czechoslovakia approached the RF for funding in 1919, it did so as a new multinational successor state. Its leadership sought to establish Czechoslovak scientific institutions that would replace the former Austro-Hungarian 'imperial' infrastructure. The RF responded favourably because it (wrongly) imagined Czechoslovakia to be a *plastic* blank slate. In contrast, the Danish relationship with the RF came to be based on the image of Denmark as a stable, neutral, Scandinavian country with strong social traditions. To Danish researchers the RF offered attractive funds as well as a chance to raise their international standing. Rather than being small and *plastic*, the shared image was of Denmark as small and *charted*: that is, as having an established social structure and a small, well-mapped population. This characterization made Denmark attractive to the RF, whose officials shared with Danish academics the idea that *charted* Denmark was a privileged laboratory for testing new forms of international science collaboration and for new research methods such as business-cycle research.

Despite these differences, in both Denmark and Czechoslovakia a small state vision for science and knowledge production gained ground as a vehicle for promoting peace and security amongst the great powers through international cooperation. As we will demonstrate, influential forms of internationalism in science, health and social science emerged in both countries. In both contexts, these forms relied heavily on both auto- and hetero-images of (increasingly conflicting) smallness.

The RF's perceptions of Denmark and Czechoslovakia

Denmark and Czechoslovakia each began to develop connections with the RF after the First World War, during a time when the RF was very new to Europe. When the RF was founded in 1913 it was only the second major philanthropic foundation in the United States. Being endowed with the massive wealth amassed by Standard Oil, the foundation was officially recognized to be promoting the aim of a particular American vision of 'the well-being of mankind throughout the world'.[9] It wedded a new faith in social reforms and research to a capitalist tradition of philanthropy. In 1917, the RF cemented its first commitment to Europe with the establishment of the Tuberculosis Commission in Paris. Two years later, its International Health Board (IHB), led by Wickliffe Rose, announced its desire to establish 'a series of schools of hygiene at strategic sites all over the world [...] including the building up of public health organizations, statistics, and public health laboratory services'.[10]

In May 1919, just one month after this intention was made public, Alice Masaryková, President Masaryk's eldest daughter and the director of the Czechoslovak Red Cross, arrived in Paris with a funding request along these very lines.[11] In the Danish case, leading scientists were instrumental in establishing the initial contacts. Amongst the RF's most significant funding efforts in Denmark were their contributions to the Institute for Theoretical Physics (*Institut for Teoretisk Fysik*), established in 1921 and directed by Niels Bohr, and to the Institute for Economics and History (*Institut for Historie og Samfundsøkonomi* (IHS)), founded in 1926.[12] Concurrently, Czechoslovakia became the first European recipient of RF public health funding. From 1920 to 1939, the RF financed dozens of fellowships and a variety of projects in both public health and the social sciences. Two of the most prominent recipients were the Institute for Public Health (*Státní zdravotní ústav* (SZÚ)) and the Social Science Research Institute (*Sociální ústav Československé republiky pro studium sociálních věd* (SÚ)). The former gained funding through the IHB, the latter through the RF's Social Science Division (SSD).

Hetero-images of Danish and Czechoslovak smallness underpinned Rose's enthusiasm for both countries' funding requests. This view of the two nations was shared by Selskar Gunn, the head of RF's Paris office. Having been convinced by Masaryková to travel to Czechoslovakia and observe its health conditions, Gunn reported his impressions of the country to the IHB and noted that the 'opportunity to have a part, and a prominent one, in laying out a public health program for thirteen million people is a unique one'; what was more, it 'could be carried out with a very small outlay'.[13] Attracted by its affordable smallness, Gunn paid a second visit to Czechoslovakia in 1920, this time joined by Rose.[14] Their joint report described Czechoslovakia as 'the most promising opportunity'. Suffering from an 'abnormally high' mortality rate, the country needed aid, but its leadership was open to 'counsel from the outside' and had shown itself eager 'to have the benefit of American experience'. Most notably, size and newness mattered. Gunn and Rose believed Czechoslovakia would be starting out 'with a clean slate'; its 'situation is plastic'.[15] In such a new, small state, the RF reasoned, their investments would make the cheapest, quickest, most enduring difference; tradition would not stand in the way.

In 1920 Gunn, accompanied by the director of the Division of Medical Sciences, travelled to Denmark, where they found the Danish science systems to be somewhat antiquated, though functional.[16] While other members of RF staff described Denmark more favourably, it was Rose, the IHB's director, who entertained the most positive view.[17] The RF considered the small northern country to be, in the words of one Danish doctor who benefitted from Rose's support for public health institutions, an especially suitable 'field site for experimentation'.[18]

Several motives lay behind the RF's preference for supporting the sciences in Denmark. Denmark was regarded as having prominent researchers who did not suffer from the 'speculative inertia' or the bitter academic quarrels that marked the institutions in the great powers.[19] The RF, considering Danish academics to be almost untouched by Nazism in the 1930s, sought to help to keep Denmark within the liberal world, free of Soviet and German influence. Moreover, officials in the University of Copenhagen, the Danish government and key Danish funding bodies were eager to help realize the ambition of interdisciplinary and internationally oriented research. Simply put, RF funds would exert a greater impact in a small country like Denmark than they would in a larger state. Denmark had a small homogenous population with a stable social system which was also unusually well registered. The last point was particularly important regardless of where the foundation sought to expand its efforts, whether it be children's health, eugenic population control, business-cycle monitoring or other areas of research. The RF realized that Denmark, an empirically manageable small country with a well-tracked population, would be a fertile ground for its projects.[20]

In sum, when evaluating its philanthropic opportunities to support science in the early 1920s, the RF was especially attracted to Denmark in its smallness because the diminutive nation appeared to offer a stable and well-established social system in miniature, which made it an ideal site for experimentation. By contrast, the appeal of Czechoslovakia's smallness came from the perceived opportunity that the country's institutions could be developed from scratch.

The prewar roots of Czechoslovak and Danish auto-images of smallness and their scientific internationalist agendas

We turn now from the small state images of Denmark and Czechoslovakia within the RF to a closer examination of the auto-images of smallness on the Czechoslovak and Danish sides. Auto-images of Czech smallness shaped Masaryková's decision to ask for RF funding in several ways. First, there were immediate financial reasons. From 1919 to 1921, the Czechoslovak Red Cross alone would spend the equivalent of 2.4 million dollars. Funding new public health infrastructure through foreign donations[21] – instead of foreign loans or citizens' contributions – alleviated the new republic's quickly escalating financial obligations. But Masaryková's leadership in nearly all of Czechoslovakia's negotiations with the RF had also resulted from prewar auto-conceptions of Czech smallness – and most of all her fierce determination to transfer American methods of social work to the Bohemian lands to help the Czech nation 'emancipate itself'.

Raised in her father's nationalist outlook, Masaryková earned her doctorate in philosophy from Prague's Charles University in 1903, and then followed her family's ties to the United States.[22] She joined Mary McDowell's University of Chicago Settlement, which assisted struggling Czech and Slovak immigrant communities. In 1904, Chicago was 'the third largest Bohemian city in the world'. As citizens of an industrialized 'freethinking' republic, these newly minted Czech- and Slovak-Americans had achieved the kind of political, religious and economic autonomy her father was envisioning for the Bohemian lands within Austria. But Chicago also taught Masaryková that the process of emancipation from 'rustic' Bohemian 'village life' and from 'bureaucratic' and 'Catholic' Austria was socially disruptive[23]; she saw 'attendant problems like child neglect, alcoholism, venereal disease, and poor nutrition'.[24] She concluded that US-style social work would be essential in overcoming these disruptions; the successful democratic emancipation and (moral) health of her 'small Czech nation' depended on this scientific transfer.

As soon as she returned home in 1905, Masaryková laid the foundations for the first social work institutions in Bohemia. She organized a coalition of students, women, workers and university leaders to pioneer a centre for sociological research that became, in 1911, the Sociological Section at Charles University.[25] Edvard Beneš (a sociologist and future political leader of Czechoslovakia) had a leading role in the Sociological Section as well.[26]

Towards the end of the First World War, with Masaryk and Beneš securing the necessary Allied support, the domestic leadership (comprising representatives of all Czech political parties) declared their full independence from Austria-Hungary on 28 October 1918. Applying prewar auto-conceptions to their new multinational republic, the government projected great optimism but also retained a sense of wariness about Czechoslovakia's long-term future. The nation's export-based economy was now more landlocked than ever and the leadership still felt surrounded by 'former enemy states' (Germany, Austria and Hungary). To secure Czechoslovakia's political and economic longevity in a manner befitting its longstanding self-image as 'inherently progressive', certain social policies were quickly agreed upon. In late 1918, the Ministry of Social Affairs and the Ministry of Public Health were founded; by December 1918, the eight-hour work day, additional protections for women's labour, the prohibition of child labour, as well as unemployment insurance (particularly for veterans) was voted into law.[27] To sustain favourable Allied hetero-images, these social policies became a cornerstone of Czechoslovakia's foreign policy. Most notably, at the first International Labour Conference in Washington D.C. in 1919, the delegation from Czechoslovakia confidently declared: 'Ladies and gentlemen, look throughout the whole world and you will find the social condition of the Czecho-Slovak Republic to be the most perfect of any country, in spite of the war.'[28]

Nevertheless, 'smallness' remained an urgent 'problem'. With its labourers now working a legal maximum of eight hours a day, 'the restoration of national health' became Masaryk's, and Masaryková's, prime concern. Declaring 'a healthy spirit and a healthy body [to be] the aim of all politics and administration', in his first New Year's Address as president, Masaryk prepared the way for the establishment of the Czechoslovak Red Cross.[29] Masaryková became its director by February 1919; by

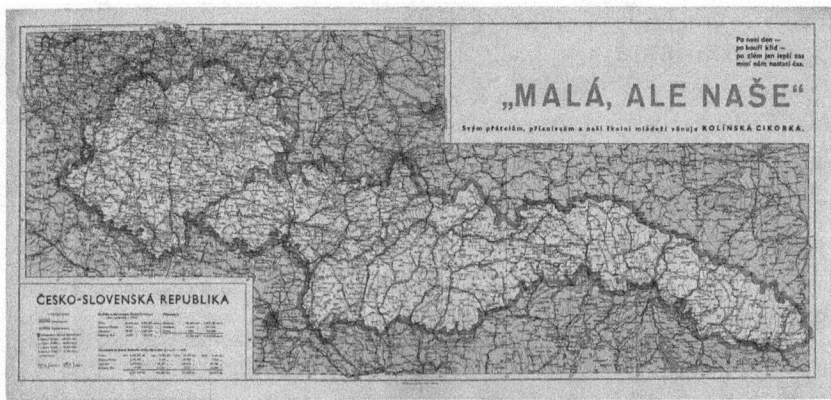

Figure 5.1 'Small, but our own'. 1938–39 advertisement for chicory by *Kolínská cikorka* (https://commons.wikimedia.org/wiki/File:Malaalenase.jpg) featuring a map of the country with its post-Munich borders and a reassuring message: 'After Night, Day; After Storm, Calm; After Evil only Good again; We Will Endure'. © Wikimedia Commons (public domain).

May 1919, as described above, she was at the RF's Paris office making her case for Czechoslovakia's 'emancipatory' new health infrastructure.

Czechoslovakia's Social Science Research Institute (SÚ) became a second beneficiary of RF funding, but only in the 1930s. With Beneš and Masaryková's Sociological Section as its precursor, the SÚ was created in 1920 as the new pre-eminent centre for sociological research in Czechoslovakia. The SÚ was formally part of the Ministry of Social Affairs but its research was largely independent.[30] To augment its scientific reputation and that of its small new republic, the SÚ established its own international network. Together with the new Geneva-based International Labour Office (ILO), the SÚ co-organized the First International Congress for Social Policy in Prague (in 1924) and helped shape the Second Social Policy Congress in Paris as well. However, the financial crises of the 1930s caused the SÚ's research budget to be cut in half.[31] In their funding request to the SSD, the SÚ argued that their shrunken $4,000 budget was too small for it to conduct solid research. In 1932, the RF granted the SÚ its first 'Grant-in-Aid' of $2,500 (a more than 50 per cent increase in the SÚ's research budget).[32]

No single person akin to Alice Masaryková in the Czech case can be pinned down as the pivotal figure in the relationship between the RF and Denmark. However, the scientists August Krogh and in particular Niels Bohr played prominent roles. In their pursuit of RF funding, these researchers were supported by policymakers equally keen to develop and internationalize Danish science and research. Alliances between scientists and politicians meant that small state scientific internationalism was enacted differently than in the Czech case – but with no less influence. During the interwar period, an internationalist agenda profoundly shaped Danish policymaking in relation to science. This agenda was based on the idea that academic collaboration could serve as a stabilizing factor in international relations.[33] As noted, scientific internationalism was a widespread idea in the interwar period, with particular salience when coupled with perceptions of smallness: for a small nation like Denmark, manoeuvring amongst powerful neighbours, the promotion of internationalism in science was considered to be an economically and politically affordable way to mobilize international recognition without jeopardizing its political neutrality. Ideally, for Denmark, a strong, internationally oriented science infrastructure could boost national development, enhance its international standing and function as a form of 'moral defence' without compromising the neutrality that had kept it out of the war. The historians Henrik Knudsen and Henry Nielsen thus argue persuasively that the commitment to internationalism in science must be seen as 'an integrated part of the neutral small state's foreign policy and as an instrument for the co-production of scientific practice and national identity both of which had international collaboration as a core component'.[34] RF support went hand in glove with this small state internationalist outlook, which prevailed amongst Danish social-liberal elites inside and outside of academia.

As in the case of Czechoslovakia, the small state vision intended to boost Denmark's place within international science began to materialize in the aftermath of the First World War. In 1917, the 'Munch committee', named after its chairman, the leading social-liberal politician Peter Munch, was established to decide how this end might be achieved. Munch, the seminal influence in Danish political and cultural internationalism during the interwar period, became the first director of the RF-supported Institute for Economics and History in 1926.[35] His ambition to make science work in concert with a progressive small-state agenda aligned well with the RF's stated aim to 'promote the well-being of Mankind throughout the world [via] the Advancement of Knowledge and Science of Man'.[36] In 1919, Munch's efforts had resulted in the establishment of the Rask-Ørsted Foundation, financed by the sale of Danish West Indies (the US Virgin Islands) to the United States in 1917. Its purpose was 'to support Danish science in association with international research' by providing means to enable researchers to come to Denmark and to support Danish researchers venturing abroad. Smallness was at the heart of the new organization's founding ethos:

> The small neutral countries that have been spared the devastations of war and have upheld their economic power [...] [owe] to themselves and the whole cultural world to find ways to serve mankind in this critical situation. By virtue of their war-time neutrality they will in the future be able to attain a proportionally greater say. Also, with regard to science, the initiative to international collaboration will have to come from them and for some time many of the threads that are going to tie the belligerents together will be placed in their hands.[37]

As it turned out, Danish physicists and social scientists were able to cash in on these favourable conditions for small state internationalism in science.

Perceptions of smallness in the deployment of Rockefeller funds. Health and physics

As depicted above, the RF started its partnership with Denmark and Czechoslovakia in the 1920s out of attraction to both countries' smallness. The RF's hetero-images of Denmark as well-charted and of Czechoslovakia as newly plastic were matched by Danish auto-images of political neutrality and Czech promises of a pro-Allied democratization of east-central Europe. In the 1930s, however, as this section will show, the RF's and Czechoslovakia's images of smallness led to conflicting expectations over the republic's new nursing programme. The situation was markedly different for Niels Bohr in Copenhagen.

In 1920, to help plan Czechoslovakia's new health infrastructure, Gunn himself moved to Prague to become an advisor to the Ministry of Health. Additionally, selected officials from the health ministry were sponsored to study the latest practices in the United States and England; nine young Czech doctors gained the first health fellowships to study in the United States.[38] These experiences initially bolstered Gunn's belief in Czechoslovakia's 'plastic' smallness. '[N]ow is the psychological time to help the project forward', Gunn assured Rose; it had the 'cooperation of all the Ministries concerned'.[39] Consequently, in 1921, the RF agreed to finance more than half of the projected cost to build the eleven departments that would make up Czechoslovakia's new Institute for Public Health. The complex was inaugurated on 5 November 1925.⁴⁰ The following year, the RF committed to another five-year investment to create a new nursing programme under the institute's auspices. The Masaryk State School of Public Health and Social Work (*Masarykova státní škola zdravotní a sociální péče*) would, however, be inaugurated only in March 1936.⁴¹ By that point, the RF had come to understand that even a small new republic like Czechoslovakia was rooted in entrenched structures and did *not* start from a clean slate.

When Elisabeth Crowell, the RF's field staff officer for Czechoslovakia, first outlined Czechoslovakia's new nursing programme in 1922, she agreed with Masaryková that Austrian traditions had to go. During the Habsburg Empire, nurses were relatively poor women or were nuns, working long hours for meagre wages in non-standardized hospital settings; all other public health work was the domain of better-paid male physicians.⁴² Both women agreed such practices were patriarchal, outdated and had no place in the new, scientifically progressive Czechoslovakia. Both women wanted well-educated professional women to become Czechoslovakia's new health workers. As mediated by Crowell, however, the RF pushed for hospital nursing and public health work to become grounded in medical science; students would be allowed to choose either specialization only after completing one full year of medical education.⁴³ By contrast, Masaryková conceived of public health as an extension of scientific social work.⁴⁴

Masaryková's concerns regarding Crowell's recommendations were rooted in her longstanding commitment to the discipline she learned at the Chicago Settlement. She remained convinced that her small independent republic needed social work to successfully forge modern, productive and self-reliant Czechoslovaks out of the remnants of Bohemia's and Slovakia's 'imperial' past. Moreover, she feared that a new RF-funded nursing school would replace her fledgling social work infrastructure. As the prewar Sociological Section was transformed into the SÚ, Czechoslovakia had created its first School of Social Work (*Vyšší škola sociálně zdravotní péče*) largely along the lines suggested by Masaryková.⁴⁵ In 1935, despite vehement protests from its female alumnae, that first School of Social Work was shuttered to prepare for a new RF-funded School for Public Health.⁴⁶

In the end, however, the new RF-funded Masaryk School for Public Health and Social Work was more of a compromise for the RF than for Czechoslovakia. With Gunn's continued support, Masaryková had been able to salvage much of her and Masaryk's conviction that uplifting national health was not just a medical but also a social and political commitment. As per Crowell's demands, the school was led by a female Czech physician, Amálie Houžvicová. But befitting Masaryková's vision, its female students spent as much time gaining sociological training as they did on medical knowledge and nursing practice combined.⁴⁷ By 1936, Crowell had learned that the new republic was not in fact plastically small, yet she still 'did not like the name of the school'. The RF, as Crowell saw it, 'had agreed to help fund only a school for public health nurses, not a school for public health and social welfare work'.⁴⁸

The Danes' relation to the RF remained less conflicted than in Czechoslovakia. In this respect, the RF's longstanding support for Niels Bohr in Copenhagen provides a notable contrast. During the interwar period, the RF helped finance new laboratory facilities, experimental equipment and scholarships for international students and researchers at Bohr's Institute for Theoretical Physics. Its contributions helped make the institute an internationally leading centre for theoretical physics renowned for the 'Copenhagen Spirit' and the promotion of international cooperation in physics.[49] For Bohr, the smallness of Denmark served as a key asset; the country's neutrality offered grounds for unified scientific endeavours in a politically divided Europe, as it enabled scientists from all over the continent to conduct research at the institute. Bohr elaborated on the advantages of a small state on numerous occasions during the interwar period.[50] As political tensions increased across Europe, Bohr stressed the importance of small nations in sustaining science's international influence to the benefit of all nations, great or small. In a 1936 speech delivered in Helsinki on behalf of the Danish delegation at the Scandinavian Meeting of Natural Scientists, Bohr, referring implicitly to the rise of Nazi Germany, noted that

> not least in times like these, when great dangers threaten our freedom and the harmonious development of the whole human culture, we feel in our small, so closely related countries that we have to turn to each other for mutual support, not only for maintaining our own independence but also for giving even a small contribution to mutual understanding and fruitful cooperation of all peoples.[51]

Nationalism and internationalism were linked for Bohr in the perception that Denmark's smallness defined a specific role for his nation. Hardly a liability to be overcome, smallness was instead a potential asset. In his introduction to an eight-volume cultural history of Denmark published in 1943 – an assertion of Danish culture in defiance of the German occupation – Bohr wrote that Denmark's specific feature was 'the immediate combination of openness to lessons brought to us from the outside – often the only option for the small amongst the large – with an adherence to our own view of life, determined by our heritage, uniting us together in the big world to which we irrevocably belong'.[52] With support from the RF, Bohr had cultivated that small role for the institute during the volatile interwar period.

In sum, neither Denmark nor Czechoslovakia altered their self-image of smallness when they lost their independence to Nazi occupation. As expressed by Bohr, the experience only intensified Denmark's commitment to neutrality and scientific internationalism; partnering with the RF had sustained that vision throughout the 1930s. Similarly, the Czech leadership of Czechoslovakia would see its own smallness – inherently democratic, yet located in a Central European 'danger zone' – confirmed when the Sudetenland was conceded to Hitler at Munich in 1938; the RF remained its partner well into 1939. Nevertheless, as part of that partnership, the IHB gradually adjusted its hetero-images of Czechoslovak smallness, since the RF's unbridled expectations of plasticity did not match the reality on the ground. The republic's leadership was rooted in longstanding (moralistic) notions of Czech smallness (and how to overcome it); for Masaryková, this conception entailed being fiercely committed to, and experienced in, 'public health as social work'.

Science, Health, and American Money 107

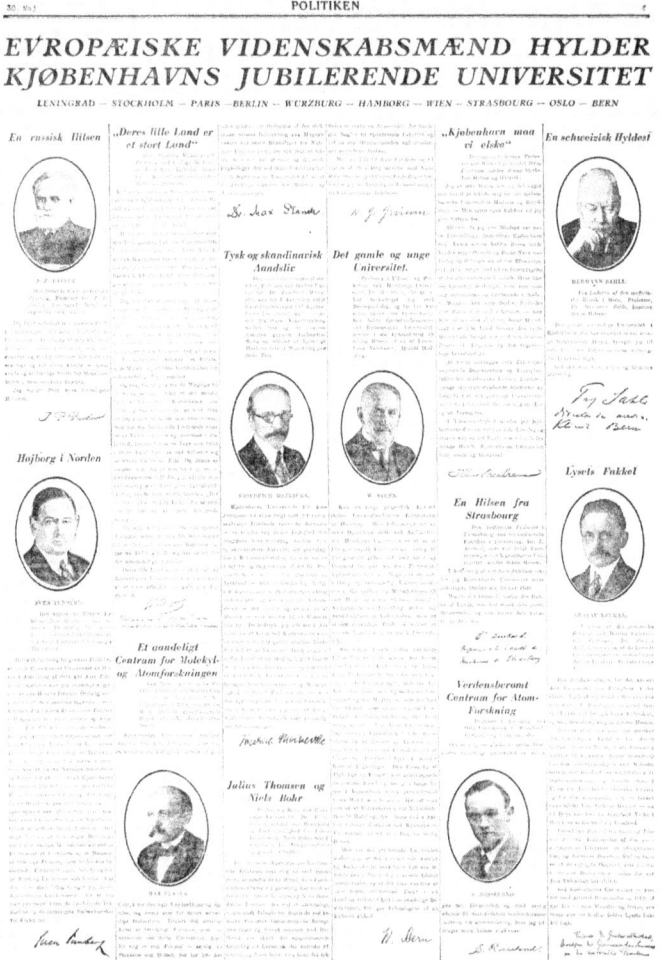

Figure 5.2 'European Scientists Honours Copenhagen Jubilee University'. At the 450-year anniversary of Copenhagen University in 1929, the social-liberal newspaper *Politiken* (30 May 1929) carried telegrams and announcements from leading European men of science hailing small Denmark's impressive scientific achievements and its progressive, internationalist outlook. © Out of copyright.

Perceptions of smallness in the use of Rockefeller funds. The social sciences

The RF's decision to cut all funding for sociology in favour of business cycle research (BCR) in the midst of the Great Depression complicated the RF's new partnership with Czechoslovakia's Social Science Research Institute (SÚ) while it benefitted

Denmark. By advocating their 'well-charted' small state, Danish economists had been working on BCR with RF funds from the beginning in 1926. By contrast, the SSD increasingly criticized the SÚ's sociological methodology and also sought to emphasize Czechoslovakia's part *Germanness*.

As explained above, Czechoslovakia's Czech leadership had defined their republic as a primarily 'Slavic' multinational democracy. It was founded with 'Czechoslovak' as the language of state and German as a minority language. The IHB official Selskar Gunn, who, as previously noted, lived in Prague in the republic's early years, saw Czechoslovakia in the way it understood itself. 'The Czechs are a progressive people [. . . who] play an important role among other Slavic peoples', Gunn maintained in 1931. To Gunn, funding the SÚ meant supporting a 'place where [RF] fellows from Bulgaria, Yugoslavia, and possibly Poland, might find good opportunities to work'.[53] But John van Sickle, the SSD's assistant director in Paris, saw Czechoslovakia differently.[54] Not only did he call the SÚ's ties to the Ministry of Social Affairs 'undesirably close', he protested against its mostly Czech publications. Van Sickle stressed that, unlike Czech, 'German is a world language of particular importance in social sciences'. He urged Edmund Day, then SSD director, to make the RF's first 'Grant-in-Aid' to the SÚ conditional on the publication of all its findings in both Czech *and* German.[55]

Just one year later (in 1933), the SÚ proudly sent a German translation of its first RF-funded research – *Der Einfluss der Krise auf Familien beschäftigungsloser Arbeiter* (The Influence of the Crisis on the Families of Unemployed Workers) – to the RF's New York headquarters,[56] but Van Sickle remained underwhelmed. That same year, the SSD had decided to narrow its mission, restricting its support to 'Economic Planning and Control', 'International Relations' and 'Community Organization and Planning'.[57] The RF, consequently, lost all interest in the SÚ's sociological mission aimed at overcoming 'Czech smallness'. It denied Masaryková funding for research the SÚ had undertaken for the Third International Conference on Social Work (1936), an international organization she had helped create in 1926.[58] Instead, Van Sickle pushed the SÚ towards producing research for the 1937 RF-funded International Studies Conference (ISC). 'Prague has for hundreds of years been in the centre of the struggle between Slav and German', Van Sickle noted. That was where the SÚ could 'contribute [something] that scholars from more homogenous areas cannot hope to contribute. If Germans and Czechs can be gotten together for a joint study of some of these problems which are at the basis of Europe's troubles, useful work may be anticipated'.[59]

With their institution's international reputation, and that of Czechoslovakia's progressive smallness, at stake, the SÚ agreed to offer the most 'objective picture of Czecho-German cooperation in this country'.[60] Pairing Czech and German (or Jewish-German) Czechoslovak authors in each chapter, the SÚ's proposed study included examples from 'industry, commerce and trade', 'agriculture', the 'free professions', the 'Czechoslovak Red Cross' and many more.[61] In 1937, the RF awarded the SÚ a second Grant-In-Aid of $2,000 to complete it.[62] In the spring of 1938, the SÚ was close to publishing their results – just as Nazi Germany was annexing Austria, Hitler was calling for the Nazi takeover of the Sudeten German areas of Czechoslovakia, and the republic's independent existence had come to an end.

Compared to the SÚ, the Danish Institute for Economics and History (*Institut for Historie og Samfundsøkonomi* (IHS)) witnessed almost the reverse in its relationship with the RF. The IHS had close ties to the Danish government, even conducting board meetings at the Ministry of Foreign Affairs, and they published almost exclusively in Danish. Yet the RF directed no criticism at the institute, as they had to the SÚ. This differing attitude can be attributed to the Danish institute's specialization in a different branch of the social sciences, which had its own roots in Denmark's historically grown auto-image of smallness. For while the SÚ focussed on sociology, the IHS specialized in economics, particularly the American tradition of Business Cycle Research (BCR). BCR sought to forecast the future through statistical inference and the use of early macroeconomic theories in order to act politically with due diligence. This discipline was what the RF came to prioritize, alongside International Relations, as an explicit precondition for funding in 1933.

IHS started out in 1926 as a brainchild of Peter Munch, funded by the Rask-Ørsted Foundation, specifically to bolster the internationalist mission of both entities. The necessity of being, or at least signalling, internationalism was often mentioned in IHS board meetings as mandatory for maintaining their Danish funding from Rask-Ørsted. This part of the institute's work was highlighted in their funding applications.[63] Attracting American money was in their sights as well, as Bohr and others from the natural sciences had already successfully procured such funding. The IHS clearly tried to emulate their strategy. The professor of history and IHS board member Erik Arup made this intention clear when he introduced the new institute to the readers of *Politiken*, Munch's party newspaper. On behalf of the social sciences, he expressed admiration and envy for the natural sciences:

The natural sciences encompass the world; For these sciences all national differences are dissolved. The Hata-Erhlich 606, Rutherford-Bohr and Nobel prizes are clear evidence to prove this fact. In all national sciences the operations are international; the grand Rockefeller-Institute (Bohr's Institute for Theoretical Physics) [...] is a visible monument to the internationalism of the natural sciences.[64]

Very much like Bohr, the IHS would become highly successful in attracting and maintaining American funding. From the beginning, the RF favoured the IHS for not belonging to a 'great' power. In 1927, the board was thus informed that two officers, from the RF and the Carnegie Foundation respectively, were working to establish an international history journal in Denmark. This placement was prioritized out of fear that establishing it in any of the great powers would immediately create animosity.[65]

Yet, unlike Bohr's institute, the IHS never seemed to completely settle into this internationalist role. As researchers began fleeing Nazi Germany in 1935, Munch noted that Bohr had hosted some of them at his institute. Munch pursued funding to have the IHS likewise host these émigré researchers, but the rest of the board refused to go beyond occasional and sparse support for them.[66] In the meantime, however, the IHS had become something approximating what they had strived for in 1927, which was to be 'reckoned with alongside the research in the natural sciences which in recent decades has contributed to the glory of Danish research and to Denmark as such'.[67]

Additionally, from the RF's perspective, the extended aim of BCR in Denmark was twofold: first, to inform the Danish public about the future state of the economy, and second, to contribute to the international network of empirical social science that the RF was building through its funding of BCR institutions around Europe, and in the League of Nations, in the 1920s and '30s. For Danish statisticians, BCR quelled the newfound anxiety that came with exposure to the world market. When meeting with their Nordic counterparts, this vulnerability was attributed to the smallness shared by all the Nordic states.[68] BCR could also be seen as a repackaging of an existing Danish research agenda, chosen explicitly by the IHS after the young and promising economist Bertil Ohlin advised them to name their economics department *Konjunkturafdelingen* [department for business cycles] in order to attract American money.[69]

Smallness had also been central to the development of the statistically driven sort of economics that had preceded BCR in Denmark. Indeed, since the late nineteenth century, smallness had been referred to as an advantage of empirical economics over theoretical 'luxury' economics:

> Denmark is too little and poor to be able to afford a luxury science in the skies, or even above the skies where it is never cloudy. Instead, we should make patient, empirical working science with both feet on the ground. If Denmark's smallness has no other advantages, it is at least possible to describe the country statistically.[70]

This tradition of describing the country statistically would come in handy once the RF started funding BCR in Denmark: forecasting business cycles demanded such readily available data. What Danish economists had seen as a product of their smallness now became an important prerequisite for establishing the burgeoning American tradition of BCR in Denmark.

In sum, unlike Czechoslovakia, with its longstanding commitment to sociology, Denmark experienced a more seamless link between the RF's funding criteria and pre-existing national economic practices from the 1920s through the 1930s. Perceptions of size and stability mattered here: Denmark's smallness and stability made BCR empirically manageable. The Danish institute, in turn, used the RF funds to achieve central, well-recognized positions in the fields of international relations and statistical economics, enabling the furthering of Munch's agenda of scientific internationalism.

Conclusion

In the aftermath of the First World War, the Czech leadership of Czechoslovakia transferred auto-images of Czech smallness to their new multinational republic. Czech smallness developed as a political strategy within Austria-Hungary, which had incorporated the (multi-ethnic) Bohemian Crownlands since the Middle Ages. Once independent, Czechoslovakia continued to depict itself as 'inherently democratic', primarily 'Slavic', with a 'problematic' landlocked position. By contrast, Danish auto-images of smallness were defined against the country's loss of territory and international rank during the nineteenth century. Against the great power rivalries of Europe, the country referenced its smallness in contrast particularly to Britain and Germany.

Arriving in Europe with little experience in philanthropy outside the United States, the RF considered small democracies to be smart bets. It was drawn to Denmark's 'well-charted' stability, while Czechoslovakia seemed to offer 'plastic' newness. The RF forged seamless partnerships with Bohr's Institute for Theoretical Physics and Munch's Institute of Economics and History, the former promoting international scientific cooperation, the latter pioneering RF-favoured BCR. The RF's partnership with Czechoslovakia was more conflicted. The nation's Institute of Public Health received generous RF funding, but the creation of a new nursing programme showed that Czechoslovakia was no 'blank slate'. By the 1930s, the RF eschewed Czechoslovakia's self-image as a small 'Slavic' democracy and redirected research into its German-Czechoslovak cooperative heritage. By comparing RF investments and their respective influence in Denmark and Czechoslovakia, this chapter has demonstrated the persistence of smallness as a concept within the realms of interwar knowledge production and international relations.

Notes

1   See Kruizinga's introduction to this volume.
2   Lettevall, Somsen, and Widmalm, 'Introduction', 9.
3   *Venkov: orgán České strany agrární*, 24 June 1928, 3: 'Česká Královna Dánů'.
4   For a more detailed study of Czech national self-identity, including its perceived roots in Medieval Bohemian history, see Holy, *The Little Czech Man and the Great Czech Nation*.
5   Kostal, 'Tjekoslovakiets Politiske Og Økonomiske Stilling', 264.
6   The Bohemian Crownlands (Bohemia, Moravia and Silesia) lost their independence to the Habsburg monarchy by the sixteenth century. The House of Habsburg resisted the Protestant reformation in all its domains, and when Empress Maria Theresa initiated the formation of a modern centralized state in the eighteenth century, German was institutionalized as the language of state and bureaucracy. Next, with the rise of nationalist movements in the nineteenth century, the Habsburg Empire became a multinational state. Lastly, the *Ausgleich* of 1867 turned Austria-Hungary into a constitutional dual monarchy. The Hungarian Crownlands regained autonomy within the Empire; the Bohemian Crownlands did not. By contrast, the Danish crown retained control over a realm gradually diminishing since the end of the Kalmar union in the sixteenth century. Absolutism, adopted juridically in 1660, lasted until 1848. German was introduced as the language of the elite during the eighteenth century; new national auto-images were consolidated during the nineteenth century, especially after a military humiliation by Prussia in 1864. Denmark turned away from its previous geopolitical ambitions in order to focus on building its cultural and national identities around a new auto-image of a small, independent and homogenous Danish speaking nation-state and people.
7   Masaryk, *Kroměříž Lectures. Problem of a Small Nation*, 29.

8   Masaryk, *The Problem of Small Nations in the European Crisis*, 10.
9   Original charter of the Rockefeller Foundation, 14 May 1913, https://www.rockefellerfoundation.org/wp-content/uploads/Rockefeller-Foundation-Charter.pdf. Last accessed 30 June 2020.
10 Cited in Page, 'The Rockefeller Foundation and Central Europe', 268.
11 Page, 269.
12 During the interwar period Danish research depended heavily on private and international funding, with the RF also contributing significantly to other fields such as physical chemistry and, not least, experimental physiology. For an overview see Kragh et al., *Science in Denmark*, 451–83.
13 Cited in Page, 'The Rockefeller Foundation and Central Europe', 270.
14 Page, 272.
15 Cited in Page, 273.
16 The RF's reasons for investing in Danish research infrastructures during the interwar period have been the subject of detailed historical research. See Buus, *Indretning og efterretning*; Koch, *Racehygiejne*; Aaserud, 'Videnskabernes København'.
17 Aaserud, 'Videnskabernes København', 204.
18 Cited in Buus, *Indretning og efterretning*, 15.
19 Craver, 'Patronage', 208–9.
20 Buus, *Indretning og efterretning*, 45.
21 Berglund, 'We Stand on the Threshold', 363–4.
22 Masaryk's wife and Alice's mother, Charlotte Garrigue, was born in Brooklyn, New York. In 1902, Masaryk lectured at the University of Chicago's School for Slavic Studies. His son Jan, Alice's brother, also lived six years in Chicago, before the First World War, through the support of Charles Crane, a Chicago industrialist and Slavophile. Kovtun, *Masaryk & America*, vii–viii; Berglund, *Castle and Cathedral*, 110.
23 Masarykova, 'The Bohemians in Chicago. A Sketch'.
24 Vickers, 'Frances Elisabeth Crowell', 60.
25 Berglund, *Castle and Cathedral*, 137.
26 Žalud, 'Das Sozialinstitut', 130.
27 Průcha and et al., *Hospodárské a Sociální Dějiny Československa, 1918–1992. Volume 1: Obdobi 1918–1945*, 75, 77.
28 International Labour Conference, *International Labor Conference, First Annual Meeting, October 29, 1919–November 29, 1919. Pan American Union Building, Washington, D.C., U.S.A.*, 55.
29 Cited in Berglund, 'We Stand on the Threshold', 360.
30 Žalud, 'Das Sozialinstitut', 130.
31 Serapionova, 'Institute of Social Studies in Prague and Its Activities in the 1920s–30s', 310–11.
32 Rockefeller Archive Center (hereafter RAC), Rockefeller Foundation Records, projects (SG1.1), Series 300, Subseries 712 S Czechoslovakia – Social Sciences, Social Science Research Institute Prague (hereafter SSRIP), 1931–1937: John van Sickle, 'Research Aids Grants-Paris', September 1932 and 'Details of Information', September 1932.
33 Somsen, 'A History of Universalism'.
34 Nielsen and Knudsen, 'Pursuing Common Cultural Ideals', 122.
35 For the moral dimension of P. Munch's influential internationalism, see Karup Pedersen, *Udenrigsminister P. Munchs Opfattelse Af Danmarks Stilling i International Politik, Volume 2*, 172–7.

36 Original charter of the Rockefeller Foundation, 14 May 1913, https://www. rockefellerfoundation.org/wp-content/uploads/Rockefeller-Foundation-Charter.pdf. Last accessed 30 June 2020.
37 Minutes of the Danish Parliament, 1919, col. 4093–94, cited in Nielsen and Knudsen, 'Pursuing Common Cultural Ideals', 123.
38 Rockefeller Foundation and Vincent, *The Rockefeller Foundation*, 37–8.
39 Cited in Page, 'The Rockefeller Foundation and Central Europe', 276.
40 Kříž and Beranová, *Historie Státního zdravotního ústavu v Praze*, 9–10.
41 Vickers, 'Frances Elisabeth Crowell', 73; Farley, *To Cast Out Disease*, 241.
42 Vickers, 'Frances Elisabeth Crowell', 65–8.
43 Vickers, 69.
44 Zaorolavá and Zaoral, 'Masarykova Státní Škola', 206.
45 Krakesová, Kodymová, and Brnula, *Sociální Kliniky*, 47; Vickers, 'Frances Elisabeth Crowell', 61.
46 Vickers, 'Frances Elisabeth Crowell', 89; Zaorolavá and Zaoral, 'Masarykova Státní Škola', 194.
47 As detailed in Zaorolavá and Zaoral, 'Masarykova Státní Škola', 206.
48 Farley, *To Cast Out Disease*, 240–1.
49 Aaserud, *Redirecting Science*.
50 See Aaserud, *Collected Works. Volume 11*; Aaserud, *Collected Works. Volume 12*.
51 Niels Bohr, 'Banquet Speech: Scandinavian Meeting of Natural Scientists, Helsinki 1936', in Aaserud, *Collected Works. Volume 11*, 506.
52 Niels Bohr, 'Danish Culture – Some Introductory Reflections', in Favrholdt, *Collected Works. Volume 10*, 119.
53 RAC, SG1.1, SSRIP: Selskar Gunn to Edmund E 'Rufus' Day, 4 May 1931.
54 Craver, 'Patronage', 210.
55 RAC, SG1.1, SSRIP: John V. van Sickle, 24 March 1931.
56 Kollar et al., *Der Einfluss der Krise auf Familien beschäftigungsloser Arbeiter in der Čechoslovakischen Republik*.
57 RAC, Rockefeller Foundation records, administration, program and policy (SG 3.1 and SG 3.2), Series 910 Social Sciences, Program and Policy – Reports – 1933–1936: 'Extract from Report of Appraisal Committee, Presented Trustees Meeting, December 11, 1934, "IV. The Social Sciences"', 65.
58 Funding request mentioned in RAC, SG1.1, SSRIP: Tracey B. Kittredge to Sydnor H. Walker, 12 August 1935 and the proposed denial in RAC, SG1.1, SSRIP: 'Extract from SHW's letter to TBK', 15 August 1935.
59 RAC, SG1.1, SSRIP: 'Memorandum, Social Institute of the Czechoslovak Republic, JVS visit to Prague, Jan 8, 1934'.
60 The National Archives of the Czech Republic (NACR), Fond Sociální ústav, Sign. 1001, 1932-7, Rockefellerova nadace: 'Report of the Research Committee of the Social Institute of the Czechoslovak Republic to be presented to the Rockefeller Foundation on the progress of work of publishing a study on the Cooperation of the Czechs and Germans in Czechoslovakia', s.d.
61 NACR, Sociální ústav, Rockefellerova nadace: 'The contents of the publication of the Social Institute of the Czechoslovak republic concerning the cooperation of Czechs and Germans in the economic and social sphere', s.d.
62 RAC, SG1.1, SSRIP: Tracey B. Kittredge to Emil Schönbaum, 18 December 1936, and 'TBK to SHW' 24 July 1936.

63 Rigsarkivet (Danish National Archives, hereafter RD), Inst. for Hist. og Samfundsøkonomi (hereafter IHS), cat.nr. 10009 (106), 1–2: Referat fra bestyrelsesmøde, 28 September 1928; Ansøgning til Rask-Ørsted, s.d.
64 Arup, 'Det Nye Historiske Institut'.
65 RD, IHS, cat. Nr. 10009 106, 1–2: Referat fra Bestyrelsesmøde 4. april 1927.
66 RD, IHS, cat. Nr. 10009 106, 1–2: Referat fra Betysrelsesmøde 23. december 1935.
67 Arup, 'Det nye historiske institut'
68 See Tudeer, 'Några Synspunkter Angående Konjunkturstatistiken'.
69 Friis, 'The Scandinavian Centre', 128.
70 Schovelin, 'Nationaløkonomiens Vilkaar I Danmark'.

6

Neutral news. Forging a small states' transnational media network, 1914-40

Vincent Kuitenbrouwer

Smallness and 'truth'

In 1955 the director of the Belgian press agency Belga, Daniël Ryelandt, gave a speech at the twentieth anniversary celebration of its Dutch 'sister', the General Dutch Press Agency (*Algemeen Nederlands Persbureau* (ANP)). He lavished praise on his good friend Herman van de Pol, the ANP's director, who at the outbreak of the Second World War in September 1939 had initiated a plan to create a joint news service comprising the press agencies of the Oslo countries, involving cooperation amongst the four Scandinavian countries, Belgium and the Netherlands. Ryelandt reflected that at that time

> the whole of the international news coverage was in hands of the big agencies, who were precisely the press agencies of the three warring countries. [...] News for those agencies had become an instrument to hit a certain target – which of course meant that they derogated from the truth [...]. This was the case with the news from the small states of Europe, who wanted to stay out of the war. News from Sweden, for example came to Belgium via English or German channel – and the other way around – which was not without danger for peace.[1]

Ryelandt's speech highlights the key dilemma facing smaller press agencies in an age of mass communication: How were they to defend themselves against the dominance of the agencies of the 'great powers' and thereby help safeguard their neutral home countries against propaganda? The war's outbreak in September 1939 gave this question burning urgency, but it was not new. The dilemma facing 'small' press agencies had emerged in the late nineteenth century, when the advent of telegraphy led to the first global electronic telecommunications network. The largest commercial press agencies of the European countries – Britain (Reuters), France (Havas) and Germany (Wolff) – formed a cartel in 1870, soon dubbed 'The Ring' or the 'Big Three', dividing amongst themselves the distribution of news throughout the entire world. Even the First World War could not cause a permanent break in the cartel's hold. The war did see a rise in propaganda messages broadcast by belligerent governments via press agencies in their own and other countries, spurring the development of rival institutions in neutral nations. But it took the outbreak of another world war for these self-described 'small', 'neutral' agencies to form a 'cartel' of their own. In the autumn of 1939, the Dutch ANP's Van de Pol set up a communal, small state news service, communicating primarily via an early form of telex technology, which allowed its members to send and receive text-based messages via a special network that gave them a greater international reach. But not long after the first messages were sent in February 1940 did the experiment come to a halt, when Germany, on 10 May, invaded the Netherlands. After 1945, however, the main participants, now baptized as 'Group 39', resumed their cooperation. This alliance, to be extended in the years that followed, still exists, dedicated to the promotion of press freedom and the independence of press agencies.[2]

This small state news alliance provides an excellent entry point to examine its members' claims that it occupied a key position in spreading the 'truth', countering the 'propaganda' of 'great' powers, and bringing a vital 'small' perspective to global affairs. As such, the correspondence amongst the representatives of these agencies provides insight into how the concept of smallness was enacted within transnational media networks. Key actors, however, rarely used the word 'small' to describe themselves or their activities. They did use 'neutral', however, to refer both to their states' efforts to remain as independent as possible in an era of great power conflict and to the trustworthiness of the news they reported – the opposite of propaganda.[3] This contribution does not seek to prove the claim that small states' representatives are more trustworthy than those of self-described great powers. One relevant factor in this respect is that the available source material, kept in the archive of the Dutch press agency ANP, does not contain the actual news reports that were circulated by the small state media network. The collection does, however, include the complete correspondence of the top management of the cooperating agencies. This material allows us to analyse the link between the two meanings of the concept 'neutrality' and connect them analytically to the auto- and hetero-images of small states, particularly in the Netherlands.

In so doing, this chapter places the Dutch press agency ANP front and centre. The ANP was the main driver behind the cooperation amongst small state news agencies on the eve of the Second World War and in the first decade after 1945. The first section will explore the national context in which the Dutch worries about the international press system emerged: as a small country with a large empire, it relied on foreign wired telegraph networks, which led to a colonial communication crisis during the First World War. As a result, actors in the Netherlands pioneered new wireless technologies in the interwar years, which made the country an important hub in global telecommunications. Although the Dutch took far longer than other small states to establish its first national press agency – the ANP was not founded until 1935 – their technological edge gave them a prominent position amongst the members of the Oslo Group, a regional pact of neutral states created in 1930. The second section explores the correspondence between the ANP and the press agencies cooperating with it. In 1939 Van de Pol managed to persuade his colleagues to work together internationally by emphasizing the need to secure national independence. After the war, this complex relation between internationalism and national interests continued in the work of Group 39, culminating in an initiative for a European organization of press agencies. As such, this chapter offers insights into the forging of a transnational media network that challenged the news cartel that had emerged in the 1870s.

The origins of the Dutch international communications network

In the second half of nineteenth century the advent of telegraphy revolutionized the international news market. Only the major press companies of the time – Reuters, Havas and Wolff – could muster enough capital to construct transoceanic telegraph cables that connected all parts of the world. Instead of competing with one another, the 'Big Three' formed a cartel and divided the world into spheres of influence, ensuring their monopoly in supplying national newspapers with international news.[4] In many ways, Reuters was the most prominent agency at the time, as it had a monopoly on news distribution over the entire British Empire as well as northwestern Europe. It created the first global telegraph network, known as the 'all red route', referring to the colour demarcating the British Empire's territories on world maps. Lacking the capital to construct an independent telegraph line between the Netherlands and its main colony in Southeast Asia, the Dutch government decided to link the Dutch East Indies (current-day Indonesia) to Reuters's global network in the 1870s. In peacetime this communication line provided an efficient way for the Dutch to organize a telegraph connection with their main colony, but in wartime it revealed its vulnerability. A first warning for the Dutch government came during the South African War (1899–1902), when the British imposed restrictions on telegraph communication from the East Indies, banning coded messages.[5]

In the early twentieth century growing geopolitical tensions also manifested themselves in the increasing strains amongst the members of the press agency cartel. Many Germans, believing that Reuters was using their dominant position in the cartel to slander their country, called for their press agency to adopt a more assertive strategy.[6] In many ways, this hostility foreshadowed what was to come in the First World War, when Germany and Great Britain engaged in an unprecedented propaganda battle. Though officially neutral because it was not directly involved in the military conflict – and therefore escaped the slaughter of the Western front – the Netherlands was severely affected by the First World War, which exposed the vulnerabilities of its position in the international system. One especially problematic facet of the situation in the eyes of Dutch officials was the war's disruptive effect on its bonds with the Dutch East Indies. The British in particular, whose dominant navy ruled the waves, imposed severe restrictions.[7] Most pressing was British dominion over the Dutch colonial telegraph lines, which they completely controlled after cutting the German line at the beginning of the war. Hence Reuters, which at the time cooperated closely with the British authorities, had full rein over the main Dutch colonial communications network for the conflict's entirety. The British imposed all sorts of restrictions to control the information passing through the network, even going so far, in October 1917, to block telegraphic communications outright.[8] This blackout caused great uncertainty amongst Dutch governing elites in the metropole and the periphery alike.[9]

Dutch woes during the First World War were not limited to the colonial communications crisis. The domestic press was under pressure as well. The Central Powers' press agencies, actively seeking to break the Reuters monopoly, engaged in a media campaign whose targets included the Netherlands, where public opinion, they argued, was being tainted by British and French propaganda. The Austrian government even hired a spin doctor who quite successfully influenced a broad group of journalists in the Netherlands.[10] Both Allied and Central Powers efforts to influence public opinion, and thereby government policy, alarmed Dutch officials, who lacked the legal instruments and institutions such as a rival information service to stop them. Their concerns aligned with wider fears that open support in the Dutch press for one of the warring blocs could cause diplomatic problems and imperil the Netherlands' neutral position through political pressure. The Dutch government wanted to avert such a situation but shied away from direct intervention through censorship laws. Instead, prominent officials asked the president of the journalists' union, L. J. Plemp van Duiveland, to discreetly instruct newspaper editors about what to publish and what support they should give to the effort to steer the country through the war without getting caught up in the fighting.[11]

When the First World War ended the direct military threats to Dutch neutrality waned, but other effects lingered for much longer. The Netherlands' international prestige suffered due to the victorious Allies' grievances about its behaviour during the war. The country, which in the first decade of the twentieth century had prided itself as a champion of international law, was now accused of '"moral bandwagoning" and [...] war profiteering'.[12] International isolation was deemed a serious threat, exemplified by Belgian demands for territory as compensation for Dutch conduct during the war.[13] As a counter to this isolation and a measure to defeat Belgian designs, Minster of Foreign Affairs H. A. van Karnebeek argued that the Netherlands should join the League of Nations and, more generally, ought to pursue a more assertive foreign policy, which he dubbed an 'autonomy policy to distinguish it from prewar and wartime "neutrality"'.[14]

This assertiveness in staking out a place for the Dutch in the world could also be seen in the field of telecommunications. The country's dependency on wired telegraphy in the First World War prompted initiatives to develop wireless telecommunications technologies. A crucial breakthrough was achieved in 1916 when C. J. de Groot, a colonial engineer on leave in the Netherlands, published his PhD thesis which argued for the theoretical possibility of a direct wireless connection between the Netherlands and the East Indies, without interference from any of the war's belligerents. The Dutch government instantly supplied him with lavish funds to set up infrastructure for longwave transmissions. In the years that followed, De Groot designed two huge radio stations that were finished in 1919 and 1923, respectively: Radio Malabar (also known as Radio Bandung) in Java and Radio Kootwijk in the sparsely populated region of the Veluwe in the Netherlands.[15] Although longwave technology had clear limits at the time – it was not well suited for radio broadcasting, for example – these stations did facilitate a regular radio-telegraphy service that was managed by the (state-owned)

Post Office in the Netherlands and the East Indies and was known under the acronym PTT (for the three services it provided: Post, Telegraphy and Telephony).[16] Moreover after the Dutch company Philips took over the *Nederlandse Seintoestellen Fabriek* (Dutch Transmitter Factory (NSF)) in 1925, it became a leading global manufacturer of radio equipment.[17] In this way, the Netherlands became an international hub of wireless telecommunication in the interwar years.

In addition to these technological advances, various Dutch actors created new organizations with the twin goals of lessening Dutch dependency on the big international press agencies and of amplifying the Dutch voice on the world stage. The first of these was the colonial press agency the General News and Telegraphy Agency (*Algemeen Nieuws-en Telegraaf-Agentschap* (ANTEA)), founded in Java in 1917 by the energetic, and unscrupulous, Eurasian businessman D. W. Berretty due to his frustration with the British telegraphy blockade. In the first years of ANTEA, Berretty managed to build up fruitful relations with both Reuters and the Dutch colonial authorities, which earned him a monopoly on wired news distribution within the Indonesian archipelago. In 1924 ANTEA received an official concession to use radio telegraphy to distribute news to the Netherlands. Via an office in The Hague it passed on its bulletins to Reuters for further distribution; as a result, the colonial press agency became the most important supplier of news from the Dutch East Indies.[18] Following Communist uprisings in the East Indies (1926-7), Berretty made a deal with Dutch colonial officials, allowing them

Figure 6.1 Radio Kootwijk, by an unknown photographer, ca. 1930 (Spaarnestad Photo SFA002007682). © Spaarnestad Photo.

to check and edit messages before they went out in exchange for subsidies and tax cuts. ANTEA made it possible for Dutch colonial authorities to spread information on a global scale under the trusted brand name Reuters. Crucially, it enabled the Dutch officials to craft their own message in reports on important events such as the 1926–7 uprisings.[19]

Metropolitan developments lagged behind those in the Dutch Empire. A former MP, F.J.W. Drion, founded the Dutch National Information Service (*Nationaal Bureau voor Documentatie Nederland* (NBDN)) just after the First World War. His intent was to create a trusted source for international journalists about the situation in the Netherlands and its colonies that would serve national interests and enhance national prestige. Drion also took more active steps to influence global public opinion: he became editor of *La Gazette de Hollande*, a periodical founded in 1911 containing English, German and French translations of Dutch newspaper articles.[20] In addition he began to employ a network of 'secret correspondents', Dutch journalists and academics residing abroad who monitored the coverage of the Netherlands in the newspapers where they lived.[21] Although on paper his bureau was private and had initially received its funding from wealthy businessmen, Drion was in close contact from the outset with officials at the Ministry of Foreign Affairs. Indeed, when the NBDN's private funding dried up in the late 1920s, it received government money via secret channels.[22] Joan Hemels argues that Drion's initiative was an experiment in the operation of a government information service, which officials regarded as useful, but he also points out that its opaque setup dissatisfied politicians and policymakers.[23] Prompted by these worries, Dutch MP called for the organization to be professionalized in 1930, which spelled its end. In 1934 it was replaced by the first official Dutch public information service, the State Press Service (*Rijkspersdienst* (RPD)).[24]

The RPD, however, was not a press agency. For most of their global news, Dutch newspapers remained dependent on the 'Big Three'. However, the cartel's high rates began to chafe once the economic crisis of the 1930s started hitting the budgets of Dutch newspapers, just as rising international tensions again raised the spectre of foreign influence on Dutch public opinion. These concerns were heightened when the ANTEA's Berretty attempted to broker a deal between Reuters and a private Dutch press agency, Vaz Diaz, prompting leading Dutch newspapers to create their own press agency, the Foundation (*Stichting*) *Algemeen Nederlandsch Persbureau* (ANP) in July 1935.[25] Later that year, Vaz Diaz amalgamated with the ANP, which also assumed the position as main agent of Reuters in the Netherlands. In 1938 ANP took over the ANTEA offices in the Netherlands proper – ANTEA having lost much of its influence and autonomy after Berretty's unexpected death in a plane crash in December 1934.[26] In the late 1930s the ANP, by then the premier press agency in the Netherlands, aspired to provide an 'independent news service' for all those interested in the Netherlands and to strive for 'a balanced, transparent division of the costs': news, henceforth, would be relatively cheap.[27]

These domestic tasks were complemented, as stipulated in the ANP's 1935 founding statute, an internationally oriented goal for the agency, namely 'the advancement of quality news coverage about the Netherlands and Dutch interests' abroad. This intention was closely aligned with the aims of the newly founded RPD, something noted in a report prepared for the ANP's founders by the Dutch diplomat A. Pelt, then the director of the Information Section of the League of Nations. Quite critical of the RPD, Pelt noted that it lacked the means to reach out to international press agencies because it had no access to telegraph networks. He therefore saw the ANP to be an important addition to the Dutch international media network.[28] As for the ANP's relations with the government, Pelt emphasized that the agency's editorial independence was crucially important; there should be 'no political or financial ties' between the organization and officials in the Netherlands or the Dutch East Indies.[29] At first glance these remarks appear to echo the idea that Dutch press organizations were 'neutral' and therefore trustworthy, in the sense that they were free from political influences.

But Pelt did see an important political role for the ANP in safeguarding the country's neutral position in a geopolitical sense. In his final recommendations, the diplomat suggested that the ANP and RPD could cooperate, which shows that he thought a strict separation between press and government was not possible in practice. The ANP's founders, however, repudiated this latter passage and only asked for 'moral' and 'legal' support from the government so that they could organize their press agency along the lines of existing bureaus.[30] In this sense, the relation between the ANP and the PTT, which managed the Dutch radio telecommunications infrastructure, was crucial. The PTT provided the press agency full access to all its facilities, including the longwave transmitter at Kootwijk. The ANP was thus granted instant access to state-of-the-art radio technology that had been, up until then, the exclusive province of the largest international press agencies, including the *Hellschreiber*, an early form of telex machine that automatically translated radio signals into printed text.[31]

In the discussion about the nature of the ANP we see how two notions of Dutch neutrality were intertwined in a complex way. Formally, the ANP was an independent, 'neutral' organization, but it is clear that from its foundation onwards, the organization was closely aligned with foreign policy goals that originated in the auto-image of the Netherlands as a 'neutral country', a conception widely shared by Dutch elites. After the First World War, the intense concern about the Netherlands' subordinate position in global telecommunication networks prompted various initiatives for improving the country's standing in this realm, which were undertaken by official and non-official actors alike. Both the development of radio technology and institutional reforms created the opportunity to sound a Dutch voice in transnational media flows. All these initiatives aimed to safeguard Dutch 'neutrality', which meant official government interference in the ANP's operation was taboo. However, the explicit adherence to 'Dutch interests' in the organization's statutes makes it clear that it aligned itself with foreign policy goals. This phrase underlines that the self-proclaimed 'neutrality' of ANP was hardly neutral: news inherently had geopolitical meanings. In this respect it is important to realize that one of the most important functions of the emergent Dutch transnational media network in the early 1930s was the bolstering of the country's colonial dominance in Southeast Asia. Later that decade the rise of Nazi Germany would pose a different challenge, threatening the very existence of the European part of the Dutch realm. The unfolding geopolitical crisis underlined the importance of the ANP as the 'voice of the Netherlands' abroad.

The Hell community

On 1 January 1936, a few months after its founding, the ANP joined the international body of press agencies, the *Agences Alliées*. This organization had been established in 1924 in reaction to the founding of numerous press agencies in the newly independent countries of Central and Eastern Europe after the Habsburg Empire had collapsed in the wake of the First World War. On the one hand, the Agences Alliées subscribed to the idealist internationalism of the era and, in that sense, marked a change in the way the cartel operated. Mimicking the League of Nations system, the press agencies from large states engaged in regular multilateral negotiations with their counterparts from smaller states who managed to secure, albeit informally, better conditions for information exchange. In addition, the attendees of the conferences emphasized the importance of placing 'objective truth above propaganda' in an effort to contribute to global peace.[32] On the other hand, however, the Agences Alliées served as a vehicle to sustain the prewar dominance of the 'Big Three'. Reuters, Havas and Wolff, known in the interwar years as the 'doyen agencies', had commanding influence within this institution and used it to control competitors that could potentially challenge their cartel.[33] Nevertheless, membership was required if the ANP was to spread 'Dutch news' globally, argued Pelt in his recommendations to the founding members of the Dutch press agency.[34] From 1936 onwards, the ANP provided a weekly bulletin of Dutch news in English and French, which it distributed to all members of the Agences Alliées.[35]

By the time the ANP joined the international conference of press agencies, the very foundation of the organization had been undermined. Several countries that wanted to revise the geopolitical status quo employed their press agencies to achieve such ends. The Nazi rise to power in Germany in 1933 had been the greatest catalyst of this process. Right after the takeover, the *Reichminsterium* for propaganda, led by Joseph Goebbels, centralized the main press agencies in Germany, including Wolff, into the *Deutsches Nachrichtenbüro* (German News Office (DNB)). Although the organization's ideological underpinnings had changed compared to those of its Weimar predecessors, the Nazis took over much of its pre-existing structures and, indeed, its staff. In contrast with the in-your-face propaganda of the domestic National Socialist German Worker's Party (NSDAP), with its characteristic mass rallies, the Nazis' manipulation of international news media was more subtle. They used existing German press agencies, which had strong connections abroad, to spread information, often formulated in moderate language, that supported Hitler's geopolitical goals.[36] In this context Nazi officials recognized the usefulness of membership in the news cartel and thus the DNB remained a member of the Agences Alliées and sent representatives to attend all its conferences.[37] The Agences Alliées continued meeting until the beginning of the Second World War on 4 September 1939 – when Great Britain and France declared war on Germany after its invasion of Poland.

For the Dutch, the sudden collapse of the Agences Alliées conjured up ghosts from the not-too-distant past. A return to a media landscape dominated by big press agencies meant that the Netherlands could again become isolated and lose control over the narrative about the country put forth via transnational media networks. Wireless technology alone could not suffice for the dissemination of news about the Netherlands: if the 'doyen agencies' did not pick it up, the information would be useless. The ANP took the initiative to prevent that from happening, contacting press agencies in countries that, like the Netherlands, had declared themselves neutral: Belgium, Norway, Sweden, Denmark and Finland – coincidentally, fellow members with the Dutch in the Oslo Group.[38]

Governments from these small states had started to cooperate in 1930 on trade and tariff policies to boost their trade in a time of protectionism. Later in the 1930s, with an eye the rising geopolitical tensions due to Nazi Germany's rise, the 'Oslo states' also began contemplating political and 'spiritual' cooperation. All the states involved adhered to a strict policy of neutrality in foreign affairs, and protecting this principle was the main priority. In addition, the idea emerged in the late 1930s that the Oslo states could, precisely because of their smallness and neutrality, act as mediators and promote international harmony. Inspired by auto-images that had developed in northern European states in the late nineteenth century, positing their special interest in and proclivity for promoting peaceful cooperation, actors from the Oslo countries launched a broad variety of initiatives to prevent all-out war, especially between the signing of the Munich Agreement in September 1938 and the outbreak of war in Western Europe in September 1940.[39] Ger van Roon's monograph on the Oslo countries argues that the bloc suffered structural weaknesses from within – due to its members' isolationist tendencies – and without – it seriously miscalculated Nazi Germany's political intentions. He briefly notes how the Oslo Group provided a framework for state and non-state actors to communicate and cooperate, but he does not expand on this facet of the alliance.[40] In that sense his one-sided analysis overlooks the more lasting effects of the Oslo Group's initiatives undertaken not long before the outbreak of the Second World War, such as the promotion of cooperation amongst press agencies.

In October 1939 the ANP's director, H.H.J. van de Pol, wrote to his colleagues in the Oslo countries asking whether they were interested in joining forces in transnational news flows. These officials met in November in Amsterdam and a final agreement was reached in December. Highlighting the prominent Dutch position in radio technology, Van de Pol proposed setting up a distribution system in which all participating agencies would send their bulletins to the ANP headquarters in Amsterdam, to be followed by dissemination via Hellschreiber through the long-distance radio transmitters at Kootwijk. This was an attractive proposition, strengthening each small state news agency's ability to provide 'neutral news' and allowing them, collectively, to become voices for moderation and the nonviolent resolution of international conflict. Referring to the technology they employed for the dissemination of their news items, Van der Pol baptized the collaboration amongst small state agencies as the Hell Community (*Hell commune*). After several tests, a regular service was inaugurated in the first week of February 1940. A memorandum from the ANP's management explained the main goals of the alliance. First and foremost: 'neutral countries will be able to receive news from each other directly without interference of the great agencies from belligerent countries.' In addition the 'participating countries are also able to make communications of national interest known to the world'. This news network was available to all that subscribed to it, but only agencies from neutral countries could send in news dispatches.[41]

Not all the national news agencies of the Oslo member states could be persuaded to join, however. The Swiss were the surprising holdout. Van de Pol's attempts to change their minds highlight the lofty ideals of the Hell Community and the immense political and cultural importance he ascribed to the network. He argued that if 'we do not succeed now, we will be cast for *ever* in the dependent position in which we have had to work, and will continue to work. It is given to us today to gain our independence in one blow and to secure a position that does not depend on anybody.'[42] The Swiss, unpersuaded, simply stopped responding to these arguments.[43] Van de Pol continued to hold out hope right up until the German invasion of the Netherlands, but to no avail.[44] The reasons behind the Swiss refusal are not evident in the source material, but considering the nation's longstanding and dogmatic tradition of neutrality in international affairs, the management of the Swiss press agency may well have been afraid that to join the Hell Community would be deemed an infringement of the hallowed principles of their country's foreign policy.

The correspondence about the financing of the Hell Community contains more explicit references to the project's political implications. Although both Havas and the DNB subscribed to the Hellschreiber service of the neutral countries, their contributions were hardly enough to cover expenses.[45] Although all parties involved in the Hell community were commercial companies, it appears that the governments of the Oslo countries were prepared to provide funds as well. In a letter to the PTT, Van de Pol wrote that the press agencies of the Hell Community received money from their governments to cover the extra costs of transmissions to Amsterdam. Although the ANP's director did not ask for a direct subsidy from the Dutch government, as this would 'go against the principles' of the agency, he did ask for financial leniency from the PTT, which initially charged not only for the hours when their radio stations transmitted the Hell messages but also the time it took to set up the facilities for such broadcasting. Van de Pol asked to cut the latter costs.[46] Although the PTT director pointed out that he was operating according to the agreed-upon conditions, he did meet these demands so as to help the ANP solve the operational problems.[47] Thanking the director for the PTT's support, Van de Pol assured him that all the allied press agencies 'expressed their feelings [and] admiration' for Dutch radio technology.[48] This correspondence shows that, despite the strong emphasis on the ANP's independence, government approval and involvement were important to the setup of the transnational news network. Neutral news, in other words, had political meaning, which was illustrated in a 'service order' (*dienstorder*) issued to ANP employees which characterized the Hell Community as 'our European home line' (*onze Europeesche huislijn*), citing an example of how a speech of the Dutch foreign minister should be distributed.[49]

By the time these words were written down, early in February 1940, the Hell Community had started its news service – without the Swiss – and Van de Pol had managed to make it work, both technologically and financially. But problems soon emerged, especially in light of the escalating geopolitical crisis. Within that context, it appeared that not all of the organization's participants shared Van de Pol's high hopes for an independent network to disseminate neutral news. There was attrition. On 30 November 1939 the Soviet Union attacked Finland, one of the Hell Community countries. During a meeting Van de Pol and the director of the Belgian press agency decided that the Finns could nonetheless contribute to the Hell Community of neutral news agencies, arguing that 'if a great power invades a country of one of the participating agencies [*Agences Participantes*], this country is not marked as belligerent'.⁵⁰ However, Van de Pol's Belgian counterpart complained in February that 'the press agency in Helsinki did not provide the most abundant collaboration'. The agency was surely working amidst difficult circumstances, but nonetheless 'everybody will understand that, exactly because of the sympathy for Finland, we want to receive more news items from Finnish sources'. In addition, he noted that certain news dispatches from Helsinki that had reached the editorial office of the Hell Community could not be used because the French agency Havas had already distributed them. He argued that such information should be communicated to 'us' first.⁵¹ These remarks suggest that the Finns had chosen to distribute news from the frontlines via the big press agencies, thus undermining the main idea behind the Hell Community.

It seems that Van de Pol particularly worried about the continued Finnish preference for the doyen agencies, all the more because other agencies also appeared to do so and even shunned the Hell service. The same day that he received the letter from Belgium about the Finnish agency, Van de Pol sent a missive to the Swedish press agency to complain that they had provided news about the Swedish stance towards the war in Finland directly to Reuters. Even worse, the Swedes did not even mention this news in their transmissions to the editorial office of the Hell Community.⁵² Ten days later he wrote a telegram to Stockholm in which he accused the Swedes of using Havas as an intermediary agency, a 'violation [of the] strictly neutral character [of the Hell] service'.⁵³ In reaction, the director of the Swedish press agency indicated that he did not understand Van de Pol's objections and claimed that he had the right to decide with whom to share its news.⁵⁴ Van de Pol countered by stressing that, in his view, participating agencies should use the Hell Community to disseminate 'national news of their countries, before such news is emitted by the doyen agencies'. He proposed to discuss this matter at a Copenhagen meeting of the Hell Community scheduled for 3–5 April.⁵⁵ During the conference the issue was tabled and the minutes stated that, although the representatives of participating agencies remained committed to the idea behind the Hell Community, they regarded the network as not yet a 'rival of the big agencies'.⁵⁶

That the small state press agencies lacked power to effectively challenge the big agencies based in the belligerent countries was a reflection of the current geopolitical crisis. The situation became painfully clear when Germany invaded Denmark and Norway a few days after the Copenhagen conference had ended. The conference reiterated the principle, as applied to the Finnish case in January, that a country under attack from a large power should be allowed to contribute to the Hell service, but it was also stipulated that were the country conquered and occupied, the remaining members should decide if it would still be allowed to participate. A few days after the invasion of Denmark it appeared that the editorial staff of the Copenhagen-based press agency Ritzau had been taken over by the Nazis; Van de Pol, opting to bite the bullet, proposed suspending it from the Hell Community. At the same time, the Germans had also begun sending news from Oslo under the name of the Norwegian press agency, although the agency's manager, having sought refuge in Stockholm, continued to transmit from there.[57] Despite these setbacks, Van de Pol decided to keep the Hell service on the air, as it were, but the disruptions resulting from the German conquest of the Nordic countries foreshadowed the network's future: on 10 May 1940 Germany invaded the Netherlands, and on the morning of that day the ANP made its last international transmission. One day later, the radio facilities at Kootwijk were sabotaged, which made further action impossible. A memorandum dated one month later concluded: 'And so the Hell Community passed away quietly and peacefully.'[58]

During the Nazi occupation of the Netherlands, the ANP was taken over by the new regime, which used it as a propaganda tool for the Third Reich. Van de Pol, who did not agree with this editorial line, was fired in 1941.[59] Engaging in clandestine activities, he was connected to a group of former ANP employees who were gathering news from the Allied press agencies via a secret radio installation.[60] These anti-Nazi credentials enabled Van de Pol to reassert his position as the ANP's director after the liberation of the Netherlands in May 1945. He quickly managed to restore its original status as an independent organization owned by the Dutch newspaper publishers.[61] Once he had secured his base at the ANP, Van de Pol got in touch with his colleagues in the former Hell Community and, finding that most of them had survived the war, he proposed that they meet again. In the following years the group met annually, and in 1949 decided to formalize their cooperation in an organization baptized (as noted above) 'Group 39', a reference to the turbulent period of their initial cooperation. In a speech at the 1949 meeting Van de Pol underscored the fundamental spirit behind the project, in the past and into the future:

> We feel it as a moral right that the national agency, and no foreign news organization, distributes the news from its own people to its own people. Because if a foreign news organization would gather and distribute home news of another country an element may welcome in the news supply which is foreign in character. It would be trespassing upon our own life and culture.[62]

Van der Pol's message in 1949 was essentially the same as it had been ten years earlier: only by working together could press agencies in small countries defend their independent position.

Having said that, Group 39 now operated under different circumstances from those of the time of the Hell Community's founding. In 1939 the threat of war had prompted the press agencies in the small states to actively distribute news from their countries in order to guard their geopolitical neutrality, which meant that they did not mingle in the doyen agencies' business. In the late 1940s, the need to safeguard the political neutrality of the northwestern European small states was less urgent and consequently the small agencies felt less restricted with regard to their larger counterparts, which they approached in a much more assertive way to defend their national interests. This attitude was illustrated in 1951 when M. Godeschalk, Van de Pol's right-hand man at the ANP, wrote a long letter to Reuters in which he listed ten of the ANP's 'objections' to how the British agency worked. Tucked in the middle, as point 5, lay the most fundamental point of criticism: 'British and American angles often prevail in reports on international events in which smaller nations take part, as well as in other news.'[63] In

Figure 6.2 The ANP telex office in 1949 (ANP collection, private). The Dutch news agency continued to employ both Hell machines and telexes up until the late 1940s. © ANP.

addition to these critical reflections on the content of the services provided by the big agencies, the small state agencies in these years cooperated on a more practical level. They formed a bloc in negotiations about tariffs and pooled resources together so that they could afford the newest technological innovations and thus be less dependent on the large press agencies. Echoing the ideals of 1939, the Belgian director Ryelandt argued in 1955 that 'our combined powers made us a new power in the international press system'.[64]

In those years it became clear that the international media landscape as had existed in the 1920s and 1930s would not return after the Second World War. Although the three main press agencies from that era continued onwards in one form or another, their grip on global news flows was less firm. In France and West Germany the press agencies were fundamentally reformed; the international body through which the doyen agencies had yielded power, the Agences Alliées, was not resurrected. In this climate, Van de Pol and his allies began working towards a new internationalist organization to manage the European news flows. In the 1950s they pointed to the process of European unification that was taking off and argued that press agencies could contribute to this project, too. Indeed, Van de Pol, in a letter to the ANP's board of directors, even touted his idea for the Hell Community in 1939 as having been 'already in embryonic form, small [*in het klein*], a European continental press agency'.[65] In the years that followed, Group 39's members were instrumental in the foundation of the Alliance Européennes des Agences de Presse, a body that also included agencies from West Germany, France, Italy and Yugoslavia.[66] This new body, which did not include Reuters, can be seen as the definitive sign of the end of the big press agencies' news cartel, ending their dominance that had begun in the late nineteenth century.

Conclusion

The story of the forging of a small state transnational news network helps us think about the politics of smallness. A crucial concept in the contemporary debate about this topic was neutrality, a term which in this context had a double meaning, referring to both geopolitical aloofness and the reliability of news. Historians need to approach this word critically. As this article shows, the Dutch initiative, begun in autumn 1939, for cooperation amongst a group of small states' press agencies was far from neutral: its main actors saw 'neutral news' to be a means to bolster their country's independence – and, indeed, to reinforce the grip on their colonial possessions. These motives go back to the experiences of the Netherlands in the late nineteenth and early twentieth centuries, when the Big Three press agencies formed a news cartel that would long dominate transnational media flows. As a small state with a large empire, the Netherlands was particularly dependent on the British transcontinental telegraphy lines that connected the country with its main colony in Southeast Asia, the Dutch East Indies. This dependency was painfully exposed during the First World War. In reaction to these predicaments, Dutch actors developed wireless radio technology and founded the press agency ANP in the interwar years. Although on the face of it the ANP was a strictly private initiative, there were political implications in play: the organization's statutes explicitly stated that it served national interests, and it received indirect support from the government. However, Dutch technological prowess notwithstanding, Dutch actors in the late 1930s were still aware that they were operating in a media landscape dominated by the doyen agencies. They realized that greater cooperation with press agencies from other small states was necessary to defend the national interest.

The geopolitical crisis in September 1939 prompted ANP director H.J.J. van de Pol to launch an initiative for cooperation amongst the press agencies of the Oslo countries. Agreeing that the belligerents' propaganda posed a threat to the neutrality of the small states of Europe, they joined the plan for the Hell Community. The main idea was to secure the news supply from participating countries; reports were gathered by the ANP and then transmitted from the Dutch wireless station in Kootwijk, using state-of-the-art technology. Van de Pol managed to overcome several organizational problems and the Hell service was initiated in February 1940. Despite the successful execution of his plan, Van de Pol did encounter scepticism from several of his partners when he asserted that the Hell Community could secure complete editorial independence for the small countries. At the conference held in Copenhagen, the consensus was that the network, for the time being, could not yet be a rival to the doyen agencies. Indeed, less than a month later, the Hell Community came to an abrupt end with the German invasion of the Netherlands. Despite the tragic end of the Hell Community in the flames of the *Blitzkrieg*, the spirit of the network, the idea that small states should work together to guard their national interests against the dominance of the doyen agencies, re-emerged after the end of the Second World War. The persistence of the main ideas behind the cooperation amongst the press agencies that had emerged in 1939 shows that if small countries work together they can exercise a sizeable impact.

From the account provided here, it appears that the main result of Van de Pol's initiative was an institutional reshuffling of transnational media networks in the mid-twentieth century. In this sense, the concept of 'neutral news' can be seen as a catalyst for the attempts of small state press agencies to challenge the Big Three's cartel, which had been in place since the late nineteenth century. One question that remains, however, concerns the extent to which these developments affected the actual content of the news coverage. The ANP archive does not contain the texts that it received and disseminated via its international network. Future research could be geared towards getting an overview of this information by gathering data on small states from digitalized media collections from various countries and by analysing this mass of material in bulk via software programmes designed to uncover semantic patterns. In this way, we might find the fingerprints of the press agencies which tried to influence the coverage of their country's affairs in international media. Such a project would sharpen our understanding of 'neutral news' and, consequently, our comprehension of the agency exercised by small state actors as it appears manifested in transnational media flows.

Notes

1. Nationaal Archief Den Haag (hereafter NL-HaNA), Stichting Algemeen Nederlands Persbureau (ANP), 2.19.212/527: Speech D. Ryelandt at the 20th anniversary of the ANP, s.d. [1955].
2. https://www.perssupport.nl/persbericht/060919055/80-years-of-group-39-independent-news-agency-alliance-expands-its-circle-of-members (accessed 4 June 2020).
3. Hellema underlines that neutrality made strategic sense for the Netherlands during the nineteenth and early twentieth centuries: Hellema, *Nederland in de Wereld : Buitenlandse Politiek van Nederland*. For a comparative reflection on the concept of geopolitical neutrality in Dutch history see Erlandsson, *Window of Opportunity*.
4. Tworek, *News from Germany*, 19.
5. Kuitenbrouwer, *War of words*, 108.
6. Tworek, *News from Germany*, chapter 1.
7. Dijk, *The Netherlands Indies and the Great War, 1914–1918*.
8. Klinkert, Kruizinga, and Moeyes, *Nederland neutraal*, 158.
9. Kuitenbrouwer, 'The Dutch East Indies during the First World War and the Birth of Colonial Radio', 29.
10. Hemels, *Een journalistiek geheim ontsluierd*, 7–180.
11. Hemels, 20–1.
12. Kruizinga, 'A Small State? The Size of the Netherlands as a Focal Point in Foreign Policy Debates, 1900–1940', 428.

13 Dijk, '"You Act Too Much as a Journalist and Too Little as a Diplomat". Pieter Geyl, the National Bureau for Documentation on the Netherlands and Dutch Public Diplomacy', 90–1.
14 Schuursma, *Vergeefs onzijdig*, 10.
15 Kuitenbrouwer, 'Ir.dr. C.J. de Groot: radiopionier in de tropen'.
16 The organization was called *Posterijen en Telegrafie* in 1915 and the last T (telephony) was added in 1928, but for the sake of clarity I will refer to it as the PTT throughout this text.
17 Blanken, *Geschiedenis van Philips Electronics N.V. Volume III: 1922–1934*, 263–5.
18 Baggermans and Hemels, *Verzorgd Door Het ANP*, 48–9; Termorshuizen and Veer, *Een groots en meeslepend leven*, 101–5.
19 Graaff, *Kalm temidden van woedende golven*, 584.
20 Dijk, 'Uithangbord van de BV Nederland. La Gazette Hollande en de Nederlandse Publieksdiplomatie, 1918–1935'.
21 Kuitenbrouwer, 'Propaganda That Dare Not Speak Its Name. International Information Services about the Dutch East Indies, 1919–1934', 246–9.
22 For the financing of the *Gazette* see: Dijk, 'Uithangbord van de BV Nederland. La Gazette Hollande en de Nederlandse Publieksdiplomatie, 1918–1935', 41–56, 96. For the financing of 'secret correspondents' see: Hemels, *Van perschef tot overheidsvoorlichter*, 32; Graaff, *Kalm temidden van woedende golven*, 577, 588.
23 Hemels, *Van perschef tot overheidsvoorlichter*, 10.
24 Hemels, 14–16.
25 Baggermans and Hemels, *Verzorgd Door Het ANP*, 64–6.
26 Baggermans and Hemels, 88–90.
27 Baggermans and Hemels, 90.
28 Baggermans and Hemels, 111–12.
29 NL-HaNA, ANP, 2.19.212/ 151: Rapport Commissie voor de Persdiensten, s.d., 12.
30 Baggermans and Hemels, *Verzorgd Door Het ANP*, 91.
31 Baggermans and Hemels, 112.
32 Tworek, 'The Creation of European News', 730–1.
33 Tworek, *News from Germany*, 111.
34 NL-HaNA, ANP, 2.19.212/ 151: Rapport Commissie voor de Persdiensten, s.d., 9–10
35 Baggermans and Hemels, *Verzorgd Door Het ANP*, 113.
36 Tworek, *News from Germany*, chapters 7 and 8.
37 Tworek, 183.
38 Luxembourg was also a member of the Oslo group, but did not have a press agency. Switzerland did not join the *Hell-commune*.
39 For a detailed account see: Roon, *Kleine landen in crisistijd*, chapters 11–13.
40 Roon, 326.
41 NL-HaNA, ANP, 2.19.212/560: Memorandum ANP 'Hellcommune', 2 February 1940.
42 NL-HaNA, ANP, 2.19.212/562: Circular by H.J.J. van de Pol, 27 December 1939.
43 This is mentioned in several documents, see for example: NL-HaNA, ANP, 2.19.212/562: Notes of meeting H.J.J. van de Pol and D. Reyelandt (Belga), 16 January 1940.
44 NL-HaNA, ANP, 2.19.212/562: Circular by H.J.J. van de Pol, 13 December 1939 and H.H.J. van de Pol to A. Pelt, 17 February 1940.
45 Baggermans and Hemels, *Verzorgd Door Het ANP*, 114.
46 NL-HaNA, ANP, 2.19.212/562: H.H.J. van de Pol to H.H. Damme, 7 February 1940.
47 NL-HaNA, ANP, 2.19.212/562: H.H. Damme to H.H.J. van de Pol, 14 February 1940.

48 NL-HaNA, ANP, 2.19.212/562: H.H.J. van de Pol to H.H. Damme, 15 February 1940.
49 NL-HaNA, ANP, 2.19.212/560: 'Dienstorder 147', 3 February 1940.
50 NL-HaNA, ANP, 2.19.212/562: Notes of meeting H.J.J. van de Pol and D. Reyelandt (Belga), 16 January 1940.
51 NL-HaNA, ANP, 2.19.212/562: D. Reyelandt to H.J.J. van de Pol, 16 February 1940.
52 NL-HaNA, ANP, 2.19.212/562: Proof of letter [by H.J.J. van de Pol] to G. Reuterswaerd, 16 February 1940.
53 NL-HaNA, ANP, 2.19.212/562: Proof of letter [by H.J.J. van de Pol] to G. Reuterswaerd, 27 February 1940.
54 NL-HaNA, ANP, 2.19.212/ 562: G. Reuterswaerd to H.J.J. van de Pol, 4 March 1940.
55 NL-HaNA, ANP, 2.19.212/562: Proof of letter [by H.J.J. van de Pol] to G. Reuterswaerd, 7 March 1940.
56 NL-HaNA, ANP, 2.19.212/563: 'Procès-verbal de la second séance de la Réunion des Agences Participantes de Service Hellcommune à Copenhague le jeudi 4 Jeune [Avril] 1940'.
57 NL-HaNA, ANP, 2.19.212/562: Memorandum with copy of telegram H.J.J. van de Pol to D. Ryelandt, 16 April 1940.
58 NL-HaNA, ANP, 2.19.212/562. Memorandum, 20 June 1940.
59 Baggermans and Hemels, *Verzorgd Door Het ANP*, 133.
60 Baggermans and Hemels, 143.
61 Baggermans and Hemels, 152.
62 NL-HaNA, ANP, 2.19.212/539: Draft speech H.J.J. van de Pol, s.d. [February 1949].
63 NL-HaNA, ANP, 2.19.212/539: M.C. Godeschalk, 'Report on Reuter's News Service', s.d. [August 1951].
64 NL-HaNA, ANP, 2.19.212/527: Speech D. Ryelandt at the 20th anniversary of the ANP, s.d. [1955].
65 NL-HaNA, ANP, 2.19.212/528: H.J.J. van de Pol to chairmen Board of Directors ANP and Association of Dutch Newspapers (De Nederlandse Dagbladpers, NDP), 15 September 1955.
66 Baggermans and Hemels, *Verzorgd Door Het ANP*, 117.

7

'Whoever says that Serbia is small is lying!' Serbia, ontological (in)security and the unbearable smallness of being

Christian Axboe Nielsen

Introduction

Since its emergence as a nation-state in the nineteenth century, Serbia has grown, shrunk, moved and generally changed shape at a rate that appears hectic even by the standards of Eastern Europe. Out of a classically irredentist agenda in the nineteenth century that envisaged the unification of all Serbs, Serbia eventually became the reluctant leader of the unification of South Slavs in Yugoslavia. Two conflicting self-images emerged in the late nineteenth century, encapsulated in two questions: Should Serbia reconcile itself to smallness and focus on improving the welfare of its population? Or should it, instead, push for the creation of a Great Serbia at the expense of its neighbours? This debate continues to resonate today at the expense of political stability and social welfare in Serbia and the Balkans. After no fewer than three iterations of Yugoslavia – the Kingdom of Yugoslavia, socialist Yugoslavia and the Federal Republic of Yugoslavia – Serbia in the twenty-first century exists in a smaller version than at any time since before the Balkan Wars of 1912–13. Avowedly pro-European, but unwilling to accept the loss of Kosovo and deeply dissatisfied with Montenegro's independence and the 'stranding' of Serbs outside Serbia, particularly in Bosnia and Herzegovina, Serbia's present-day leadership bears a self-image that remains stuck in a somewhat schizophrenic frame of mind. Ambitions of EU membership and an acceptance of smallness collide on an almost daily basis with an obsession with Serbia's alleged perpetual victimization and a persistent fear that European unification is a stalking horse for the further partition of Serbian territory. Combining a succinct overview of the last two centuries with analysis of present-day policy in Serbia, this chapter will analyse why Serb elites have such a difficult time reconciling themselves to smallness.

'National rebirth'

Together with Greece, Serbia was the first area of the Balkan portion of the Ottoman Empire to experience rebellions in the early nineteenth century. In 1804, a group of Serbs led by Karađorđe ('Black George') Petrović rose up against what they viewed as the rapacious and oppressive rule of local Ottoman officials. The initial revolt of the Serbs, suppressed in 1813, has come to be known as 'the First Serbian Uprising'. The grievances of Karađorđe and his associates were socioeconomic in nature. Notions of economic and social justice along with law and order most likely mattered much more to the peasantry than any fanciful and – at the time – newfangled notions of nationhood.[1] Simply put, 'the Serb peasant fought not for an abstract state or, perish the thought, for the leader Karađorđe'.[2] His goal was the restoration of what the historian Barbara Jelavich has called 'the circle of equity', with the Ottoman sultan's authority restored as the guardian of all the Empire's inhabitants, regardless of their identities.[3] There is no doubt that 'the uprising evolved into a movement for political autonomy in search of international guarantees', and particularly during and after the 'Second Serbian Uprising' (1815–17) the situation became part of the larger 'Eastern Question' concerning the future of 'Turkey in Europe'.[4] However, the uprising has been consistently and teleologically portrayed in Serbian historiography as a national revolution that from the outset sought to free the Serb nation from 'the Ottoman yoke' (*osmanski jaram*) and establish a strong state encompassing all Serbs.[5] Historians in Serbia also utilized religious metaphors of a Serbian nation-state being 'resurrected' from the long martyrdom of 'Ottoman slavery' (*osmansko ropstvo*) since the Battle of Kosovo in 1389, where Serbs, according to legend, accepted defeat in exchange for heavenly greatness.[6] The historian Radovan Samardžić wrote that this loss inaugurated a process of disintegration for the Serb nation.[7] More recently, in a sign of the times, his colleague Dušan Bataković has indulged in exaggeration by presenting the 1804 uprising within a European context as a 'Balkan-style French revolution'.[8]

The upshot of the two uprisings was the establishment of an autocratic Serbian vassal state that enjoyed some degree of autonomy with respect to the Ottoman Empire. Territorially speaking, compared in size to both other contemporary political units and later iterations of Serbia, it was definitely a small state, centred around Belgrade and Smederevo and covering approximately 38,000 km², thus slightly smaller than present-day Switzerland. Serbian politics after the two uprisings were characterized by bitter feuding not only between two rival dynasties – Obrenović and Karađorđević, where the former in particular displayed many common traits with feudal Ottoman forms of rule – but also with a tiny but growing, politically active bourgeoisie. The members of this class had typically spent time in cities like Vienna, Leipzig and Paris, absorbing in particular romantic notions of nationalism and democracy and, later, strains of socialism and nihilism from both Germany and Russia.[9]

Despite their rivalry, a common element of the two dynasties was a desire to grow the size of the state, not least in the name of encompassing those Serbs residing outside Serbia. The challenge for those politicians and state officials who wished to prioritize the expansion of the Serbian state in the nineteenth century was that the peasantry – which made up by far the bulk of the population – was uninterested in, if not hostilely inclined towards, such expansionism. Generally speaking, the peasants were doubtless not keen to substitute exorbitant late Ottoman rates of taxation with extortionist taxes and intervention from the nascent Serbian state apparatus, against which they repeatedly rebelled as early as the 1820s.[10]

In 1835, following a rebellion against his autocratic rule, Miloš Obrenović agreed to adopt the Candlemas constitution (*Sretenjski ustav*). This constitution, quite liberal for the time, incurred the wrath of the conservative Great Powers. Owing in part to this pressure, Obrenović only three years later abolished the constitution, replacing it with the more conservative 'Turkish constitution'. But even this proved unacceptable to Obrenović. In the 1840s, his autocratic rule ceded way to the 'defenders of the constitution' (*ustavobranitelji*) who wanted to bring Serbia onto a more modern path of statehood and facilitate its 'return to Europe'.[11] It is during this period that a plan for the creation of a larger Serbian state began to crystallize. Serbia faced a classic irredentist problem: at this point, those persons defined by the leaders of the Serbian state as being Serbs – and here it is important to note the lack of any clear consensus regarding this definition – were distributed widely outside the borders of Serbia. The great Serbian language reformer Vuk Stefanović Karadžić propounded the slogan 'Serbs all and everywhere' (*Srbi svi i svuda*), which adopted an expansive – and expansionist and (potentially aggressive) assimilationist – stance towards membership in the Serb nation.[12] There were 'Serbs' in the Habsburg Empire (in present-day Croatia, Vojvodina, Hungary and Romania), in Montenegro and in the Ottoman Empire (in present-day Bosnia and Herzegovina, North Macedonia and Kosovo). Clearly, were Serbia to fulfil the ambition of an irredentist nation-state, a lot of borders would have to be moved, and those not voluntarily identifying as Serbs would have to be persuaded or be forced to assimilate to Serb national identity.

The man who tried to convert the ideas of irredentist 'mental mapping' floating around in the region into some kind of concrete plan was Ilija Garašanin.[13] A 'defender of the constitution', Garašanin served as head of the Serbian government (1852–3 and 1861–7) and, like many young Serbs, was convinced that the Ottoman Empire was in terminal decline. This view was, of course, not at all unique in a time when the 'Eastern Question' asked what would become of the territories currently controlled by the 'sick man of Europe'. In this sense, the 'Serbian question' was merely one entry in a long list alongside its Greek, Romanian, Bulgarian, Albanian and (later) Macedonian counterparts. It is important to note that Garašanin and likeminded Serb elites viewed such ideas as being emancipatory with respect to those who remained in a state of alleged oppression in various empires, although of course the objects of these thoughts may have held quite different perceptions.

Garašanin's second conviction was that smallness was not a viable option for the Serbian state. Serbia either had to grow proactively or else it risked being partitioned in the Great Power contest between the Russian and Habsburg empires.[14] Garašanin's answer to this dilemma took the form of a draft plan (*načertanije*) inspired in particular by the Polish nobleman Adam Czartoryski and the Czech military theorist František Zach. Czartoryski's memorandum 'Conseils sur le conduite à suivre par la Serbie' had been provided by a Polish agent to Garašanin. This memorandum 'pointed out that expansionism was a sine qua non for Serbia's future existence'.[15] Garašanin's *Načertanije* therefore proposed re-establishing Serbian statehood on the territory of Tsar Dušan's medieval Serbian state. This state, which was of course erroneously presented as a nation-state, had in fact stretched deep into present-day Greece. This anachronistic misrepresentation conveniently allowed Garašanin to portray the many centuries of Ottoman presence as an unfortunate interruption of (great) Serbian statehood – and even to indulge the messianic notion that Serbia was a successor to the Byzantine Empire. Seen from this perspective, the *Načertanije* would merely right a historical wrong, though it was vague as to who the Serbs actually were and assumed a benevolent reaction by those who were not Serbs. Significantly, Garašanin replaced Czartoryski's and Zach's broader references to South Slavs with 'Serbs'.[16] Garašanin's plan was in fact vague on quite a number of points, but its haziness has not prevented many people – particularly in Croatia and in Bosnia and Herzegovina – from teleologically and facilely depicting it as a master plan for the establishment of 'Great Serbia'.[17] More accurately, the *Načertanije* was emblematic of similar ideas elsewhere in Europe, not least the Μεγάλη Ιδέα (Great Idea) introduced the same year in Greece.[18] On a practical level, Garašanin, like his colleagues in Greece, used covert networks of 'patriots' to foment pro-Serbian sentiment – and later actions – for the irredentist cause. However, it is important to emphasize that this plan was more or less shelved until the early twentieth century, when it was rediscovered by a later generation of Serb nationalist elites.

By becoming the prime and initial mover amongst the South Slavs, Serbia had the potential to become not just a growing nation-state at the expense of the Ottoman Empire but also to become the Piedmont for those South Slavs – many of them not Serbs – who lived in the Habsburg Empire.[19] That is, the Serbs would play a leading role in gathering the South Slavs, just as the Piedmont had done for Italian national unity. Indeed, the military camarilla known as the Black Hand published a newspaper called *Pijemont* precisely because of this proclivity. However, Serbia's expansion between the early nineteenth and early twentieth centuries also set the stage for what Holm Sundhaussen has called a collision of historical rights and national self-determination.[20] Likewise, the idea of an expanding Serbian state exposed tensions between narrower Serbian nationalism and the nascent notion of Yugoslavism.[21] For example, when Serbia expanded considerably as a result of the Congress of Berlin in 1878, it gained – 'liberated', in patriotic parlance – territories where large numbers of non-Serbs (including many non-Slavs such as Albanians and Turks) resided. The reality of the Balkans' incredible ethnic and religious diversity tended to get in the way of imagined national unity. Moreover, it all too easily fed into a sense of what the Hungarian legal theorist István Bibó later called 'misery' and 'political hysteria', plaguing the relationship amongst fragile and small nation-states and their minorities.[22]

Seen from the perspective of Serb leaders, the complex ethnic demography of 'southern Serbia' was a nuisance and could not complicate or cast doubt upon the legitimacy of Serbia's territorial claims.[23] Gathering all Serbs in a single state would solve most of the problems confronting Serbia. Irredentism, not social revolution, was the goal. The historian Paul Hehn therefore considers the *Načertanije* to have been the 'the demand of the Serbian bourgeoisie for a national rather than a social transformation in the creation of a Serbian state'.[24]

In the second half of the nineteenth century, Serbia's leaders and its small number of intellectuals thus in many senses seemed inclined to pursue 'greatness', though there were certainly disagreements regarding the appropriate strategy and timing for pursuing this goal. Yet Svetozar Marković (1846–75), a short-lived proto-socialist and co-founder of the Serbian Radical Party, proved to be the eloquent main articulator of the acceptance of smallness. Marković believed in the principle of self-determination and regarded 'great ideas' based on historical rights as misguided. Marković also believed that the Serbian state had failed to modernize adequately during its period of (semi-)autonomous existence.[25] 'It is better to have good courts and good schools than to keep an enormous army for the oppression of the people and for the selfish intentions of the ruler [...] better to build roads, hospitals and other buildings for the general good than to spend millions on the court suite, court balls, royal lovers, etc.'[26]

It was not that Marković lacked feelings for Serbs outside the borders of Serbia. Indeed, his ponderings regarding some form of Balkan federation show him capable of pursuing arguments against smallness in another, more benevolent form. However, he believed that the young Serbian state needed to prioritize development and economic growth over (irredentist) expansion. 'We are only beginning to build a house when old nations are already big bosses [*velike gazde*].' Marković did not exclude the possibility that Serbia would grow to greatness – and indeed hoped it would, albeit only in cooperation with the other South Slavs.[27] Yet somewhat paradoxically, Marković also had quite negative things to say about Prussia, which had used might to unite Germany. Marković seemed much keener to have Serbia play a leading role in a progressive Balkan federation of states rather than serve as a Prussian-type creator of a great state.

Marković died in February 1875. Although a few other figures espoused similar ideas, Sundhaussen is correct in arguing that the small Serbian solution which would have favoured development and welfare instead of militarism and expansionism largely died with Marković.[28] In the decades between his death and the outbreak of the First World War, Serbia underwent rapid territorial expansion.[29] As a consequence of the Russo-Turkish War of 1877–8, Serbia obtained – again, 'liberated', in the nationalist narrative – large sections of what is today southern Serbia. The Congress of Berlin in the summer of 1878 angered Serb nationalists by awarding Austria-Hungary custody of Bosnia and Herzegovina, but it also secured Serbia's existence as a state and Austria-Hungary had left the door relatively open to the expansion of Serbia into Macedonia.[30] (The minority rights embedded in the treaty, ignored by Serbia, were never enforced.)

In 1903, the pro-Austrian Obrenović dynasty in Serbia was violently toppled and was replaced by the Karađorđević dynasty, thereby finally resolving the feud originating in the Second Serbian Uprising but simultaneously setting the stage for the fateful confrontation that would spark the First World War. In the meantime, the next dramatic step in Serbia's territorial expansion arrived in 1912 and 1913 with the Balkan Wars. In the first war, Serbia united in a coalition with Montenegro, Greece and Bulgaria and almost succeeded in dislodging the Ottoman Empire from Europe. In the second war, provoked by an unsatiated and irredentist Bulgaria, the members of the erstwhile coalition, in an ironic twist, joined forces with the Ottoman Empire and Romania to crush Bulgaria. The upshot of the Balkan Wars for Serbia was the 'recovery' of Kosovo and large portions of Macedonia – referred to in the jargon of the time as 'Old Serbia' (*Stara Srbija*) or 'Southern Serbia' (*Južna Srbija*). For obvious reasons, the inclusion of Kosovo carried with it special weight and seemed to underscore the nearly millennialist resurrection of Serbia from 'the Ottoman yoke'.[31] Bosnia and Herzegovina stood out as the major missing piece in the creation of a 'Great Serbia'. Another great frustration for Serbia was the creation of an Albanian state, with which Austria-Hungary sought to thwart the expansion of Serbia and to prevent it from attaining an Adriatic port.

Serbia was undoubtedly the big winner of the Balkan Wars, expanding its territory by 81 per cent (from approximately 48,000 to 87,000 km^2) and increasing its population from approximately 3 million to 4.3 million people.[32] However, Serbs constituted a minority of the inhabitants of the annexed areas of the vastly larger state, which now included non-Serbs as approximately 25 per cent of the population. This did not give the leaders of the Serbian state any reason to adjust their policies, which still aimed – as elsewhere in Europe – at the creation of a strong nation-state.

Here it needs emphasizing that Serbia's dramatic territorial expansion during the Balkan Wars – semi-voluntary and forced migrations of Muslims of various ethnicities in particular notwithstanding – dramatically increased the number of ethnic minorities in the Kingdom of Serbia.

The period from 1875 to 1914 proved that Svetozar Marković had been visionary in prophesying that Serbia's expansion would take place at the expense of its socioeconomic and political development and its relations with most of its neighbours. Yet from the nationalist point of view, things were proceeding quite nicely until the outbreak of war in 1914. Seen from this perspective, Serbia's greatness and democratic development were tragically stunted by the catastrophe of the nation's 'Golgotha' marked by a massive loss of life and the Austro-Hungarian occupation which lasted from 1915 until 1918.[33] When 'resurrection' came at the end of the war, Serbia would emerge a new, much larger state but with concomitant new challenges.

Between hegemony and imprisonment. The Kingdom of Yugoslavia and Socialist Yugoslavia

At the end of the First World War, Serbia joined the newly created Kingdom of Serbs, Croats and Slovenes. [Illustration 2: Cover of newspaper *Velika Srbija* (Great Serbia) during the First World War.] This state was formed as an uneasy edifice built on a foundation of Serbian statehood, with the Serb prince regent and later king Aleksandar Karađorđević as its head of state. Serbia certainly did not enter the war with the establishment of such a state in mind, but a very complex set of events and factors brought together the Slovenes and Croats – as well as other officially unrecognized South Slav ethnicities – as parts of a common state.[34] Officially renamed the Kingdom of Yugoslavia in 1929, this new state endured a painful and protracted birth. Indeed, some historians have argued that the promulgation of the country's constitution – adopted only in June 1921 with critical abstentions from the main Croatian political party in particular – occurred under circumstances that were essentially fatal to it.[35]

Nevertheless, from the point of Serbian statehood, interwar Yugoslavia was the first state which united virtually all Serbs within the borders of a single state. The obvious 'problem' was that Serbs were far from alone in this new state and that the competing agendas of other nations – of which the Croats were the most numerous and restive – risked subsuming or submerging Serbia within Yugoslav statehood. Thus the long delay in officially adopting the Yugoslav name, despite its contemporary popular usage, was precisely due primarily to Nikola Pašić's adamant opposition to the notion that Serbia would 'drown in a sea of Yugoslavia'.[36]

Outside Serbia at least, there is a strong historiographic consensus that Serbia and Serbs so dominated interwar Yugoslavia that it is correct to speak of Serbian hegemony.[37] King Aleksandar's Yugoslav identity project, though undoubtedly including many earnestly Yugoslav components, suffered from a heavy surplus of Serbian elements and in the end proved acceptable to no one.[38] Paradoxically, however, Serb nationalists have not only bristled at the notion of Serbian hegemony but have maintained that Serbia selflessly sacrificed its own ambitions and interests by agreeing to be part of Yugoslavia. According to this view, which was present from the outset in the interwar period, the Croats in particular were ungrateful. Not only had the Serbs agreed to create a joint country notwithstanding the Croats having been on the 'wrong side' in the First World War, but the Croats excelled in making unreasonable demands of the Serbs, up to and including advocating secession from Yugoslavia. By the end of the interwar period, the most assertive Serb nationalist voices congealed in the Serbian Cultural Club, whose slogan was 'strong Serbdom, strong Yugoslavia'. These voices were reacting to the establishment of a large Croatian province, Banovina Hrvatska, in 1939, and they believed that 'when a Croatian ethnic unit is defined, inevitably a Serbian ethnic unit must be defined [...]. When the Croatian question is raised, inevitably so is the Serbian question, and we must, with united forces, defend what is ours'.[39] During the interwar period the Serb historian Vladimir Ćorović published a book entitled *Velika Srbija* (Great Serbia).[40]

In 1941, Yugoslavia was invaded by an Axis coalition spearheaded by Germany and Italy and including Hungary and Bulgaria. Summarized briefly, the ensuing, very brutal occupation was accompanied by protracted internecine warfare, not just between the occupiers and the occupied but also between various nationalist collaborationist movements and the communist-led resistance in the form of the Partisan movement. The upshot was that more citizens of Yugoslav were killed by other citizens of Yugoslavia than were killed by the occupying forces. With Serbia prostrate during the war, the main priority was the very survival of the state and the Serbs under Axis occupation. Amongst the nationalist Chetnik guerrilla movement, Stevan Moljević, a member of the Serbian Cultural Club, did find time to articulate a plan for the postwar establishment of an ethnically homogenous Great Serbia. However, as Jasna Dragović-Soso notes,

> even Moljević envisaged the establishment of this 'homogenous Greater Serbia' as the first step in the creation of a 'federal' Yugoslavia of three units (Serbia, Croatia and Slovenia). The idea of Serbia as an *alternative* to Yugoslavia was only articulated in a series of unsuccessful memoranda to the German authorities by members of

the pro-German collaborationist Nedić regime and the fascist-inspired followers of Dimitrije Ljotić in occupied Serbia.⁴¹

(though not by Ljotić himself)

Against this dystopian background and against considerable odds, the Partisans in 1943 officially decided to re-establish Yugoslavia in a more egalitarian form under the slogan 'Brotherhood and Unity'. This second, socialist Yugoslavia existed from 1945 until 1991. Its leaders keen to avoid the problems that had beset interwar Yugoslavia, the official ideology recognized and encouraged the reasonable development of national identities as long as they did not take on 'chauvinistic' and antagonistic forms towards other national identities in Yugoslavia. Indeed, socialist Yugoslavia actively encouraged the recognition and nurturing of newer national identities such as those of the Macedonians and the Bosnian Muslims. Moreover, Yugoslavia adopted a federal structure comprising six republics, of which Serbia was one. Alone amongst the republics, Serbia included two provinces, Kosovo and Vojvodina. It is also worth noting that Yugoslav leader Josip Broz Tito's interest in pursuing a possible Balkan federation was one of the factors contributing to the Tito-Stalin split in 1948.⁴²

During its first two decades, socialist Yugoslavia was ruled in a very centralist manner. All important decisions were taken in Belgrade, again both the Yugoslav and the Serbian capital. Serbs played a prominent role in the bureaucracy, although to a lesser degree than during the interwar period, and were particularly and disproportionately present in the security services. To a significant extent, therefore, centralist- (or nationalist-)minded Serbs could choose to disregard the internal administrative boundaries.⁴³ However, in 1966, the most powerful Serb communist, Aleksandar Ranković, founder of the Yugoslav State Security Service and later the country's vice president, a man widely seen as a potential successor to the supreme leader Josip Broz Tito, was purged. Ranković was alleged to have abused the power of the security services. With his purge, a process of liberalization and decentralization commenced.

A possible acceptance of smallness flourished in the late 1960s in the manifestation of a liberal current within the League of Communists of Serbia. Marko Nikezić, the League's chairman from 1968 until 1972, prioritized Serbia's modernization over national(ist) thinking, believing that 'economic development […] would ultimately resolve all of Serbia's and Yugoslavia's problems, including the national ones; and, that their mission should be limited to their own republic – Serbia, not Serbdom or Yugoslavia'.⁴⁴ Yet in 1972 Tito purged Nikezić and the other liberals. Their fall was to some extent due to their own outpacing of Tito's own appetite for reforms, and in part they became 'collateral damage' of the mass purge of the League of Communists of Croatia that followed the crushing of the liberal-nationalist movement known as the Croatian Spring.⁴⁵

The aforementioned decentralization culminated in 1974 with the promulgation of what would turn out to be Yugoslavia's last constitution. It devolved power massively to the six republics and two autonomous provinces: only foreign policy and defence policy remained the exclusive remit of the federal state. And the autonomous provinces experienced such an expansion of jurisdiction that they became tantamount to republics. Because Serbia was the only republic that included autonomous provinces, its own increased power was balanced, and in the eyes of many Serbs effectively annulled, by the greatly augmented autonomy of Kosovo and Vojvodina. The 1974 constitution came to be portrayed by a generation of Serb politicians and scholars as a fundamentally unjust act aimed at neutering Serbian influence in Yugoslavia.[46] Indeed, not a few Serb politicians and scholars pointed to the constitution as one of the primary factors, in their view, leading to Yugoslavia's collapse.

The constitution reinforced the idea, as uttered by the Serb writer Dobrica Ćosić, that 'Serbia won its wars but lost the peace'. In the 1950s, Ćosić had been something of a court muse for Tito, but Ćosić became increasingly dissatisfied with the direction that Yugoslavia had taken. At the beginning of the 1960s, Ćosić engaged in a protracted public debate with the Slovene intellectual Dušan Pirjevec regarding Yugoslavia's direction and Serbia's place in the state.[47] Ćosić came to regard Yugoslavia as a sort of betrayal of the Serbs, holding that the Serbs had been subjected to a process in which they entered the twentieth century as leaders in the Balkans but had been reduced to underdevelopment and had come to stand as 'the only Balkan nation without its own sovereign state'.[48]

By contrast, the Kosovo Albanians remained dissatisfied for their part because Kosovo had not been promoted to the status of a republic. Not long after Tito's death in May 1980, Kosovo Albanians launched demonstrations demanding, amongst other things, republic status. Many Serb intellectuals and Serbs in the military and security services regarded the Kosovo Albanians' demands as merely a pretext for Kosovo's eventual secession from Yugoslavia and the creation of a 'Great Albania'.[49]

The notion of a Serb nation under assault within Yugoslavia was articulated in the leaked 1986 draft memorandum of the Serbian Academy of Sciences and Arts. This document painted a dire landscape of Serbs under assault. Indeed, the document (in) famously asserted that Serbs in Kosovo were being submitted to 'genocide' and were effectively being eliminated from the province. Socialist Yugoslavia as a whole was portrayed as a project that had discriminated against the Serbs, who had been held back by others.

Make Serbia Great Again: The Great Serbian idea and Slobodan Milošević

In the late 1980s Slobodan Milošević, who took control of the Serbian League of Communists in September 1987, began to work to reassert Serbia's role within Yugoslavia. Initially a colourless apparatchik, Milošević essentially stumbled upon the opportunity offered him by nationalism. After he blurted out that no one would be allowed to 'beat Serbs' in Kosovo, his admirers harnessed the state media to project Milošević as the figured destined to make Serbia great again.

Jasna Dragović-Soso has noted that, while the aforementioned draft memorandum was a descriptive 'repository of Serbian nationalist grievances', only in 1988 was a prescriptive political platform issued.[50] Prior to taking the helm of the Serbian League of Communists, Milošević had adhered, as a party stalwart, to the doctrine of 'brotherhood and unity', but by 1989 he had effectively co-opted the nationalist agenda, as shown by his staging of a massive political rally at Gazimestan in Kosovo to mark the six-hundredth anniversary of the Battle of Kosovo. Although the co-opting of nationalist discourse by Milošević made the event famous, Milošević's speech also included implicit references to smallness. Bojan Savić writes that, 'Speaking before thousands of supporters in Kosovo, Milošević told the story of a small country of brave people who live at the crossroads of civilisations'.[51] Yet this nation was also a chosen nation, one which would not accept the loss of territory and would respond with force if necessary were it confronted with hostility. 'Serbian geopolitical exceptionalism was thus constructed around the spatialised nexus of smallness, sanctity, and heroic physical prowess. [...] In the economy of self-victimising narratives, a collective social equilibrium is pursued: Serbia's fortune is the cause of its misfortunes, yet every misfortune is perversely welcome, as it reinforces the martyrdom and sanctity of Serbs.'[52]

More practically, in terms of Serbian statehood Milošević pushed through a series of 'antibureaucratic revolutions' which resulted in cadres loyal to him replacing the leaderships of Vojvodina, Kosovo and Montenegro.[53] This process culminated in the revocation of autonomy for Kosovo and Vojvodina, recentralizing political power in Serbia and thereby addressing one of the Serb nationalists' main grievances. From the constitutional point of view, these changes effectively granted Milošević control of four of the eight votes in the Yugoslav presidency. This agglomeration of power provoked profound disquiet and dismay elsewhere, particularly in Slovenia and Croatia, where the republican leaderships viewed any attempt to revert to centralized rule as unacceptable. By the spring of 1990, the Yugoslav League of Communists for all intents and purposes had ceased to function.

Three key factors must be mentioned to understand subsequent developments. First, while shrewdly catering to Serb nationalist interests, Milošević stubbornly maintained publicly that he was in fact defending Yugoslavia. This claim allowed him not only to court international public opinion concerned about a possible breakup of the country but also, more importantly, to secure the backing of the powerful Yugoslav People's Army (JNA). Second, the ethnic demography of Yugoslavia meant that significant settlements of Serbs could be found not only in Serbia (including, of course, Kosovo and Vojvodina) but also in Bosnia and Croatia. Third, the living memory of systematic persecution and mass atrocities committed against Serbs during the Second World War meant that keeping all Serbs in one state figured as the primary claim of Serb nationalists. In time this evolution led to considerable political schizophrenia, with Serbia claiming to be both a victim of Yugoslavia and the sole actor intent on saving the country.[54]

Summarized briefly, the events from 1989 to 1991 represent a power struggle between Serb centralizers on the one hand and Slovene and Croat federalists or autonomists on the other. As the political rhetoric became more aggressive on both sides, and particularly with the election of Croat nationalists under the leadership of the dissident historian Franjo Tuđman in April 1990, this power struggle ratcheted up continuously. Events began to look like elements in a chain reaction, a potential violent detonation growing ever more likely.

The subsequent story of Yugoslavia's collapse and road to war, told countless times, need not be recounted here, but suffice it to say that the 1990s witnessed the violent consequences caused by the resurrection of the Great Serbia (*Velika Srbija*) project. In Croatia and Serbia, Serbs organized politically in 1990 and 1991, primarily along ethnic lines. As noted, their primary motivation was to avoid being 'stranded' in newly independent Croatian or Bosnian states in which, they feared, they would become the victims of renewed oppression or atrocities.[55] The most extreme advocates of an irredentist solution to the Yugoslav crisis represented by the Serb politician Vojislav Šešelj and his Serbian Radical Party, founded in 1991, literally adopted the slogan 'Great Serbia' as the title of their party's magazine. For these nationalists, the acceptance of smallness was treason; the only acceptable smaller version of a state had to include every settlement in Yugoslavia in which Serbs lived.[56] Meanwhile, the Milošević regime's insistence that it was fighting not on behalf of Serbian nationalism but instead to defend Yugoslavia was symbolized by the fact that Serbia (with Vojvodina and Kosovo) and Montenegro, after April 1992, officially clung to the name Federal Republic of Yugoslavia.

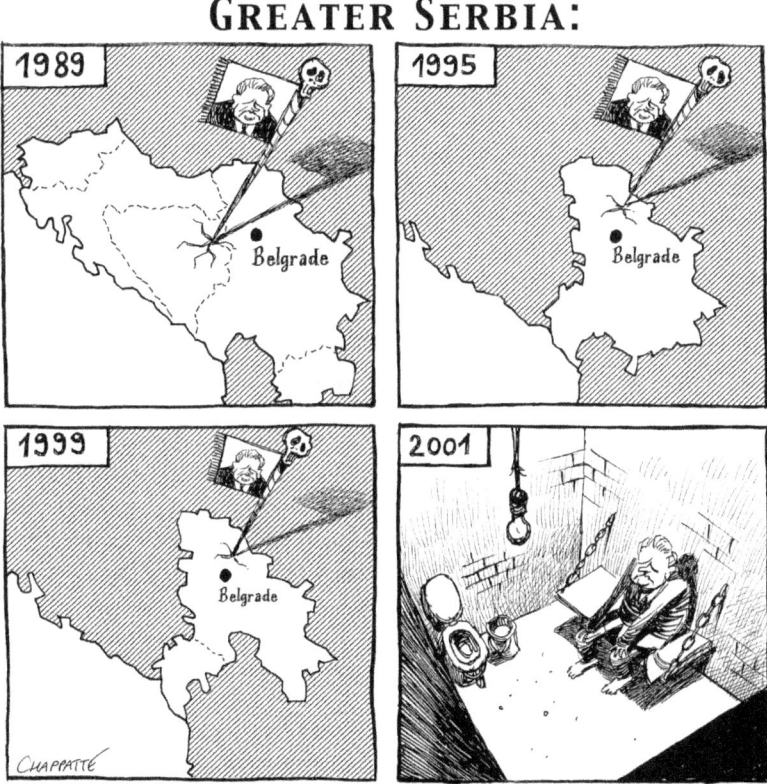

Figure 7.1 Cartoon by Patrick Chappatte. Printed in *Die Weltwoche*, 5 April 2001. © Chappatte.

Events in the wars of Yugoslav succession did not proceed as Serb nationalists had hoped. In 1991 and 1992, first the Croatian Serbs and then the Bosnian Serbs did succeed in carving out Serb entities, Republika Srpska Krajina and Republika Srpska, respectively. However, by the autumn of 1995, the Croatian army had overrun the Republika Srpska Krajina, and most of its inhabitants had fled to Bosnia or Serbia. Croatia was left with a much smaller Serb minority than had been the case in 1991, and hundreds of years of Serb settlement in what had been the old Habsburg military frontier was put to an end. In Bosnia, by contrast, the Serbs received the recognition of Republika Srpska through the war-ending Dayton Accords, but only at the cost of massive 'ethnic cleansing' and a war costing approximately 100,000 lives. Finally, NATO launched its 1999 military intervention in Kosovo, resulting in the Kumanovo Peace Treaty that removed Kosovo from Serbia and paved the way for Kosovo's independence – still bitterly contested by Serbia – in 2008. In the end, the dream of a Great Serbia emerging from the 'prison' of socialist Yugoslavia, which had been enthusiastically propounded by Serb nationalists and opportunistically implemented by the Milošević regime, has yielded the smallest Serbian state since 1912–13. As of 2022 Serbia – without Kosovo – covered 77,474 km^2.

Between Great Serbia and the EU

Before summarizing more recent events, it is necessary to provide an account of the somewhat confusing manifestations of Serbian statehood since the dissolution of Yugoslavia. On 27 April 1992, Serbia (with Kosovo and Vojvodina) and Montenegro proclaimed the Federal Republic of Yugoslavia (Savezna Republika Jugoslavija), which during the 1990s was also popularly and ignominiously known, in English, as 'rump Yugoslavia'. The name of the state allowed the Milošević regime to pursue the fiction that it was preserving and protecting what was left of Yugoslavia, when what was occurring would be more accurately described as the opportunistic destruction of Yugoslavia and the pursuit of Serb nationalist goals in Croatia and Bosnia. As Bojan Savić puts it, the implicit new slogan became 'Yugoslavia is where Serbs are'.[57] After the loss of Kosovo and the fall of Milošević, Serbia (with Vojvodina) and Montenegro formed a looser state union called Serbia and Montenegro on 4 February 2003. Given the tensions between Belgrade and Podgorica, this state proved short-lived and was dissolved in May 2006 when Montenegro declared its independence. Kosovo became independent in February 2008. It is therefore easy to see how a significant number of Serbs became obsessed with the idea that their state would continue shrinking until it ceased to exist outright. Indeed, in a society with a strong tradition of cynical and self-deprecatory humour, people quipped that Serbia was like Nokia's mobile telephones, which kept getting smaller every year.[58]

Although there is debate regarding the extent to which the defeat in the Kosovo war led to the political fall of Milošević, the fact is that he was ousted only sixteen months later, on 5 October 2000. Although Serbia was spared any direct military damage during the wars in Slovenia, Croatia and Bosnia, and was 'only' hit directly during NATO's seventy-eight-day bombing campaign in 1999, the 1990s proved devastating to Serbia because the Federal Republic of Yugoslavia had effectively subsidized Serb forces in Croatia and Bosnia and had engaged in systematic economic mismanagement and kleptocracy, leading to severe hyperinflation.[59] But conventional wisdom in Serbia held that the real problem was not the goal pursued by Milošević but instead the fact that an opportunistic 'cryptocommunist' and not a genuine nationalist had led Serbia. In other words, the irredentist project was not discarded. The enormous coalition which had opposed Milošević, it turned out, agreed about only one thing – that they wanted to get rid of Milošević, who was in June 2001 extradited to face the United Nation's (UN) International Criminal Tribunal for the Former Yugoslavia (ICTY) and stand trial on charges of genocide, war crimes and crimes against humanity.

The immediate post-Milošević years featured a power struggle between Serbian prime minister Zoran Đinđić and the new Yugoslav president, Vojislav Koštunica. Although Đinđić had himself flirted with nationalism during the 1990s, his reformist and pro-European utterances as prime minister at times seemed to paraphrase some of the more pacific declarations of Svetozar Marković.[60] By contrast, Koštunica was a dour constitutionalist lawyer who stubbornly asserted Serbia's national and territorial claims.[61]

The period since Đinđić's death has shown Serbia to be a reluctant and at times ornery and malcontent traveller on the road to what is euphemistically known as 'Euro-Atlantic integration', which includes amongst other things EU and NATO membership.[62] For obvious reasons linked to the events of 1999, Serbia has consistently opposed joining NATO and has instead stressed that it wishes to remain neutral but cooperative with both the alliance and with Russia. This stance seems a reasonable balance given the strong (but often abstract and unrequited) Russophilic tendencies present in Serbian society, but such a balance has also proved increasingly difficult to maintain after the Russo-Georgian war of 2008 and to an even greater extent afterwards, given the issues and tensions raised by Russia's invasion of Ukraine and occupation of Crimea.[63]

Serbian attitudes towards the EU have also been markedly more sceptical than those of any other country in the Balkans. Part of the scepticism derives from the EU's effective application of the conditionality principle, which linked Serbia's progress towards European integration to its cooperation with the ICTY.[64] Broad swathes of the Serbian public were – and remain – convinced that the 'international community' has unjustly vilified Serbia and Serbs and that the ICTY was a fundamentally political and anti-Serb institution. As can also be seen in Croatia, any assertion that crimes have been committed in the name of the state or nation is treated not as claims to be investigated seriously and conscientiously but instead as threats to the continued existence of the nation-state.[65] The more shrill and paranoid voices – in what is by no means a fringe phenomenon – propagate an image of a (German-led) European Union bent on dismantling and effectively neutering the country. Such portrayals sometimes invoke pan-German and Habsburg precedents from the twentieth century but of course cite more recent developments as well. In this nightmare scenario, the campaign against Serbian statehood will stop only when Vojvodina and perhaps even the area of Sandžak, populated by many Muslim Slavs, are no longer under the control of Serbia's sovereignty.[66] Generally speaking, these fears represent a continuation of popular (conspiracy) theories that cast Serbia as a victim of great power politics, where only Russia can, at least on occasion, be trusted to defend Serbia's interests.

Serbia (stuck) at a crossroads between European smallness and Great Serbia

Aleksandar Vučić, who became Serbia's president in 2017, embodies to a considerable extent the contradictions of Serbia's relationship to smallness. In the 1990s, Vučić was a high-ranking member of the aforementioned ultranationalist Serbian Radical Party (SRS). In 2008, Vučić and another prominent SRS member, Tomislav Nikolić, broke with the SRS and formed their own party, the Serbian Progressive Party (*Srpska napredna stranka* (SNS)). Nikolić and Vučić steered away from extreme nationalism and professed to want Serbia to enter the EU. From 2012, Vučić served first as deputy prime minister and then as prime minister before becoming president of Serbia in May 2017.

Although Vučić maintains a declaratively pro-EU course, his statements about Serbian history, national identity, Kosovo and the wars of the 1990s – not to mention his own personal background – exude a profoundly complicated relationship to Serbia's status and size. Like his predecessors, Vučić maintains that Kosovo seceded illegally and that Serbia should not recognize its independence. Tabloid newspapers in Serbia are subsidized by and are slavishly loyal to the regime, serving up a steady stream of hysterical headlines about Croatian, Albanian, Islamic and other alleged threats to Serbian security. Even the EU is frequently portrayed as a villain, as in a 2018 headline in the tabloid *Informer* in which EU Commission President Jean-Claude Juncker is shown cackling next to the headline 'Serbia Must Lose Everything – Kosovo, Republika Srpska, Russia and the Border'.[67] And in November 2018, *Politika*, a serious newspaper with a reputation for always supporting the regime *du jour*, published an editorial cartoon depicting Marilyn Monroe wearing a skirt with the EU's logo. As she strikes her most famous pose, the European skirt lifts to reveal a garter belt holding stockings emblazoned with the flags of Kosovo and Albania.[68] Hence, the EU is a (sexy) stalking horse for 'Great Albania', another frequent trope in the contemporary Serbian media. Such articles, combined with a stream of articles about historical and more recent real and alleged atrocities committed against Serbs, reinforce a pervasive popular sense of ontological insecurity. The message is clear: Serbia risks becoming even smaller, and if and when this happens, new bloodshed and suffering will accompany its partitioning. From nationalist intellectual circles, the tone remains that of a defiant Serbia. To quote the Serbian academician Matija Bećković in November 2019, 'No force exists that will remove [the thought] from our heads that we are a great power'.[69]

Could they see such headlines, Svetozar Marković and Marko Nikezić would recognize them as cynical attempts to heighten the population's fears in order to distract and discourage them from asking critical questions about more mundane issues: widespread corruption and clientelism, broken political promises, economic instability, unemployment and dilapidated infrastructure. The leaders of Serbia effectively wield the fear of (increased) smallness or even extermination as an instrument of power.

By way of conclusion, this chapter will close with a brief summary of two recent speeches by President Vučić. In September 2018, Vučić travelled to Kosovska Mitrovica, a de facto divided city in northern Kosovo and delivered a speech. He spoke about compromise, the need to emerge victorious 'without blood, deaths, horrors and graves', and about 'the necessity of our common existence with the Albanians'.[70] The twentieth century had 'killed us, not even in the next two centuries will we be able to compensate for the people whom we have lost'. Yet at the same time Vučić invoked Milošević's 1989 speech, noting how people back then had sung the old song 'Whoever Says That Serbia Is Small Is Lying' (*ko to kaže, ko to laže, Srbija je mala*), and spoke of Milošević as a 'great leader' whose 'intentions were surely the best, but our results were very bad'. And Vučić warned, at the end of his speech, that Serbia would resolutely stop those 'who think that they can threaten and persecute our nation'.

Eight months later, in May 2018, Vučić with great pomp gave a speech in the Serbian parliament.[71] This time, Vučić spoke of the necessity to choose between 'sweet lies and bitter truths'. After emphasizing that he would strive for compromise with Kosovo's Albanians, Vučić then dramatically predicted that it was only a matter of time before they would attack Serbia. Moreover, Vučić's speech dwelled at length on the kind of zero-sum demographics that has informed much nationalist thought and many policies in the Balkans over the previous century. After going through various historical statistics, he extrapolated to the future, speaking of how Albanians in the Balkans were becoming ever more numerous while Serbs were demographically dwindling. Vučić assigned blame for these developments almost exclusively to external factors, particularly the actions of the West, various great powers and Serbia's neighbours. Precisely such rhetorical contradictions – seen by some as evidence of duplicitousness – reverberate throughout the Balkans and leave politicians in the EU and in neighbouring states wondering whether Serbia has really reconciled itself to its present smallness. In the meantime, like other states in the region, Serbia at the beginning of the twenty-first century faces the far greater and far more real threat of demographic smallness, and no amount of nationalist bluster can parry this reality.[72]

Notes

1 For a summary of the novelty and limited traction of national identity in the Balkans in the nineteenth century, see Mazower, *The Balkans*.
2 Miedlig, 'Patriarchalische Mentalität Als Hindernis Für Die Staatliche Und Gesellschaftliche Modernisierung in Serbien Im 19. Jahrhundert', 172.
3 Jelavich, *History of the Balkans. Volume 1: Eighteenth and Nineteenth Centuries*, 43–4.
4 Meriage, 'The First Serbian Uprising (1804–1913) and the Nineteenth-Century Origins of the Eastern Question', 422.
5 For a newer overview of the 'rebirth' of the Serbian state written by a foreign historian, see Sundhaussen, *Geschichte Serbiens*, 65–230.
6 Novaković, *Vaskrs države srpske*; Ejdus, *Crisis and Ontological Insecurity: Serbia's Anxiety of Kosovo's Secession*; Čolović, *Smrt Na Kosovu Polju*.
7 Djilas, Bulatović, and Samardžić, 'Istorijski Karakter Srba'.

8   Bataković, 'A Balkan-Style French Revolution? The 1804 Serbian Uprising in European Perspective'. Cf. Sundhaussen, *Geschichte Serbiens*, 68. Today, Serbia observes 15 February not only as Sretenje (Candlemas) according to the Serbian Orthodox calendar but also as the anniversary of the First Serbian Uprising and the 1835 constitution and hence Serbia's national day. At receptions at Serbian embassies, Bataković's thesis – he himself served as an ambassador – is sometimes mentioned.
9   Malešević, 'Did Wars Make Nation-States', 301.
10 Malešević, 'Did Wars Make Nation-States'. Needless to say, nationally inclined Serb historians do not cite any of the rebellions against the Serbian state as examples of nationalism's shortcomings.
11 Sundhaussen, *Geschichte Serbiens*, 77–80.
12 Karadžić published his treatise *Srbi svi i svuda* in 1849, and he acknowledged the challenge that many Muslim or Catholic 'Serbs' did not identify as such. See also Hajdarpašić, *Whose Bosnia? Nationalism and Political Imagination in the Balkans, 1840–1914*, 18–37; Banac, *The National Question in Yugoslavia*, 80. Sundhaussen is correct in placing what he calls Karadžić's 'integrative linguistic nationalism' (*integrativer Sprachnationalismus*) into proper historical context, but Sundhaussen goes too far in denying the link to aggressive strains of Serb nationalism. Sundhaussen, *Geschichte Serbiens*, 93.
13 MacKenzie, *Ilija Garašanin: Balkan Bismarck*; Hehn, 'The Origins of Modern Pan-Serbism'. See also Ljušić, *Knjiga o Načertaniju*.
14 Sundhaussen, *Geschichte Serbiens*, 116.
15 Hehn, 'The Origins of Modern Pan-Serbism', 153–4.
16 Jelavich, 'Garašanins Načertanije Und Das Großserbische Problem'.
17 Grmek, Gjidara, and Šimac, *Le nettoyage ethnique*.
18 Sundhaussen, *Geschichte Serbiens*, 117.
19 MacKenzie, 'Serbian National and Military Organizations and the Piedmont Idea, 1844–1914'.
20 Sundhaussen, *Geschichte Serbiens*, 120.
21 Hehn, 'The Origins of Modern Pan-Serbism', 155.
22 Bibó, *Die Misere Der Osteuropäischen Kleinstaaterei*.
23 It should be remembered that not only was the ethnic demography complex, there were also arguably large swathes of the local population who were either highly uncertain of their ethnic identity or rather ambivalent or even hostile towards the very notion of ethnic identity in the modern sense. Roudometof, 'From Rum Millet to Greek Nation: Enlightenment, Secularization, and National Identity in Ottoman Balkan Society, 1453–1821'.
24 Hehn, 'The Origins of Modern Pan-Serbism', 157.
25 Marković, 'Šta Treba Da Radimo', 59–61.
26 Marković, 66–7.
27 Marković, 68.
28 Sundhaussen, *Geschichte Serbiens*, 136. Other thinkers critical of irredentism and largeness were Ilarion Ruvarac (1832–1905) and Dimitrije Tucović (1881–1914) and Živojin Perić. Antolović, 'Modern Serbian Historiography between Nation-Building and Critical Scholarship: The Case of Ilarion Ruvarac (1832–1905)'; Tucović, *Srbija i Arbanija: Jedan Prilog Kritici Zavojevačke Politike Srpske Buržoazije*; Perić, *La Confédération Balkanique*.
29 See also Sundhaussen regarding the Serb geographer Jovan Cvijić, who had broad views regarding the borders of Serbdom and, by extension, the Serbian state. Sundhaussen, *Geschichte Serbiens*, 192–4.

30 Sundhaussen, 200.
31 On the importance of Kosovo, see Ejdus, Filip and Subotić, 'Kosovo as Serbia's Sacred Space: Governmentality, Pastoral Power, and Sacralization of Territories'.
32 Sundhaussen, *Geschichte Serbiens*, 215–16.
33 Mitrović, *Serbia's Great War 1914–1918*; Gumz, *The Resurrection and Collapse of Empire in Habsburg Serbia, 1914–1918*.
34 For detailed treatment of this complex process, see Banac, *The National Question in Yugoslavia*; Lederer, *Yugoslavia at the Paris Peace Conference: A Study in Frontiermaking*; Nielsen, *Making Yugoslavs*.
35 Banac, *The National Question in Yugoslavia*.
36 Cited in Gligorijević, *Kralj Aleksandar Karađorđević u Ratovima Za Nacionalno Oslobođenje*, 422.
37 This view was also the consensus view of the historiography produced in the era of socialist Yugoslavia, but it fell into disfavour in the 1980s and 1990s in direct correlation with the rehabilitation of the notion of Serbian primacy and greatness. However, since then some Serb historians have taken a more critical view.
38 Nielsen, *Making Yugoslavs*.
39 Quoted in Dragović-Soso, 'Rethinking Yugoslavia', 2004, 174.
40 Ćorović, *Velika Srbija*.
41 Dragović-Soso, 'Rethinking Yugoslavia', 2004, 176, emphasis in original. See also Pavlowitch, *Hitler's New Disorder: The Second World War in Yugoslavia*.
42 Perović, 'Tito-Stalin Split'.
43 Dragović-Soso, 'Rethinking Yugoslavia', 2004, 176–7.
44 Helfant-Budding, 'Yugoslavs into Serbs', 412.
45 Batović, *The Croatian Spring*.
46 Vujačić, 'Institutional Origins of Contemporary Serbian Nationalism'.
47 Helfant-Budding, 'Yugoslavs into Serbs'.
48 Ćosić seems to have arrived at this conclusion by simultaneously accepting the sovereignty vested in the Yugoslav republics but denying that it applied to the Socialist Republic of Serbia. Ćosić, *Srpsko Pitanje u XX Veku. Lična Istorija Jednog Doba*.
49 The best treatment of nationalist ideology amongst Serb intellectuals in the 1980s is Dragović-Soso, *Rethinking Yugoslavia*, 2002.
50 Dragović-Soso, 'Rethinking Yugoslavia', 2004.
51 Savić, 'Where Is Serbia?' 685.
52 Savić, 685.
53 Vladisavljević, *Serbia's Antibureaucratic Revolution*.
54 I recall a conversation in 2001 with a Belgrade historian who told me of a Serbian history textbook in which Yugoslavia was portrayed at once as the prison of the Serb nation but also as a nation nonetheless where Serbs were the only group willing to defend Yugoslavia from 'foreign aggressors' and traitorous 'internal enemies'.
55 Needless to say, equally extreme solutions abounded amongst Croat nationalists bent on including all Croats from Bosnia and Herzegovina – if not the actual territory itself – within the future independent Croatian state.
56 In a particularly morbid twist, the most extreme nationalists even insisted that the Great Serbian state should include all Serbian graves. On necrophilic nationalism, see Anzulovic, *Heavenly Serbia. From Myth to Genocide*; Verdery, *The Political Lives of Dead Bodies: Reburial and Postsocialist Change*.
57 Savić, 'Where Is Serbia?' 702.
58 Of course, the fact that Nokia later abandoned the production of mobile phones altogether casts a particularly dire light on this bit of humour.

59 Dinkić, *Ekonomija Destrukcije: Velika Pljačka Naroda*. It should be noted that up through today, the NATO intervention in 1999 is referred to by many Serbs and Serb politicians and journalists as 'NATO aggression', with some even claiming genocidal intent against the Serb nation.
60 Not coincidentally, Đinđić in 1996 published a collection of his writings under the title *Srbija ni na Istoku ni na Zapadu* (Serbia Neither in the East Nor in the West), echoing the title of Svetozar Marković's famous *Srbija na Istoku* (Serbia in the East). For an excerpt Đinđić, 'Srbija, Ni Na Istoku, Ni Na Zapadu'.
61 The co-author of the work that had made a name for Koštunica was Kosta Čavoški, who had become an advisor to Radovan Karadžić, the leader of the Bosnian Serbs subsequently convicted at the ICTY. Koštunica and Čavoški, *Party Pluralism or Monism: Social Movements and the Political System in Yugoslavia, 1944–1949*.
62 Nielsen, 'From Nightmare to Pragmatic Partnership: Serbia and the EU'.
63 Nielsen, 'Kosovo Precedent'. Bojan Savić points out that some Serb nationalists have paradoxically seemed willing to accept smallness within a framework in which Russia instead of the West would dominate. Citing several quotes from former Serb president (and semi-reformed ultranationalist) Tomislav Nikolić in which he lavishes praise on Russia and even spoke on one occasion of Serbia as a Russian province, Savić writes that 'unlike the "small Serbia of the West", the "small Serbia of the East" is re-infused with spiritual ontologies'. Savić, 'Where Is Serbia?' 711.
64 Subotić, *Hijacked Justice. Dealing with the Past in the Balkans*.
65 This is also true of the collective memory of crimes committed during the Second World War, including the Holocaust. Subotić, 'Political Memory, Ontological Security, and Holocaust Remembrance in Post-Communist Europe'.
66 Ejdus, 'Critical Situations, Fundamental Questions and Ontological Insecurity in World Politics', 24.
67 *Informer* 16 May 2018, 'Srbija mora da izgubi sve'.
68 *Politika* 29 November 2018.
69 *Večernje novosti* 4 November 2019, Interview with Mateja Bećković.
70 Aleksandar Vučić's speech, 8 September 2018, quoted at http://mondo.rs/a1130925/Info/Srbija/Vucic-na-Kosovo-govor-u-Mitrovici.html. Last accessed 28 May 2019.
71 Aleksandar Vučić's speech, 27 May 2019, https://www.predsednik.rs/lat/pres-centar/vesti/govor-predsednika-republike-srbije-aleksandra-vucica-u-narodnoj-skupstini-republike-srbije-27052019-godine. Last accessed 28 May 2019.
72 *BalkanInsight* 24 October 2019, Tim Judah, 'Too Late' to Halt Serbia's Demographic Disaster, https://balkaninsight.com/2019/10/24/too-late-to-halt-serbias-demographic-disaster/. Last accessed 26 May 2020.

8

Iceland's smallness. Acceptance or denial?

Baldur Thorhallsson and Guðmundur Hálfdanarson

Introduction

This chapter aims to trace the part played by smallness in Iceland's political life from around 1918, when the country became a sovereign state, up to the present. The focus primarily centres on the domestic political discourse about Iceland's small size – or, more precisely, its absence in public debates – and how 'smallness' influenced the decision to create an independent state and the construction of the country's foreign policy. We will analyse how the Icelandic political elite has used Iceland's size, or its perceived size, to support its preferred policies at home and abroad, even as it has frequently overlooked problems related to the nation's smallness.

Iceland, with a little more than 360,000 inhabitants, is one of the smallest member states of the United Nations.[1] Maintaining no armed forces, and possessed of a small and volatile domestic market and a small public administration (including a very modest foreign service), it is a typical small state, as we find the term defined in small state studies.[2] Nevertheless, the notion of Iceland as a small state has not been a dominant feature in Icelandic political discourse. Moreover, policymakers' use of Iceland's smallness in public discourse and in Iceland's foreign policy is paradoxical. Thus, while Icelandic policymakers seem to recognize the obvious facts of Iceland's small population and political power relative to almost any other country, the political elite has picked up or dropped the concept of smallness variously and inconsistently, according to context and convenience. Policymakers are often silent about Iceland's small size, especially at home, although they occasionally flaunt it in domestic debates to win support from voters. Iceland's smallness therefore often seems taboo, something one simply does not speak of. True during the long struggle for Icelandic independence from Denmark, this attitude of silence is equally true now in the debates about the country's relations with superpowers like China. The inherent dangers of simply ignoring the nation's smallness became evident in the 2008 economic crash, when Iceland's lack of economic diversification and its dependency on others became painfully obvious. On other occasions, however, Iceland's small size has in fact been used politically, but in a highly opportunistic manner. 'Smallness' was and is invoked as an argument for or against membership in international organizations such as NATO and the European Union (EU) or as a way to gain sympathy from the world in the country's fishing disputes (the so-called Cod Wars) with much larger states and to gain the financial support of international organizations. Iceland's auto-image, therefore, does not seem to feature smallness. Rather, the issue of its size can be a means to an end, but when this reality is inconvenient it is utterly ignored.

Nonetheless, we can identify a common theme in the policymakers' language of smallness within domestic discourses on the one hand, and a common, albeit tacit understanding of 'smallness' by Icelandic foreign policy elites on the other. Policymakers shy away from referencing smallness domestically, as the notion of a 'small Iceland' undermines the nationalist claim that the nation possesses a natural right to self-determination and should act as an independent player in the international arena. Using 'small' to refer to Iceland within a political context is not likely to attract many votes, as the term contradicts Iceland's auto-image as a fully sovereign member of the international community, not reliant on other international actors to sustain its independence. Internationally, however, Icelandic agents abroad seem driven by a different auto-image. From the moment the country became sovereign in 1918, its foreign policy elites took the country's need to overcome the limits that its smallness was deemed to impose on it as a given. Iceland's reliance on the Danish Royal Navy to protect its territorial waters, as well as on Danish trade policy during the interwar period, is as emblematic of this tendency as Iceland's more recent drive for membership in the International Monetary Fund (IMF), the World Bank, NATO, the European Free Trade Area (EFTA) and the European Economic Area (EEA), efforts motivated by the need to secure development grants, guarantee defence and strengthen the small volatile domestic market. Moreover, Icelandic policymakers have acknowledged and continue to grant Iceland's need to seek forms of 'shelter' together with larger states and international organizations, a necessity now ever more pressing after the United States closed its military base in the country in 2006 and refused to offer Iceland financial assistance in the wake of the 2008 economic collapse. The United States, which had granted Iceland essential economic support to deal with many of the serious economic crises plaguing the country in the postwar period, had previously served as both a military and an economic guarantor; its withdrawal from Iceland (though the countries still have a bilateral defence treaty and the United States is currently increasing its military activity in and around Iceland) was regarded as a betrayal by a large portion of the Icelandic political elite. Their response indicates a form of policymaking based on an auto-image of the country as small, although this view is rarely acknowledged publicly.

Thus, Icelandic policymakers present Iceland's size in one way at home and in another way abroad: in domestic public discourse, they tend not to acknowledge weaknesses and restraints that could be associated with Iceland's smallness, whereas these considerations very much inform their foreign policy orientation. The paradoxical situation emerges in which Iceland's smallness, however instrumental in and indeed fundamental to its foreign policy and therefore essential to the hetero-images of Iceland constructed abroad, is represented quite differently at home. To complicate things even further, the ideological leanings of foreign policy elites have largely determined perceptions about consequences that result from Iceland's smallness. It also seems to matter whether the parties they align themselves with are in government or in the opposition in the *Alþingi*, the Icelandic national parliament. This chapter seeks to shed light on this double paradox.

Its first section offers an explanation for the key role played by smallness in Iceland's auto- and hetero-images with regard to the country's decision to seek independence at the end of First World War. At the time, it was generally believed that ethnic groups needed both to be of certain size and to have a requisite economic strength to exercise their supposed right of self-determination. To outside observers, and to some Icelandic politicians as well, Iceland lacked both requirements and therefore the only sensible strategy would be to continue to exist under the aegis of the Danish monarchy. This route proved to be an impossible proposition, as Icelandic political discourses were – and still are – heavily influenced by cultural nationalism.

The second section focuses on discourses of smallness and their interaction with Iceland's foreign policy since the end of the Second World War. It will examine how Iceland's policymakers have interpreted Iceland's smallness as necessitating – to compensate for its perceived weaknesses – a search for shelter that would be provided both by larger states (Nordic states, the UK and China) and international organizations (the EU, the IMF and the Nordic Council).

'They are too small'

At the beginning of the twentieth century, Iceland had been ruled by Danish kings for over half a millennium, first as a royal fief but later as an integral part of the Danish monarchy. During most of this long period, Danish rule had met only limited resistance in Iceland, as the Icelandic elites viewed it as both a natural and generally beneficial arrangement for the remote, sparsely populated island to be a part of a larger, more powerful polity. The political relations between the dependency and the metropole began to change, however, in the early nineteenth century, as romantic cultural nationalism spread to various parts of the Danish empire. This period was characterized by what Joep Leerssen has called 'viral nationalism', referring to a pandemic-like wave of romantic nationalist ideas and ideals that swept the European continent during the first decades of the nineteenth century, moving from one community to another through tightly knit networks of intellectuals and political figures.[3] Inspired by Danish cultural nationalism, which primarily focused on curbing German influences in the Danish part of the monarchy, a small cadre of Icelandic university students and intellectuals living in Copenhagen began to redefine Icelandic as an identity distinct from Danish. In the spirit of the era, they accentuated the linguistic boundaries separating Iceland from the rest of the monarchy while rebranding well-known mediaeval literary texts, preserved in manuscripts originating in Iceland but stored in various European libraries, as a specifically Icelandic national treasure rather than an expression of a common Scandinavian or European cultural heritage. In this manner, a cohesive Icelandic national community was imagined, its internal cultural coherence and fixed geographic boundaries separating it from the rest of the world.[4]

The complex political consequences of this nationalist turn emerged slowly over the latter half of the nineteenth century. According to pervasive political discourses popular in liberal circles in Europe, nations – defined in cultural terms – formed the most natural framework for democratic state authority. Thus, to quote the influential liberal philosopher and political economist John Stuart Mill, free institutions are 'next to impossible in a country made up of different nationalities. Among a people without fellow-feeling, especially if the they read and speak different languages, the united public opinion, necessary to the working of representative government, cannot exist.'[5] This nationalist ideology, Leerssen points out, sought its inspiration in '[Johann Gottfried] Herder's belief in the individuality of nations, [and Jean-Jacques] Rousseau's belief in the sovereignty of the nation'[6]; that is, it was believed that humanity is 'naturally divided into nations, each with their different culture and character, each deserving a separate nation-based sovereignty, each commanding the overriding allegiance of their members'.[7]

Mill's liberal 'principle of nationality' came, however, with an important caveat as, in his opinion, it applied only to a limited group of potential national communities. Mill claimed, for example, that the European colonial powers were entitled to control 'the less advanced people' of the world, as the former would – through their *mission civilisatrice* – improve people's lives by spreading European civilization around the globe. Similarly, Mill argued, the small and less developed national minorities in Europe were best served by accepting total integration into larger and more advanced nations. 'Nobody can suppose', Mill stated, 'that it is not more beneficial to a Breton, or a Basque of French Navarre, to be brought into the current of the ideas and feelings of a highly civilized and cultivated people [...] than to sulk on his own rocks, the half-savage relic of past times'.[8] This is what historian Eric Hobsbawm later called 'the threshold principle', meaning that the 'principle of nationality' applied only to population groups of a certain size and economic vigour. 'Self-determination for nations', he argued, 'applied only to what were considered to be viable nations: culturally, and certainly economically (whatever exactly viability meant)'.[9]

Similar concerns motivated the Danish opposition to growing demands in Iceland for national self-determination in the years leading up to the First World War. Most Danish commentators fully accepted Icelandic claims to separate nationhood, as they had great respect for the mediaeval heritage preserved in Icelandic manuscripts and regarded the Icelandic language to be a living remnant of an ancient Scandinavian *Ursprache*.[10] At the same time, they brushed off all calls for a separate Icelandic state as a utopian fallacy or at least as utterly premature. Iceland simply lacked, they argued, the economic and cultural means to operate its own polity. It was a sheer 'madness for a population of 70,000 to request an independent statehood', wrote, for example, the eminent Danish literary critic Georg Brandes in a letter to an Icelandic friend in 1907. 'You have no trade, no industry, no army, no fleet, you are altogether as many as a small, fifth rate town in England and Germany; the only thing you have is a famous past.'[11] Ten years later, the Danish prime minister Carl Theodor Zahle expressed a similar opinion in a meeting of his cabinet convened to discuss the political situation in Iceland. 'There is hardly any desire up there to secede from us', Zahle informed his fellow ministers, 'because they are too small to establish themselves as a state'. The foreign minister, Erik Scavenius, concurred: 'Now they are really free and very independent. If they separate from us, they will become a colony. Their financial circumstances are, after all, very difficult.'[12] In other words, for the leaders of the Danish government, Iceland was not part of Denmark – as was clearly expressed by their use of the pronouns 'us' and 'them' (*os* and *de*) – but because of the country's small size and economic vulnerability,

Figure 8.1 A real puzzle? Few outside Iceland believed in the 'madness' of a nation of less than 100,000 with 'no trade, no industry, no army, no fleet' to establish a sovereign state in the first two decades of the twentieth century. Composition by Mykhailo Polenok (Getty Images 1198200422) © Mykhailo Polenok / EyeEm / Getty Images.

they thought that Iceland's nationalist dreams were doomed to fail. In fact, leaving the shelter provided by the Danish would inevitably force the island into the hands of another, much less benevolent protector – most likely Britain.[13]

From the late nineteenth century until the end of the First World War, the predominant theme of Icelandic politics was the question of how to negotiate between two seemingly irreconcilable political positions: the universally accepted belief that Iceland possessed the historical and moral right to control its own sovereign state, set against serious doubts that the country could do so in practice.

The former position was most forcefully expressed through an immensely popular historical narrative, in which the story of the Icelandic nation was emplotted, to use Hayden White's term, as a Romance, meaning that it was recounted as 'a drama of the triumph of good over evil, of virtue over vice, of light over darkness, and of the ultimate transcendence of man over the world in which he was imprisoned by the Fall'.[14] In the Icelandic context, this view of the Icelandic past – and future – was communicated through a continuous stream of patriotic utterances and acts, where the story of the Icelandic nation, from its alleged birth in the tenth century onwards towards its imminent liberation one millennium later, was recounted as a continual struggle for the nation's freedom from foreign control. Such a conception followed a familiar narrative pattern, its story closely resembling what the Jamaican anthropologist David Scott calls twentieth-century 'anticolonial utopias'. These stories, he writes, 'have tended to be narratives of overcoming, often narratives of vindication; they have tended to enact a distinctive rhythm and pacing, a distinctive direction, and tell stories of salvation and redemption. They have largely depended upon certain (utopian) horizon toward which the emancipationist history is imagined to be moving.'[15] In the Icelandic version of this teleological story, Iceland not only possessed the right, as a truly 'civilized' (albeit impoverished) nation, to establish its own home in an independent nation-state; its independence was believed to be *necessary* so that the nation could redeem its rightful place in the world. In other words, if the Icelandic nation were to move from its present state of poverty and lethargy towards a prosperous future, it would have to free itself from foreign colonial bondage.[16]

The more pragmatic position countering these aspirations – summed up in the claim that Iceland did not really possess the material and cultural means to run an independent nation-state on its own – was harder to articulate, because it directly contradicted the Icelandic anti-colonial Romance. In the first years of the twentieth century, as calls for sovereignty grew ever louder, several conservative politicians in Iceland did in fact urge the nation to slow its march towards full sovereignty, though they were eventually silenced in the euphoria that accompanied 'viral nationalism'. Some of these cautionary voices advocated a permanent union with Denmark because they 'thought it would always be beneficial for the Icelandic nation to be in league with its most closely related nations' – of which the Danes were the most obvious choice.[17] Others advised the nation not to declare its independence until the economy had improved and the population had substantially increased. 'Let us till the earth, use the sea, strengthen the economy', wrote an anonymous author in the newspaper *Reykjavík*, 'so the population will grow, and the country's prosperity will increase. In this manner we will prepare the ground for the coming generations of our descendants, so *they* will be capable to do the things that are beyond *us now*.' Heeding this recommendation, the article predicted, would allow Iceland to perhaps become an independent state when the country's population had reached a quarter-million or so – a threshold surpassed only in the late 1980s.[18]

The issue came to a head in a fiercely contested parliamentary election in 1908, which resulted in a clear majority of the Icelandic electorate rejecting a draft of a new union treaty with Denmark on the grounds that it failed to establish a sovereign Icelandic state.[19] To accept this draft was equal to revoking the nation's sacred right to manage its own affairs, its opponents argued, a path that would inevitably lead to the country's demise.[20] From then on, it was clear that the Icelandic political elite would settle for nothing less than full sovereignty, which it indeed acquired with a new Danish-Icelandic Act of Union in 1918.[21] The new act was, in most respects, very similar to the draft from 1908, excepting its first clause that explicitly stated that Denmark and Iceland were two 'free and sovereign states, in a union under the same king'. For the Icelanders, this was the most important part of the act, as it meant the Danish authorities' formal recognition of Iceland as an equal partner in a coalition of two sovereign states.

Therefore, the question whether Iceland was large enough to run its own state was pushed to the side as what the historian C. A. Macartney once called 'national determinism' – the belief the 'every nation must form an independent state' – conquered

Figure 8.2 A view from the centre of Reykjavík, the capital of Iceland, around 1900. Photo by Frederick W. W. Howell (Fiske Icelandic Collection, Cornell University Library, 1923.1.11). © Out of copyright.

Icelandic politics.[22] If we read the Act of Union we can, however, discern some of the problems facing the small nation-states formed during the 'Wilsonian moment' at the end of the First World War.[23] Unlike many of them, Iceland had both well-defined and uncontested territorial boundaries and, by that point, there was a clear understanding that Icelandic was a cultural entity separate from Denmark. Meanwhile, though its ability to exercise its newfound sovereignty in the international arena was severely limited. Thus, Iceland entrusted its former ruling nation to administer its foreign affairs and to police its territorial waters, while the country's only defence strategy was to declare permanent and absolute neutrality.[24] The fact was, as Georg Brandes had pointed out, Iceland had neither an army nor a naval fleet, and it had no intention of creating even a rudimentary military force to defend the country. It seemed that, nationalist bluster aside, the Icelandic nation could talk but not act as a fully sovereign entity.

Smallness in Iceland's foreign policy

Despite Iceland's formal status as an equal partner to Denmark, in practice the former's newfound formal sovereignty was dependent on the latter, as Denmark provided it with political, economic and social shelter.[25] Denmark gave Iceland political shelter by protecting its territorial waters from unwanted foreign incursions; patrolling the waters around the island nation, Danish vessels performed police and rescue duties for foreign and Icelandic fishermen alike.[26] Denmark also graced Iceland with significant political and economic shelter through valuable diplomatic support in the negotiation of trade agreements with other states and by regarding Iceland as a part of the Danish market in order to secure exports from Iceland to other countries, which could, in return, export goods to Denmark. Furthermore, Denmark continued to provide Iceland with an essential form of social shelter in its granting Icelandic students free and open access to Danish universities, along with specialized education and training, though the liberal pre-1918 scholarships proffered by the Danish state had been abolished.[27] Small states' access to innovation, research and development outside their boundaries is essential for the prosperity of such nations.[28]

After the German invasion of Denmark in 1940, relations between Iceland and Denmark were severed. Iceland had no other option than to take full control of its foreign policy, albeit under the watchful eyes of British and American forces during the war years, and to establish its own foreign service. In 1940, the UK occupied Iceland, with the United States taking over the country's defence a year later. At the war's end the Icelandic government rejected the security guarantees proposed by the United States, claiming that the presence of a foreign military in Iceland would jeopardize its sovereignty and requesting that American forces leave the country.

In the postwar period, the United States replaced Denmark as Iceland's primary shelter provider and practically carried Iceland over what can be called the sovereignty threshold, guaranteeing the nation's defence, providing the country with essential diplomatic assistance, and dispensing much-needed economic aid through generous grants made under the aegis of the Marshall Plan.[29] Iceland, moreover, abandoned its neutrality and was a founding member of NATO in 1949. Further underscoring its increasing dependence on the United States, the two countries signed a bilateral defence treaty in 1951.[30]

Iceland's dependence on the United States and its abandonment of neutrality quickly proved controversial. The decision to seek shelter was taken by foreign policy elites who had felt that Iceland needed to compensate for its 'smallness'. Many Icelandic politicians, along with their domestic bases, appealed to the auto-images created in the early twentieth century, in which sovereignty, independence and neutrality were inherently linked. They argued that the country should stay out of the Cold War rather than risk becoming involved in a nuclear war.

Iceland's neutrality policy had been firmly intertwined with its sovereignty and independence, and the country's defencelessness was not regarded as a weakness in public political discourse. On the contrary, during the Cold War many Icelandic politicians, especially those left of centre, viewed the country's smallness as a strength rather than a vulnerability. Iceland would be more secure as a small neutral state, they argued, than as a potential target in a military alliance.[31] Soon Iceland's relationship with the United States, symbolized above all by the US military base at Keflavík Airport, and its membership in NATO became more divisive flashpoints than the economic and social issues that had originally given the Icelandic political parties their respective alignments.[32] But although its two Cold War–era left-wing governments (1956-8 and 1971-4) planned to revoke the defence agreement with the United States, each backtracked from these plans, illustrating the need for the political and economic shelter provided by the superpower. 'The need to achieve shelter was more important than the need to satisfy nationalist sentiments.'[33]

In fact, until the mid-1970s, the United States lent Iceland crucial diplomatic assistance in disputes surrounding the Cod Wars with the UK. Without this help, the Icelandic fisheries industry and its maritime exports would have suffered dramatically.[34] The United States was also instrumental in helping Iceland achieve the financial support, when necessary, of international organizations such as the World Bank, the IMF, and the Organization for European Economic Co-operation (OEEC). Finally, the United States bestowed upon Iceland direct economic assistance, either through direct transfers or via investments as part of its military commitments to the island, which included the building and operation of Reykjavik's international airport, Keflavík, as well as an advanced early warning system for air surveillance and military and civilian infrastructural projects. This assistance became even more important since Iceland's economy was in constant flux, due to increasing difficulties in stabilizing its small domestic market and its growing reliance on a single export: fish.[35]

One can say, however, that Icelandic policymakers did not publicly recognize the volatility of the country's small domestic market in the international economy. Politicians across the political spectrum, except for the Social Democrats (which formed the smallest of the four traditional political parties in Iceland), simply argued that Iceland could – and should – stand on its own and make bilateral trade agreements with its main trading partners; it needed neither join the Common Market nor liberalize its economy.[36] The other traditional political parties, the centre-right Independence Party, the centre-agrarian Progressive Party and the Socialists (currently, forming the Left Green Movement) 'prefer to evade the discourse of smallness or at least insist that it cannot undermine the power and legitimacy of Icelandic home-grown values'.[37]

Not even the United States' decision to close its military base in Iceland seemed to make a dent in the unspoken assumption that Iceland could always count on American assistance. So in 2008, when the country was hit so hard by the international financial crisis that its financial system nearly collapsed, the Icelandic government appealed for US aid to compensate for the effects of a severe economic downturn. Now, however, the United States declined Iceland's request for financial support. For US policymakers, now that the Cold War had ended, Iceland's strategic importance had simply vanished.[38] Their Icelandic counterparts, meanwhile, realized that Iceland could not hope to weather the crisis alone but were reluctant to make this admission openly, lest the limited capacity of the Icelandic Central Bank and the state's coffers in general be seen as an acknowledgement that Iceland was too small to survive.[39] The governing parties were also loathe to admit that Icelandic companies and banks had taken on enormous overseas debts to fuel expansions that the domestic market simply could not support. These so-called *útrásarvíkingar* ('Outvasion Vikings') had used borrowed money to aggressively acquire foreign businesses up until the sudden and unexpected economic crash of October 2008 led to the default of the three largest Icelandic banks. These defaults, in turn, brought down the *króna* and much of the economy, as major Icelandic companies could not pay their debts and went into bankruptcy.

Ironically, in the boom years before the crash, Icelandic commentators and policymakers across the political spectrum had suddenly begun invoking Icelandic smallness, arguing that with smallness came flexibility, informality and the capacity for innovation. These features were regarded as greatly advantageous in the new, globalized economy, bestowing a nimbleness unavailable to larger, lumbering states. The risks taken by the 'Outvasion Vikings' were not seen as dangers but rather hailed as outgrowths of Icelandic independent-mindedness and the 'Viking spirit', and as validation of its ability to go it alone.[40] The globalized economy, argued Minister of Foreign Affairs Halldór Ásgrímsson in 2002, had freed Iceland from the constraints associated with smallness and transformed its diminutive size into an asset.[41] In this rhetoric we can see a clear continuity with the auto-image of Iceland as a country that is fully independent, as well as the heroic culmination of the romantic 'anticolonial utopian' idea, begotten in the nineteenth century, of a small country overcoming obstacles on its way to success and glory.

So when the house of cards collapsed in October 2008, some politicians tried to divert attention away from the domestic causes of the crash, placing the blame squarely on the international financial system instead.[42] The refusal of leading centre-right Icelandic politicians to engage critically with any image of their country where its perceived smallness might have negative effects also fuelled their reluctance to ask for IMF assistance in dealing with the fallout of the crisis. Abiding by the IMF's rules would reveal Iceland's systemic financial-economic weaknesses, it was feared, and revive the old anxieties that the country was really just too small to be truly independent. On 8 October 2008, at the height of the economic crisis, the Icelandic Central Bank and the prime minister, desperate for a way out of the country's dire straits, even strongly hinted that they would turn away from the West by asking, rhetorically, 'Why shouldn't Iceland call on the Russians if they could help?'[43] The Russian loan offer led nowhere, but the interesting fact remains that Icelandic policymakers were willing to entertain the possibility of a Russian rescue package rather than accepting support from the IMF – apparently, Russian 'shelter' befitted a proudly independent state more than being beholden to international organizations. Ultimately, their request for financial support denied by the United States, and the Russian loan out of the picture, Iceland turned to the EU for assistance. However, the EU also declined Iceland's request for aid, citing the fact that Iceland was not a member state: its membership in the European Economic Area (EEA) and Schengen did not equate to formal EU membership.

Six months after the economic crash, which had caused momentous economic and political impact, voters delivered a crushing verdict on the traditional political parties deemed responsible for the mishandling of the ensuing crisis. The country's very first left-wing government, consisting of the Social Democratic Alliance and the more orthodox Left Green Movement, applied for Icelandic membership in the EU, representing a major turnaround in the country's international politics.

The initiative to apply for EU membership came from the traditionally pro-European Social Democrats, who had earlier successfully advocated for Iceland's entrance into EFTA and EEA. But joining the EU went significantly further than membership in these two bodies; it meant delegating sovereignty to EU institutions, albeit in return for representation within them. The main Social Democrat argument for membership was that the 2008 crisis had proved that Iceland was simply too small to continue as it had been. The country needed to secure the economic shelter provided by the EU and its institutions to its member states, mainly the European Central bank as a lender of last resort.[44] The notion that the European countries are individually too small but together add up to something great is an idea shared all over the continent – especially by those, like the citizens of the Benelux countries, who consider their own member state to be small – but this position was, for a long time, not widely shared in Iceland outside Social Democratic circles.[45]

The other traditional political parties (the Conservatives, the Progressives and the Left Greens) remained united in their Euroscepticism. Their auto-image of Iceland, informed by both unrepentant nationalism and exceptionalism, could not abide EU membership, which they felt would subsume Icelandic interests and morals within larger and muddier wholes.[46] The decision to start the EU accession process narrowly passed in the Icelandic parliament in July 2009. The Left Greens continued to oppose EU membership but reluctantly accepted the EU application in order to secure a seat in government and create the first left-wing government in Iceland. The main argument put forth by opponents of the membership application was that Iceland should not transfer power to EU institutions. Iceland had always, they argued, stood on its own in the international system and, as such, had been victorious in international disputes without external assistance, including the Cod Wars.[47] Academic findings, however, indicate the opposite.[48] Ironically, opponents of EU membership also argued that Iceland would be too small to be able to defend its interests within the Union. For that reason, prominent members of the centre-right in Iceland also opposed Iceland's candidacy for the United Nation Security Council (UNSC) for the 2009–10 term.[49]

In the 2013 parliamentary elections, voters returned an anti-EU, nationalist majority to the Alþingi, and the traditional governing parties once again took up the reins of government. They halted the EU accession process, and thereafter seemed to return to the *status quo ante*: domestically, Iceland was portrayed as large enough to manage its own affairs, while behind the scenes, Icelandic politicians continued to seek arrangements with larger states and inter- and supranational organizations in order to compensate for what they perceived as their country's smallness and associated vulnerability. They also argued that Iceland's relative rapid economic recovery, as well as the Euro crisis that badly hit some small EU member states, supported their traditional rhetoric and policy: Iceland, they insisted, could succeed on its own, and joining the Union would have devastating consequences for the nation.[50]

Since American aid was diminished and the EU accession project was halted, Iceland has continued to seek shelter through its relations with larger nations. Its government has made civil security agreements – mainly concerning its territorial waters – with the UK, Denmark, Norway and Canada. The aim of these agreements is to exchange information, discuss common security concerns and plan various projects regarding training and military exercises. Furthermore, airspace surveillance arrangements have been made with various NATO member states, including France, Germany and the UK, as well as the non-NATO Nordic states Sweden and Finland, that allow for the temporary presence of their jet fighters in the country. Alongside its pursuit of new bilateral agreements, Iceland has sought to strengthen its ties with

NATO in an effort to shore up the organization's provision of shelter to the country. Central to achieving this aim is its participation in the NATO Infrastructure Fund as well as an ongoing commitment to its international operations. The release of the country's first-ever defence budget, as well as its offer to cover all substantial costs for military exercises in the region, further emphasizes that Iceland is increasing its own contribution to sustain its political shelter.[51] Additionally, Iceland has put greater emphasis on Nordic cooperation in recent years than before, and Nordic norms and values have also become more visible in Iceland's foreign policy. Thus, the country closely cooperates with the Nordic states in international organizations, and a recently developed security collaboration amongst the Nordic states has added a new and important layer of shelter-related components to Iceland's relations with its closest neighbouring states.[52]

The Icelandic government has also been looking to non-traditional sources for support – namely China. In the aftermath of the crash, when it had become clear that none of Iceland's long-term allies were willing to provide financial assistance, the Icelandic government approached China and requested assistance in its time of need. In 2010, the Icelandic Central Bank and the Central Bank of China made a currency-swap agreement. The agreement may not have been financially important, but it increased Iceland's much-needed credibility at the time and was a statement of trust. This agreement was renewed in 2013 and again in 2016. Moreover, China gave unbroken support to Iceland's attempt to obtain a rescue package from the IMF at the same time when Iceland's European allies blocked IMF assistance for over a year. According to the Chinese prime minister, Wen Jiabao, China took a deliberate decision to help Iceland at the time of the crash.[53] These events have led to close cooperation between the countries, according to Iceland's former president, Ólafur Ragnar Grímsson. First, Iceland and China signed a memorandum of understanding concerning closer collaboration and more extensive business relations at the same time they signed the currency-swap agreement. Second, in 2013, Iceland became the first European country to sign a free-trade agreement with China. The foreign minister at the time described the document as the most important agreement since Iceland became part of the internal market of the EU in the mid-1990s. Third, Iceland and China have also signed several other important cooperation agreements, including on geothermal energy, and the countries work closely together on Arctic affairs.[54]

Interestingly, Icelandic policymakers have an easier time advocating for closer cooperation with China than for membership in supranational organizations such as the EU. Centre-right rhetoric asserts that Iceland is fully in charge of its bilateral relations with China but, as a member of the European project, the country would lose its ability to operate freely. This stance also reflects how political parties' rhetoric on Icelandic 'smallness' often reflects their political position, that is, whether they are in government or in the opposition in parliament. Parties in opposition, for example, frequently demand an end to Iceland's membership in NATO and the EEA on the basis that joining a military organization for defence purposes or becoming a part of a larger economic association jeopardizes or even betrays the hard-fought sovereignty secured in 1918. They paint an image of Iceland positing that the country has grown to be 'large enough' to stand outside of alliances committed to ensuring its military or economic security. Once in government, these same parties often quietly drop those demands – while taking pragmatic action. Such behaviour limits serious political debate about Iceland's political future and about its identity, role and mission in a globalizing world.

Most recently, prominent Icelandic politicians have welcomed the UK's exit from the EU, claiming that it provides significant opportunities for Iceland. The then foreign minister, Guðlaugur Þór Þórðarson, hoped that the UK, as the fifth largest economy in the world, would become a European leader in free trade in its post-Brexit incarnation. Iceland in turn might be allowed – being the UK's neighbour and an established trade partner – to utilize the opportunity and engage in free-trade relations worldwide, thus strengthening the Icelandic economy.[55] In addition, Iceland and the UK have already strengthened their security and defence ties. Thus Iceland's policymakers continue in practice to search for a shelter provider (or providers) in order to compensate for its smallness, but do so without making references to the country's limitations in the public discourse.

Conclusion

To summarize, the withdrawal of American military forces from Iceland and the 2008 economic crash exposed fundamental challenges which have occupied Iceland's policymakers from the foundation of the state in 1918. These two events proved once again to the political elite that Iceland, as a small state, needs the economic and political shelter provided by larger states and international organizations. This view has always been a cornerstone of Icelandic foreign policy, as Iceland's political leaders have largely agreed on the importance of seeking closer engagement with Iceland's larger neighbouring states such as the United States and the Nordic states. Nonetheless, politicians have been very reluctant to address Iceland's smallness and its associated vulnerability in their search for shelter providers. One reason is because the shelter-seeking behaviour of Icelandic governments has always conflicted with the nationalist discourse on Iceland's sovereignty and independence, which has focused on the importance of full national self-determination for the economic and cultural welfare of the Icelandic nation. Hence, governments continue their shelter-seeking behaviour without referring explicitly to Iceland's smallness in relation to the small domestic market and the country's limited defence capacity. There has only been one exception to this pattern. Drawing a lesson from the economic crash, Europhiles in Iceland have explicitly adopted the notion that Iceland must address its smallness by seeking the economic and political shelter provided by the EU. According to their rhetoric, Iceland cannot afford to go it alone, least of all if it desires an active role in the globalized economy.[56] The Europhiles' rhetoric, however, is firmly rejected by the vast majority of politicians across the Icelandic political landscape. The Eurosceptic majority continues to oppose formal power-sharing with other European states within the Union; they claim that Iceland, as a small state, would not be able to defend its interests and have a say within the EU. The current government, a Left-Right coalition government composed of the Independence Party, the Progressive Party and the Left Green Movement, advocates an independent, flexible, self-reliant and market-oriented approach to prosperity. The coalition parties actively avoid mentioning Iceland's 'smallness' when discussing its present challenges, since doing so might highlight the limits of its self-sufficiency and the lack of an alternative to a pro-European approach.[57] Following the traditional policy approach of Icelandic governments, the current government continues to try to compensate for diminishing American protection through a search for economic and political shelter provided by other important international actors.

Notes

1. Iceland had 364,000 inhabitants on 1 January 2020; Statistics Iceland, 'Population, Key Figures 1703–2020', https://statice.is/statistics/population/inhabitants/overview/. Last accessed 18 May 2020.
2. See e.g. Thorhallsson, *Small States and Shelter Theory*.
3. Leerssen, 'Viral Nationalism: Romantic Intellectuals on the Move in Nineteenth-Century Europe'; Leerssen, *National Thought in Europe*.
4. Hálfdanarson, 'Severing the Ties – Iceland's Journey from a Union with Denmark to a Nation-State'.
5. Mill, *Considerations*, 289.
6. Leerssen, *National Thought in Europe*, 125.
7. Leerssen, 101.
8. Mill, *Considerations*, 293–5.
9. Hobsbawm, *Nations and Nationalism*, 31–2.
10. Hálfdanarson and Thisted, 'The Specter of an Empire', 113–16.
11. Bull and Landquist, *Georg og Edv. Brandes*, 412–14.
12. Kaarsted, *Ministermødeprotokol 1916–1918*, 215.
13. This was a common claim in the Danish media; see for example 'Møde Om Island'.
14. White, *Metahistory*, 9.
15. Scott, *Conscripts of Modernity*, 7.
16. Hálfdanarson, 'Icelandic Modernity'.
17. *Lögrjetta* 11 April 1908, Guðmundur Björnsson, 'Framtíð Íslands', 57.
18. *Reykjavík* 27 October 1906, 'Betri er krókur and kelda', 189.
19. Gunnar Þór Bjarnason, *Upp með fánann!*
20. See for example *Ísafold* 5 September 1908, 'Opnar það ekki augun á öllum', 217.
21. 'Dansk-Íslensk Sambandslög'.
22. Macartney, *National States and National Minorities*, 100.
23. Manela, *The Wilsonian Moment*.
24. See 'Dansk-Íslensk Sambandslög', clauses 7 and 19.
25. Thorhallsson, *Iceland's Shelter-Seeking Behaviour: From Settlement to Republic*.
26. Icelandic Coast Guard, 'Saga LHG', www.lhg.is/sagan/. Last accessed 25 May 2017.
27. Pétur J. Thorsteinsson, *Utanríkisþjónusta Íslands og utanríkismál*, 101–14; Hálfdanarson, 'Embættismannaskólinn 1911–1961', 99–100, 179, 208–9.
28. Mokyr, 'Cardwell's Law and the Political Economy of Technological Progress'.
29. Thorhallsson et al., 'Shelter during the American Period'.
30. Ingimundarson, *Í eldlínu kalda stríðsins*.
31. Ingimundarson.

32 Hardarson and Kristinsson, 'The Icelandic Parliamentary Election of 1987'.
33 Thorhallsson et al., 'Shelter during the American Period', 73.
34 Jóhannesson, *Troubled Waters*, 58, 116–18; Ingimundarson, *I eldlínu kalda stríðsins*; Jóhannesson, 'How "Cod War" Came: The Origins of the Anglo-Icelandic Fisheries Dispute, 1958–61', 77:198 (2004) 459, 543–74.
35 Jakob F. Ásgeirsson, *Þjóð í hafti*.
36 Thorhallsson, 'European Integration'.
37 Thorhallsson and Bailes, 'Small States'.
38 US Government Accountability Office, 'Federal Reserve System: Opportunities Exist to Strengthen Policies and Processes for Managing Emergency Assistance', Report to Congressional Addressees, July 2011, www.gao.gov/assets/330/321506.pdf. Last accessed 24 March 2011; Central Bank of Iceland, 'Norrænir seðlabankar framlengja gjaldmiðlaskiptasamninga', 20 November 2008, https://www.sedlabanki.is/utgefid-efni/frettir-og-tilkynningar/frettasafn/frett/2008/11/20/Norraenir-sedlabankar-framlengja-gjaldmidlaskiptasamninga/. Last accessed 24 May 2020.
39 Thorhallsson, 'The Icelandic Economic Collapse: How to Overcome Constraints Associated with Smallness?'
40 See President Ólafur Ragnar Grímsson's lecture, 'Icelandic Ventures, presented at the Icelandic Historians' Society, 10 January 2006, http://wayback.vefsafn.is/wayback/20061114195222/http://www.forseti.is/media/files/06.01.10.Sagnfrfel.utras.enska.pdf. Last Accessed 14 May 2020.
41 Halldór Ásgrímsson, 'Alþjóðavæðing' ('globalization'). Speech at the Trade Council of Iceland. 8 May 2002, www.utanrikisraduneyti.is/frettaefni/raedurHA/nr/1751. Accessed 6 June 2013.
42 Alþingi, 'Report of the Special Investigation Commission'. Chapter 21, 'Causes of the Collapse of the Icelandic Banks – Responsibility, Mistakes and Negligence', https://www.rna.is/media/skjol/RNAvefurKafli21Enska.pdf. Last accessed 24 May 2020; see also Hannes Hólmsteinn Gissurarson, 'The 2008 Icelandic Bank Collapse: Foreign Factors. A Report for the Ministry of Finance and Economic Affairs', 19 September 2018, https://www.stjornarradid.is/lisalib/getfile.aspx?itemid=29cca5ac-c0c6-11e8-942c-005056bc530c. Last accessed 24 May 2020.
43 US Embassy in Reykjavik, 'Icelandic Economics Crisis, Time for USG to Get Involved?' October 2008, https://www.wikileaks.org/plusd/cables/08REYKJAVIK225_a.html. Last accessed 24 March 2018.
44 *Morgunblaðið* 12 October 2010, Össur Skarphéðinsson, 'Framtíðin og frelsið til að velja', 17; Ingibjörg Sólrún Gísladóttir, 'Skýrsla Ingibjargar Sólrúnar Gísladóttur utanríkisráðherra um utanríkis- og alþjóðamál', Report by the Minister of Foreign Affairs to Alþingi, 8 January 2008, http://www.utanrikisraduneyti.is/media/Skyrslur/Skyrslan.pdf. 1 June 2013. Last accessed 6 July 2020.
45 Thorhallsson and Bailes, 'Small States', 126.
46 Thorhallsson and Bailes, 126.
47 For instance, see Thorhallsson, 'European Integration'.
48 For instance, see Jóhannesson, *Troubled Waters*.
49 Thorhallsson, 'Small States in the UN Security Council: Means of Influence?'
50 For instance, see Thorhallsson, 'European Integration'.
51 Thorhallsson et al., 'Shelter during the American Period', 78–9.
52 Thorhallsson, 'Nordicness as a Shelter: The Case of Iceland'.
53 *Evrópuvaktin* 13 September 2010, 'Kínverjar vilja færa tengslin við Ísland á hærra stig', www.evropuvaktin.is/frettir/16262/. Last accessed 14 May 2020.

54 Thorhallsson and Steinsson, 'European Integration'.
55 *Vísir* 11 January 2017, 'Nýr utanríkisráðherra sér tækifæri í útgöngu Breta úr ESB', https://www.visir.is/g/20171950703d. Last accessed 14 December 2021.
56 Össur Skarphéðinsson, *Utanríkis- og alþjóðamál* (Althingi 14 May 2010), www.althingi.is/altext/138/s/pdf/1070.pdf; Össur Skarphéðinsson *Utanríkis- og alþjóðamál* (Althingi 14 May 2010), www.althingi.is/altext/139/s/pdf/1416.pdf. Last accessed 3 June 2020.
57 Thorhallsson and Bailes, 'Small States', 126.

9

Great Britain and Little Ireland. Reimagining British and Irish relations in BIPA, Brexit and beyond

Sara Dybris McQuaid

Introduction

The withdrawal of the UK from the European Union (Brexit) has exposed anew an ongoing crisis of 'Britishness' and heralded an unwelcome return of the 'Irish Question' in the British body politic. At the centre of both these challenges are increasingly strained relationships amongst territorial, national and political communities across the two islands, driven by asymmetrical sizes, powers and outlooks. Here, the relative dominance of England over the smaller partners of the UK and the neighbouring country of Ireland is a specific source of grievance in the political economy of the Isles.

Current evidence of this asymmetrical relationship lies in the withdrawal of the entire UK, as a result of the overall dominant electoral force in England voting to leave the EU even though sizable territorial majorities in Scotland and Northern Ireland voted to remain. At the same time, the majority decision to leave the EU has serious implications for Ireland as a whole, not least because of the ongoing peace process in Northern Ireland, which critically rests on British and Irish bilateral cooperation and integration being nested within European integration. The Brexit referendum managed to raise and re-awaken all hues of nationalism in the Isles and has paved the way for shape-shifting constitutional discourses of independence and unification all-round. In this chapter, I examine these relations and processes through the lens of smallness, understood not as a distinct quality of given entities but as a relative and contextual political position, produced in particular institutional structures which themselves are product of the intertwined and sometimes strained relations and histories in the Isles.

Amidst the unfolding series of Brexit crises, parliamentarians from across the UK and Ireland have continued to meet twice a year to discuss the shifting shapes of British-Irish relations. These specific dialogues have taken place under the aegis of a small, non-legislative, transnational institution, which is rarely mentioned or even noticed in public debates: the British Irish Parliamentary Assembly – or simply, BIPA. This institution's particular significance lies in the unique shared political space it provides for democratically elected politicians across Britain and Ireland, who would have otherwise remained isolated in their respective national parliaments and assemblies. BIPA first and foremost draws members from one sovereign state widely considered small (Ireland) and another sovereign union state that is considered to be much larger (UK).[1] However, since 2001 it has also included members from the minor devolved parliaments and assemblies in Scotland, Northern Ireland and Wales, as well as administrations in the Channel Islands. Importantly, since the UK's formal withdrawal from the European Union in 2020, BIPA is now the only parliamentary site of British-Irish association, and given the constitutional stresses in the UK it might very well become a key arena for future discussions amongst former members of the UK. Moreover, it is an institution perhaps uniquely suited to give expression to the fluidity of political communities, nations and states of various sizes across Britain and Ireland and, as such, it is a prime site for studying discourses and hierarchies of smallness.

As a whole, this book conceptualizes different relational dynamics of smallness. In this chapter, I am particularly interested in investigating the 'shifting shapes of smallness' and the images that accompany such discourses of 'becoming', as they are articulated and reformed in a *regional* system of states and nations across the British Isles and as they have weathered the eruptive context of Brexit. Brexit is, of course, an event with enormous consequences for debates on the relative 'size' of Britain, its constituent nations, and Ireland. Therefore, this examination also focuses on how smallness is conceptualized to reposition the constituent parts of the UK in relation to one another, to the two parts of Ireland and to the EU. In doing so, it is inspired by the transnational Pocockian idea of studying the several peoples, nations and histories of Britain and Ireland (as geographic entities) both as they are shaped in interaction with one another and as they appear when contextualized by one another.[2] For in both historical and contemporary terms, 'shape-shifting' has been a pervasive political dynamic across the UK and Ireland. The UK is of course founded on movements of accession (i.e. the Act of Union between England and Scotland in 1707 and between the UK of Great Britain and Ireland in 1801) and was later reshaped by nationalist and anti-colonialist movements of secession (e.g. Irish independence in 1922, wider imperial retreat and the recent conflict in Northern Ireland, and the growing support for Scottish independence). Since the rise of nationalist politics in the late 1960s and the accession of the UK and Ireland to the European Community in 1973, political relationships and questions of size, self-determination and sovereignty have been navigated in the tensions emerging from devolving more power to the sub-national level in Northern Ireland, Scotland and Wales at the same time as transferring more power to the supranational European level.

Engaging BIPA as the site of analysis allows the examination of how size and the meaning-making of 'small' continues to be an ongoing negotiation in the volatile political economy created by Brexit, but also how institutional design can work to create a more level playing field amongst highly asymmetric powers and positions. BIPA is a particularly useful prism to study such political positioning because the institution both refracts overlapping and competing alliances amongst communities, nations and states (all with different powers, legal statuses, international obligations and even constitutional designs for the future) and provides a shared space to articulate auto- and hetero-images that accompany, reflect and help shape these positionings.[3]

Key in this regard is notions about size which is, per this volume's central thesis, both a relative and a perspectival term. You are small or large relative to other entities, just as apparent size is a product of perspective (or distance/location). In the complex political context of the Isles and the chaotic force of Brexit, particular political actors may articulate their smallness in multiple and shifting ways relative to other actors and institutional structures. Moreover, in the British-Irish context we are working with complex layerings of selves and others, not just in having a British identity 'superimposed' onto the national identities of English, Scottish, Welsh and Northern Irish, but also in the historical constructions of Anglo-Ireland, Anglo-Scotland and Anglo-Wales and in the contemporary constitutional recognition of people in Northern Ireland as both British and Irish. Moreover, the UK's decision to leave the EU has exacerbated certain differences as seen in the rise of English nationalism, calls for a second independence referendum in Scotland (the first was in 2014), and re-articulated mainstream political ambitions to bring about a united Ireland.

The chapter will open with a brief introduction to the kind of political arena BIPA is and the nature of exchanges that have taken place there since 1990. Drawing primarily on the transcripts of the plenary sessions, which are held two times a year, I will examine the period from 2016 to 2019 in order to capture Brexit's impact in redistributing power relations and discourses across the Isles. The chapter then turns to the idea of smallness as a political construct.[4] Specifically, I examine how BIPA members have articulated references to smallness in debates after Brexit so as to reshape relationships across the Isles within a 'politics of smallness'. In the following, I pursue these discussions of what it means to be small and how to navigate tensions between influence and autonomy, nationalism and cosmopolitanism, across three main categories: (1) small as a driver of integration across the isles (internal interdependence); (2) small as a motor for the 'Celtic Fringe' to unhinge England; and (3) small as an argument for pursuing independence only through international frameworks (external interdependence). The boundaries of these categories are quite permeable: arguments for integration might be reserved to the two parts of Ireland and thus entail the disintegration of the UK. Similarly, arguments for interdependence beyond the Isles might be used to pursue a first instance of independence, as in the case of Scotland. The final section sizes up the current state of British-Irish relations and returns to the pervasive Questions – 'Irish' and 'British' – which also reveals a pressing 'English Question' in which England is forced to come to terms with its own smallness.

The British Irish Parliamentary Assembly: 'This little institution'

It seems to me that it [BIPA] is the only body that brings parliamentarians together from Ireland, the United Kingdom, the dependencies and the devolved Administrations, but this body will take on a much greater role post-Brexit than it has at the moment.
        The Lord Murphy (BIPA 55th plenary, 15-17 October 2017, 134)

During the 1980s and 1990s the British and Irish governments took steps to introduce a bilateral approach to conflict resolution in Northern Ireland. In this context, a number of Anglo-Irish and British-Irish institutions were set up to promote macro-regional cooperation. The institutionalization ranged from the highest level of intergovernmental cooperation (the British-Irish Intergovernmental Conference, 1985, 1998) down through the ministerial level (the British Irish Council, 1998) and the parliamentary level (BIPA, 1990), as well as the formalizations of existing forms of civil society engagement. These vertical and horizontal political infrastructures were aimed at improving and giving institutional recognition to British-Irish relations and thus at undergirding the peace process in Northern Ireland. During the twentieth century, it had become more and more evident that the 'three solitudes' (Paul Arthur) which had formed around administrations in Belfast, Dublin and London following Irish independence and partition in 1920–1 had to be broken in order to bridge political cultures and build mutual trust.[5] These joint institutions have helped transform and frame British-Irish relations far beyond the main problem they were conceived to address, as the scope of dialogue and cooperation has extended to include newly emerging constitutional and cultural debates.[6]

BIPA, established in 1990, became the first instalment of this brand of zealous institution-making.[7] Its inaugural meeting, the first joint assembly of British and Irish parliamentarians in seventy years, provided a symbolic and public display of cooperation and conflict resolution. Since 2001 BIPA has brought together not just parliamentarians from the two sovereign governments of the UK and the Republic of Ireland (each bringing twenty-five members) but also representatives from the devolved local parliament and assemblies in Scotland, Wales and Northern Ireland (each with five members) and the Crown Dependencies in Jersey, Guernsey and the Isle of Man (each with one member). Therefore, BIPA is itself a significant shape-shifter in the sense that it reconfigures proportional representation and political power. Despite their relative sizes on other scales, in BIPA Ireland is thus equal to the UK and superior to Scotland. Here, the size of representation becomes a question of relative powers (sovereignty, devolution, dependence) rather than relative populations. I will return to how this impacts capacity and capability in terms of participation, debates and relationships.

BIPA's plenary sessions take place twice a year, in a location somewhere in 'The Isles'. The sessions usually consist of a couple of themed headline presentations by invited dignitaries and ministers from the sovereign governments, followed by debates and progress reports from BIPA's subcommittees: sovereign matters; European affairs; economic matters; and environmental and social matters. The wide scope of the committee work in Brexit's aftermath can be gauged from the reports presented in the October 2017 assembly: 'Trade and the border in the context of Brexit'; 'British/Irish relations post-Brexit'; 'Implications of Brexit on the agri-food sector'; 'Cross-jurisdictional aspects of abortion practice'.[8]

The plenary sessions are always infused with a sense of local history and a transnational perspective. For example, at the 2017 plenary in Liverpool, the parliamentarians heard a presentation from a local historian on the Irish community in Britain, then discussed the common ancestry and common historical experiences of Welsh and Irish migrant labour, and how their different allegiances to the Labour and the Liberal parties, respectively, had shaped their experiences of integration in Liverpool. These reflections on a shared past led onto presentations from policy research institutes and business schools for a discussion of Brexit's implications for the economies of Britain and Ireland in the present.[9] As this example begins to illustrate, a key motif in BIPA's efforts is to link the different parts of the Isles together, not just by moving from the local to the transnational level but also by moving up and down history, thus implicating otherwise more separate narratives in one another and creating a sense of common purpose in addressing issues of joint concern.

Part of what enables these transnational dialogues is precisely the redistribution of parliamentary representation (equalizing the UK and Ireland and including sub-national parliamentary representation), which to a certain extent 'short-circuits' the otherwise dominant power and presence of England to make room for more hybrid interests. In 1975, J.G.A. Pocock argued that it was difficult to write a British history of increasing English domination in other than English terms.[10] However, precisely because the size of England is indirectly reduced through the levelling of UK representation, BIPA offers a site where it becomes possible to study transnational exchanges and patterns of engagement beyond purely English terms. This has particular effects, not only for the volume at which different participants can speak but also for the issues that can take centre stage. Themes that resonate in the round and are the result of centuries of co-mingling are privileged, and the members can relate to one another on a more direct and equal footing.

At the same time, it is important to note that England, in both historical and contemporary terms, remains *a very* significant other for the creation of nationalist hetero- and auto-images in Northern Ireland, Ireland, Scotland and Wales.[11] Conversely, England's *British* other has as often been France, Germany and now arguably the EU.[12] The politics of imaging are correspondingly asymmetrical, and particular discourses and imagologies emerge from these asymmetries of power and populations. They appear in the BIPA proceedings in interesting ways for discussing the shifting shapes of small.

Smallness as a driver of integration

'Ní dhéanfaidh aon ní buillí ag tarraingt le chéile'. It means: 'Nothing beats pulling together'.
John McGrane, Director General of the British Irish Chamber of Commerce
(BIPA 52nd plenary, 4-5 July 2016, 77)

Smallness is often invoked by BIPA members as a motor driving both cooperation and integration, with different political implications. It is commonly said that it is because the nations are small that they must cooperate, but by the same token their cooperation is predicated on a continual articulation of smallness. In BIPA, cooperation is mostly seen as inherently valuable, particularly when driven by pragmatic concerns. Integration, by contrast, can be a bit more tricky in a geography where some nations have seceded (Ireland from the UK), been partitioned (Ireland), may aim for further political separation (Scotland) or have contested futures (Northern Ireland). In this context, perimeters of sovereignty and self-determination can be guarded jealously even when there is also a shared sense of practical reasoning and emotional belonging. At the same time, the deep historical and accelerating exchanges across the islands propels politicians to develop policies that accommodate the mobile practices and co-mingled identities of their constituents. As one member puts it: 'As politicians, we owe it to our citizens to reflect the type of lives that they lead. That is why BIPA is so important because it is reflecting all those citizens in the various parts and it is doing it well.'[13]

One important aspect of BIPA's debates, which relays smallness directly to integration, is concerned with economic cooperation. Small businesses make up a large part of the economy on the island of Ireland and of the 'all-Ireland' economy which has developed as part of the European single market. It makes business sense to join forces in small peripheral economies, but in the Irish case there is also an inherently political element to arguing for economic integration between the North and South of Ireland. Since the implementation of the European Single Market in 1993 and the paramilitary ceasefires in 1994, successive EU programmes (the UK-Northern Ireland Peace Programme (PEACE I-IV) and the Interregional Community Initiative (INTERREG)) have combined funding for economic integration and sociocultural peacebuilding to reconstruct relationships across the border region of Ireland. The UK Brexit promise to redraw borders and markets thus undermines the EU premise of promoting trade and peace together. Social Democratic and Labour Party MP Mark Durkan, representing the border constituency Foyle, told BIPA in 2016 that '[b]usinesses in my constituency are concerned about the degree to which all sorts of complicated borderism could flow from a situation where Northern Ireland, as part of the UK, is out of the EU and the South is in the EU'.[14]

Health is another sector in which 'being small' is used to pave the way for cooperation and integration in Ireland. In a presentation at BIPA in 2018, the Northern Ireland Commissioner for Children and Young People, Ms Koualla Yiasouma, discussed the integration of social care on the Island. 'Because the island of Ireland is quite small, we have small island networks, particularly involving paediatric and cardiac care, and that is incredibly important where the surgery is now being done in Dublin and some of the outpatient work is being done in Belfast.'[15] Moving to the field of education, she laid out how many children crossed the border to go to school every day and how important it was for them to be able to live across the border and, not least, to have their qualifications recognized across jurisdictions. Her address to BIPA ended up hammering home that '[y]oung people wanted to send that clear message. They do not see their future on the borders either north, south, east or west. They see it beyond them'.[16]

The functionalist integration *and* enlargement of the all-Irish socioeconomic territory is fuelled by considerations of limited size and has been enabled by wider European cooperation. In BIPA debates, a similar argument about the imperatives of smallness is conceived in relation to East-West integration. As we will see, both types of arguments work to reposition and reconceptualize nations and states across the Isles and inside the European Union.

Embracing smallness in the 'Celtic Periphery'

I think the future for relations between Ireland and Scotland is very positive and fruitful, because there is now a Scottish Government who our Ministers can deal with. Irish Ministers regularly go to Scotland and Scottish Ministers come to Ireland, because we recognize the things we have in common and we want to develop them for the future.

Willie Coffey, Member of the Scottish Parliament (MSP)
(BIPA 53rd plenary, 27-29 November 2016, 76)

In the cases of both businesses and services, smallness is introduced as a rationale for integration. However, there are overlapping ideas about how exactly to configure 'The Isles' as one shared space. As the quote above indicates, devolution in the UK has gone far beyond changing the political relations amongst Scotland, Wales, Northern Ireland and the centre of power in the UK parliament. Importantly, devolution has also enabled the establishment of discrete links between the small states and nations in the Isles. In 1998, Ireland opened a Consulate General in Edinburgh and Cardiff with the objectives of developing economic links and identifying common interests in the EU. Although the consulate in Cardiff was closed in 2009 amidst the financial crisis, it reopened on 23 June 2019 (exactly three years after the referendum to leave the EU) with the aim of maintaining 'strong economic links with Wales whatever the outcome of Brexit'.[17] These links also build on a succession of Ireland-Wales EU INTERREG programmes in place from 1994 to 2020.[18] Part of the integrationist approach seems to be about the small nations/states mobilizing to short-circuit England as the main power supplier in the political economy. For Scotland and Northern Ireland, which voted to remain in the EU, manoeuvring around England's majority decision makes sense in the context of Brexit.

At the BIPA session in July 2016 a panel of tourism experts discussed 'Tourism and Interconnectivity between the Two Islands' in light of Brexit.[19] Parliamentarians from Scotland and Wales repeatedly forwarded the idea of marketing a 'Celtic Experience' to tourists, that is, to a 'Celtic Fringe' which excludes England. One BIPA member suggested an initiative to 'open up the Celtic arc that is Scotland, Northern Ireland, the Republic of Ireland and Wales, and to produce joint itineraries for visitors from other markets who can enjoy thoroughly the shared experience of our great culture, our sports, our music, our brilliant food and our service offerings as well'.[20] The image of a 'Celtic Fringe' at once draws on and transcends theories about asymmetrical developments in the 'core and periphery' of modern British society.[21] Here, despite increasing interactions brought on by industrialization and expanded infrastructure, cultural differences have not ceased to be socioeconomically meaningful. Being small and remote becomes a badge of authenticity, which is remarkable and marketable. 'Celtic' is also used to express a particular form of political solidarity shared by the smaller nations of the British Isles when they band together. This connection becomes apparent in the phrase 'the diplomatic [Celtic] corridor', exemplified by the Irish representations in Edinburgh and Cardiff introduced above and the special representations of Scotland and Wales through the British Embassy in Dublin. Indeed,

Figure 9.1 EU Council staff members remove the United Kingdom's flag from the European Council building in Brussels on Brexit Day, 31 January 2020 (Getty Images 1197807625). Photo by Olivier Hoslet. © Getty Images.

the Irish consulate in Edinburgh and the Scottish and Welsh representations in Ireland are often referred to as sites of gestation for such joint ventures.

At the first plenary after the referendum in 2016, the Sinn Féin Teachta Dála (TD)[22] Aengus o Snodaigh proposed a radical territorial solution to solve the democratic problem created by England and Wales voting to leave and Scotland and Northern Ireland voting to remain in the EU:

> Obviously, from my point of view as a Republican, the logic for those in the North who voted to remain should be to campaign for a united Ireland. If they wish to remain in the EU, the quickest and easiest way to do so would be to join with us. The same could be said for Scotland, and we might have the resurrection of the Dalriada Kingdom of many moons ago. If Scotland votes for independence, as it should, it will have to apply to the EU, with everything that that entails. Maybe a quick route would be to join with us, and the same goes, as I said, for the North.

Such a mischievous intervention was, of course, partly made in jest, but it contains the narrative of older alliances and allegiances existing long before the UK came into being (albeit Gaelic rather than Celtic solidarities in this instance). It draws attention to how the size and shapes of political domains have fluctuated in history and may be made to do so again.

Another way of reconfiguring relations within the British Isles – next to, of course, those of a United Ireland – is to promote the continuity of current British-Irish relations post-Brexit by moving Ireland closer to, rather than away from, Britain and England. In the Irish *Seanad*, on 21 June 2016, Senator Frank Feighan suggested that the debate on the Brexit referendum presented the perfect opportunity for the Republic of Ireland to re-evaluate its relationship with its closest neighbour and rejoin the Commonwealth (which it officially left in 1949 upon becoming a republic). The idea that Ireland should contemplate returning to the Commonwealth has regularly been trotted out as part of the negotiation of British-Irish relations in the context of conflict resolution in Northern Ireland. In 1998, the year of the peace agreement, Taoiseach Bertie Ahern suggested that Ireland should have a debate on rejoining the Commonwealth.[23] Leaving the commonwealth was considered a key act of Irish self-determination in 1949, whereas rejoining it now is construed as a recognition of British-Irish interdependence, which might go some ways towards accommodating unionist national and political identities in a potential united Ireland of the future. This debate has also been transplanted to BIPA, where longstanding member Senator Feighan has brought up the question several times. At the plenary in July 2016 he was seconded by Lord Bew, who argued that 'the Commonwealth is an institution that brings more soft power to Ireland [and] that there would be greater respect for Ireland's material interests in the event that it seriously reconsidered rejoining the Commonwealth'. Reactions to these suggestions in BIPA are stratified: unionists in Northern Ireland and conservatives in Scotland note it with interest, Irish nationalists dismiss it as a distraction.[24]

Within BIPA, these discussions aimed at reconfiguring the shape and size of territories and spheres of influence in the Isles are not taken in national isolation. Rather, they can avail themselves of a broad spectrum of national political voices and positions. Imagining the future as a return to the Kingdom of Dalriada or as a re-entry into a reconstructed commonwealth both entail coming together in different constellations consisting of complicated relationships between unionist and nationalist selves and others. Further, the debates sketched here illustrate the conceptualization of independence as a form of broader interdependence, to which I now turn.

Small as a vehicle for interdependence

My immediate reaction to the Brexit vote, to use the Latin phrase, was this: festina lente *– hasten slowly. In all of this, there needs to be huge respect for each other. We are far too small island nations to be talking about independence. I believe that we should be talking around the whole issue of interdependence.*
Declan Breathnach, TD for Fianna Fáil (BIPA 52nd plenary, 4-5 July 2016, 17)

A key epistemological and strategic question in the work of BIPA has always been whether the remit of British-Irish cooperation was exclusively to maintain, deepen and develop relationships across the Isles, or whether the consolidation of links and joint understandings in BIPA should also serve as building blocks to launch more international positions, for instance, as a macro-region in relation to the EU.[25]

These considerations also have to do with the growth of the EU, in which partners who share many interests (as Ireland and the UK have in the past) may well pool forces and develop joint stances. However, Brexit has brought the UK and Ireland onto different trajectories, each with implications for how they imagine and therefore interact with each other. Specifically, Irish actors and political concerns have been at the forefront of the multi-year diplomatic process to negotiate the future political and economic relationship between the UK and the European Union. As the senator Catherine Noone told BIPA in 2017:

> We may be a small country with a small population, but we punch far above our weight in Europe at all levels, not just amongst politicians; we have senior civil servants. There are Irish people who have infiltrated all the institutions of the EU at all levels, and work will continue. It will be relentless until we feel that we have done everything in our power to help the situation.[26]

The reversal of sizeable fortune and relative proportions, which kicks in when Ireland forms part of the 'EU27' (the EU member states minus the UK, which from 2016 to 2020 nominally remained its twenty-eighth member), echoes BIPA debates about scopes and spheres of influence. It means that interdependence is conceived in different ways. For some, independence is a *stratified continuum*: that is, interdependence at once between the Isles *and* between EU member states. For others, interdependence is seen *as exclusive*: that is, either British and Irish interdependence *or* European interdependence without the UK, or following the breakup of the UK. Arguments in support of cooperation and interdependence (at all levels) vary in their emphasis on size and similarities. Positions tend to crystalize around a combination of defensive ideas of 'being too small to succeed' and more positive articulations of having 'so much in common'.

For Ireland, shifting the context of British-Irish relations, so that they are encompassed and framed by a wider interdependence of European cooperation, has changed the perspective to mitigate sizable differences. As Dan Mulhall, the Irish Ambassador to the UK told the BIPA plenary in November 2016:

> Our relations during the past 40 years have broadened and deepened as the UK and Ireland have dealt with each other not in an exclusively bilateral context, which is always unsatisfactory between a large country and a smaller country, but on a range of topics that arise naturally on the European Union agenda.[27]

However, with Brexit, the UK seems to be effectively removing itself from a layered version of institutional interdependence, creating a floating gap in British-Irish relations. Within this gap new auto- and hetero-images emerge. Knowing that for the rest of the EU the Irish point of view might always be an obscure vision from the periphery, Irish diplomats quickly set out to bring their concerns to the attention of the EU27 in the immediate aftermath of the vote.[28] As a result, Ireland has been able to use its conceptualization of what it means to be small as a way to exert a large impact on the international Brexit debates, changing its auto-image in the process. At the same time, the UK's belittling hetero-image of Ireland as its small dependent neighbour has had severe consequences for the UK's ability to navigate the Brexit negotiations. This image has led them to downplay the centrality of Ireland in the withdrawal negotiations and has rendered them blind to the foreign policy agility of Irish diplomats and politicians and the corresponding shift of initiative and power. Thus, while Ireland is a small country with a vulnerable economy, it has become a significant power in the political economy of Brexit, exemplified by the EU's chief negotiator Michel Barnier's dictum that 'in this negotiation Ireland's interest will be the Union's interest'.[29] Clearly Ireland is asserting itself as a symbol of interdependence, solidarity and peacebuilding to be rallied around. Arguably, it has become such a symbol not least because of its size, where the EU's position becomes one of rallying around its smaller members so as to join forces against the derangements of their larger, ruthless neighbours.

These debates about shifting size and identity also arguably concern the tension between independence and interdependence, which were not and are not experienced the same way across the Isles. For Ireland, membership in the European Union is viewed not as diluting independent statehood – as it is for English Brexiteers – as much as confirming and guaranteeing it. For Scottish and Welsh nationalists, the pursuit of independence is almost exclusively conceptualized within a wider European framework of interdependence.[30] As is illustrated by the introductory quote to this section, the dynamics of Brexit are now leading BIPA members to increasingly posit the UK as *another* small nation, which equally needs to rethink ideas about independence as something not radically different from interdependence. Despite this 'shrinking to size' of the UK, BIPA members may of course continue to have diverging ideas about the layers, scales and directions of future independence and interdependence.

Sizing up the shifting shapes of British-Irish Relations

> When I think back to 2013, 2014 and 2015, the big debate was about whether there was a need for this particular forum. We were discussing whether it was needed at all because the peace process was sorted and everything was grand and rosy. I think we need it more than ever now [...]
>
> Joe McHugh TD, Irish Minister of State for the Diaspora and Overseas Development Aid (BIPA 52nd Plenary, 4–5 July 2016, 11)

Since the referendum in 2016, the British and Irish governments have found themselves on opposite sides of the table in the Brexit negotiations. At the same time, ongoing tensions amongst the devolved institutions in Scotland, Wales, Northern Ireland and the sovereign parliaments in Dublin and London have brought about serious and deepening fault lines as a UK-wide debate erupted as to the shape of EU-UK relations post-Brexit.

In this final section, the chapter explores the hardening attitudes vis-à-vis British-Irish relations understood at once as the bilateral relationship between the British and Irish governments and as the asymmetrical relations amongst the nations in the Isles.

It locates the current situation with regard to the otherwise historically good relations which had developed between Britain and Ireland over the past twenty-five years and the wider crisis in Britishness, which predates Brexit. It looks particularly at the political languages still available to BIPA, which remains a political arena dedicated to finding common ground and reason in a transnational conceptualization of identity and political community.

Before Brexit, British-Irish relations were considered to have been fundamentally changed from their acrimonious past due to the countries working together in the EU and on behalf of the peace process in Northern Ireland.[31] The official and symbolic peak was reached when the Queen went on a hugely successful visit to Ireland in 2011 (the first royal visit to Ireland in one hundred years!) followed by the first-ever state visit of an Irish president to the UK in 2014 by Michael D. Higgins.[32] At the 58th BIPA plenary in 2019, His Excellency Robin Barnett, Ambassador of the UK to Ireland, assured the assembly that 'the bilateral relationship remains absolutely undimmed. Officials in London and in Dublin and our respective embassies have continued to work closely together on a wide range of issues, all designed to underpin our special and unique relationship'.[33] This reassurance, however, came after three years of strain and tear on the British-Irish relationship and an increasingly toxic, and 'size-ist', media discourse on the role of the Irish government and English nationalism in respectively frustrating and hardening Brexit. In the Irish mediascape, there was quite a bit of schadenfreude attached to finally having the UK not have the upper hand in its dealings with Ireland. For its part, the UK press was positively fuming over Ireland's central position in the negotiations and on the international stage, in what they saw as the tail wagging the dog. There is an uncomfortable return to 'Brit' and 'Paddy-Bashing' discourses, in which size is a consistent feature. Headlines such as 'Bought by Brussels, little Ireland's ridiculous leaders have landed it in a Brexit crisis',[34] 'Britain is uncomfortable because Ireland has the upper hand for the first time'[35] and 'UK must come to terms with being a "small country" after Brexit'[36] all speak to historical auto- and hetero-images of dominance and deference and the contemporary contestations around them.

There are clear differences between the confrontational discourses in the national presses and the reconciliatory portrayals of British-Irish relationships so diplomatically crafted in BIPA. Nonetheless, BIPA is also an arena for airing concerns about sharpening tones and ulterior motives – particularly when it pertains to discourses attempting to re-imagine Ireland. Already in July 2016, former Fianna Fail Minister Martin Mansergh cautioned BIPA that it would be unfortunate were it to appear that Irish nationalists sought to use Brexit to advance an all-Ireland agenda, instead of dealing constructively with the fallout and maintaining British-Irish relations in the round.[37] The concern was not least for maintaining relationships beyond Brexit and not saying things that would damage those relationships. Here we see highlighted how, through the centrality and exceptionalism of the 'Irish Question' in the Brexit negotiations, the Irish state has clearly become a force to be reckoned with. In BIPA debates, this prominence has been underscored by successive calls for the Irish Government to use its influence to protect British-Irish relationships and emphasize the point that 'a bad Brexit for Britain, is an even worse Brexit for Ireland'.[38] Here, the protection of the historical oppressive other is reconceptualized as a protection of self and each other.

The Irish question, the British question and the English question

I live near the border so I am keen on having a soft border. Nevertheless, we are talking about two separate nations, the United Kingdom and the Republic of Ireland, and the main trade between the Republic of Ireland and the United Kingdom is across the water into Wales.
Lord Kilclooney (House of Lords (HoL)), 56th plenary, Sligo June 2018

At the heart of Brexit and British-Irish relations alike stand contending and overlapping ambitions to erase and/or redraw borders and thereby redefine, grow or diminish national identities, political cultures, economic integrity and legal jurisdictions. The border, re-emerging between Northern Ireland and the Republic of Ireland now that the UK has left the EU, was a particular fierce point of contestation since the referendum in 2016. Indeed, the challenges Brexit presented for continuing the existing flows of trade, movement and political cooperation between the 'North' and 'South' of Ireland were identified by the EU as one of three key issues to be resolved in the first phase of negotiations for the UK's departure.[39] The importance of this relationship – and its nesting within wider European cooperation – was further underscored in the Joint Report issued in December 2017 by the negotiators of the European Union and the UK's government. In the resolution on Ireland and Northern Ireland, the report stated: 'Cooperation between Ireland and Northern Ireland is a central part of the 1998 Agreement and is essential for achieving reconciliation and the normalisation of relationships on the island of Ireland' and further that 'North-South cooperation relies to a significant extent on a common European Union legal and policy framework. Therefore, the United Kingdom's departure from the European Union gives rise to substantial challenges to the maintenance and development of North-South cooperation'.[40] In this context, any re-emergence of a land border in Ireland would have immediate economic, pragmatic and ideological consequences for the ongoing peace process as well as tapping, of course, into a more historical reservoir of grievances stemming from the partition of Ireland in 1920.

As an institution created in the peace process, BIPA is a very resonant forum for discussing developing British-Irish relations and its members are extremely lucid in their thinking about bridging borders. Here images of power are more about density and texture (soft/hard) than about shape and size. Owing to BIPA's transnational nature, the terms employed are also part of a more plural language that captures multiple borders, a discourse where the fate of the border in Ireland is discussed relative to a potential future border between England and Scotland as well as the consequences for Scottish and Welsh ports should a border run down the Irish Sea.[41]

Members of BIPA generally agree that a hard border would be detrimental to British-Irish relations but, as can be gleaned from Lord Kilclooney's remarks, the border's significance can be interpreted in different ways. The unionist interpretation holds that the border between the Republic of Ireland and Northern Ireland separates distinct nations, whereas a more nationalist interpretation would view this border as dividing the nation. Debates between 2016 and 2019 pivot around pragmatic and ideological concerns. On the one hand, that means considering the experience of the border population and the practical and economic impact of interrupting border-crossing

Figure 9.2 Following Brexit Day, Northern Ireland remains aligned to the European Single Market in a limited way for goods, while also forming part of the United Kingdom customs territory and internal market. Legally, a customs border exists between Northern Ireland and the Republic of Ireland, but in order to prevent a 'hard border' it has been moved de facto to the Irish sea, seen here in this photo taken by the author from Carrickfergus (NI). © Sara Dybris McQuaid.

flows which have integrated the island in less than political terms. On the other hand, it means discussing the political and ideological implications of 're-bordering' Ireland for British-Irish relations. It goes to the heart of how the nation is constituted and the legitimacy of the Brexit votes in Northern Ireland and Scotland. As Irish Minister Joe McHugh said at the plenary in July 2016:

> The fact is that 56% of those who voted in Northern Ireland did so to remain [...] and they now face their preference being set aside as a result of the overall result across the UK. That raises some profound issues, as we know it also does in Scotland.[42]

Clearly, Brexit has created rifts not just in the relationship between Britain and Ireland but also amongst the constituent parts of the UK. Beyond the fact that the populations in Northern Ireland and Scotland clearly expressed a different democratic will to remain within the EU than did England and Wales, there are also fears that Brexit will have consequences for the local assemblies and parliament in Belfast, Cardiff and Edinburgh. In the 'Great Repeal Bill' to 'repatriate' all existing EU legislation and copy it into British law, the devolved institutions fear a more permanent power grab from Westminster. As the First Minister of Wales Mr Carwyn Jones put it to BIPA in 2016: 'The replacement of Brussels with Whitehall is not an acceptable situation. We want to see devolution respected. There is no UK agriculture. Everything is in Brussels, devolved or, as far as England is concerned, run in Whitehall.'[43] This fear and the stratification of interests within the UK were echoed by Member of the Legislative Assembly of Northern Ireland (MLA) David Ford in 2017, when he argued that

> there are certainly some fears that, if the UK Government do not repatriate policy back to the devolved nations, as has been the case up to now, we will not necessarily do well in Northern Ireland, given the political balance of where agriculture lies for the UK Government as opposed to the Celtic fringe.[44]

In this way, BIPA delivers a space where ministers and parliamentarians from Wales, Scotland and Northern Ireland can voice joint concerns which are not as easily drowned out as they are in Westminster. Throughout the period 2016–20, a major concern was that local administrations were neither properly consulted nor given sufficient access to the Brexit negotiations. As Linda Fabiani, MSP for the Scottish National Party (SNP), tersely snapped in response to a speech by the minister Robin Walker from the Department of Exiting the European Union in October 2017:

> I am very interested in the terminology that is used all the time by the UK Government, which is about the devolved Administrations being fully engaged. I ask the Minister, whether he thinks withholding analysis that refers to Scotland as being very badly affected by Brexit and refusing to publish it represents being fully engaged.[45]

In January 2020 all three devolved administrations voted overwhelmingly against giving their consent to the Withdrawal Agreement Bill, demonstrating the ever widening gulf between levels and territories of government in the UK. Crucially, political tensions amongst the constituent parts of the UK are not created by Brexit but, like British-Irish relations, have a much longer history. In the 1880s, the struggle for Irish independence occasioned debates about the possibility of 'Home Rule all-round'.[46] In the late 1960s, the election of the first Scottish and Welsh nationalists to the UK parliament led to (unsuccessful) referenda on devolution in 1979,[47] but when New Labour came to power in 1997, it did so on a manifesto committed to constitutional reform and devolution[48] – which finally came to pass in 1999, when governments were established in Northern Ireland, Scotland and Wales. However, devolution did not 'kill nationalism stone dead' as much as occasion a new crisis of 'Britishness'[49] in which the nations reimagined themselves in relation to one another. In a BIPA debate about 'Implications of Brexit for British-Irish Relations', the First Minister of Wales recognized the challenge and also identified the role of 'the dog that didn't bark':

> [I]f we turn away and file it in the 'too difficult' or 'maybe later' categories, we risk the scenario of the four nations each drifting off alone and individually into an uncertain future. There needs to be the recognition of the special status of the devolved nations and also appropriate recognition for England, a nation that is often forgotten about in these considerations.

In many ways, devolution helped conjure the elusive 'Englishness' into being. This has been compounded by the territorial fragmentation of the UK political-party landscape in which the Conservative party is now overwhelmingly elected in England. If Scotland, Wales and Northern Ireland increasingly cease to contribute to the definition of Britishness, what is left is, of course, England. BIPA members' understand the rise of English nationalism within the context not only of imperial decline and European cooperation but also of political devolution in the UK, where England is the only nation that does not enjoy a measure of self-governance.[50] With devolution, Northern Ireland, Scotland and Wales have come to practise a different sort of political culture with different electoral systems and have come to expect a different kind of constitutional accountability. Amassing institutional experience not available to England, they have thus entered into a position where they can provide blueprints and guidance as trailblazers. In this context, having auto-images of being small might actually mean that they have a better handle on the democratic direction to travel.

Conclusion

This chapter has tracked the shifting shapes of British-Irish relations as they are conjured within a particular institutional and contextual politics of size. Applying a lens of smallness to the transnational and macroregional setting of 'the Isles' brings into sharper focus how political actors use size in shifting and multiple ways in order to reposition the constituent parts of the UK in relation to one another, to the two parts of Ireland and to the EU. Focusing on the dynamics of size and the constant remaking of what it means to be small in British-Irish relations enables a broader and deeper understanding of contemporary debates about independence and interdependence as well as variables of unionism and nationalism in the Isles. Situating the analysis in BIPA reveals how national members articulate and navigate representations of selves and others through languages of both solidarity and difference, specifically in the context of Brexit. Identifying as small and being identified as small are simultaneously used to push for integration, disintegration and realignment depending on the level such aims are pitched at. Here, overlapping and competing allegiances spanning communities, nations and states at once give rise to apparently 'national questions' (the Irish Question, the British Question, the English Question) and deny their firm response, since the imagined other is also a part of the self at different levels. In future shifting shapes of the UK, a potentially united Ireland, and a developing European Union, attention to these multiple levels of selves in a politics of size will remain crucial.

Notes

1   Many people have argued that the UK should more accurately be considered a union state rather than a unitary state (particularly after devolution in 1999). See e.g. Bogdanor, *Devolution in the United Kingdom*; Mitchell, *Devolution in the UK*, 220–1.
2   Pocock, 'The Union in British History', 181.

3   Leerssen, 'Imagology. History and Method'.
4   Wendt, 'Anarchy Is What States Make of It: The Social Construction of Power Politics'
5   Arthur, *Special Relationships*.
6   Coakley, 'British Irish Institutional Structures: Towards a New Relationship'; McQuaid, 'Nordic Horizons for a Council of the Isles', in *After Independence*, Ed. Gerry Hassan and James Mitchell (Edinburgh, Luath Press, 2013); McQuaid, 'Better Together?'.
7   Initially named the British-Irish Inter-Parliamentary Body, it changed its name to the British Irish Parliamentary Assembly in 2006.
8   BIPA 55th Plenary, 15–17 October 2017. Transcripts of the BIPA Plenaries are available for download at http://www.britishirish.org/plenary-transcripts/. Last accessed 6 July 2020.
9   Ibid.
10 Pocock, 'British History: A Plea for a New Subject'.
11 Rose, 'Do the British Exist?'
12 Colley, *Britons. Forging the Nation, 1707–1837*.
13 Joe McHugh, TD, in BIPA 56th Plenary, 11–12 June 2018, 18.
14 BIPA 52nd Plenary, 4–5 July 2016, 35.
15 Ibid., 18.
16 Ibid., 45.
17 BBC 23 June 2019, 'New consulate to boost Welsh-Irish trade', https://www.bbc.com/news/uk-wales-48722001. Last accessed 30 April 2020.
18 'Ireland and Wales Programme 2007–2013', s.d., https://gov.wales/docs/wefo/publications/territorialcooperation/irelandwales/070925irelandwalesoperationalprogrammeen.pdf. Last accessed 30 April 2020.
19 BIPA 52nd Plenary, 4–5 July 2016.
20 Ibid., 76.
21 Hechter, *Internal Colonialism. The Celtic Fringe in British National Development (1999 [1975])*.
22 *Teachta Dála* (TD) is the equivalent Irish term for Member of Parliament.
23 *The Times*, 26 November 1998, Martin Fletcher, 'Commonwealth option for Ahern'. For a fuller analysis see Lloyd, *Diplomacy with a Difference*, 283.
24 BIPA 52nd Plenary, 4–5 July 2016, 25, 'Developments in British-Irish Relations: EU Referendum in the UK'.
25 McQuaid, 'Better Together?' 165–7.
26 BIPA 55th Plenary, 15–17 October 2017, 72.
27 BIPA 53rd Plenary, 27–29 November 2016, 62.
28 Connelly, *Brexit and Ireland: The Dangers, the Opportunities, and the Inside Story of the Irish Response*.
29 'Speech by Michel Barnier at the Joint Houses of the Oireachtas (Houses of Parliament of Ireland), Dublin', 11 May 2017, https://www.europa-nu.nl/id/vke4idepxtyq/nieuws/speech_by_michel_barnier_at_the_joint?ctx=vgg41g1vpcsp&tab=0. Last accessed 30 April 2020.
30 McCrone, *The Sociology of Nationalism. Tomorrow's Ancestors*, 146.
31 For example, in March 2012, then Prime Minister David Cameron and then Taoiseach Enda Kenny gave a joint statement on British Irish Relations, in which it was said: 'The relationship between our two countries has never been stronger or more settled, as complex or as important, as it is today'. 'British-Irish relations statement in full',

12 March 2012, https://www.politics.co.uk/comment-analysis/2012/03/12/british-irish-relations-statement-in-full. Last accessed 30 April 2020.
32. Commons Foreign Affairs Committee analysis of the UK-Ireland bilateral relationship, s.d. [2017], https://www.parliament.uk/documents/commons-committees/foreign-affairs/Correspondence/2017-19/OFFICIAL-Analysis-of%20UK-Ireland-bilateral-relationship-(FAC)-Final.pdf. Last accessed 29 May 2020.
33. BIPA 58th Plenary, 13–15 May 2019, 36.
34. *The Telegraph*, 31 July 2019, Bruce Arnold, 'Bought by Brussels, little Ireland's ridiculous leaders have landed it in a Brexit crisis'.
35. *The Irish Times*, 28 February 2020, Finn McRedmond, 'Post-Brexit UK still doesn't get Ireland; The UK remains unable to conceive of Ireland as a nation with its own voice'.
36. *The Telegraph*, 27 January 2020, Gordon Rayner, Amy Jones and Tony Diver, 'UK must come to terms with being a "small country" after Brexit, says Leo Varadkar'.
37. BIPA 52th Plenary, 4–5 July 2016, 77. Paul Girvan from the Democratic Unionist Party in Northern Ireland echoed this concern: BIPA 57th plenary, 22-23 October 2018, 77.
38. Lord Bew, BIPA 55th plenary, 15–17 October 2017, 64.
39. 'Guiding principles transmitted to EU27 for the Dialogue on Ireland/Northern Ireland', 6 September 2017, https://ec.europa.eu/commission/sites/beta-political/files/guiding-principles-dialogue-ei-ni_en.pdf. Last accessed 7 July 2020.
40. 'Joint report from the negotiators of the European Union and the United Kingdom Government on progress during phase 1 of negotiations under Article 50 TEU on the United Kingdom's orderly withdrawal from the European Union', 8 December 2017, https://ec.europa.eu/commission/sites/beta-political/files/joint_report.pdf. Last accessed 7 July 2020.
41. Undersecretary of State, Chloe Smith (MP), in BIPA 55th plenary, 15–17 October 2017, 43.
42. BIPA 52nd plenary, 4–5 July 2016, 4.
43. BIPA 53rd plenary, 27–29 November 2016, 6.
44. BIPA 54th plenary, 17–18 July 2017, 107.
45. BIPA 55th plenary, 15–17 October 2017, 29.
46. See e.g. Mitchell, *The Scottish Question*.
47. See e.g. Nairn, *The Break-Up of Britain*.
48. Labour Party (Great Britain), *New Labour*.
49. See e.g. D'Ancona, *Being British*; Hazell, *Constitutional Futures Revisited*.
50. BIPA 58th plenary, 13–14 May 2019.

10

From David to Goliath? The question of size in Israel's identity politics

Alexei Tsinovoi

Introduction

The image of Israel as a small state surrounded by a hostile environment plays a central role in Israeli identity narratives. For significant part of its history, the state has been popularly recognized as 'David' confronting 'Goliath'.[1] However, towards the end of the 1990s – with the stagnation of the peace process, the events of the second Intifada, the expansion of West Bank settlements and a series of controversial military operations – Israel's privileged meta-image of smallness began to invert itself, becoming a prime matter of political concern not only in foreign policy circles but also in the country's public debates.[2] Drawing on insights from the poststructuralist tradition in IR theory, in which national images are discursive formations intertwined in mutually constitutive relations with foreign policy, I will analyse, in this chapter, the transformations in Israel's imaginal politics in recent decades.[3]

Specifically, focusing on the construction of Israel's smallness through three primary identity narratives commonly discussed in the literature – namely *Western democracy*, *Jewishness* and *security provider* – the chapter highlights not only the complex and fragile social construction of Israel's smallness but also how this particular articulation of smallness creates the conditions of possibility for its foreign policy goals to be realized.[4] Moreover, the chapter examines how Israel's discourses of smallness have been destabilized in recent years, leading to the consolidation of a new discourse of international misrecognition, associated with the alleged misrepresentation of the state's image by foreign press and civil society organizations operating online. The chapter concludes by suggesting that due to the transformations in the media environment, imaginal politics are becoming a central dimension of contemporary international relations. However, Israel's discourse of misrecognition, which these transformations have ignited, might further estrange Israel's international relations and narrow the conditions of possibility for a reconciliatory foreign policy.

National identity and the construction of Israel's smallness

Understanding a state's smallness as part of its national image and identity – as the present volume seeks to grasp – requires a post-positivist approach. Within IR theory, poststructuralist discourse analysis has long been considered a central method in examining the relations between national identity and foreign policy.[5] This approach regards foreign policies and national identities as discursive formations and, as such, national images of smallness and their political salience in the making of foreign policy are essentially understood as constructed through language. The relations between foreign policy and national identity are *constitutive*, because 'foreign policies rely upon representations of identity, but it is also through the formulation of foreign policy that identities are produced and reproduced'.[6] In turn, understanding how the smallness of a state is constructed and *performed* through language can be central in understanding that state's foreign policy choices.

Israel is a particularly instructive case study for this approach and for the significance of national images and identities to foreign policy more broadly. Indeed, scholars often point out that various ideational national identity concerns, rather than material factors traditionally discussed in the mainstream IR literature, are what often end up playing a decisive role in Israel's foreign policy. For example, Lupovici discusses the centrality of national identity concerns in the unilateral steps taken towards the Palestinians during the 2000s, such as the West Bank separation wall and the disengagement plan from Gaza; Löwenheim and Heimann suggest that the destabilization of Israel's identity was one of the causes behind the 2006 Lebanon war; Waxman argues that issues pertaining to national identity played a central role in the inability of Israeli leaders to make certain concessions during the Camp David peace negotiations in 2000. At the same time, a common Israeli identity has never been stabilized and its narratives are riven with internal conflicts and divisions – some dating back to the beginning of the Zionist movement in late nineteenth-century Europe and continuing to evolve up through the present.[7]

As we will see, with identity narratives and cultural values split between secular and religious conceptions, under the sway of socialist, ethno-nationalist, and Western and Eastern influences, it required a great deal of political imagination to envision not only a common Israeli identity but also the implementation of policies that attempted to reconcile the multitude of divisions and tensions. As declared by Israel's first prime minister, David Ben-Gurion, in 1948: 'It is necessary to melt down the debris of Jewish humanity which is scattered throughout the world and will come to Israel, in the melting-pot of Independence and national sovereignty.'[8] It is clear, however, that Israel's institutional 'melting pot' doctrine has failed in its task of creating a national identity that reflects broad consensus.[9] Identity politics, which still dominates Israeli public debates, culminated in one peak at the end of the 1990s, following the First Intifada and the Oslo peace process, in what some dubbed an acute 'identity crisis'.[10] Nonetheless, despite the tensions, there are, amongst the Jewish-Israeli population that constitutes the population's dominant majority, three identity narratives that appear to be consistently central to the Israeli self-image: Israel as a *security* provider, Israel as a

Jewish homeland and Israel as a *democracy*.[11] Understanding these identity narratives is essential for tracing how Israel's smallness has been constituted.

Israel's Jewishness

Since the early days of the Zionist movement, Jewishness has been a constitutive component in Israel's national identity narratives. Yet throughout the years there was very little agreement about what 'Jewishness' actually meant. Traditionally, being Jewish was understood in religious terms, but in the nineteenth century the Zionist movement aspired to create a new, secular, ethno-national Jewish identity.[12] However, although secular (and predominantly socialist) Zionist factions, dominant in the foundation of the state of Israel, were often antagonistic towards religion, they eagerly repurposed many Jewish texts, symbols and myths for the purpose of nation-building. As such, while different Biblical narratives, such as the mythic image of David and Goliath, played central roles in the formation of the new Israeli identity, Jewishness – as a religious category – was downplayed up through the end of the 1960s in favour of a more civic-oriented identity that placed the state above all other political commitments.[13] For example, in explicit negation of the sense of Jewish victimhood in the diaspora, the new Israeli identity was embodied in the mythic image of the 'sabras' – the new 'Jewry of the muscle' renowned for their courage, patriotism and devotion to physical labour in peacetime and for self-sacrifice in war.[14]

After decades of ideological dominance by the socialist Labour party, which defined Israel's identity in secular and statist Western terms, towards the end of the 1960s and onwards the religiosity of the Jewish component of Israel's national identity began taking an increasingly prominent role. Motivated by ideological and cultural changes, such as an increasing societal alienation from Labour values and the mass migration of the more religiously inclined Mizrahi Jews, this process culminated in the dramatic 1977 electoral victory of the Likud Party, whose leader, Menachem Begin, strategically sought to unite the nation around traditional and religious Jewish values. Today, the majority of Israelis are not religious in the orthodox sense, but Jewishness still plays a central role in Israeli identity narratives, where religious motifs are often intertwined with ethno-nationalist and historical terms. As we will see with the discourse concerning Israel's policies in the West Bank and Gaza, the increasing predominance of a more religiously inclined discourse of Israel's Jewish identity had profound implications on Israel's foreign policy choices pertaining to Israel's size, such as the justifications given for the continuation of the settlement project and its leadership's inability to make certain concessions during the peace negotiations.[15]

Israel as security provider

While, in principle, all sovereign states are committed to provide security for their citizens, scholars note that national security concerns in Israel extend well beyond traditional military issues, ranging from energy supplies to immigration and even to national image and reputation.¹⁶ Some scholars note that due to Israel's continuous state of war since 1948, combined with the history of Jewish victimhood in the diaspora, national security concerns have gained a mythic status in Israel as a kind of a 'religion of security' in which national security policies are not only the results of rational calculation by experts but are also an outgrowth of a complex constellation of cultural, historical and ideological dynamics.¹⁷ For example, a sense of Jewish history has been said to play a central role in the perceptions affecting Israel's security policy: collective memories of prosecution, victimhood and existential threats in the diaspora have facilitated a certain 'siege mentality' embodying a core societal belief that the country is 'standing alone against the hostile world'.¹⁸ Such generally accepted beliefs that the international domain is profoundly hostile and that 'the whole world is against us' has led not only to the sanctification of military strength and self-reliance on the part of Israel's political leaders but also to broad societal acceptance of frequent encroachments on civil liberties made in the name of national security.¹⁹

National security concerns, and the military-civil apparatus that has formed around them, continue to play a primary part in the constitution and reproduction of Israel's identity narratives. For example, in the early years, the Israeli leaders regarded mandatory military service to be a central tenet of the aforementioned 'melting pot' doctrine envisioned by Ben-Gurion, through various activities such as instruction in Jewish history and the Hebrew language.²⁰ This way, according to Ben-Gurion, the army would serve as 'the cultural instrument of the ingathering of the exiles, their unification and spiritual uplifting'.²¹ In turn, this cultural dimension of security has helped facilitate what some critics call a 'garrison state', imbued with 'civil militarism' characterized by porous boundaries between the civil and the military domains and a 'security network' consisting of informal associations between active and retired military experts who play a central role in making political decisions well beyond the military domain.²² Combined with Israel's prolonged state of war with its neighbours – it is 'a nation that lives by its sword', in famed Israeli commander Moshe Dayan's words – being a *security provider* is thus a primary dimension of Israel's national identity.²³

Specifically, in this identity narrative, Israel is conceived as to be 'defensive-warrior' – that is, a warrior committed only to fighting 'no alternative' wars, while maintaining 'purity of arms' in battle.²⁴ This dimension of Israeli identity is often captured through the Biblical 'myth of David and Goliath – the few versus the many'.²⁵ As explained by Sucharov, 'As a single, fledging Jewish state in the predominantly Arab Middle East, from its birth Israel fostered the myth of heroic struggle against those bent on its destruction.'²⁶ In reviewing the dominant themes in the Israeli commemorative narratives of state foundation, Strömbom similarly notes that the imagery 'of "few against the many", of the Israeli David defeating an Arab Goliath' became central to Israeli national identity, depicting 'a righteous struggle by a defensive and weak Jewish collective against a strong and ruthless enemy'.²⁷ This myth was widely adopted domestically as part of Israel's auto-image and at times even internationally as a hetero-image. As claimed by Moshe Dayan, Israel's 'victory over the Arabs in four wars, is a perfect expression of the symbolism in the David-Goliath duel', not only in terms of the weak against the strong but as 'the struggle for the way of life [...]. The Arabs come to us with sword [...] while we seek to live with them in peace'.²⁸ This conception is not limited to Israel's image of itself. Some note that internationally as well, particularly in the United States, Israel's victory in 1967 'elicited a euphoric response [that was] nothing short of a modern iteration of "the old story of David and Goliath"', supported by iconic war images (see Figure 10.1) that 'bolstered the perception of the heroic Israeli soldier as "the epitome of Jewish masculinity and valor"'.[29]

Figure 10.1 An Israeli soldier takes a celebratory bath after his country has achieved an 'astounding' victory against the numerical superiority of Arab coalition forces. Cover of *Life Magazine*, 23 June 1967. © Life Magazine.

This image of Israeli identity, combining a sense of profound insecurity with assertions of moral superiority, remained mainly unchallenged within Israel until the end of the 1980s. However, as we will see, beginning with the war in Lebanon and the first intifada in the 1980s, and later, following the failure of the peace process in the late 1990s, the second intifada in the early 2000s, the continuation of the settlement project in the West Bank, and a series of controversial military campaigns in Gaza, this meta-image of smallness became increasingly destabilized, its volatility becoming a matter of prime concern within Israeli foreign policy debates. '[T]he David and Goliath myth can be understood as forming a central part of Israel's role-identity', notes Sucharov, but it also contains 'the seeds of that identity's most painful challenge'.[30]

Israel as a Western state

Perhaps the final politically salient dimension of Israeli identity is its self-perception as a Western state, which is often articulated through differentiating the country, both explicitly and implicitly, from its non-Western Arab neighbours. Indeed, at the same time that the Zionist movement sought to differentiate itself from certain dimensions of Jewish history and identity in order to constitute the new Israeli identity – a process often referred to as the *negation of exile* – a parallel process took place, marked by another constitutive differentiation, in this case the distinction of Israelis from the native Arab population in Palestine.[31] In line with Edward Said's discussion of the constitution of European identity, the local Arab population were often depicted, in early Zionist and later in Israeli accounts 'within the confines of orientalist discourse' as being 'either violent, irrational, and evil, or authentic and antiquated', serving as a constitutive Other for the new Israeli (Western) self.[32] In the 1950s, Jews emigrating from Arab countries were often framed within the parameters of the same orientalist discourse, leading to years of alienation and resentment, which was central to the demise of the secular, socialist understanding of Jewishness promoted by the Labour party and the rise of a more religiously inclined interpretation promoted by the revisionist Likud.[33] While explicit orientalist discourse is less common today, differentiation from the Arab Other is still important for Israeli identity and at times is even enacted implicitly in Israel's public diplomacy efforts, projected strategically by the state both domestically and internationally.[34]

For example, as frequently expressed by politicians through phrases such as 'villa in the jungle', the narrative that Israel is the only democracy in the Middle East can be seen as playing an important role in Israeli national identity.[35] As noted by Kook, 'Israeli governments have commonly prided themselves in granting [...] the right to participate in elections, as voters, and as potential candidates (to) both Arabs and Jews'.[36] At the same time, as argued by Smooha, although the argument 'that Israel is no different from Western countries, which are nation-states and liberal democracies [...] is widespread among the Israeli Zionist left', the ethnic component is much more predominant in Israel than in many other Western democracies, leading him to conclude that unlike the Western model, Israel is more of an *ethnic democracy* than a liberal one.[37]

Besides appealing to Israel's democratic character, which some argue is currently in decline,[38] the differentiation from the Arab Other has frequently been constituted in recent years by strategic appeals to other Western values, such as pluralism, tolerance and technological progress. For example, various nation-branding campaigns began promoting Israel – and particularly the city of Tel Aviv – as a gay-friendly destination which, in contrast to the surrounding Arab states, provides a safe haven of tolerance for the Lesbian, Gay, Bi, Trans, Queer (LGBTQ) community.[39] Moreover, following a best-selling book with the same title, in a new discourse eagerly adopted by Prime Minister Benjamin Netanyahu and the late President Shimon Peres, Israel is increasingly depicted in various political performances as a 'Start-Up Nation', second only to Silicon Valley in its level of technological innovation and ingenuity.[40] In this emerging discourse, a particularistic concern with being a security provider is often reframed as a universalistic concern with scientific and technological innovation. As was argued by Peres, Israel's security necessities foster innovation and creativity, and it was 'creativity on the security front [that] laid the foundations for civilian industries'.[41] By rearticulating the role of the military – which is no longer a mere *security-provider* but can now claim to be a 'technological incubator' for 'dual-purpose technologies'[42] – this discourse expresses Israel's 'desire to be *Or Lagoim* (a light unto other nations)' as part of its national self-image.[43]

Imaginal tensions

These narratives of Israeli identity, and the images of the Israeli self they attempt to project, are rife with internal contradictions and tensions that have been subject to continuous academic, political and popular debate. While there is not sufficient space here to cover these debates, the tension at the core of all of them seems to be an uneasy relation between universalism and particularism.[44] For example, as argued by Smooha, the ethnic dimension is particularly central in Israeli democracy, which 'combines the extension of civil and political rights to individuals […] with institutionalization of majority control over the state'.[45] In turn, scholars often note how the state's Jewish character manifests itself at the expense of democratic commitments. As noted by Kook, due to 'the lack of separation between religion and nationality, membership in the nationality is not co-terminus with citizenship'. Thus non-Israeli Jews are included within the parameters of the national self and Israeli non-Jews are excluded.[46] Though the same individual rights are, in principle, granted to the non-Jewish population, one finds considerable exclusions on a collective level. For example, the members of the state's Arab population 'are systematically written out of both the commemorative and written symbols of the Israeli […] national identity', such as the flag, monuments, the national anthem and various collective rights such as the Law of Return, which enables foreigners with Jewish ancestry to immigrate to Israel and automatically become citizens, even as members of other groups, such as Palestinian refugees, are excluded from such treatment.[47] Some argue that this tension between universal democratic values and ethnic particularism has been exacerbated in recent years and that today's 'Israel is in the midst of a democratic recession'.[48]

Moreover, the aforementioned trade-off between universalism and particularism frequently manifests itself in the tension between security practices and democratic principles. As has often been noted by critical security studies scholars, security practices not only respond to objective threats but represent a political choice of governance which legitimizes the suspension of 'regular' democratic procedures.[49] Indeed, as argued by Peri, the Arab-Israeli conflict and considerations of national security have exerted a 'predominant influence on the shape of politics' in Israel; security concerns have become part and parcel of societal domains that extend well beyond the military sector and have caused severe ramifications for various democratic principles.[50] For decades, as part of these dynamics, elites depicted seemingly 'regular' issues such as energy supplies or demographics in existential terms, as matters of 'life or death' for Israel. Exclusionary governance practices preventing parliamentary oversight and public debate, as well as various forms of anti-democratic legislation, were thus legitimized.[51] Commenting on this tension, Barak and Sheffer argue that Israel's 'security network' helped place the security agenda above other societal concerns, thus posing 'a major obstacle to the advancement of (Israel's) democratic regime'.[52] At the same time, due to the 'religion of security', according to Peri, the Israeli public could also be more disposed to accept encroachments on civil liberties in the name of national security, 'view[ing] themselves as ignorant in the area of security, powerless to affect decisions made on security matters, and prepared to adopt those decisions'.[53]

The construction of Israel's smallness

This account is far from exhaustive, but suffice it to say that these identity narratives and their imaginal tensions are pivotal to begin understanding how Israel's smallness has been socially constructed and contested, and to grasp the role it has played in Israel's foreign policy. Indeed, while many outside commentators would doubtless now consider Israel to be a military and economic superpower in its region, it had precisely been the various dimensions of Israel's smallness – understood in both territorial and demographic terms – that for many years preoccupied Israeli policymakers.[54] Constituted through complex intertextual relations with Israel's predominant identity narratives, different enactments of Israel's smallness have discursively framed the conditions of possibility for Israel's foreign policy. Specifically, the constitution of Israel's smallness has been pivotal in the Israeli-Palestinian conflict and the various attempts at conflict resolution.

For most part, the linkage of size, identity and foreign policy was perhaps most evident and politically salient within the context of the *security provider* narrative. Questions of Israel's size have been at the heart of the country's policies directed towards the Palestinians, as evinced through the refusal to retreat to the 1967 demarcation line and the continuation and expansion of the settlement project, amongst other examples. Specifically, within this identity narrative, the political argument often promulgated by central actors is that Israel's smallness, as expressed in terms such as 'narrow waistline' or its lack of 'strategic depth' – referring to its lack of a hinterland and the geographical proximity between the border and its large centres – represents a persistent existential threat. The late Ariel Sharon, for example, has been said to bring foreign visitors to an observatory in a West Bank settlement, from where one can see all the way to Tel Aviv and can behold Ben-Gurion Airport and other strategic locations. Without the settlements, he argued, 'we will be left with a narrow waistline of only a few kilometres separating the east from the sea'.[55] From a military perspective, the Israeli Defence Force's (IDF) former chief of staff Moshe Yaalon argued that 'with all the new weaponry and technological developments available to its enemies', having such a 'waistline [...] would make [Israel] not only more vulnerable and inviting of attack, but virtually indefensible'.[56]

Over the years a political formula was thus stabilized in Israeli public debates, in which Israel's smallness requires military control over larger territories in order to create and maintain defensible borders. Within this logic, after 1967, 'the territories formed a protective belt around the state and provided necessary strategic depth'.[57] This point was perhaps most famously made in 1969 by the late Israeli foreign minister Abba Eban. Rejecting the possibility of a post–Six Day War Israeli retreat to the pre-1967 demarcation known as the Green Line, he declared that '[t]he June map is for us equivalent to insecurity and danger. I do not exaggerate when I say that it has for us something of a memory of Auschwitz'.[58] This 'Auschwitz borders' argument, as it came to be known – equating geographical smallness with indefensibility, the real possibility of death and one of the most traumatic events in Jewish history – has since been made on numerous occasions by leading Israeli politicians, enacting the question of smallness as a matter of survival and national security in order to legitimize the refusal to retreat from the occupied territories and thus enabling the military occupation to continue.[59] As Prime Minister Netanyahu remarked in 2020, within the context of new plans for the annexation of the West Bank, the 'great victory' in the 1967 war ensured that Israel 'cancelled the narrow and dangerous [...] "Auschwitz borders"'; the borders had now 'moved from the suburbs of Tel Aviv to the protective wall of Judea and Samaria' and hence '[w]e are here to stay – forever'.[60]

Within the parameters of this discourse, the settlement project – perhaps one of the most controversial aspects of Israel's foreign policy under international law – drew its political legitimacy from security arguments associated with Israel's smallness. As explained by Bar'el, 'Security reasons [...] were adopted as a rationale for establishing the settlements (as) part of Israel's security defense line. This *civil wall* was to absorb the first possible attack by any enemy coming from the East'.[61] For this purpose, from 1967 onwards the idea promoted and implemented by the Labour party was 'to establish a string of agricultural Kibbutz and Moshav settlements' in order to 'fortify' the eastern border with Jordan as a kind of 'hybrid military/civilian zone'.[62] According to Yigal Alon – one of the central figures behind this plan – this arrangement would provide 'maximum security and maximum territory for Israel with a minimum number of Arabs'.[63] In itself, the notion that hybrid civic/military settlements can be used for defensive purposes was not a new idea, as is illustrated by the construction of 'Wall and Tower' (*homa umigdal*) settlements in the 1930s.[64] However, though the security arguments attempt to frame the occupation and the West Bank settlements as an objective material necessity stemming from geographical and political factors, Bar'el notes that in practice '[q]uestions such as how exactly the settlements were supposed to protect the State of Israel [...] were never seriously discussed'.[65] As critical security scholars have long argued, this dearth of discussion illustrates that discursive articulations of security concerns need not reflect objective material necessity in order to possess political salience, and indeed many of these new fortification settlements were evacuated during the 1973 war instead of serving as an actual military buffer zone during a moment of conflict.

The security argument nonetheless continued to infuse Israel's foreign policy, enabling the legal 'confiscation of lands for *security reasons*, and granting the settlers and settlement's with a proper Israeli aura and legitimacy'.[66] At the same time, the continuation and expansion of the settlement project were increasingly enacted in the years that followed within the parameters of a different discursive formation, in which Biblical and religious myths, in the place of the former security arguments, were mobilized in various ethno-nationalist arguments. Regarding this transformation, scholars often point out the increasing 'Judaicization' of Israeli national identity from the 1960s onwards, concurrent with a distancing from the secular Zionist vision of Israel's founders. The culmination of this process was perhaps reached in the 1977 electoral victory of the Likud Party, whose revisionist and ethno-nationalist vision of Zionism came to replace the secular, socialist Zionism of the Labour party. Under the leadership of Prime Minister Menachem Begin, the Jewish dimensions of Israeli identity – enacted more through an appeal to various popular traditions and ethnic myths than to orthodox religiosity as such – became increasingly central to Israel's national identity.[67] The proliferation of this identity narrative as part of the Israeli self-image created favourable conditions of possibility for a different kind of settlement activity to emerge, that drew legitimacy not only from security and various economic considerations but also from Jewish religion, tradition and myths.

Indeed, the notion of Greater Israel, its size indicated via various biblical myths, has long been at the core of the revisionist Zionist ideology which Begin subscribed to, where 'Judea and Samaria' – the Biblical terms adopted in Israel for the territories of the West Bank – were deemed 'an integral part of the area of Jewish sovereignty'.[68] In this discursive formation, as Waxman points out, 'Israeli possession of the West Bank [...] and Gaza was based on the historical rights of the Jewish people' to their 'ancestral home': 'to forsake these territories would be to forsake Israeli national identity'.[69] The settlement project thus began changing its character in Israeli public debate. While under the Labour government a small number of ideologically driven religious settlements had been established – at times 'illegally near supposedly biblical sites'[70] – as Weizman points out '[t]he number of settlers and settlements in the West Bank rose, no doubt, after Likud was elected to power in May 1977'.[71] Moreover, while Labour predominantly 'regraded settlements as a means to guarantee military defensible borders (according to topographic conditions)', Begin's government began providing support to ideological settler groups such as Gush Emunim, religious Zionists who wanted to build settlements 'not only according to military-strategic or economic-suburban logic, but also according to a national-religious one'.[72] As Pappe notes, within their 'messianic discourse' about the occupied territories, greater state size was 'not only vital for Israel's survival but also for the advent of the Messiah'. This discourse began slowly moving from the fringes of the Israel's right wing towards its mainstream.[73]

The increasing predominance of religiosity in the Jewish dimension of Israeli national identity, and its influence on the state's policies in the occupied territories, emphasized a tension in Israel's identity narratives related to the questions of size, the ethnic constitution of the enlarged state and its democratic commitments. The 'demographic demon' – that is, the fear of losing the ethnic Jewish majority within Israel's boundaries – has been a central concern for the Zionist movement for many years.[74] From the state's beginning, however, there was a clear tension between maintaining a Jewish majority – a goal that all Zionist factions agreed on – and enlarging the size of the state in its democratic form. As argued by Ben-Gurion in 1949: 'the IDF could easily occupy the territory between the Jordan River and the sea, but what kind of state shall we have? Assuming there are elections [...] we will have a Knesset [...] with an Arab majority. Between the Greater Israel and a Jewish State, we have chosen a Jewish State'.[75] However, as explained by Abulof, the 'clear Jewish majority within the [...] 1949 borders was eroded by the 1967 war and its territorial gains', and towards the end of the 1980s this new demographic status quo was increasingly depicted as a security threat, becoming an 'existential drive for territorial compromise' that later inserted itself into the peace process.[76] Tensions involving size, democracy and the issue of the Jewish majority continued to play a central role in Israeli foreign policy during the 2000s, resulting in various unilateral steps taken by Israel towards the Palestinians, such as the disengagement from Gaza in 2005, where reducing the size of the state became a means to stabilize Israel's identity narratives as still being centred on its Jewish and democratic character.[77]

With the occupation of the West Bank and the Gaza Strip, along with the expansion of the settlement project, the narrative about maintaining a demographic Jewish majority by democratic means became starkly contrasted with the other narratives that centred on the state's territorial enlargement due to security and religious reasons. As summarized by Sucharov, the question of size trapped Israeli identity within 'what has come to be known as the "triangle dilemma" of democracy, Greater Israel, and the Jewish character of the state: Israel could have any two, but not all three'.[78] On the one hand, in an enlarged Israel, as we can see from the previous statements, the granting of citizenship to the Palestinian population in the occupied territories would eliminate the Jewish majority in Israel. But not doing so would eliminate its democratic character. In turn, to remain both Jewish and democratic, Israel would then have to become *smaller*. On the other hand, becoming smaller contradicts not only elements of the *security provider* identity narratives, with larger size associated with the defensibility of the state due to Israel's 'narrow waistline' and its need for 'strategic depth', but also some of the new *Jewishness* narratives, where larger size is bound up with history, national identity and religion.

Concerns with the 'demographic demon', along with broader societal changes, were at the forefront in the creation of the conditions necessary for the 1990s peace process to begin. Questions of size – of both Israel and a future Palestinian state – were front and centre in these negotiations, necessitating significant concessions from both sides. Israel's ability and willingness to make such foreign policy concessions, however, was to a large degree constrained by the conditions of possibility constituted by its identity narratives. On the one hand, within the discursive formation of being a *security provider*, the territories were held mainly for strategic defence purposes. Hence, if security could be provided by other means, such as a peace agreement, there should be no problem with withdrawing from the occupied territories – as implied by the 'land for peace' formula that was at the basis of the bilateral peace negotiations between Israel and the Palestinians.[79] On the other hand, within the Jewishness identity narrative, as it had been reconstituted since the 1970s, the occupied territories were deemed part of Jewish history and identity, limiting considerably the legitimacy of any territorial concessions because to do so would be to contradict the ethno-nationalist narratives and to deprive Israel of its Jewish identity. As stated recently by Prime Minister Netanyahu with regard to the West Bank settlements: 'We returned to the lands of our forefathers […]. This is our identity; this is our heritage and here is our future.'[80]

The question of size, as enacted in these competing discursive formations, became a central matter of concern in Israeli public debates during the 1990s, with immediate implications for both the enabling and the constraining of Israel's foreign policy choices. For example, as suggested by Waxman, during the peace negotiations with Egypt in 1978 even the revisionist Prime Minister Begin had no problem with reducing the state's territorial size by returning the strategically important Sinai Peninsula in exchange for a peace agreement, since this area did not play a central role in the *Jewish* identity narratives. However, during the 2000 Camp David summit between the Israeli and the Palestinian delegations, the Labour Prime Minister Ehud Barak was unable to make any concessions over the strategically insignificant Temple Mount area in Jerusalem precisely because it was so integral to Israel's *Jewishness* identity narrative; any such moves would lack public support.[81] As the question of Israel's size remained unresolved following the failure of the peace process negotiations and the eruption of the second Intifada in the 2000s, the tensions between Israel's identity narratives became particularly acute.

The violence that erupted in the beginning of the 2000s not only challenged Israel's self-perception as a *security provider* capable of protecting its citizens but also raised renewed concerns about the 'demographic demon' and the nation's ability to maintain its democratic character in its enlarged state. The unilateral steps taken towards the Palestinians during this time, such as the disengagement from Gaza and the construction of a wall separating Israel from the West Bank, can in turn be seen as a strategy 'aimed to deal with threats to each identity without challenging the other identities'.[82] That is to say, by strategically modifying its size through the disengagement from Gaza and the construction of the West Bank wall, Israel could maintain the territories essential to the *Jewishness* narrative and, at the same time, through physical separation from the Palestinian population, quarantine the 'demographic demon' and restore its image as a *security provider*. However, as Lupovici summarizes the matter, 'Far from solving the Israeli-Palestinian conflict, the unilateral steps preserve the enmity and to some extent perpetuate the Israeli occupation in the West Bank'.[83]

The international dimension of Israel's imaginal politics

As concerns with conflict resolution were increasingly replaced with unilateral conflict management,[84] Israel's foreign policy towards the Palestinians began attracting considerable international critique. Taking a distinctly normative tone, much of this critique focused on the various ramifications of these unilateral steps, such as the West

Bank checkpoints and the siege of the Gaza Strip. As explained by Adler, 'the occupation [...] and in particular, the growth of settlements in the occupied territories, helped change Israel's image in the world from "David" to "Goliath"'.[85] Indeed, while Israel's privileged auto-image of smallness has been challenged over the years, not until the beginning of the 2000s did 'Israel's reputation abroad [...] dramatically deteriorate[]'.[86] For example, according to the 2003 Eurobarometer public opinion survey, Israel was perceived as the world's biggest threat to peace by European publics; the British Broadcasting Company (BBC) public opinion surveys in 2007 and 2012 conducted across several continents showed Israel chosen as one of the worst influences on world politics amongst the nations – with Israel's foreign policy explicitly identified as the main cause of such a sentiment.[87]

As Israel's constitutive meta-image of smallness began to invert itself, the international dimensions of Israel's identity politics became more politically salient, resulting in new policies and institutional arrangements. Developments in media technologies and their translation into political practice played a central role in this regard. International conflicts are now experienced by most around the globe in mediated form, with a significance already evident during the first intifada at the end of the 1980s. As noted by Sucharov, 'images of Palestinian children facing down the barrel of an Israeli gun forced Israeli and international opinion to be moved by the uprising', and the intifada became, to a large degree, 'a battle fought for the media'.[88] Corresponding to what some IR scholars refer to as the *CNN effect* (after the *Cable News Network*), where the constant flow of real-time news can become a force that influences foreign policy, Prime Minister Yitzhak Rabin argued that 'the Intifada [...] has focused international attention on the Palestinian problem. Therefore, it also obligates us (to reach a settlement)'.[89]

However, as peace negotiations with the Palestinians came to a halt and the second intifada began in the beginning of the 2000s, followed by a series of controversial military operations, the flow of images (e.g. see Figure 11.2) through old and new media, challenging Israel's self-image as a small, democratic and morally superior '*security provider*' – that is, a *David* – increasingly became a prime foreign policy concern. The communications scholar Eytan Gilboa discusses several examples frequently mentioned in this regard, such as the Muhammad al-Durrah incident in 2000, involving controversial footage of a twelve-year-old boy and his father caught in the crossfire between Israeli and Palestinian forces, and the media coverage of the military operation 'Defensive Shield' in 2002, in which media outlets often employed terms such as 'massacre' and 'war crimes' instead of adopting the vocabulary of the official Israeli counterterrorism argument.[90] Expressing a widespread view amongst Israeli practitioners and the public, he concludes that '[t]he media has decided that Palestinians are the victims and Israel the aggressor' and thus '[m]edia coverage [...] severely damages Israel's image and reputation'.[91] Illustrating this perception further is another event frequently mentioned in this regard: the second war in Lebanon, in 2006.[92] As a former official argues, from the Israeli perspective '[t]he facts were clear: Hizbullah was the aggressor and Israel was defending itself, but the impression received from the foreign media was that Israel was [...] the "neighbourhood bully" [because] the foreign media blindly bought the Arab propaganda'.[93] In this narrative, media representations, rather than Israel's policies, are responsible for the inversion in Israel's hetero-image from 'defensive warrior' to 'bully', from *David* to *Goliath*. As argued by the former minister of foreign affairs Tzipi Livni, this inversion has clear political implications: 'In conversations with other foreign ministers I could see that they know that we are right [but] the pictures from Lebanon have created a twisted image in public opinion, and they just had to respond [...] by criticizing Israel.'[94]

The years that followed saw the frequent articulation of such gaps between the international remediation of controversial events and the predominant Israeli narratives. As argued by an influential Israeli think-tank report, during this period a 'significant gap between Israel's stance amongst the political leadership across the globe and the public' developed, where in parallel with good official relations, Israel's international public image 'is under a persistent attack'.[95] Such views became widespread and many Israeli practitioners began expressing their conviction that a

Figure 10.2 A young Palestinian protestor faces an Israeli tank, during clashes at the Karni crossing point between Israel and the Gaza Strip, on the outskirts of Gaza City. Photo by Laurent Rebours, 29 October 2000. © Associated Press.

gap has opened up between the global representations of Israel (its hetero-image) and the image many Israelis have of themselves (the auto-image). For example, according to the former director of the Government Press Office, 'Those foreign journalists [...] accusing [Israel's] defense forces of war crimes [...] paint a picture so different from the reality in the eyes of Israelis, and with such little regard for their point of view'.[96] In turn, as expressed by Livni, 'there is a very big gap, created over the years, between the image of Israel and who we really are. While we keep our values, shared also by the international community, a totally different image of us has been created'.[97] As elaborated elsewhere, the challenges to Israel's self-image and the responses they have ignited have led in recent years to the consolidation of a certain discourse of *international misrecognition* in Israeli foreign policy debates, where a variety of Israeli actors regularly articulate an objectified gap between the Israeli privileged self-image and the way the state is represented globally.[98]

Traditionally, Israel's approach to international public opinion was dismissive and pragmatist.[99] As argued by the late Shimon Peres, '[i]f a country has good policies, it does not need public relations (PR), and if the policy is bad, the best PR in the world will not help'.[100] Within the parameters of the misrecognition discourse, however, this logic seems to have become inverted, so that image management has in recent years been transformed into a panacea for foreign policy choices. New Public Diplomacy, nation-branding and Digital Diplomacy – often discussed in Israel using the term *Hasbara* – became increasingly central to Israeli foreign policy, leading to a plethora of new image management initiatives which mobilized the affordances of the new media environment and the participation of civil society. As Mendel writes, in this new approach 'the starting point is that we are OK. Now we just need to explain it'.[101] As argued elsewhere, this discourse's consolidation helps Israel stabilize its privileged auto-image and creates the conditions of possibility for it to circumvent international critique and continue its current foreign policy.[102] However, this discourse may also help perpetuate Israel's conflictual international relations and deepen its international estrangement.

Reconciliatory dynamics of conflict resolution require identity destabilization and transformation. Indeed, as argued by Sucharov, during the 1980s, due to the 'dissonance' between Israel's auto-image as a 'defensive-warrior' and the visibility of its policies towards the Palestinians, 'significant segments of the Israeli polity began to see itself as a Goliath vis-à-vis the Palestinians' David', and this perception has played a crucial role in paving the way for the peace process.[103] For example, as illustrated by Strömbom, during this period the so-called Israeli New Historians began producing 'critical historical accounts questioning the Israeli master commemorative narratives' such as the myth of David versus Goliath, leading to '*a destabilization of the self-other split*' and the creation of new 'openings' for narratives of *recognition* and identity transformation.[104] Their work exerted significant influence on Israeli society in the 1990s, leading *inter alia* to a revision of curriculum and of textbooks used in educational institutions. In turn, this transformation arguably changed the conditions of possibility for policymaking and to some degree 'trickled down to the peace negotiations'.[105] However, with the halt of the peace process and the eruption of the second intifada in the beginning of the 2000s, this opening for new narratives of recognition began to close. Instead, the emergent discourse of misrecognition has seemed to reproduce the old self-other divisions and entrenched societal beliefs such as 'the whole world is against us', thus narrowing down the conditions of possibility for reconciliatory foreign policies in the future.

Conclusion

This chapter has analysed the construction of Israel's national identity through three predominant identity narratives: those of *security provider*, *Jewishness* and *Western democracy*. It has argued that over the years the question of Israel's size, insofar as it pertains to Israel's foreign policy, was constructed through these identity narratives and that the enactment of this question of size within each of these narratives has constituted different conditions of possibility for Israel's foreign policy. Specifically, within the *security* narrative, Israel's geographical 'narrow waistline' is deemed to constitute an existential threat to the state, legitimizing foreign policy actions which seek the expansion of Israel's size in order to create a greater strategic buffer zone through land annexation and the building of settlements. At the same time, within the *Jewishness* narrative, the enlargement of Israel's size through expansion into those territories is not only a question of strategic imperative but is – indeed mainly – an ideological and religious endeavour, with the territories depicted as an integral part of Jewish history and identity. The clash between these identity narratives, insofar as they pertain to Israel's size, became apparent during the peace negotiations with the Palestinians in the 1990s and the underlying 'land for peace' formula, leading to a deep domestic schism and eventually contributing to the halting of the peace process.

Moreover, the chapter has also examined how, with the breakdown in the peace process and the eruption of violence in the beginning of the 2000s, the international dimensions of Israel's identity politics increasingly occupied centre stage in Israel's foreign policy debates. Specifically, the chapter discussed how during this period Israel's foreign policy debates were increasingly imbued with a discourse of *international misrecognition*, articulating a gap between Israel's predominant identity narratives and the global representation of these narratives. Media technologies, disseminating images of the conflict globally in real time, were pivotal in this discourse, where media representations, rather than Israel's foreign policies, were said to be responsible for the inversion of Israel's hetero-image, leading to a plethora of new image management initiatives. However, while the consolidation of this discourse helps Israel stabilize its auto-image at home, it can also contribute to perpetuating and deepening its international estrangement.

Notes

1. Adler, 'Israel's Unsettled Relations', 3; Gertz, 'Social Myths in Literary and Political Texts'.
2. Gilboa, 'Public Diplomacy'; Adler, 'Israel's Unsettled Relations'; Adler-Nissen and Tsinovoi, 'International Misrecognition'.

3   Hansen, *Security as Practice*. On the concept of imaginal politics and the link between images and political imagination see Bottici, *Imaginal Politics: Images beyond Imagination and the Imaginary*.
4   Cf. Lupovici, 'Ontological Dissonance'.
5   Campbell, *Writing Security*; Neumann, *Uses of the Other*; Wæver, 'Identity, Communities and Foreign Policy: Discourse Analysis as Foreign Policy Theory'; Hansen, *Security as Practice*.
6   Hansen, *Security as Practice*, 1.
7   Lupovici, 'Ontological Dissonance'; Löwenheim and Heimann, 'Revenge in International Politics'; Waxman, *Pursuit of Peace*.
8   Cited in Waxman, *Pursuit of Peace*, 22.
9   Ya'ar, 'Continuity and Change in Israeli Society'.
10 See Carmon, 'Political Education in the Midst of a National Identity Crisis: The Compatibility of Judaism and Democracy as a Pedagogical Theme'.
11 Lupovici, 'Ontological Dissonance'.
12 Waxman, *Pursuit of Peace*.
13 See Waxman; Shapira, 'The Religious Motifs of the Labor Movement'; Sucharov, *The International Self*; Gertz, 'Social Myths in Literary and Political Texts'.
14 Almog, *The Sabra. The Creation of the New Jew*.
15 Waxman, *Pursuit of Peace*; Melchior, 'Judaism and Islam in the World'.
16 See e.g. Bialer, 'Top Hat, Tuxedo and Cannons: Israeli Foreign Policy from 1948 to 1956 as a Field of Study'; Tsinovoi, 'The Sacred, the Secular, and the Profane'; Adler-Nissen and Tsinovoi, 'International Misrecognition'; Olesker, 'Law-Making'; Abulof, 'Deep Securitization'.
17 Peri, 'Arab-Israeli Conflict', 346.
18 Bar-Tal and Antebi, 'Siege Mentality in Israel', 251.
19 Peri, 'Arab-Israeli Conflict', 346.
20 Sucharov, *The International Self*, 72.
21 Cited in Waxman, *Pursuit of Peace*, 32.
22 Barak and Sheffer, 'Israel's "Security Network"'; Kimmerling, 'Patterns of Militarism in Israel'.
23 Peri, 'Arab-Israeli Conflict', 343.
24 Sucharov, *The International Self*, 45.
25 Gertz, 'Social Myths in Literary and Political Texts', 622.
26 Sucharov, *The International Self*, 57.
27 Strömbom, 'Thick Recognition', 177–8.
28 Cited in Raider, 'Moshe Dayan', 41–2.
29 Raider, 32.
30 Sucharov, *The International Self*, 58.
31 Walzer, 'Negation of the Exile'.
32 Cited in Mendel and Ranta, *From the Arab Other to the Israeli Self: Palestinian Culture in the Making of Israeli National Identity*, 10. See also Peleg, *Orientalism and the Hebrew Imagination*; Said, *Orientalism*.
33 Waxman, *Pursuit of Peace*, 41.
34 Explored in more detail in Adler-Nissen and Tsinovoi, 'International Misrecognition'.
35 *The Guardian* 20 August 2013, Aluf Benn, 'The Jewish majority in Israel still see their country as "a villa in the jungle"', https://www.theguardian.com/commentisfree/2013/aug/20/jewish-majority-israel-villa-in-the-jungle. Last accessed 8 December 2016.
36 Kook, 'Between Uniqueness and Exclusion', 214.

37   Smooha, 'Ethnic Democracy', 211.
38   E.g. Chazan, 'The Democracy Factor'.
39   E.g. *Haaretz*, 12 June 2009, Cnaan Liphshiz, 'Israel Advocates Play Gay Card', https://www.haaretz.com/1.5063670. Last accessed 31 March 2020. These efforts were often criticized as a form of 'pinkwashing' that strategically invokes certain liberal values in order to conceal other illiberal and controversial policies. See Schulman, *Israel/Palestine and the Queer International*.
40   Senor and Singer, *Start-Up Nation*.
41   Cited in Senor and Singer, xii.
42   Cited in Senor and Singer, xii–xiii.
43   Adler, 'Israel's Unsettled Relations', 1.
44   See Adler, 'Israel's Unsettled Relations'.
45   Smooha, 'Ethnic Democracy', 199.
46   Kook, 'Between Uniqueness and Exclusion', 202.
47   Kook, 217.
48   Chazan, 'The Democracy Factor', 73.
49   Buzan, Wæver, and Wilde, *Security: A New Framework for Analysis*; Aradau, 'Security and the Democratic Scene'; Tsinovoi, 'The Sacred, the Secular, and the Profane'.
50   Peri, 'Arab-Israeli Conflict', 343.
51   David Ben-Gurion cited in Bialer, *Oil and the Arab-Israeli Conflict*, 221–2. See also Abulof, 'Deep Securitization'; Olesker, 'Law-Making'; Bialer, *Oil and the Arab-Israeli Conflict*; Cohn, 'Fuzzy Legality'.
52   Barak and Sheffer, 'Israel's "Security Network,"' 238.
53   Peri, 'Arab-Israeli Conflict', 349.
54   Jones, 'The Foreign Policy of Israel'.
55   Cited in *Haaretz*, 4 April 2001, Daniel Ben Simon, 'למה שרון לא עושה סדר' [Why Sharon does not fix it]', https://www.haaretz.co.il/misc/1.691995. Last accessed 1 April 2020.
56   Moshe Yaalon, 'Introduction: Restoring a Security-First Peace Policy', Jerusalem Center for Public Affairs (s.d.), https://jcpa.org/requirements-for-defensible-borders/security-first_peace_policy/. Last accessed 3 April 2020.
57   Waxman, *Pursuit of Peace*, 73.
58   Cited in *Haaretz*, 31 December 2007, Bradley Burston, 'Here's to the '67 Borders, the New Middle of the Road', https://www.haaretz.com/1.4973999. Last accessed 30 March 2020.
59   *Haaretz*, 2 January 2014, Barak Ravid, 'Deputy Foreign Minister: 1967 Borders Are Auschwitz Borders', https://www.haaretz.com/1967-borders-are-auschwitz-borders-1.5307464; *The Jerusalem Post*, 26 May 2023, Lahav Harkov, 'Landau: 1967 lines are "Auschwitz borders"', https://www.jpost.com/Diplomacy-and-Politics/Landau-1967-lines-are-Auschwitz-borders-314393. Last accessed 31 March 2020.
60   Cited in *The Jerusalem Post*, 8 February 2020, Lahav Harkov, 'Israel begins mapping out West Bank land for annexation after election', https://www.jpost.com/Israel-News/Israel-begins-mapping-out-West-Bank-land-for-annexation-after-election-616961. Last accessed 31 March 2020.
61   Bar'el, 'Four States', 111.
62   Weizman, *Hollow Land*, 59.
63   Cited in Weizman, 58.
64   Rotbard, 'Wall and Tower. The Mold of Israeli Adrikhalut'.
65   Bar'el, 'Four States', 111.
66   Bar'el, 112.

67 Waxman, *Pursuit of Peace*, 36–7.
68 Shavit, 'Ideology, World View, and National Policy', 107.
69 Waxman, *The Pursuit of Peace*, 58–9.
70 Pappe, *A History of Modern Palestine*, 200.
71 Weizman, *Hollow Land*, 92.
72 Waxman, *Pursuit of Peace*, 61; Weizman, *Hollow Land*, 94.
73 Pappe, *A History of Modern Palestine*. See also Shavit, 'Ideology, World View, and National Policy'.
74 Abulof, 'Deep Securitization'.
75 Cited in Abulof, 405.
76 Abulof, 405.
77 Lupovici, 'Ontological Dissonance'.
78 Sucharov, *The International Self*, 114.
79 Duncan, 'Land for Peace'.
80 Cited in *The Jerusalem Post*, 8 February 2020, Lahav Harkov, 'Israel begins mapping out West Bank land for annexation after election', https://www.jpost.com/Israel-News/Israel-begins-mapping-out-West-Bank-land-for-annexation-after-election-616961 Last accessed 31 March 2020.
81 Waxman, *Pursuit of Peace*, 189; Melchior, 'Judaism and Islam in the World', 126–7.
82 Lupovici, 'Ontological Dissonance', 831.
83 Lupovici, 833.
84 Lupovici, 830.
85 Adler, 'Israel's Unsettled Relations', 3.
86 Gilboa, 'Public Diplomacy', 715.
87 European Commission Directorate General Press and Communication, 'Flash Eurobarometer: IRAQ and PEACE IN THE WORLD' (2003), http://ec.europa.eu/public_opinion/flash/fl151_iraq_full_report.pdf; BBC World Service, 'Views of Europe Slide Sharply in Global Poll, While Views of China Improve' (2012), https://web.archive.org/web/20121017040610/http://www.worldpublicopinion.org/pipa/pdf/may12/BBCEvals_May12_rpt.pdf; Knesset Research and Information, מערך ההסברה של ישראל ותדמיתה בעולם [Israel's Hasbara apparatus and its global image] (2010), https://fs.knesset.gov.il/globaldocs/MMM/d2c18d55-f7f7-e411-80c8-00155d010977/2_d2c18d55-f7f7-e411-80c8-00155d010977_11_9703.pdf; *The Jerusalem Post*, 6 March 2007, 'BBC poll: Israel has worst world image', https://www.jpost.com/printarticle.aspx?id=53623. Last accessed 8 July 2020. See also Gilboa, 731–5.
88 Sucharov, *The International Self*, 129. See also Adler-Nissen and Tsinovoi, 'International Misrecognition'.
89 Cited in Sucharov, *The International Self*, 129. See also Robinson, 'The CNN Effect'.
90 Gilboa, 'Public Diplomacy', 726–8.
91 Gilboa, 731.
92 Israeli State Comptroller, דוח שנתי 58א [Annual Report 58A]' (2007), http://www.mevaker.gov.il/he/Reports/Pages/293.aspx. Last accessed 8 July 2020.
93 Shoval, 'Why Israel Lost the Hasbara War', 16–17.
94 *nrg*, 24 October 2006, Barak Ravid, מותג ושמו ישראל - חופי ים במקום הטנקים [Brand Israel: beaches instead of tanks]',https://www.makorrishon.co.il/nrg/online/1/ART1/495/761.html. Last accessed 6 July 2020.
95 The Reut Institute, 'Building a Political Firewall against Israel's Delegitimization. Conceptual Framework' (2010), 14, http://reut-institute.org/Data/Uploads/PDFVer/20100310%20Delegitimacy%20Eng.pdf. Last accessed 8 July 2020.

96 *The Jerusalem Post*, 3 March 2010, Daniel Seaman, 'Opposing the digital pogrom', http://www.jpost.com/printarticle.aspx?id=170128. Last accessed 8 July 2020.
97 Cited in *Walla News*, 14 May 2007, 'לבני: כניסה לעזה תחזק את הקיצונים' [Entering Gaza will reinforce the extremist]', https://news.walla.co.il/item/1106579. Last accessed 8 July 2020.
98 See Adler-Nissen and Tsinovoi, 'International Misrecognition'.
99 As detailed in Adler, 'Israel's Unsettled Relations'.
100 Cited in Gilboa, 'Public Diplomacy', 735.
101 *Walla News*, 9 March 2010, Yonatan Mendel, 'מדינת ישראל זקוקה לשוק חשמלי' [The State of Israel needs an electric shock]', http://news.walla.co.il/item/1651294. Last accessed 8 July 2020.
102 As detailed in Adler-Nissen and Tsinovoi, 'International Misrecognition'.
103 Sucharov, *The International Self*, 57–8.
104 Strömbom, 'Thick Recognition', 178–9.
105 Strömbom, 182.

Conclusions

Samuël Kruizinga and Karen Gram-Skjoldager

The politics of smallness

Over the more than three years we have been working on this book, the following scenario has played out countless times when discussing its slow but steady progress with co-workers, friends and family members. Having explained that the book is about smallness in European history and in the present, the reply would often go something like: 'Oh, you mean it's about European small states!' The confusion is understandable.[1] Not only is small state studies a recognizable field of study, but the notion that some states are small and others are 'big' or 'great' is widespread, both inside and outside academia. But this book has not been about small states – or about a discrete set of states that share a set of commonly agreed-upon characteristics that set it apart from other categories of states. It is, rather, about what people thought or think a small state is. And, to repeat a key phrase from this volume's introduction, it focuses on the effects of such an attribution, on what smallness 'does': What sorts of things should a small state, once so identified, do or not do? What is its proper place, its appropriate behaviour? What rights and duties accompany its diminutive size? Through several case studies, this volume's authors have set out to operationalize smallness as a new way of understanding how something perceptual and malleable – ideas about size – can and does influence outlook and thereby policy. The ensuing insights entail more than just a new way of saying that 'small states behave differently than great powers', because smallness means different things to different actors. Moreover, individual and group beliefs about what constitutes a given size, and what size in fact means, change over time. Thus this book has explored both how smallness is constructed politically and how smallness influences international politics.

The book's individual essays have focused on a range of case studies spanning the nineteenth, twentieth and early twenty-first centuries. By intervening in and contributing substantially to important scholarly and contemporary debates, they have demonstrated the utility of an explicit research focus on issues of smallness. Moreover, these essays invite us to explore a wider variety of source materials than is common in either political history or political science.

We have found implicit and explicit references to smallness not only in the minutes of political bodies, in opinion pieces, and in the ego-documents of politicians but also in the works of literary canons, in newspaper advertisements, and in the files of non-Government Organisations (NGO) and scientific bodies. Through these sources, this volume's chapters have pointed to new ways of understanding the nineteenth-century 'belittlement' of Spain – based on much older stereotyping – the way political elites framed the relationships of smaller national units within the larger multinational European empires before 1914, and the construction by Romanian politicians of a national identity for Romania as the small Belgium-of-the-East, in the process allowing us to seriously question the supposed divergence of eastern nationalisms from their Western counterparts. Others contributions offered analyses of how a gendered 'smallness' was instrumental in mobilizing 'great' American support for the relief of small, dependent Belgium during the First World War, and then for military intervention against Belgium's oppressors, or how American think-tanks and funding agents quite differently perceived the possibilities and limits of the smallness of Czechoslovakia and Denmark, respectively – and how such perceptions shaped their attempts to influence each country's scientific and public health agenda. Still others highlighted how the nexus between smallness and neutrality inspired governments and businesses to create press agencies tasked with providing news that was 'neutral' in more than one sense of the word: they were intended not only to break up existing cartels but also to make the international case that their home states had the right to exist and should help foster international understanding.

'Smallness' also emerged as a long-running current in Serbian political culture, serving chiefly as a focal point for fears that the nation would be imprisoned, submerged or destroyed within a hostile political, cultural or ethnic environment. In Icelandic political culture, smallness served a similarly negative function, but there it is conspicuous by its absence. Smallness was seen as the antithesis to Icelandic independence and sovereignty, and references to its modest size or its possible consequences were and remain anathema for most of its mainstream political parties. Much more evident was the use of smallness in the re-imaging and reconfiguration of political relations within the British Isles after the Brexit vote of 2016, as the countries that make up the UK and the Republic of Ireland, which remains part of the European Union, refer to size to discuss perceived asymmetries in the relationships within their constituent territorial, national and political communities. Finally, Israeli smallness in the twentieth and twenty-first centuries was constructed out of the notion that its Jewishness, its ability to provide security for its inhabitants and its democracy were embattled due to the state's precarious existence within a hostile regional environment dominated by autocracies. However, these three pillars of Israeli identity formation have increasingly been at odds with one another and with smallness – particularly because of debates on the pros and cons of decreasing or increasing Israel's size as part of either a peace settlement or related to security arrangements with the Palestinians – and have exposed deep schisms.

Images of Smallness

The individual chapters of this book have also demonstrated how the relationship between the politics of smallness on the one hand, and discourses on smallness on the other, is mutually constitutive. To once again repeat a phrase from this volume's introduction: 'small' politics rely upon representations of 'small' identity, which is in turn produced and reproduced through political action. In an effort to capture something of this dynamic, we have introduced the metaphoric language of auto-, hetero- and meta-images of smallness.

Auto-images refer to common themes in discourses and policies related to one's own polity or another form of collective Self. Political elites in Habsburg Bohemia, Ottoman Albania and Tsarist Georgia, for example, understood the position of their own respective nations within larger empires in the late nineteenth and early twentieth centuries as constituting a necessary compensation for weaknesses – expressed in geopolitical, economic and/or cultural terms – and therefore argued against the creation of a separate nation-state and for the maintenance of the status quo. But certain figures in these elites, notably including the future Czechoslovak leader Tomáš Masaryk, changed tack during the First World War, arguing that the war had provided indisputable proof that the great imperial centre no longer served to shield the small nation from the dangers of the outside world but had instead dragged it to an unwanted destination. Freed from what was now domination rather than protection, the independent small states of central Europe, Czechoslovakia first and foremost, had a duty, according to postwar elites, to give voice to their innate progressiveness and love of freedom and democracy. Similarly, in the Netherlands of the late 1930s, Dutch auto-images focusing on the country's smallness and its neutrality propelled the formation of a transnational news network dedicated to neutral news, both to safeguard the Netherlands' precarious independence and to bring a disinterested ('neutral', and therefore 'typically' Dutch) voice to an overheated war of words between the Allies and the Axis powers.

Hetero-images, for their part, are common themes in discourses on and policies aimed at Others. British and Dutch hetero-images of the Spanish, for example, were influenced by the Black Legend, which painted Spain and its inhabitants as intolerant, fanatical and therefore incapable of contributing anything to European culture or civilization; the narrative consistently generated was of an ever-shrinking, negligible country. Nineteenth-century Romanian elites, by way of contrast, had a much more positive impression of small Belgium. These elites connected its smallness to its ability to function, apparently quite successfully, as at once a bridge between civilizations and a barrier against various forms of barbarism, inhabiting a dual identity that Romania could aspire to and, it was hoped, one day achieve. The relentless press campaign waged in the United States during the First World War saw less agency amongst the Belgians than the Romanian elites did. Instead, what was highlighted was a hetero-image of Belgium that depicted the country as unable to withstand the onslaught of war generally, or its German occupier specifically, without American help. Belgium's portrayal as great America's 'little sister', moreover, helped to evoke a sense of 'brotherly' devotion and commitment. Just a few years later, American philanthropists imagined two kinds of smallness existing side by side in Europe: developed, and therefore well-charted, Denmark was portrayed as an ideal laboratory environment-in-miniature, whereas newly created Czechoslovakia seemed to offer itself up as a small, empty canvas that could be painted upon quickly.

Meta-images, our third category, are second-order projections. They refer to discourses and policies related not to the (collective) Self or the Other but instead based on *expectations* of what the Other thinks of the Self. In the Serbian media landscape, for example, we can detect a persistent thread of meta-images related to purported designs of Others – the Habsburgs, Germans, NATO and most recently the European Union – on Serbian statehood or even the Serbians' right to exist. These, in turn, influenced auto-images, strengthening narratives of Serbia as a state continually on the verge of becoming smaller, thus complicating Serbian-EU accession talks. Similarly, in Israel, the notion that, by and large, the outside world cannot or refuses to grasp the complexities of its unique security situation and draws unfair conclusions from biased media representations – painting it as a lumbering, aggressive Goliath rather than 'little guy' David fighting the good fight against all odds – has resulted in domestic shifts away from conciliatory politics vis-à-vis the Palestinians.

Finally, this volume has included several examples of discourse and policy appearing to be at odds with each other. In Iceland, for example, the most prominent strand of (political) identity construction emphasized independence and autonomy, even if in practice Icelandic politicians throughout the twentieth and into the twenty-first centuries have sought shelter so as to protect the country against the geopolitical, economic and financial storms that its political elites apparently believe the country cannot hope to weather alone. This dichotomy between identity and foreign policy has made 'smallness' a taboo subject, and debate about Icelandic dependence on other political entities became, and remains, a bridge too far for the country's major political groupings. And on the British Isles, Brexit enflamed rhetoric about who is great and who is small – even as the overlapping and competing allegiances owed by the isles' inhabitants to a multitude of communities, nations and states muddies the waters significantly. Here, we see smallness 'acted out' in practice rather than being the explicit subject of, and something sustained by, political discourse.

Patterns of smallness

The essays that make up this book thus demonstrate the utility of our approach by showing how a focus on the politics of smallness questions assumptions, introduces new research questions, allows for a focus on new types of source materials and leads to key new insights while introducing a new metaphorical language to help analyse 'smallness'. In what remains of this final chapter, we will first explore the various ways that smallness itself has been imaged in European political and identity discourses since the early nineteenth century. Crucially, this endeavour is a first attempt to move beyond single instances or comparative case studies and to look at the broader patterns evident as the politics of smallness have played out over the last two centuries.

First of all, it is important to distinguish situations in which smallness is contested – or when smallness is seen to not accurately reflect a state's proper status within a size-based hierarchy – from those where it is not. When accepted or even embraced, smallness seems to be a much more stable element of identity formation, and something that is also more readily recognized in 'like-minded' others. Those peers form part of a reference group and are then held to similar standards with the expectation that they will act and/or respond to particular situations in similar ways.[2] The Scandinavian experience of smallness in the nineteenth and twentieth centuries, for example, offers prime examples here. However, in late nineteenth-century Spain, twentieth-century Iceland, and twenty-first-century Serbia, smallness was contested in each instance as being at odds with the country's historical achievements, its sovereignty and/or its future prospects.

Likewise, smallness is experienced differently in a situation experienced as adversarial or asymmetrical. If the international system is perceived ultimately to be driven by a preponderance of military or economic power, smallness will be seen as a liability or will be reconfigured to increase its defensive potential. Small states' press agencies, as we have seen, were first formed out of an increasing sense of vulnerability and would continually stress the right of smallness to exist in a world increasingly dominated by the force of arms. But such vulnerability can also lead smallness to be rejected outright, or, as in the case of Serbia, contribute to situations involving costly military offensives and ethnic cleansing campaigns.

Third, smallness seems to be intimately connect to imagined geography, and more specifically to the perception of centrality. Whether a state is thought to occupy a 'central' position or is instead placed on the 'periphery' will co-determine a state's size on the mental maps of those considering such a state and its position vis-à-vis other states. Obviously, the inevitability of such judgements is aligned with the idea that size is perceptual and subjective. But it also ties into the notion that the international system is made up of changing and overlapping hierarchies: and these hierarchies, in determining our mental maps of the globe and influencing our conceptions of what is central and peripheral within them, also help shape our ideas of (relative) size, and what these gradations of size mean. The attraction of Belgium's smallness was, for nineteenth-century Romanian elites, closely related to its centrality, which is to say its position near the cultural and political power centres of Europe, over which it could wield a benign influence. And during the First World War, Americans saw in diminutive Belgium a country central to European culture and civilization, its smallness making it both incapable of helping itself in times of war and invasion and eminently worthy of aid when its borders were violated. And in the 1930s, small, peripheral Czechoslovakia was imagined by American donors as a blank slate, and later as little more than an annex to Germany, whereas Denmark was seen as an established, older state, more modern and therefore closer to the 'centre'. Imagined geography also played key roles, as we have seen, in the reconfiguration of relations amongst the various political entities occupying the British Isles, as questions of centrality and peripherality as well as 'natural' connections and axes are affected by the political event of Britain's exit from the European Union.

Fourth, there seems to be a close connection between smallness and spheres of action. Of course, hetero- and meta-images abounded that cast small states as essentially passive. American aid appeals painted First World War-era Belgium, for example, as a nation almost devoid of agency: rendered powerless by the invading Germans, its population, which seemed to consist nearly exclusively of women and children, simply needed American men to swoop in and rescue them. And in twenty-first-century Israel, a foreign policy and an internal defence policy both seen as being too active – too violent, too expansionist – have been at odds with conscious attempts to portray the country as small. A kind of necessary, inherent passivity on the part of small states has been one key reason why neutrality was so long thought to be a perfect fit for them. And yet the connection between passivity and smallness is far from automatic: smallness might be accompanied by spurious activity, but this has never been so across the full political spectrum. What exactly the 'right' areas were, in which agency and smallness could go hand in hand, differed according to (changing perceptions of) the shape of the international system.

Finally, and flowing from all that has been stated above, the politics of smallness differs not only from place to place but also from era to era. For example, the political and intellectual elites of the self-proclaimed proto-nations embedded within the larger central European empires seemed, prior to 1914, content to exist within the given political framework of the time, since (so the argument went) their smallness left no room for true sovereignty. That perception started to change in 1914 and decisively altered at the end of the First World War, when these same elites reconfigured their politics of smallness so as to align with new understandings of the (changed) hierarchies of the international system: they now saw their nations as having the space to inhabit independent political units. We see here a distinction emerging between established and new small states, as the twin examples of Czechoslovakia's and Denmark's experience with their American benefactors show. In the Netherlands, meanwhile, smallness and neutrality were considered to be two sides of the same coin throughout the nineteenth and the early part of the twentieth centuries. However, the experience of occupation during the Second World War and the onset of the Cold War convinced subsequent governments and voters alike that Dutch smallness needed to be divorced from a stance of neutrality, which was to be replaced with participation in European and Atlantic security arrangements. Tellingly, however, in Sweden the foreign policy elites interpreted their geopolitical circumstances differently, opting to continue their policy of neutrality as the two superpower-based blocs emerged post-1945.[3] In Iceland, moreover, foreign policy elites sought shelter to compensate for their smallness where they could, displaying an eagerness to replace American with Chinese or Russian aid that is (as yet) unknown in other European states, whereas policy elites in the UK and Ireland (Northern Island as part of but distinct within the UK, and the Republic) continue their existential debates about what smallness means either within Europe or globally up through the time of this writing.

Smallness, size, hierarchies and institutions

In this last section, we will consider some of the avenues of further research that this volume has opened up. We would like to point to three possible strands of future research in particular, namely those related to *size*, *hierarchies* and *institutions*.

Smallness, first, is but one size-class, and size is an integral part of the construction of any state's identity. We suggest therefore that it would yield real benefits to develop a more comprehensive understanding of how these debates and processes play out in relation to other size categories – be they 'great powers', 'superpowers', 'medium powers' or 'microstates' – in much the same way that this volume has done with regard to 'small states'. The approach of this volume, at its core, is not about specific issues or policies but about new ways of reconstructing and analysing size-related mental maps based primarily on beliefs. In essence, such an orientation connects with and reinvigorates much older notions that international relations are primarily concerned with beliefs about Self and Other and their proper relation to each other.[4] This linkage, in turn, helps us to anchor debates about specific issues and policies in much deeper, more stable (but not immobile!) debates about worldviews and identity.[5]

Second, we suggest looking not simply at the analysis of size-based state categories but more specifically at the relationships amongst them. If all states are not created equal and state size (however constructed) is widely understood to enable and limit certain spheres of international political activity, then the questions of which hierarchies exist that order (and often subordinate) these states, and how they are reproduced, contested, and renegotiated become signally important. Whether a particular size category and status are accepted or rejected can be attributed to one's own state or to that of another – these deliberations play out in a relational and hierarchical context where considerations about the comparative size and status of a state is important and has implications for the possibilities and the limits of interstate interactions. For these reasons, future research on state size and size-based categorization might benefit from engaging with the concept of hierarchy, drawing inspiration from the rich field of hierarchy studies that has gained prominence in international relations studies over the last two decades. Hierarchy studies, in challenging neorealism's fundamental assumption that the ordering principle of the international system is anarchy, disputes the inference that since an international system is anarchic, all relations within that system must also be so.[6] Rather, so the argument goes, hierarchies governing units are consistent with and possible within an anarchic system – whether these hierarchies are organized around social norms, status or authority.[7] Without going into too much detail, a couple of observations from this literature can be used to demonstrate the potential of engaging with this scholarship in future historical work on state size and its role in international politics. As David A. Lake points out in his succinct overview of the field, it is productive to distinguish broad hierarchies based on social norms from more specific hierarchies based on status. According to Lake, what defines a broad hierarchy is its foundation upon social norms of inequality 'that are often beyond consciousness, or at least have been so thoroughly "normalized" that they typically are left unexamined'.[8] Racial hierarchies and hierarchies of gender are two core examples of these pervasive and implicit forms of hierarchy.[9] Status hierarchies, by contrast, are the types of hierarchies that evolve around diplomats' and scholars' typologies of international actors – such as the concepts of small states and great powers that are addressed in this volume. This strand of literature takes as given that collectives of individuals organized into states have the same psychological propensity as individuals do for ranking other groups relative to themselves in order to establish how these groups should be regarded and treated in social interactions. In IR, as in small state studies, status most often appears as a characteristic associated with the distribution of capabilities. However, an alternative strain of literature, more constructivist in its orientation, examines strategies for building and subverting hierarchy.[10]

The distinction between broad hierarchies of social norms and the more specific and explicit hierarchies of status may be analytically useful, as it prompts us to be more attentive to the types of hierarchies that are sublimated and normalized and thus form the subtext to the explicit and politically conscious forms of status-building in international politics. This will be particularly helpful as we move the exploration of size in international politics beyond the Anglo-European sphere and venture into a terrain where other forms of hierarchies – for example, those created by the legacies of Empire and other structures of dependency – still linger.[11] Likewise, the constructivist approaches to status hierarchies prompt us to supplement the mappings of images in international politics with attempts to trace and conceptualize the active status-seeking strategies employed by states in order to maintain and improve their standing in the international system.[12]

Finally, the contributions in this volume have focused mainly on inter-state relationships and perceptions, whether bilateral or multilateral. They have discussed how the international system and its composite parts have been imagined but have done so almost exclusively from the vantage point of, and in between, state (or sub-state) units, mainly in and around Europe. A logical next step would be to bring the analytical lens introduced in this book to the institutions where these multiple hierarchies overlap, intersect and crystallize, namely international organizations and international law. Although there is a rich literature on the codification of the status and hierarchies of states in diplomatic law and practice,[13] systematic historical studies of how international organizations and international public law reflect and reproduce various kinds of state typologies and hierarchies through formal procedure and informal day-to-day practices still await scholars to delve into them.

Each of these avenues, we believe, is worth pursuing. We hope that this book has not only demonstrated new ways to conceptualize and understand the nexus linking size, politics and identity but has also provided an impetus and encouragement to ongoing discussion on how states are seen to differ from each other, and how the formation and constant re-creation of the international system connect to patterns of identity construction. This book will definitely not be the last word on 'smallness', or even on 'small states'. But we do hope that we have reframed the discussions about smallness and, in doing so, have opened up new avenues for studying 'size' and its importance in understanding the ways states 'see' themselves, others and their place amongst them.

Notes

1 Inspired by Proctor, *Civilians in a World at War, 1914–1918*, 267.
2 Cf. Clunan, 'Status Is Cultural', 294.
3 Erlandsson, *Window of opportunity*.
4 E.g. Jervis, *The Logic of Images in International Relations*, esp. 4–5, 14.
5 Although this is an argument that needs to be developed much further, a key reason to embark on such a project could be to help solve what has been a key issue in the

study of international relations (history): the connection between policy on the one hand and 'public opinion' on the other. It has been very hard, even for time periods and locales where regular polls were conducted and are available for study, to establish firm links between what people thought about international politics and the international conduct of a country, or of transnational organizations and NGOs. See Hucker, *Public Opinion and Twentieth-Century Diplomacy*; Eichenberg, 'Public Opinion on Foreign Policy Issues'; Bishop, *The Illusion of Public Opinion*.

6   Lake, *Hierarchy in International Relations*, 17–43.
7   Lake, 'Hierarchy and International Relations'.
8   Lake, 3.
9   For one prominent example of this approach, see: Towns, *Women and States*. In international history there is a rich tradition for analysing the role of cultural assumptions and norms in the making of foreign policy, see for instance Costigliola, 'Unceasing Pressure for Penetration'; Costigliola, 'The Nuclear Family',
10 Lake, 'Hierarchy and International Relations', 4–5. Lake 2017 p. 4–5.
11 On the relationship between authority and hierarchy, see Lake, *Hierarchy in International Relations*, 45ff.
12 For a few example of this approach, see Renshon, *Fighting for Status. Hierarchy and Conflict in World Politics*; Zarakolu, *After Defeat*.
13 See for instance Satow, *A Guide to Diplomatic Practice*. Satow's guide has been published in consecutive editions since 1917.

Bibliography

Aa, A.J. van der, ed. 'Petrus van Limburg Brouwer'. In *Biographisch Woordenboek Der Nederlanden. Deel 2. Derde En Vierde Stuk*, 1446-9. Haarlem: J.J. van Brederode, 1855.
Aaserud, Finn. *Niels Bohr – Collected Works. Volume 11: The Political Arena (1934-1961)*. Amsterdam: North Holland, 2005.
Aaserud, Finn. *Niels Bohr – Collected Works. Volume 12: Popularization and People (1911-1962)*. Amsterdam: North Holland, 2006.
Aaserud, Finn. *Redirecting Science: Niels Bohr, Philanthropy, and the Rise of Nuclear Physics*. Cambridge/New York: Cambridge University Press, 2002.
Aaserud, Finn. 'Videnskabernes København i 1920'erne Belyst Af Amerikansk Filantropi'. In *Videnskabernes København*, edited by Thomas Söderqvist, Jan Faye, Helge Kragh and Frans Allan Rasmussen, 201-22. Roskilde: Roskilde Universitetsforlag, 1998.
Abulof, Uriel. 'Deep Securitization and Israel's "Demographic Demon"'. *International Political Sociology* 8, no. 4 (2014): 396-415.
Adler, Emanuel. 'Israel's Unsettled Relations with the World: Causes and Consequences'. In *Israel in the World. Legitimacy and Exceptionalism*, edited by Emanuel Adler, 1-23. London: Routledge.
Adler-Nissen, Rebecca and Alexei Tsinovoi. 'International Misrecognition: The Politics of Humor and National Identity in Israel's Public Diplomacy'. *European Journal of International Relations* 25, no. 1 (2019): 3-29.
Alford, Jonathan. 'Security Dilemmas of Small States'. *The World Today* 40, no. 8-9 (1984): 363-9.
Almog, Oz. *The Sabra. The Creation of the New Jew*. Berkely, CA: University of California Press, 2000.
Amara, Michaël. 'La Propagande Belge et l'image de La Belgique Aux Etats-Unis Pendant La Première Guerre Mondiale'. *Belgisch Tijdschrift Voor Nieuwste Geschiedenis/Revue Belge d'Histoire Contemporaine* 30, no. 1-2 (2000): 173-226.
Amstrup, Niels. 'The Perennial Problem of Small States. A Survey of Research Efforts'. *Cooperation and Conflict* 11, no. 3 (1976): 163-82.
'An Appeal to Americans'. In *The Need of Belgium. A Few Words*, Third edition, 32. New York: Commission for Relief of Belgium, 1915.
Antolović, Michael. 'Modern Serbian Historiography between Nation-Building and Critical Scholarship: The Case of Ilarion Ruvarac (1832-1905)'. *Hungarian Historical Review* 5, no. 2 (2016): 332-56.
Anzulovic, Branislav. *Heavenly Serbia. From Myth to Genocide*. London: Hurst & Co., 1999.
Aradau, Claudia. 'Security and the Democratic Scene: Desecuritization and Emancipation'. *Journal of International Relations and Development* 7, no. 4 (2004): 388-413.
Archer, Mary, ed. *Belgian Relief Cook Book*. Reading, PA: Belgian Relief Committee, 1915.
Arthur, Paul. *Special Relationships. Britain, Ireland and the Northern Ireland Problem*. Belfast: Blackstaff Press, 2000.
Arup, Erik. 'Det Nye Historiske Institut'. *Politiken*, 1 December 1927, 11-12.

Ásgeirsson, Jakob F. *Þjóð í hafti: Þrjátíu ára saga verslunarfjötra á Íslandi*. Reykjavík: Almenna bókmenntafélagið, 1988.
Ashton, Rosemary. 'Lewes, George Henry (1817–1878)'. In *Oxford Dictionary of National Biography*. 2008. Accessed 13 January 2020. https://doi.org/10.1093/ref:odnb/16562.
Baehr, Peter R. 'Small States: A Tool for Analysis'. *World Politics* 27, no. 3 (1975): 456–66.
Baggermans, J. and Joan Hemels. *Verzorgd Door Het ANP. Vijftig Jaar Nieuwsvoorziening*. Utrecht/Antwerpen: J.A. Veen, 1984.
Bailes, Alyson J.K., Jean-Marc Rickli and Baldur Thorhallsson. 'Small States, Survival and Strategy'. In *Small States and International Security. Europe and beyond*, edited by Clive Archer, Alyson J.K. Bailes and Anders Wivel, 26–45. London and New York: Routledge, 2014.
Baker Fox, Annette. *The Power of Small States. Diplomacy in World War II*. Chicago: University of Chicago Press, 1959.
Bakić-Hayden, Milica. 'Nesting Orientalisms: The Case of Former Yugoslavia'. *Slavic Review* 54, no. 4 (1995): 917–31.
Bakradze, Akaki. *Ilia Chavchavadze*. Tbilisi: Pegasi, 2006.
Baldacchino, Godfrey. 'Mainstreaming the Study of Small States and Territories'. *Small States & Territories* 1, no. 1 (2018): 3–16.
Banac, Ivo. *The National Question in Yugoslavia. Origins, History, Politics*. Ithaca, NY: Cornell University Press, 1984.
Barak, Oren and Gabriel Sheffer. 'Israel's "Security Network" and Its Impact: An Exploration of a New Approach'. *International Journal of Middle East Studies* 38, no. 2 (2006): 235–61.
Bar'el, Zvi. 'Four States, Two People, One Solution: Can Israel Maintain Its Identity'. In *Israel in the World. Legitimacy and Exceptionalism*, edited by Emanuel Adler, 110–23. London: Routledge, 2013.
Barston, R.P. 'Introduction'. In *The Other Powers. Studies in the Foreign Policies of Small States*, edited by R.P. Barston, 13–28. London: George Allen & Unwin Ltd., 1973.
Bar-Tal, Daniel and Dikla Antebi. 'Siege Mentality in Israel'. *International Journal of Intercultural Relations* 16, no. 3 (1992): 251–75.
Bataković, Dušan. 'A Balkan-Style French Revolution? The 1804 Serbian Uprising in European Perspective'. *Balcanica* 36 (2005): 113–29.
Batović, Ante. *The Croatian Spring. Nationalism, Repression and Foreign Policy under Tito*. London: I.B. Tauris, 2017.
Baudet, H. 'Nederland En de Rang van Denemarken'. *Bijdragen En Mededelingen Betreffende de Geschiedenis Der Nederlanden / Low Countries Historical Review* 90, no. 3 (1975): 430–43.
Bažantová, Iliona. 'Karel Kramář a Jeho Zájem o Národohospodářskou a Finační Vědu'. In *Karel Kramář (1860–1937): Život a Dílo*, edited by Jan Bílek and Luboš Velek, 58–74. Prague: Historický ústav, 2009.
The Belgian People's War. A Violation of International Law. Translations from the Official German White Book. New York: Press of John C. Rankin Co., 1915.
Belgium's Need. San Francisco, CA: Commission for Relief in Belgium, 1916.
Beller, Manfred. 'Perception, Image, Imagology'. In *Imagology. The Cultural Construction and Literary Representation of National Characters. A Critical Survey*, edited by Manfred Beller and Joep Leerssen, 3–16. Amsterdam/New York: Rodopi, 2007.
Bennett, Arnold. 'The Prodigious Problem of Belgium, with a Few Words to the Kind Heart'. In *The Need of Belgium. A Few Words*, Third edition, 8–10. New York: Commission for Relief of Belgium, 1915.

Benwell, Richard. 'The Canaries in the Coalmine: Small States as Climate Change Champions'. *The Round Table* 100, no. 413 (2011): 199–211.

Berezhnaya, Liliya and Heidi Hein-Kircher, eds. *Rampart Nations: Bulwark Myths of East European Multiconfessional Societies in the Age of Nationalism*. New York: Berghahn Books, 2019.

Berglund, Bruce R. *Castle and Cathedral. Longing for the Sacred in a Skeptical Age*. Budapest/New York: Central European University Press, 2016.

Berglund, Bruce R. 'We Stand on the Threshold of a New Age: Alice Masaryková, the Czechoslovak Red Cross, and the Building of a New Europe'. In *Aftermaths of War: Women's Movements and Female Activists*, edited by Ingrid Sharp and Matthew Stibbe, 377–96. Leiden/Boston: Brill, 2011.

Bialer, Uri. *Oil and the Arab-Israeli Conflict, 1948–63*. Basingstoke: Palgrave Macmillan, 1999.

Bialer, Uri. 'Top Hat, Tuxedo and Cannons: Israeli Foreign Policy From 1948 to 1956 as a Field of Study'. *Israel Studies* 7, no. 1 (2002): 1–80.

Bibó, István. *Die Misere Der Osteuropäischen Kleinstaaterei*. Frankfurt am Main: Verlag Neue Kritik, 1992.

Bishop, George F. *The Illusion of Public Opinion. Fact and Artifact in American Public Opinion Polls*. Lanham, MD: Rowman & Littlefield, 2005.

Blanken, Ivo. *Geschiedenis van Philips Electronics N.V. Volume III: 1922–1934*. Leiden: Martinus Nijhoff, 1992.

Blom, Frans R.E. 'Enemy Treasures: The Making and Marketing of Spanish Comedia in the Amsterdam Schouwburg'. In *Literary Hispanophobia and Hispanophilia in Britain and the Low Countries (1550–1850)*, edited by Yolanda Rodríguez Pérez, 115–44. Amsterdam: Amsterdam University Press, 2020.

Blom, Frans R.E. and Olga van Marion. 'Lope de Vega and the Conquest of Spanish Theater in the Netherlands'. *Anuario Lope de Vega* 23 (2017): 155–77.

Bogdanor, Vernon. *Devolution in the United Kingdom*. Oxford: Oxford University Press, 2001.

Bondallaz, Patrick. 'Entre propagande et action humanitaire: l'exemple des secours suisses en faveur des Belges'. *Relations internationales* 159, no. 4 (2014): 17–33.

Bosbach, Franz. *Monarchia Universalis: Ein Politischer Leitbegriff Der Frühen Neuzeit*. Göttingen: Vandenhoeck & Ruprecht Gm, 1988.

Bottici, Chiara. *Imaginal Politics: Images beyond Imagination and the Imaginary*. New York: Columbia University Press, 2014.

Brisku, Adrian. *Bittersweet Europe: Albanian and Georgian Discourses on Europe, 1878–2008*. New York/Oxford: Berghahn Books, 2013.

Brisku, Adrian. *Political Reform in the Ottoman and the Russian Empires: A Comparative Approach*. London: Bloomsbury Academic, 2017.

Browning, Christopher S. 'Small, Smart and Salient? Rethinking Identity in the Small States Literature'. *Cambridge Review of International Affairs* 19, no. 4 (2006): 669–84.

Bull, Francis and John Landquist, eds. *Georg og Edv. Brandes: Brevveksling med nordiske Forfattere og Videnskabsmænd, Volume III*. Copenhagen: Gyldendal, 1940.

Burguera, Mónica and Christopher Schmidt-Nowara. 'Introduction: Backwardness and Its Discontents'. *Social History* 29, no. 3 (2004): 279–83.

Buus, Henriette. *Indretning og efterretning: Rockefeller Foundations indflydelse på den danske velfærdsstat 1920–1970*. København: Museum Tusculanum, 2009.

Buzan, Barry and Ole Wæver. *Regions and Powers. The Structure of International Security*. Cambridge [etc.]: Cambridge University Press, 2003.

Buzan, Barry, Ole Wæver and Jaap de Wilde. *Security: A New Framework for Analysis.* Boulder, CO: Lynne Rienner, 1998.
Caine, Hall, ed. *King Albert's Book. A Tribute to the Belgian King and People from Representative Men and Women throughout the World.* s.l.: Daily Telegraph, 1914.
Campbell, David. *Writing Security. United States Foreign Policy and the Politics of Identity.* Minneapolis, MN: University of Minnesota Press, 1992.
Carlsnaes, Walter. 'How Should We Study the Foreign Policies of Small European States?' *Naçao & Defesa* 118, no. 3 (2007): 7–20.
Carmon, Arye. 'Political Education in the Midst of a National Identity Crisis: The Compatibility of Judaism and Democracy as a Pedagogical Theme'. In *Israeli Democracy under Stress*, edited by Ehud Sprinzak and Larry Diamond, 293–308. Boulder, CO: Lynne Rienner Publishers, 1993.
Carr, E.H. and Michael Cox. *The Twenty Years' Crisis.* Second edition, reissued. Basingstoke: Palgrave Macmillan, 2010.
Cârstocea, Raul. 'Historicising the Normative Boundaries of Diversity: The Minority Treaties of 1919 in a Longue Durée Perspective'. *Studies on National Movements* 5, no. 7 (2020): 43–79.
Cârstocea, Raul. 'Uneasy Twins? The Entangled Histories of Jewish Emancipation and Anti-Semitism in Romania and Hungary, 1866–1913'. *Slovo* 21, no. 2 (2009): 64–85.
Case, Holly. *Between States: The Transylvanian Question and the European Idea during World War II.* Stanford, CA: Stanford University Press, 2013.
Chakrabarty, Dipesh. *Provincializing Europe: Postcolonial Thought and Historical Difference.* Princeton, NJ: Princeton University Press, 2000.
Chapnick, Adam. 'Middle Power No More? Canada in World Affairs since 2006'. *Seton Hall Journal of Diplomacy and International Relations* 14, no. 2 (2013): 102–11.
Chavchavadze, Ilia. *Publitsisturi Tserilebi.* Tbilisi: Gamomtsemloba 'Sabchota Sakartvelo', 1987.
Chavchavadze, Ilia. *Tserilebi Literaturisa Da Khelovnebaze.* Tbilisi: Sakartvelos SSR Sakhelmtsipo Gamomtsemloba, 1957.
Chazan, Naomi. 'Israel and the World: The Democracy Factor'. In *Israel in the World. Legitimacy and Exceptionalism*, edited by Emanuel Adler, 73–96. London: Routledge, 2013.
Checa Beltrán, José. 'Lecturas Sobre La Cultura Española En El Siglo XVIII Francés'. In *Lecturas Del Legado Español En La Europa Ilustrada*, edited by José Checa Beltrán, 105–37. Madrid/Frankfurt am Main: Iberoamericana/Vervuert, 2012.
Checa Beltrán, José. 'Leyenda Negra y Leyenda Rosa'. In *Lecturas Del Legado Español En La Europa Ilustrada*, edited by José Checa Beltrán, 7–12. Madrid/Frankfurt am Main: Iberoamericana/Vervuert, 2012.
The Children's Plight. New York: The Commission for Relief in Belgium, 1916.
Chong, Alan. 'Small State Soft Power Strategies: Virtual Enlargement in the Cases of the Vatican City State and Singapore'. *Cambridge Review of International Affairs* 23, no. 3 (2003): 383–405.
Cibulka, Pavel, Jan Hájek and Martin Kučera. 'The Definition of Czech National Society during the Period of Liberalism and Nationalism (1860–1914)'. In *A History of Czech Lands*, edited by Jaroslav Pánek and Oldřich Túma, 313–38. Prague: Karolinum Press, 2009.
Clark, Ian. *The Hierarchy of States: Reform and Resistance in the International Order.* New York: Cambridge University Press, 1989.

Clercq, Willem de. *Verhandeling Ter Beandwoording Der Vraag: Welken Invloed Heeft Vreemde Letterkunde, Inzonderheid de Italiaansche, Spaansche, Fransche En Duitsche, Gehad Op de Nederlandsche Taal- En Letterkunde, Sints Het Begin Der Vijftiende Eeuw Tot Op Onze Dagen?* Amsterdam: Pieper en Ipenbuur, 1824.

Clunan, Anne L. 'Why Status Matters in World Politics'. In *Status in World Politics*, edited by Deborah Welch Larson, T.V. Paul and William C. Wohlforth, 273–96. Cambridge: Cambridge University Press, 2014.

Coakley, John. 'British Irish Institutional Structures: Towards a New Relationship'. *Irish Political Studies* 29, no. 1 (2014): 76–97.

Cohn, Margit. 'Fuzzy Legality and National Styles of Regulation: Government Intervention in the Israel Downstream Oil Market'. *Law & Policy* 24, no. 1 (2002): 51–88.

Colley, Linda. *Britons. Forging the Nation, 1707–1837*. Third edition. New Haven: Yale University Press, 2009.

Čolović, Ivan. *Smrt Na Kosovu Polju. Istorija Kosovskog Mita*. Belgrade: Biblioteka XX veka, 2016.

Connelly, Tony. *Brexit and Ireland: The Dangers, the Opportunities, and the Inside Story of the Irish Response*. Dublin: Penguin Ireland, 2017.

Cooper, Andrew F. and Timothy M. Shaw. 'The Diplomacies of Small States at the Start of the Twenty-First Century: How Vulnerable? How Resilient?' In *The Diplomacies of Small States. Between Vulnerability and Resilience*, edited by Andrew F. Cooper and Timothy M. Shaw, 1–18. Houndsmills/New York: Palgrave Macmillan, 2009.

Ćorović, Vladimir. *Velika Srbija*. Novi Sad: Budućnost, 2009.

Ćosić, Dobrica. *Srpsko Pitanje u XX Veku. Lična Istorija Jednog Doba*. Belgrade: Službeni glasnik, 2009.

Costigliola, Frank. 'The Nuclear Family: Tropes of Gender and Pathology in the Western Alliance'. *Diplomatic History* 21, no. 2 (1997): 163–83. https://doi.org/10.1111/1467-7709.00062.

Costigliola, Frank. '"Unceasing Pressure for Penetration": Gender, Pathology, and Emotion in George Kennan's Formation of the Cold War'. *The Journal of American History* 83, no. 4 (1997): 1309–39. https://doi.org/10.2307/2952904.

Craver, Earlene. 'Patronage and the Directions of Research in Economics: The Rockefeller Foundation in Europe 1924–1938'. *Minerva* 24, no. 2 (1986): 205–22.

Crowards, Tom. 'Defining the Category of "Small" States'. *Journal of International Development* 14, no. 2 (2002): 143–79.

Crump, Laurien and Susanna Erlandsson. 'Introduction. Smaller Powers in Cold War Europe'. In *Margins for Manoeuvre in Cold War Europe. The Influence of Smaller Powers*. London/New York: Routledge, 2020: 1–10.

Dainotto, Roberto. *Europe (in Theory)*. Durham: Duke University Press, 2007.

D'Ancona, Matthew. *Being British. The Search for the Values That Bind the Nation*. Edinburgh/London: Mainstream Publishing, 2009.

'Dansk-Íslensk Sambandslög'. In *Stjórnartíðindi Fyrir Ísland*. Volume A, 75–9. Reykjavík: Ísafoldarprentsmiðja, 1918.

Dibdin, Charles. *A Complete History of the English Stage; Introduced by a Comparative and Comprehensive Review of the Asiatic, the Grecian, the Roman, the Spanish, the Italian, the Portuguese, the German, the French, and Other Theatres, and Involving Biographical Tracts and Anecdotes*. London: s.l., 1800.

Dibdin, Charles. *The Professional Life of Mr. Dibdin, Written by Himself. Together with the Words of Six Hundred Songs Selected from His Works and Sixty Small Prints Taken from*

the Subjects of the Songs, and Invented, Etched, and Prepared for the Aqua Tint by Miss Dibdin. London: s.l., 1803.
Dijk, Kees van. *The Netherlands Indies and the Great War, 1914–1918*. Leiden: KITLV Press, 2007.
Dijk, Pelle van. 'Uithangbord van de BV Nederland. La Gazette Hollande En de Nederlandse Publieksdiplomatie, 1918–1935'. MA Thesis, University of Amsterdam, 2016.
Dijk, Pelle van. '"You Act Too Much as a Journalist and Too Little as a Diplomat". Pieter Geyl, the National Bureau for Documentation on the Netherlands and Dutch Public Diplomacy'. In *Shaping the International Relations of the Netherlands, 1815–2000. A Small Country on the Global Scene*, edited by Ruud van Dijk, Samuël Kruizinga, Vincent Kuitenbrouwer and Rimko van der Maar, 80–96. London: Routledge, 2018.
Dijk, Ruud van, Samuel Kruizinga, Vincent Kuitenbrouwer and Rimko Van Der Maar. 'Conclusions and Outlook. Small States on the Global Scene'. In *Shaping the International Relations of the Netherlands, 1815–2000. A Small Country on the Global Scene*, edited by Ruud van Dijk, Samuël Kruizinga, Vincent Kuitenbrouwer and Rimko van der Maar, 240–4. London: Routledge, 2018.
Đinđić, Zoran. 'Srbija, Ni Na Istoku, Ni Na Zapadu'. *Helsinška Povelja*, 2013.
Dinkić, Mlađan. *Ekonomija Destrukcije: Velika Pljačka Naroda*. Belgrade: Stubovi kulture, 1995.
Djilas, Aleksa, Ljiljana Bulatović and Radovan Samardžić, eds. 'Istorijski Karakter Srba'. In *Srpsko Pitanje*, 7–26. Beograd: Politika, 1991.
Doubek, Vratislav. *T. G. Masaryk: A Česka Slovanska Politika, 1882–1910*. Prague: Academia, 1999.
Dragović-Soso, Jasna. 'Rethinking Yugoslavia: Serbian Intellectuals and the "National Question" in Historical Perspective'. *Contemporary European History* 13, no. 2 (2004): 170–84.
Dragović-Soso, Jasna. *'Saviours of the Nation'. Serbia's Intellectual Opposition and the Revival of Nationalism*. Montreal: McGill-Queen's University Press, 2002.
Drinker Bullit, Ernesta. *An Uncensored Diary from the Central Empires*. Garden City, NY: Doubleday, Page & Company, n.d.
Duchesne, Albert. *Le Prince Philippe de Belgique, Comte de Flandre (1837–1905)*. Brussels: Koninklijke academie voor overzeese wetenschappen, 1972.
Duka, Ferit. *Shekujt Osmanë Në Hapsirën Shqiptare*. Tirana: UET Press, 2009.
Duncan, Andrew. 'Land for Peace: Israel's Choice'. *Israel Affairs* 2, no. 1 (1995): 59–72.
East, Maurice A. 'Size and Foreign Policy Behavior: A Test of Two Models'. *World Politics* 25, no. 4 (1973): 556–76.
Eichenberg, Richard C. 'Public Opinion on Foreign Policy Issues'. *Oxford Research Encyclopedia of Politics*, 5 April 2016. https://doi.org/10.1093/acrefore/9780190228637.013.78.
Ejdus, Filip. *Crisis and Ontological Insecurity: Serbia's Anxiety of Kosovo's Secession*. Houndsmills: Palgrave Macmillan, 2020.
Ejdus, Filip. 'Critical Situations, Fundamental Questions and Ontological Insecurity in World Politics'. *Journal of International Relations and Development* 21 (2018): 883–908.
Ejdus, Filip and Jelena Subotić. 'Kosovo as Serbia's Sacred Space: Governmentality, Pastoral Power, and Sacralization of Territories'. In *Politicization of Religion, the Power of Symbolism. The Case of Former Yugoslavia and Its Successor States*, edited by Gorana Ognjenović and Jasna Jozelić, 159–83. London: Palgrave, 2014.

Ellerman, Bruce A. 'Starvation Blockade and Herbert Hoover's Commission for Relief in Belgium, 1914-1919'. In *Navies and Soft Power. Historical Case Studies of Naval Power and the Nonunse of Military Force*, edited by Bruce A. Ellerman and S.C.M. Paine, 47-67. Newport, RI: Naval War College Press, 2015.

Elliott, John. *Spain, Europe and the Wider World, 1500-1800*. London: Yale University Press, 2009.

Elman, Miriam Fendius. 'The Foreign Policies of Small States: Challenging Neorealism in Its Own Backyard'. *British Journal of Political Science* 25, no. 2 (1995): 171-217.

Erlandsson, Susanna. *Window of Opportunity: Dutch and Swedish Security Ideas and Strategies 1942-1948*. Uppsala: Uppsala University Press, 2015.

Étienvre, Françoise. 'Montesquieu y Voltaire: Sus Visiones de España'. In *Lecturas Del Legado Español En La Europa Ilustrada*, edited by José Checa Beltrán, 67-101. Madrid/Frankfurt am Main: Iberoamericana/Vervuert, 2012.

Eyre Hunt, Edward. *War Bread. A Personal Narrative of the War and Relief in Belgium*. New York: Henry Holt and Company, 1916.

Farley, John. *To Cast Out Disease. A History of the International Health Division of the Rockefeller Foundation (1913-1951)*. New York/Toronto: Oxford University Press, 2007.

Favrholdt, D. *Niels Bohr – Collected Works. Volume 10: Complementarity beyond Physics (1928-1962)*. Amsterdam: North Holland, 1999.

Filimon, A. 'Quelques Donnees Concernant Les Relations Entre La Roumanie et La Belgique Au 19e Siecle'. *Belgisch Tijdschrift Voor Nieuwste Geschiedenis/Revue Belge d'histoire Contemporaine* 2, no. 1 (1970): 21-6.

Flemming, Thomas. *The Illusion of Victory. America in World War I*. New York: Basic Books, 2003.

Frashëri, Sami. *Shqipëria Çka Qënë, çështë e Çdo Të Bëhet*. Tirana: Reklama, 2010.

Friis, Søren. 'The Scandinavian Centre: Denmark and the Early Years of International Studies under the League of Nations'. In *The League of Nations: Perspectives from the Present*, edited by Karen Gram-Skjoldager and Haakon A Ikonomou, 123-36. Aarhus: Aarhus University Press, 2019.

Fuchs, Barbara. 'The Black Legend and the Golden Age Dramatic Canon'. In *La Leyenda Negra En El Crisol de La Comedia: El Teatro Del Siglo de Oro Frente a Los Estereotipos Antihispánicos*, edited by Yolanda Rodríguez Pérez and Antonio Sánchez Jiménez, 218-36. Madrid/Frankfurt am Main: Iberoamericana/Vervuert, 2016.

Fuchs, Barbara. *The Poetics of Piracy: Emulating Spain in English Literature*. Philadelphia: University of Pennsylvania Press, 2013.

Galsworthy, John. 'To the Rescue – AMERICA!' In *The Need of Belgium. A Few Words*, Third edition, 15-18. New York: Commission for Relief of Belgium, 1915.

García Cárcel, Ricardo and José Javier Ruiz Ibáñez. 'Reflexiones Sobre La Leyenda Negra'. In *Las Vecindades de Las Monarquías Ibéricas*, 43-80. Madrid: Fondo de Cultura Económica, 2013.

Gay, George and H.H. Fisher, eds. *Public Relations of the Commission for Relief in Belgium. Documents, Vol. II*. Palo Alto, CA: Stanford University Press, 1929.

Georgescu, Vlad. *The Romanians. A History*. Columbus, OH: University of Ohio Press, 1991.

Gertz, Nurith. 'Social Myths in Literary and Political Texts'. *Poetics Today* 7, no. 4 (1986): 621-39.

Gilboa, Eytan. 'Public Diplomacy: The Missing Component in Israel's Foreign Policy'. *Israel Affairs* 12, no. 4 (2006): 715-747.

Ginderachter, Maarten Van. *The Everyday Nationalism of Workers. A Social History of Modern Belgium*. Stanford, CA: Stanford University Press, 2019.
Gligorijević, Branislav. *Kralj Aleksandar Karađorđević u Ratovima Za Nacionalno Oslobođenje*. Belgrade: Zavod za udžbenike i nastavna sredstva, 2002.
Goddeeris, Idesbald. 'Les Relations Entre La Belgique et La Roumanie, 1859-1939(-1989)'. *Studia Politica. Romanian Political Science Review* 8, no. 1 (2008): 47-55.
Graaf, Beatrice de. 'The Allied Machine. The Conference of Ministers in Paris and the Management of Security, 1815-18'. In *Securing Europe after Napoleon. 1815 and the New European Security Culture*, edited by Beatrice de Graaf, Ido de Haan and Brian Vick, 130-49. Cambridge [etc.]: Cambridge University Press, 2019.
Graaf, Beatrice de. 'The Legacy of the Wars for the International System'. In *Cambridge History of the Napoleonic Wars*. Cambridge: Cambridge University Press, Forthcoming.
Graaff, Bob de. 'Kalm temidden van woedende golven'. In *Het ministerie van Koloniën en zijn taakomgeving, 1912-1940*. Den Haag: SDU Uitgevers, 1997.
Gram-Skjoldager, Karen. 'The Other End of Neutrality. Denmark, the First World War and The League of Nations'. In *Caught in the Middle: Neutrals, Neutrality and the First World War*, edited by Johan Den Hertog and Samuël Kruizinga, 155-72. Amsterdam: Amsterdam University Press, 2012.
Gram-Skjoldager, Karen, Haakon A. Ikonomou and Torsten Kahlert. 'Scandinavians and the League of Nations Secretariat, 1919-1946'. *Scandinavian Journal of History* 44, no. 4 (2019): 1-30.
Grazia Profetti, Maria. 'Para La Fortuna de Lope En El Siglo XVIII'. In *Una de Las Dos Españas. Homenaje a Manfred Tietz*, edited by Arno G. Arnscheidt and P. Tous, 728-41. Madrid/Frankfurt am Main: Iberoamericana/Vervuert, 2007.
Green, Leanne. 'Advertising War: Picturing Belgium in First World War Publicity'. *Media, War & Conflict* 7, no. 3 (2014): 309-25.
Greer, Margaret R., Walter D. Mignolo and Maureen Quilligan, eds. *Rereading the Black Legend: The Discourses of Religious and Racial Difference in the Renaissance Empires*. Chicago: University of Chicago Press, 2007.
Griffin, Eric. *English Renaissance Drama and the Scepter of Spain: Ethnopoetics and Empire*. Philadelphia: University of Pennsylvania Press, 2009.
Grmek, Mirko Dražen, Marc Gjidara and Neven Šimac. *Le nettoyage ethnique: documents historiques sur une idéologie serbe*. Paris: Fayard, 1993.
Guillen, P. 'La Crise Franco-Allemande de 1886-7 et Les Relations Franco-Belges'. In *Les Relations Franco-Belges de 1830 à 1934: Acte Du Colloque de Metz, 15-16 Novembre 1974*, 87-96. Metz: Centre de recherches relations internationales de l'Université de Metz, 1975.
Gullace, Nicoletta F. 'Sexual Violence and Family Honor: British Propaganda and International Law during the First World War'. *The American Historical Review* 102, no. 3 (1997): 714-47.
Gumz, Jonathan E. *The Resurrection and Collapse of Empire in Habsburg Serbia, 1914-1918*. Cambridge: Cambridge University Press, 2009.
Gunnar Þór Bjarnason. *Upp með fánann! Baráttan um uppkastið 1908 og sjálfstæðisbarátta Íslendinga*. Reykjavík: Mál og menning, 2012.
Hajdarpašić, Edin. *Whose Bosnia? Nationalism and Political Imagination in the Balkans, 1840-1914*. Ithaca, NY: Cornell University Press, 2015.
Hálfdanarson, Guðmundur. 'Embættismannaskólinn 1911-1961'. In *Aldarsaga Háskóla Íslands*, edited by Gunnar Karlsson, 17-282. Reykjavík: Háskólaútgáfan, 2011.

Hálfdanarson, Guðmundur. 'Icelandic Modernity and the Role of Nationalism'. In *Nordic Paths to Modernity*, edited by Jóhann Páll Árnason and Björn Wittrock, 251–73. New York: Berghahn Books, 2015.

Hálfdanarson, Guðmundur. 'Severing the Ties – Iceland's Journey from a Union with Denmark to a Nation-State'. *Scandinavian Journal of History* 31, no. 3–4 (2006): 237–54.

Hálfdanarson, Guðmundur and Kirsten Thisted. 'The Specter of an Empire'. In *Denmark and the New North Atlantic: Narratives and Memories in a Former Empire*, edited by Kirsten Thisted and Ann-Sofie N. Gremaud, 93–180. Aarhus: Aarhus University Press, 2020.

Hall, Stuart. 'The West and the Rest: Discourse and Power'. In *Formations of Modernity*, edited by Stuart Hall and Bram Gieben, 184–227. Oxford: Polity Press in association with Blackwell and the Open University, 1992.

Hall, Stuart, Jessica Evans and Sean Nixon. *Representation: Cultural Representation and Signifying Practices*. London: The Open University/SAGE, 2013.

Hansen, Lene. *Security as Practice. Discourse Analysis and the Bosnian War*. London/ New York: Routledge, 2006.

Hardarson, Ólafur Th. and Gunnar H. Kristinsson. 'The Icelandic Parliamentary Election of 1987'. *Electoral Studies* 6, no. 3 (1987): 219–34.

Harline, Craig E. *Pamphlets, Printing, and Political Culture in the Early Dutch Republic*. Dordrecht/Boston: Martinus Nijhoff, 1987.

Hasquin, Hervé. *Historiographie et politique en Belgique*. Third edition. Brussels/Charleroi: Editions de l'Université de Bruxelles/Institut Jules Destrée, 1996.

Hastings, Adrian. *The Construction of Nationhood: Ethnicity, Religion and Nationalism*. Cambridge: Cambridge University Press, 1997.

Hazell, Robert, ed. *Constitutional Futures Revisited. Britain's Constitution to 2020*. Houndsmills: Palgrave Macmillan, 2008.

Hechter, Michael. *Internal Colonialism. The Celtic Fringe in British National Development (1999 [1975])*. Second edition. New Brunswick, NJ: Transaction Publishers, 1999.

Hehn, Paul N. 'The Origins of Modern Pan-Serbism – the 1844 Načertanije of Ilija Garašanin'. *East European Quarterly* 9, no. 2 (1975): 153–71.

Helfant-Budding, Audrey. 'Yugoslavs into Serbs: Serbian National Identity, 1961–1971'. *Nationalities Papers* 25, no. 3 (1997): 407–26.

Hellema, Duco. *Nederland in de Wereld : Buitenlandse Politiek van Nederland*. Fourth edition. Houten [etc.] : Spectrum, 2010.

Hellemans, Jacques. '"La Belgique de l'Orient". Les Relations Belgique–Roumanie à Travers l'imprimé Au Milieu Du XIXe Siècle'. In *Actes Du Symposium International 'Le Livre. La Roumanie. L'Europe'*, edited by Frédéric Barbier, 298–300. Bucharest: Editura Biblioteca Bucureştilor, 2012.

Hellemans, Jacques. 'L'Imprimé Bruxellois Dans La "Belgique de l'Orient" (1830–1865)'. *Revista Bibliotecii Academiei Române* 2, no. 2 (2017): 39–50.

Hemels, Joan. *Een journalistiek geheim ontsluierd. De Dubbelmonarchie en een geval van dubbele moraal in de Nederlandse pers tijdens de Eerste Wereldoorlog*. Apeldoorn/ Antwerpen: Spinhuis Uitgevers, 2010.

Hemels, Joan. *Van perschef tot overheidsvoorlichter. De grondslagen van overheidsvoorlichting*. Alphen aan den Rijn: Samsom, 1973.

Hemphill, Alexander J. *Belgium under the Surface. Personal Observations of Alexander J. Hemphill, Treasurer of the Commission*, n.d.

Hey, Jeanne A.K. 'Introducing Small State Foreign Policy'. In *Small States in World Politics. Explaining Foreign Policy Behavior*, edited by Jeanne A.K. Hey, 1–12. Boulder, CO: Lynne Riener, 2003.

History of the Woman's Section of the Commission for Relief in Belgium. New York: Commission for Relief in Belgium, 1915.
Hitchins, Keith. *Rumania, 1866–1947.* Oxford: Clarendon Press, 1994.
Hobsbawm, Eric. *The Age of Empire: 1875–1914.* London: Weidenfeld & Nicolson, 1987.
Hobsbawm, Eric J. *Nations and Nationalism since 1780. Programme, Myth, Reality.* Second edition. Cambridge: Cambridge University Press, 1990.
Holdar, Sven. 'The Ideal State and the Power of Geography the Life-Work of Rudolf Kjellén'. *Political Geography* 11, no. 3 (1992): 307–23.
Holy, Ladislav. *The Little Czech Man and the Great Czech Nation. National Identity and the Post-Communist Transformation of Society.* Cambridge/New York: Cambridge University Press, 1996.
Hope, Anthony. 'The Fleet of Mercy'. In *The Need of Belgium. A Few Words*, Third edition, 19–22. New York: Commission for Relief of Belgium, 1915.
Horne, John and Alan Kramer. *German Atrocities, 1914: A History of Denial.* New Haven, CT: Yale University Press, 2001.
Horst, Daniel. *De Opstand in Zwart-Wit: Propagandaprenten Uit de Nederlandse Opstand (1566–1584).* Zutphen: Walburg Pers, 2003.
Hroch, Miroslav. *Social Preconditions of National Revival in Europe: A Comparative Analysis of the Social Composition of Patriotic Groups among Smaller European Nations.* New York [etc.]: Cambridge University Press, 1986.
Hucker, Daniel. *Public Opinion and Twentieth-Century Diplomacy: A Global Perspective.* London/New York: Bloomsbury Academic, 2020.
Hull, Isabel V. *A Scrap of Paper. Breaking and Making International Law during the Great War.* Ithaca: Cornell University Press, 2013.
Iarocci, Michael. *Properties of Modernity: Romantic Spain, Modern Europe, and the Legacies of Empire.* Nashville: Vanderbilt University Press, 2006.
Iglesias, Carmen. 'España Desde Fuera'. In *España. Reflexiones Sobre El Ser de España*, edited by Real Academia de la Historia, 377–428. Madrid: Real Academia de la Historia, 1998.
Iii, William L. Chew. 'What's in a National Stereotype? An Introduction to Imagology at the Threshold of the 21st Century'. *Language and Intercultural Communication* 6, no. 3–4 (15 August 2006): 179–87. https://doi.org/10.2167/laic246.0.
Ingimundarson, Valur. *Uppgjör við umheimin.* Reykjavik: Vaka-Helgafell, 2002.
International Labour Conference, ed. *International Labor Conference, First Annual Meeting, October 29, 1919–November 29, 1919. Pan American Union Building, Washington, D.C., U.S.A.* Washington, DC: Government Printing Office, 1920.
Iordachi, Constantin. 'Citizenship, Nation and State-Building: The Integration of Northern Dobrogea into Romania, 1878–1913'. *Carl Beck Papers in Russian and East European Studies.* 1607 (2002). https://doi.org/10.5195/CBP.2002.93.
Iordachi, Constantin. 'From Imperial Entanglements to National Disentanglement: The "Greek Question" in Moldavia and Wallachia, 1611–1863'. In *Entangled Histories of the Balkans. Volume One: National Ideologies and Language Policies*, edited by Roumen Dontchev Daskalov and Tchavdar Marinov, 67–148. Leiden: Brill, 2013.
Irwin, Julia. 'The Disaster of War: American Understandings of Catastrophe, Conflict and Relief'. *First World War Studies* 5, no. 1 (2014): 17–28.
Irwin, Will. 'The Babes of Belgium'. In *The Need of Belgium. A Few Words*, Third edition, 11–14. New York: Commission for Relief of Belgium, 1915.
Irwin, Will. *A Reporter at Armageddon. Letters from the Front and behind the Lines of the Great War.* New York/London: D. Appleton and Company, 1918.

Janelidze, Mikheil. 'Address'. Edited by Ministry of Foreign Affairs of Georgia and LEPL Information Centre of NATO and EU. *Georgia's European Way* 14 (2018): 1–53.

Jaskułowski, Krzysztof. 'Western (Civic) "versus" Eastern (Ethnic) Nationalism. The Origins and Critique of the Dichotomy'. *Polish Sociological Review* 17, no. 1 (2010): 289–303.

Jelavich, Barbara. *History of the Balkans. Volume 1: Eighteenth and Nineteenth Centuries.* Cambridge: Cambridge University Press, 1983.

Jelavich, Charles. 'Garašanins Načertanije Und Das Großserbische Problem'. *Südostforschungen* 28 (1968): 131–47.

Jensen, Lotte. 'In verzet tegen "Duitschlands klatergoud". Pleidooien voor een nationaal toneel, 1800–1840'. *Tijdschrift voor Nederlandse Taal-en Letterkunde* 122 (2006): 289–302.

Jervis, Robert. *The Logic of Images in International Relations.* New York/Oxford: Princeton University Press, 1970.

Jesse, Nel G. and John R. Dreyer. *Small States in the International System. At Peace and at War.* Lanham, MD: Lexington Books, 2016.

Johannes, Gert-Jan and Inger Leemans. *Worm en Donder, Geschiedenis van de Nederlandse Literatuur 1700–1800: De Republiek.* Amsterdam: Prometheus, 2013.

Jóhannesson, Guðni Th. 'How "Cod War" Came: The Origins of the Anglo-Icelandic Fisheries Dispute, 1958–61'. *Historical Research* 77, no. 198 (2004): 459, 543–74.

Jóhannesson, Guðni Th. *Troubled Waters. Cod War, Fishing Disputes, and Britain's Fight for the Freedom of the High Seas, 1948–1964.* Reykjavik: North Atlantic Fisheries History Association, 2007.

Jones, Clive. 'The Foreign Policy of Israel'. In *The Foreign Policies of Middle East States*, edited by Raymond Hinnebusch and Anoushiravan Ehteshami, Second edition, 289–314. Boulder, CO: Lynne Rienner Publishers, 2004.

Jones, Stephen F. *Socialism in Georgian Colours: The European Road to Social Democracy 1883–1917.* Cambridge [etc.]: Harvard University Press, 2005.

Juderías, Julián. *La Leyenda Negra.* Madrid: Atlas, 2007.

Kaarsted, Tage, ed. *Ministermødeprotokol 1916–1918. Kirkeminister Th. Povlsens referater.* Aarhus: Universitetsforlaget i Aaarhus, 1973.

Kakachia, Kornely and Salome Minesashvili. 'Identity Politics: Exploring Georgia's Foreign Policy Behaviour'. *Journal of Eurasian Studies* 6 (2015): 171–80.

Kamen, Henry. *Imagining Spain. Historical Myth and National Identity.* Yale: Yale University Press, 2008.

Kaniok, Peter and Robert Majer. 'Small Countries in the EU: The Czech Republic Case'. *Journal of Contemporary of Central and Eastern Europe* 24, no. 1 (2016): 17–35.

Karup Pedersen, Ole. *Udenrigsminister P. Munchs Opfattelse Af Danmarks Stilling i International Politik, Volume 2.* Copenhagen: Gads Forlag, 1970.

Keene, Jennifer D. 'Americans Respond. Perspectives on the Global War, 1914–1917'. *Geschichte Und Gesellschaft* 40, no. 2 (2014): 266–86.

Kellogg, Charlotte. *Women of Belgium. Turning Tragedy to Triumph.* New York/London: Funk & Wagnalls Company, 1917.

Kellogg, Vernon. *Fighting Starvation in Belgium.* Garden City, NY: Doubleday, Page & Company, 1917.

Kellogg, Vernon. *Headquarters Nights. A Record of Conversations and Experiences at the Headquarters of the German Army in France and Belgium.* Boston: The Atlantic Monthly Press, 1917.

Kelsen, Hans. 'The Principle of Sovereign Equality of States as a Basis for International Organization'. *Yale Law Review* 53, no. 2 (1944): 207–20.
Kemal, Ismail. *The Memoirs of Ismail Kemal Bey*. Edited by Sommerville Story. London: Constable, 1920.
Khundadze, Simon. *Kartuli Inteligentsiis Evronuli Profili Metskhramete Saukuneshi*. Tbilisi: s.n., 1927.
Kimmerling, Baruch. 'Patterns of Militarism in Israel'. *European Journal of Sociology/ Archives Européennes de Sociologie/Europäisches Archiv Für Soziologie* 34, no. 2 (1993): 196–223.
Klinkert, Wim, Samuël Kruizinga and Paul Moeyes. *Nederland neutraal. De Eerste Wereldoorlog 1914–1918*. Amsterdam: Boom, 2014.
Kluge, Sophie. 'Ambiguous Allegories: What the Mythological Comedia Reveals about Baroque Tragedy'. *Comparative Drama* 47, no. 2 (2012): 187–207.
Koch, Lene. *Racehygiejne i Danmark 1920–56*. Third edition. Copenhagen: Information, 2014.
Kohn, Hans. *The Idea of Nationalism*. New York: The MacMillan Company, 1944.
Kohn, Hans. 'Western and Eastern Nationalisms'. In *The Idea of Nationalism*, edited by John Hutchinson and Anthony Smith, 162–5. Oxford: Oxford University Press, 1994.
Kollar, Robert, Heinrich Hoffmann, Marie Nečasová-Poubová and Stanislav Režný. *Der Einfluss der Krise auf Familien beschäftigungsloser Arbeiter in der Čechoslovakischen Republik*. Prague: Forschungssektion des Sozialinstitutes der Čechosl Republik, 1933.
Konitza, Faik. *Selected Correspondence, 1896–1942*. London: Centre for Albanian Studies, 2000.
Kook, Rebecca. 'Between Uniqueness and Exclusion: The Politics of Identity in Israel'. In *Srael in Comparative Perspective. Challenging the Conventional Wisdom*, edited by Michael N. Barnett, 199–225. Albany, NY: State University of New York Press, 1996.
Kořalka, Jiří. *Tschechen im Habsburgerreich und in Europa, 1815–1914: Sozialgeschichtliche Zusammenhänge der neuzeitlichen Nationsbildung und der Nationalitätenfrage in den böhmischen Ländern*. Munich: R. Oldenbourg Verlag, 1991.
Koselleck, Reinhart. 'The Historical-Political Semantics of Asymmetric Counterconcepts'. In *Futures Past: On the Semantics of Historical Time*, edited by Reinhart Koselleck, translated by Keith Tribe, 155–91. New York: Columbia University Press, 2004.
Kostal, Karel. 'Tjekoslovakiets Politiske Og Økonomiske Stilling'. *Økonomi Og Politik* 9, no. 4 (1935): 264–72.
Koštunica, Vojislav and Kosta Čavoški. *Party Pluralism or Monism: Social Movements and the Political System in Yugoslavia, 1944–1949*. Boulder, CO: East European Monographs, 1985.
Kovtun, George J. *Masaryk & America: Testimony of a Relationship*. Washington, DC: United States Government Printing Office, 1988.
Kragh, Helge, Peter Kjærgaard, Henry Nielsen and Kristian Hvidtfeldt-Nielsen. *Science in Denmark: A Thousand-Year History*. Aarhus: Aarhus University Press, 2008.
Krakesová, Marie, Pavla Kodymová and Peter Brnula. *Sociální Kliniky: Z dějin Sociální Práce a Sociálního Skolství*. Prague: Karolinum Press, 2018.
Kramář, Karel. *Paměti Dr. Karla Kramáře*. Edited by Karel Hoch. Prague: Nakladatelství Pražské Akciové Tiskárny, 1938.
Krauel, Javier. *Imperial Emotions: Cultural Responses to Myths of Empire in Fin-de-Siecle Spain*. Liverpool: Liverpool University Press, 2013.
Kříž, Jaroslav and Renata Beranová. *Historie Státního zdravotního ústavu v Praze*. Prague: Státní zdravotní ústav, 2005.

Kruizinga, Samuël. 'A Small State? The Size of the Netherlands as a Focal Point in Foreign Policy Debates, 1900-1940'. *Diplomacy & Statecraft* 27, no. 3 (2016): 420-36.
Kruizinga, Samuël. 'Neutrality'. In *The Cambridge History of the First World War. Volume II: The State*, edited by Jay Winter, 542-75, 712-14. Cambridge: Cambridge University Press, 2014.
Kuitenbrouwer, Vincent. 'The Dutch East Indies during the First World War and the Birth of Colonial Radio'. *World History Bulletin* 31, no. 1 (2015): 28-31.
Kuitenbrouwer, Vincent. 'Ir.dr. C.J. de Groot: radiopionier in de tropen'. In *Na de catastrofe. De Eerste Wereldoorlog en de zoektocht naar een nieuw Europa*, edited by Frits Boterman, Arnold Labrie and Willem Melching, 255-66. Amsterdam: Nieuw Amsterdam, 2014.
Kuitenbrouwer, Vincent. 'Propaganda That Dare Not Speak Its Name. International Information Services about the Dutch East Indies, 1919-1934'. *Journal of Media History* 20, no. 2 (2014): 239-53.
Kuitenbrouwer, Vincent. *War of Words. Dutch Pro-Boer Propaganda and the South African War (1899-1902)*. Amsterdam: Amsterdam University Press, 2012.
Kunczik, Michael. 'Forgotten Roots of International Public Relations: Attempts of Germany, Great Britain, Czechoslovakia, and Poland to Influence the United States during World War I'. In *Pathways to Public Relations: Histories of Practice and Profession*, edited by Burton St. John III, Margot Opdycke Lamme and Jacquie L'Etang, 91-107. London/New York: Routledge, 2014.
Labour Party (Great Britain). *New Labour. Because Britain Deserves Better*. London: Labour Party, 1997.
Laczó, Ferenc and Luka Lisjak Gabrijelčič, eds. *The Legacy of Division: East and West after 1989*. Budapest/New York: Central European University Press, 2020.
Lafit. 'Belgia… Orientului'. *Belgia Orientului* 1, no. 1 (1903): 2.
Lagasse, Charles-Étienne. 'Le Modèle Constitutionnel Belge'. *Studia Politica. Romanian Political Science Review* 8, no. 1 (2008): 13-14.
Lake, David A. 'Hierarchy and International Relations: Theory and Evidence'. *Oxford Research Encyclopedia of Politics*, 26 September 2017. https://doi.org/10.1093/acrefore/9780190228637.013.324.
Lake, David A. *Hierarchy in International Relations*. Ithaca, New York/London: Cornell University Press, 2009.
Lake, David A. 'Laws and Norms in the Making of International Hierarchies'. In *Hierarchies in World Politics*, edited by Ayşe Zarakol, 17-42. Cambridge [etc.]: Cambridge University Press, 2017.
Lederer, Ivo. *Yugoslavia at the Paris Peace Conference: A Study in Frontiermaking*. New Haven, CT: Yale University Press, 1963.
Leerssen, Joep. 'Imagology. History and Method'. In *Imagology. The Cultural Construction and Literary Representation of National Characters. A Critical Survey*, edited by Manfred Beller and Joep Leerssen, 3-16. Amsterdam/New York: Rodopi, 2007.
Leerssen, Joep. 'Imagology: On Using Ethnicity to Make Sense of the World'. *Iberic@l, Revue d'études Ibériques et Ibéro-Américaines* 10 (2016): 13-31.
Leerssen, Joep. *National Thought in Europe*. Amsterdam: Amsterdam University Press, 2006.
Leerssen, Joep. 'Viral Nationalism: Romantic Intellectuals on the Move in Nineteenth-Century Europe'. *Nations and Nationalism* 17, no. 2 (2011): 257-71.
Lem, Anton van der. 'Het nationale epos. Geschiedenis in één greep'. In *De Palimpsest: Geschiedschrijving in de Nederlanden, 1500-2000*, edited by Jo Tollebeek, Tom Verschaffel and Leonard H.M. Wessels, 177-96. Hilversum: Verloren, 2002.

Lenarduzzi, Carolina. '"De oude geusen teghen de nieuwe geusen". De dynamiek van het oorlogsverleden ten tijde van het Twaalfjarig Bestand'. Special Issue of *Holland. Historisch Tijdschrift* 43, no. 2 (2011): 65–80.
Lettevall, Rebecka, Geert Somsen and Sven Widmalm. 'Introduction'. In *Neutrality in Twentieth-Century Europe. Intersections of Science, Culture, and Politics after the First World War*, edited by Rebecka Lettevall, Geert Somsen and Sven Widmalm, 1–16. London: Taylor & Francis, 2012.
Levy, Jacob T. 'Beyond Publius: Montesquieu, Liberal Republicanism and the Small-Republic Thesis'. *History of Political Thought* 27, no. 1 (2006): 50–90.
Lewes, G.H. *The Spanish Drama. Lope de Vega and Calderon*. London: Charles Knight & Co., 1846.
Limburg Brouwer, P. van. *Verhandeling over de Vraag: Bezitten de Nederlanders een nationaal tooneel met betrekking tot het Treurspel?* Rotterdam: D. Du Mortier en zoon, 1823.
Little, Branden. 'Band of Crusaders. American Humanitarians, the Great War, and the Remaking of the World'. PhD Thesis, University of California, 2009.
Little, Branden. 'Humanitarian Relief in Europe and the Analogue of War, 1914–1918'. In *Finding Common Ground. New Directions in First World War Studies*, edited by Jennifer D. Keene and Michael S. Neiberg, 139–58. Leiden/Boston: Brill, 2011.
Little, Branden. 'The Humanitarian Mobilization of American Cities for Belgian Relief, 1914–1918'. *Cahiers Bruxellois/Brusselse Cahiers* 46, no. 1 (2014): 121–39.
Lizcova, Zuzana. 'USA Ani Čína Se Nechtějí o Pozici Supervelmoci Dělit, to Je Hlavni Problém Světové Politiky, Říká Německý Expert'. *Hospodářské Noviny*, 8 June 2019. https://zahranicni.ihned.cz/c1-66586200-usa-ani-cina-se-nechteji-o-pozici-supervelmoci-delit-to-je-hlavni-problem-svetove-politiky-rika-nemecky-expert?fbclid=IwAR3yHr9pJ-UqiBjiPDUfzvIKQIv6gnqthcJMizBg_76ocKdFtGaIUMy6gD0.
Ljušić, Radoš. *Knjiga o Načertaniju*. Belgrade: BIGZ, 1993.
Lloyd, Lorna. *Diplomacy with a Difference: The Commonwealth Office of High Commissioner, 1880–2006*. Leiden/Boston: Martinus Nijhoff, 2007.
London, April. *Literary History Writing: 1770–1820*. Basingstoke: Palgrave Macmillan, 2010.
Long, Tom. 'Small States, Great Power? Gaining Influence through Intrinsic, Derivative, and Collective Power'. *International Studies Review* 19, no. 2 (2017): 185–205.
López Madera, Gregorio. *Excelencias de La Monarchia y Reyno de España*. Valladolid: por Diego Fernandez de Cordoua impresor, a costa de Martin de Cordoua, 1597.
Löwenheim, Oded and Gadi Heimann. 'Revenge in International Politics'. *Security Studies* 17, no. 4 (2008): 685–724.
Lupovici, Amir. 'Ontological Dissonance, Clashing Identities, and Israel's Unilateral Steps towards the Palestinians'. *Review of International Studies* 38, no. 4 (2012): 809–33.
Luykx, Theo and Marc Platel. *Politieke Geschiedenis van België. Vol. 1: Van 1789 Tot 1944*. Antwerpen: Kluwer, 1985.
Macartney, Carlile Aylmer. *National States and National Minorities*. Oxford: Oxford University Press, 1934.
MacGinty, Roger. 'War Cause and Peace Aim? Small States and the First World War'. *European History Quarterly* 27, no. 41 (1997): 41–55.
MacKenzie, David. *Ilija Garašanin: Balkan Bismarck*. Boulder, CO: East European Monographs, 1985.
MacKenzie, David. 'Serbian National and Military Organizations and the Piedmont Idea, 1844–1914'. *East European Quarterly* 16 (1982): 153–82.

Mahieu-Hoyois, Françoise. *Ĺévolution Du Mouvement Socialiste Borain (1885–1895)*. Louvain-Paris: Nauwelaerts, 1972.
Maiorescu, Titu. 'În Contra Direcţiei de Astăzi În Cultura Română'. In *Critice*, edited by Domnica Filimon, 101–13. Bucharest: Editura Albatros, 1998.
Malešević, Siniša. 'Did Wars Make Nation-States in the Balkans? Nationalisms, Wars and States in the 19th and Early 20th Century South East Europe'. *Journal of Historical Sociology* 25, no. 3 (2012): 299–330.
Maltby, William S. *The Black Legend in England: The Development of Anti-Spanish Sentiment, 1558–1660*. Durham: Duke University Press, 1971.
Manela, Erez. 'International Society as a Historical Subject'. *Diplomatic History* 44, no. 2 (2020): 184–209.
Manela, Erez. *The Wilsonian Moment: Self-Determination and the International Origins of Anti-Colonial Nationalism*. Oxford: Oxford University Press, 2007.
Marholeva, Krasimira. 'Kramářův a Masarykův Předválecný Federalismus v Kontextu České Federalistické Tradice'. In *Karel Kramář (1860–1937): Život a Dílo*, edited by Jan Bílek and Luboš Velek, 314–35. Prague: Historický ústav, 2009.
Marín Pina, María Carmen and Victor Infantes, eds. *Poesía y Prosa Contra España: Emblemas Del Perfecto Español y Rodomuntadas Españolas*. Capellades: José J. de Olañeta, 2013.
Markland, Russell, ed. *The Glory of Belgium. A Tribute and a Chronicle*. London: Erskine MacDonald, 1915.
Marković, Svetozar. 'Šta Treba Da Radimo'. In *Sabrani Spisi. Volume 1*, edited by Svetozar Marković, 58–69. Belgrade: Kultura, 1960.
Martínez Luna, Fernando. 'Las Monarquías de Campanella: Una Propuesta de Enfoque Imagológico'. In *España Ante Sus Críticos: Las Claves de La Leyenda Negra*, edited by Yolanda Rodríguez Pérez, Antonio Sánchez Jiménez and Harm den Boer, 193–208. Madrid/Frankfurt: Iberoamericana/Vervuert, 2015.
Marton, Silvia. '"La Belgique de l'Orient" et Les Chemins de Fer: Les Raisons d'une Comparaison: La Construction Politique de l'État-Nation Dans Le Parlement Roumain (1866–1871)'. *Studia Politica. Romanian Political Science Review* 8, no. 1 (2008): 27–44.
Masaryk, Thomas G. *Česka Otázka: Snahy a Tužby Národního Obrození*. Prague: Melantrich, 1969.
Masaryk, Thomas G. *Kroměříž Lectures. Problem of a Small Nation*. Prague: Trigon, 2010.
Masaryk, Thomas G. *Nová Evropa: Stanovisko Slovanské*. Brno: Doplněk, 1994.
Masaryk, Thomas G. 'O Českém Státním Právu'. *Čas* 2, no. 18 (1888): 274–7.
Masaryk, Thomas G. *O Democracii*. Prague: Melantrich, 1991.
Masaryk, Thomas G. *Otázka Sociálni: Základy Marxismu Filozofické a Sociologické*. Prague: Čin, 1947.
Masaryk, Thomas G. *Parliamentní Projevy, 1891–1893*. Prague: Masarykův ústav AV ČR, 2001.
Masaryk, Thomas G. *Parliamentní Projevy, 1907–1913*. Prague: Masarykův ústav AV ČR, 2001.
Masaryk, Thomas G. *Student a Politika*. Prague: Nakladatelstiví Svoboda, 1990.
Masaryk, Thomas G. *The Problem of Small Nations in the European Crisis*. London: he Council for the Study of International Relations, 1916.
Masaryk, Thomas G. *The Voice of an Oppressed People*. Chicago: Bohemian National Alliance, 1917.
Masarykova, Alice G. 'The Bohemians in Chicago. A Sketch'. *Charities* 13, no. 10 (1904): 206–10.

Mason, A.E.W. 'Not Bread Alone, but Bread before All Else'. In *The Need of Belgium. A Few Words*, Third edition, 23–5. New York: Commission for Relief of Belgium, 1915.
Masson de Morvilliers, Nicolás. 'Espagne'. In *Encyclopédie Méthodique Ou Par Ordre Des Matières. Géographie Moderne. Vol. I*, 554–68. Paris: Pandoucke, 1782.
Maurice, Arthur B. *Bottled Up in Belgium. The Last Delegate's Informal Story*. New York: Moffat, Yard & Company, 1917.
Mazower, Mark. *The Balkans: A Short History*. New York: Modern Library, 2000.
McCrone, David. *The Sociology of Nationalism. Tomorrow's Ancestors*. London: Routledge, 1998.
McQuaid, Sara Dybris. 'Better Together? Comparative Perspectives on Regional Cooperation'. In *Ireland and the North*, edited by Fionna Barber, Heidi Hansson and Sara Dybris McQuaid, 149–76. Oxford: Peter Lang, 2019.
McQuaid, Sara Dybris. 'Nordic Horizons for a Council of the Isles'. In *After Independence: The State of the Scottish Nation Debate*, edited by Gerry Hassan and James Mitchell, 246–58. Edinburgh: Luath Press Limited, 2013.
Meisel, August Heinrich. *Cours de Style Diplomatique, Volume II*. Paris: J.P. Aillaud, 1826.
Melchior, Michael. 'Judaism and Islam in the World'. In *Israel in the World. Legitimacy and Exceptionalism*, edited by Emanuel Adler, 124–34. London: Routledge, 2013.
Mendel, Yonatan and Ronald Ranta. *From the Arab Other to the Israeli Self: Palestinian Culture in the Making of Israeli National Identity*. London: Routledge, 2016.
Meriage, Lawrence P. 'The First Serbian Uprising (1804–1913) and the Nineteenth-Century Origins of the Eastern Question'. *Slavic Review* 37, no. 3 (1978): 421–39.
Miedlig, Hans-Michael. 'Patriarchalische Mentalität als Hindernis für die staatliche und gesellschaftliche Modernisierung in Serbien im 19. Jahrhundert'. *Südostforschungen* 50 (1991): 163–90.
Mill, John Stuart. *Considerations on Representative Government*. London: Parker & Bourn, 1861.
Milo, Paskal. *Politika e Jashtme e Shqipërisë*. Tirana: Botimet Toena, 2013.
Mishkova, Diana and Roumen Daskalov. '"Forms without Substance": Debates on the Transfer of Western Models to the Balkans'. In *Entangled Histories of the Balkans Vol. 2: Transfer of Political Ideologies and Institution*, edited by Diana Mishkova and Roumen Daskalov, 1–97. Leiden: Brill, 2014.
Mitchell, James. *Devolution in the UK*. Manchester: Manchester University Press, 2009.
Mitchell, James. *The Scottish Question*. Oxford: Oxford University Press, 2014.
Mitrović, Andrej. *Serbia's Great War 1914–1918*. West Lafayette, IN: Purdue University Press, 2007.
'Møde Om Island'. *Atlanten* 2, 1909.
Mokyr, Joel. 'Cardwell's Law and the Political Economy of Technological Progress'. *Research Policy* 23, no. 5 (1994): 561–74.
Mombauer, Annika. *The Origins of the First World War: Controversies and Consensus*. London [etc.]: Longman, 2002.
Montesquieu. *The Spirit of the Laws*. Edited by Basia Carolyn Miller, Harold Samuel Stone and Anne M. Cohler. Cambridge: Cambridge University Press, 1989.
Muller, Herbert J. *The Spirit of Tragedy*. New York: Knopf, 1956.
Munro, Dana C., George C. Sellery and August C. Krey. *German War Practices. Part 1. Treatment of Civilians*. Washington, DC: Committee on Public Information, 1918.
Nairn, Tom. *The Break-Up of Britain. Crisis and Neo-Nationalism*. Twenty-fifth anniversary edition. Champaign, IL: Common Ground Publishing, 2015.

Nash, George H. *The Life of Herbert Hoover. Master of Emergencies, 1917–1918*. New York: W.W. Norton, 1996.
Nash, George H. *The Life of Herbert Hoover. The Humanitarian, 1914–1917*. New York: W.W. Norton, 1988.
'Návrh Programu Lidového'. *Čas* 4, no. 44 (1890): 689–94.
Neumann, Iver B. 'Status Is Cultural: Durkheimian Poles and Weberian Russians Seek Great-Power Status'. In *Status in World Politics*, edited by Deborah Welch Larson, T.V. Paul and William C. Wohlforth, 85–112. Cambridge: Cambridge University Press, 2014.
Neumann, Iver B. *Uses of the Other. 'The East' in European Identity Formation*. Minneapolis, MN: University of Minnesota Press, 1998.
Neumann, Iver B. and Sieglinde Gstöhl. 'Introduction: Lilliputians in Gulliver's World?' In *Small States in International Relations*, edited by Christine Ingebritsen, Iver B. Neumann, Sieglinde Gstöhl and Jessica Beyer, 3–36. Seattle: University of Washington Press, 2012.
Niculescu, Andrei. 'Andrei Rădulescu, La Belgique et Le Constitutionnalisme Roumain'. *Studia Politica. Romanian Political Science Review* 8, no. 1 (2008): 190–206.
Nielsen, Christian Axboe. 'From Nightmare to Pragmatic Partnership: Serbia and the EU'. In *Playing Second Fiddle: Contending Visions of Europe's Developmen*, edited by Hans-Åke Petersson and Cecile Stokholm Banke, 137–58. Malmö: Universus Academic Press, 2015.
Nielsen, Christian Axboe. 'The Kosovo Precedent and the Rhetorical Development of Former Yugoslav Analogies in the Case of Abkhazia and South Ossetia'. *Journal of Southeast European and Black Sea Studies* 9, no. 1 (2009): 171–89.
Nielsen, Christian Axboe. *Making Yugoslavs. Identity in King Aleksandar's Yugoslavia*. Toronto: University of Toronto Press, 2014.
Nielsen, Henry and Henrik Knudsen. 'Pursuing Common Cultural Ideals: Niels Bohr, Neutrality, and International Scientific Collaboration during the Inter-War Period'. In *Neutrality in Twentieth-Century Europe. Intersections of Science, Culture, and Politics after the First World War*, edited by Rebecka Lettevall, Geert Somsen and Sven Widmalm, 115–39. London: Taylor & Francis, 2012.
Nikoladze, Niko. *Kartuli Mtserloba*. Vol. 14. Tbilisi: Nakaduli, 1997.
Nikoladze, Niko. 'Mamashviluri Rcheva'. *Klde* 38 (1913): 1–6.
Nikoladze, Niko. 'Sachiro-Dzala'. *Moambe* 8 (1894): 130–5.
Nikoladze, Niko. 'Safrangetis Sakmeebzed'. *Moambe* 8 (1894): 152–5.
Nikoladze, Niko. *Tkhzulebani, 1872–1873*. Edited by M. I. Kandelaki. Vol. 3. Tbilisi: Tbilisis Universitetis Stamba, 1966.
Noli, Fan. *Faqe Të Panjohura Te Nolit*. Edited by Koço Bihiku. Tirana: Albin, 2002.
Novaković, Stojan. *Vaskrs države srpske: političko-istorijska studija o prvom srpskom ustanku 1804–1813*. Second edition. Belgrade: Štampano u Državnoj Štampariji Kraljevine Srbije, 1904.
Nünning, Ansgar. 'On the Englishness of English Literary Histories as a Challenge to Transcultural Literary History'. In *Studying Transcultural Literary History*, edited by Gunilla Lindberg-Wada, 158–68. Berlin: Walter de Gruyter, 2006.
Nye, Jr., Joseph S. *Soft Power. The Means to Success in World Politics*. New York: PublicAffairs, 2004.
O'Brien, Patrick. 'The American Press, Public, and the Reaction to the Outbreak of the First World War'. *Diplomatic History* 37, no. 3 (2013): 446–75.
Olesker, Ronnie. 'Law-Making and the Securitization of the Jewish Identity in Israel'. *Ethnopolitics* 13, no. 2 (2014): 105–21.

Osterhammel, Jürgen. *The Transformation of the World: A Global History of the Nineteenth Century*. Princeton, NJ: Princeton University Press, 2014.
Pagden, Anthony. *Lords of All the World: Ideologies of Empire in Spain, Britain and France c.1500–c.1800*. New Haven: Yale University Press, 1995.
Page, Benjamin. 'The Rockefeller Foundation and Central Europe: A Reconsideration'. *Minerva* 40 (2002): 265–87.
Pánek, Jaroslav and Oldřich Tůma, eds. *A History of Czech Lands*. Prague: Karolinum Press, 2009.
Panke, Diana. 'Small States in EU Negotiations: Political Dwarfs or Power-Brokers?' *Cooperation and Conflict* 46, no. 2 (2011): 123–43.
Pappe, Ilan. *A History of Modern Palestine: One Land, Two Peoples*. Second edition. Cambridge: Cambridge University Press, 2006.
Parker, Geoffrey. *The Grand Strategy of Philip II*. Yale: Yale University Press, 2000.
Pavlowitch, Stevan K. *Hitler's New Disorder: The Second World War in Yugoslavia*. London: Hurst & Co., 2008.
Peleg, Yaron. *Orientalism and the Hebrew Imagination*. Ithaca, NY: Cornell University Press, 2005.
Peri, Yoram. 'The Arab-Israeli Conflict and Israeli Democracy'. In *Israeli Democracy under Stress*, edited by Ehud Sprinzak and Larry Diamond, 343–57. Boulder, CO: Lynne Rienner Publishers, 1993.
Perić, Živojin. *La Confédération Balkanique*. Paris: Librairie générale de droit et de jurisprudence, 1912.
Perović, Jeronim. 'The Tito-Stalin Split: A Reassessment in Light of New Evidence'. *Journal of Cold War Studies* 9, no. 2 (2007): 32–63.
Peterson, Genevieve. 'Political Inequality at the Congress of Vienna'. *Political Science Quarterly* 60, no. 4 (1945): 532–54.
Pétur J. Thorsteinsson. *Utanríkisþjónusta Íslands og utanríkismál: sögulegt yfirlit*. Volume I. Reykjavík: Hið íslenska bókmenntafélag, 1992.
Piller, Elisabeth. 'American War Relief, Cultural Mobilization, and the Myth of Impartial Humanitarianism, 1914–1917'. *The Journal of the Gilded Age and Progressive Era* 17 (2018): 619–35.
Piller, Elisabeth. 'To Aid the Fatherland. German-Americans, Transatlantic Relief Work and American Neutrality, 1914–17'. *Immigrants & Minorities. Historical Studies in Ethnicity, Migration and Diaspora* 35, no. 3 (2017): 196–215.
Plamenatz, John. 'Two Types of Nationalism'. In *Nationalism: The Nature and Evolution of an Idea*, edited by Eugene Kamenka. New York: St. Martin's Press, 1976.
Plaschka, Richard G. 'The Political Significance of František Palacký'. *Journal of Contemporary History* 8, no. 3 (1973): 35–55.
Pocock, J.G.A. 'British History: A Plea for a New Subject'. *The Journal of Modern History* 47, no. 4 (1975): 601–21.
Pocock, J.G.A. *The Machiavellian Moment: Florentine Political Thought and the Atlantic Republican Tradition*. Princeton, NJ [etc.]: Princeton University Press, 1975.
Pocock, J.G.A. 'The Union in British History'. *Transactions of the Royal Historical Society* 10 (2000): 181–96.
Preda, Cristian. 'L'influence Belge, Hier et Aujourd'hui'. *Studia Politica. Romanian Political Science Review* 8, no. 1 (2008): 9.
Proceedings of Meeting to Protest Against Deportation of Belgian Citizens into Servitude in Germany. Philadelphia: Academy of Music, 1917.

Proctor, Tammy M. *Civilians in a World at War, 1914–1918*. New York: New York University Press, 2010.
Průcha, Václav, et al. *Hospodárské a Sociální Dějiny Československa, 1918–1992. Volume 1: Období 1918–1945*. Brno: Doplněk, 2004.
Puissant, Jean. *Sous La Loupe de La Police Française, Le Bassin Industriel Du Centre*. Haine-Saint-Pierre: Cercle d'histoire et de folklore Henri Guillemin, 1988.
Puto, Artan. 'The Idea of Nation during the Albanian National Movement, 1878–1912'. PhD Dissertation, Università degli Studi di Firenze, 2009.
Rădulescu, Andrei. 'L'influence Belge Sur Le Droit Roumain'. *Studia Politica. Romanian Political Science Review* 8, no. 1 (1932–2008): 191–206.
Raider, Mark A. 'Moshe Dayan: "Israel's No. 1 Hero" (in America)'. *Journal of Israeli History* 37, no. 1 (2019): 21–59.
Rappard, William E. 'Small States in the League of Nations'. *Political Science Quarterly* 49, no. 4 (1934): 544–75.
Ratzel, Friedrich. *Politische Geographie, Oder Die Geographie Der Staaten Des Verkehres Und Des Krieges*. Munich: Oldenbourg, 1903.
Ravenhill, John. 'Entrepreneurial States: A Conceptual Overview'. *International Journal* 73, no. 4 (2018): 501–17.
Renshon, Jonathan. *Fighting for Status. Hierarchy and Conflict in World Politics*. Princeton, NJ/Oxford: Princeton University Press, 2017.
Rider, Jacques le. *Modernity and Crises of Identity: Culture and Society in Fin-de-Siècle Vienna*. Cambridge: Polity, 1993.
Robinson, Piers. 'The CNN Effect: Can the News Media Drive Foreign Policy?' *Review of International Studies* 25, no. 2 (1999): 301–9.
Rochau, August Ludwig von. *Grundsätze der Realpolitik, angewendet auf die staatlichen Zustände Deutschlands*, Vol. 1. Stuttgart: Göpel, 1859.
Rockefeller Foundation, and George E. Vincent. *The Rockefeller Foundation. A Review for 1920, the Program for 1921*. New York: Rockefeller Foundation, 1921.
Rodríguez Pérez, Yolanda. '"Covering the Skeletons with Flesh and Blood": Spanish Golden Age Drama in English and Dutch Early-Nineteenth-Century Literary Histories'. In *Literary Hispanophobia and Hispanophilia in Britain and the Low Countries (1550–1850)*, edited by Yolanda Rodríguez Pérez, 317–40. Amsterdam: Amsterdam University Press, 2020.
Rodríguez Pérez, Yolanda. *The Dutch Revolt through Spanish Eyes. Self and Other in Historical and Literary Texts of Golden Age Spain (ca. 1548–1673)*. Oxford/Bern: Peter Lang, 2008.
Rodríguez Pérez, Yolanda. 'On Hispanophobia and Hispanophilia across Time and Space'. In *Literary Hispanophobia and Hispanophilia in Britain and the Low Countries (1550–1850)*, edited by Yolanda Rodríguez Pérez, 11–45. Amsterdam: Amsterdam University Press, 2020.
Rodríguez Pérez, Yolanda. '"The Spanish Seignor" or the Transnational Peregrinations of an Anti-Hispanic Dutch Broadsheet'. Edited by Jan Bloemendal, James A. Parente Jr., and Nigel Smith. *Renaissance Studies, Special Issue: Transnational Exchange in the Early Modern Low Countries* 35, no. 4 (2021). https://doi.org/10.1111/rest.12739.
Rodríguez Pérez, Yolanda, Antonio Sánchez Jiménez and Harm den Boer, eds. *España Ante Sus Críticos: Claves de La Leyenda Negra*. Madrid/Frankfurt am Main: Iberoamericana/Vervuert, 2015.
Rodríguez-Salgado, M.J. 'Patriotismo y Política Exterior En La España de Carlos V y Felipe II'. In *La Proyección Europea de La Monarquía Hispánica*, edited by Felipe Ruíz Martín, 49–105. Madrid: Editorial Complutense, 1996.

Romani, Roberto. 'Political Thought in Action: The Moderates in 1859'. *Journal of Modern Italian Studies* 17, no. 5 (2012): 593-607.
Roon, Ger van. *Kleine landen in crisistijd: van Oslostaten tot Benelux, 1930-1940*. Amsterdam: Elsevier, 1985.
Rose, Richard. 'Do the British Exist?' *Journal of Ethnic and Migration Studies* 1, no. 4 (1972): 271-6.
Rotbard, Sharon. 'Wall and Tower. The Mold of Israeli Adrikhalut'. In *City of Collision. Jerusalem and the Principles of Conflict Urbanism*, edited by Philipp Misselwitz, Tim Rieniets, Zvi Efrat, Rassem Khamaisi and Rami Nasrallah, 102-12. Basel: Birkhäuser, 2006.
Roudometof, Victor. 'From Rum Millet to Greek Nation: Enlightenment, Secularization, and National Identity in Ottoman Balkan Society, 1453-1821'. *Journal of Modern Greek Studies* 16, no. 1 (1998): 11-48.
Said, Edward W. *Orientalism*. New York: Pantheon Books, 1978.
Sánchez Jiménez, Antonio. *Leyenda Negra: La Batalla Sobre La Imagen de España En Tiempos de Lope de Vega*. Madrid: Cátedra, 2016.
Saroléa, Charles. *How Belgium Saved Europe*. London: William Heinemann, 1915.
Satow, Ernest. *A Guide to Diplomatic Practice*. Cambridge: Cambridge University Press, 2011.
Savić, Bojan. 'Where Is Serbia? Traditions of Spatial Identity and State Positioning in Serbian Geopolitical Culture'. *Geopolitics* 19, no. 3 (2014): 684-718.
Schaepdrijver, Sophie De. 'Champion or Stillbirth? The Symbolic Uses of Belgium in the Great War'. In *How Can One Not Be Interested in Belgian History. War, Language and Consensus in Belgium since 1830*, edited by Benno Barnard, Martine van Berlo, Geert van Istendael, Tony Judt, Marc Reynebeau and Sophie De Schaepdrijver, 55-81. Gent: Academia Press, 2005.
Schaepdrijver, Sophie De. *De Groote Oorlog. Het Koninkrijk België Tijdens de Eerste Wereldoorlog*. Antwerpen/Amsterdam: Atlas, 1997.
Schaepdrijver, Sophie De. 'Liège 1914 et l'opinion Publique Américaine'. *Ulletin d'Information Du Centre Liégeois d'Histoire et d'archéologie Militaires* 10, no. 5 (2008): 41-53.
Schaepdrijver, Sophie De. 'Occupation, Propaganda, and the Idea of Belgium'. In *European Culture in the Great War. The Arts, Entertainment, and Propaganda, 1914-1918*, edited by Aviel Roshwald and Richard Stites, 267-94. Cambridge [etc.]: Cambridge University Press, 1999.
Schenkeveld, Margaretha H. *Willem de Clercq En de Literatuur*. Groningen: Wolters, 1962.
Schmidt, Peter. *Spanische Universalmonarchie Oder 'Teutsche Libertet'. Das Spanische Imperium in Der Propaganda Des Dreissigjahrigen Krieges*. Stuttgart: Franz Steiner Verlag, 2001.
Schovelin, Julius V. 'Nationaløkonomiens Vilkaar I Danmark'. *Nationaløkonomisk Tidsskrift* 9 (1891): 321-49.
Schulman, Sarah. *Israel/Palestine and the Queer International*. Durham, NC: Duke University Press, 2012.
Schulz, Matthias. 'Cultures of Peace and Security from the Vienna Congress to the Twenty-First Century. Characteristics and Dilemmas'. In *Securing Europe after Napoleon. 1815 and the New European Security Culture*, edited by Beatrice de Graaf, Ido de Haan and Brian Vick, 21-39. Cambridge [etc.]: Cambridge University Press, 2019.

Schulz, Matthias. 'La Société Des Nations et La Résolution Pacifique Des Différends: Règles, Normes et Pratiques'. In *Commentaire Sur Le Pacte de La Société Des Nations*, edited by Robert Kolb, 1247–99. Brussels: Bruylant, 2015.

Schulz, Matthias. *Normen Und Praxis. Das Europäische Konzert Der Großmächte Als Sicherheitsrat 1815–1860*. Munich: Oldenbourg Verlag, 2009.

Schuursma, Rolf. *Vergeefs onzijdig. Nederlands neutraliteit 1919–1940*. Utrecht: Matrijs, 2005.

Scott, David. *Conscripts of Modernity: The Tragedy of Colonial Enlightenment*. Durham, NC: Duke University Press, 2004.

Scott, Hamish. *The Birth of a Great Power System 1740–1815*. Abingdon [etc.]: Routledge, 2006.

Scott, Hamish. 'The Seven Years War and Europe's Ancien Régime'. *War in History* 18, no. 4 (2011): 419–55.

Sedláček, Tomáš. 'Politici Tvrdí, Že Jsme Malý Národ, Který Potřebuje Uchránit Před Neexistující Hrozbou'. *IROZHLAS*, 8 May 2019. https://www.irozhlas.cz/zivotni-styl/spolecnost/tomas-sedlacek-demokracie-politika-rozhovor-sametova-revoluce-historie_1905081600_lac.

Senor, Dan and Saul Singer. *Start-up Nation. The Story of Israel's Economic Miracle*. New York/Boston: Twelve, 2009.

Sens, Andrew D. 'The Newly Independent States, the United Nations, and Some Thoughts on the Nature of the Development Process'. *The Journal of Politics* 30, no. 1 (1968): 114–36.

Serapionova, Yelena Pavlvna. 'Institute of Social Studies in Prague and Its Activities in the 1920s–30s'. In *Theory and Practice of the Welfare State in Europe in 20th Century*, edited by Zlatica Zudová-Lešková, Emil Voráček and et al., 303–12. Prague: Historický ústav, 2014.

Shapira, Anita. 'The Religious Motifs of the Labor Movement'. In *Zionism and Religion*, edited by Shmuel Almog, Jehuda Reinharz and Anita Shapira, 251–72. Hanover, NH: Brandeis University Press, 1998.

Shavit, Yaacov. 'Ideology, World View, and National Policy: The Case of the Likud Government'. *The Jerusalem Journal of International Relation* 9, no. 2 (1987): 101–15.

Shaw, George Bernard. 'The Case of Belgium'. In *The Need of Belgium. A Few Words*, Third edition, 26–31. New York: Commission for Relief of Belgium, 1915.

Shoval, Zalman. 'Why Israel Lost the Hasbara War'. *Israel Journal of Foreign Affairs* 1, no. 2 (2007): 15–18.

Shulman, Stephen. 'Challenging the Civic/Ethnic and West/East Dichotomies in the Study of Nationalism'. *Comparative Political Studies* 35, no. 5 (2002): 554–85.

Sierp, Aline and Christian Karner. 'National Stereotypes in the Context of the European Crisis'. *National Identities* 19, no. 1 (2 January 2017): 1–9. https://doi.org/10.1080/14608944.2016.1209646.

Sinclair, May. 'America's Part in the War'. In *The Need of Belgium. A Few Words*, Third edition, 4–7. New York: Commission for Relief of Belgium, 1915.

Smith, Joseph. 'The "Splendid Little War" of 1898: A Reappraisal'. *History* 80, no. 258 (1995): 22–37.

Smith, Nicola, Michelle Pace and Donna Lee. 'Size Matters: Small Studies and International Studies'. *International Studies Perspectives* 6, no. 3 (2005): ii–iii.

Smooha, Sammy. 'Ethnic Democracy: Israel as an Archetype'. *Israel Studies* 2, no. 2 (1997): 198–241.

Somsen, Geert. 'A History of Universalism: Conceptions of the Internationally of Science from the Enlightenment to the Cold War'. *Minerva* 46, no. 3 (2008): 361–79.

Sorescu, Andrei. 'National History as a History of Compacts: Jus Publicum Europaeum and Suzerainty in Romania in the Mid-Nineteenth Century'. *East Central Europe/ L'Europe Du Centre-Est* 45, no. 1 (2018): 63–93.

Sorescu, Andrei. 'Visions of Agency: Imagining Individual and Collective Action in Nineteenth-Century Romania'. PhD Thesis, University College London, 2018.

'Speech by the Prime Minister of Albania, Edi Rama at the Annual NATO Military Committee Conference Attended by the Chiefs of Staff of Alliance Member Countries, Tirana, Albania'. *North Atlantic Treaty Organisation*, 12 October 2017. https://www.nato.int/cps/en/natohq/opinions_146877.htm?selectedLocale=en.

Steinmetz, Robert and Anders Wivel. 'Introduction'. In *Small States in Europe. Challenges and Opportunities*, edited by Robert Steinmetz and Anders Wivel, 3–14. Farnham/Burlington, VT: Ashgate, 2010.

Stengers, Jean. 'La Belgique de 1830, Une "Nationalité de Convention"?' In *Histoire et Historiens Depuis 1830 En Belgique*, edited by Hervé Hasquin, 7–19. Brussels: Éditions de l'Université de Bruxelles, 1981.

Stern, Fritz. *The Politics of Cultural Despair. A Study in the Rise of the Germanic Ideology*. Berkeley, CA: University of California Press, 1974.

Streeten, Paul. 'The Special Problems of Small Countries'. *World Development* 21, no. 2 (1993): 197–202.

Strömbom, Lisa. 'Thick Recognition: Advancing Theory on Identity Change in Intractable Conflicts'. *European Journal of International Relations* 20, no. 1 (2014): 168–91.

Subotić, Jelena. *Hijacked Justice. Dealing with the Past in the Balkans*. Ithaca, NY: Cornell University Press, 2009.

Subotić, Jelena. 'Political Memory, Ontological Security, and Holocaust Remembrance in Post-Communist Europe'. *European Security* 27, no. 3 (2018): 296–313.

Sucharov, Mira M. *The International Self. Psychoanalysis and the Search for Israeli-Palestinian Peace*. Albany, NY: State University of New York Press, 2005.

Sundhaussen, Holm. *Geschichte Serbiens, 19–21. Jahrhundert*. Vienna: Böhlau Verlag, 2007.

Suny, Ronald G. *The Making of the Georgian Nation*. Bloomington: Indiana University Press, 1994.

Swart, K.W. 'The Black Legend during the Eighty Years War'. In *Britain and the Netherlands Vol. V: Some Political Mythologies*, edited by J.S. Bromley and E.H. Kossmann, 36–57. Dordrecht: Springer, 1975.

Taglia, Stefano. 'The Feasibility of Ottomanism as a Nationalist Project: The View of Albanian Young Turk Ismail Kemal'. *Die Welt Des Islams* 56 (2016): 336–58.

Teichova, Alice. 'Continuity and Discontinuity: Banking and Industry in Twentieth-Century Central Europe'. In *Economic Transformation in East and Central Europe*, edited by David F. Good, 63–74. London: Routledge, 1994.

Termorshuizen, Gerard and Coen van 't Veer. *Een groots en meeslepend leven: Dominique Berretty, Indisch persmagnaat*. Zutphen: Walburg Pers, 2018.

Thiel, Jens. '*Menschenbassin Belgien*'. *Anwerbung, Deportation und Zwangsarbeit im Ersten Weltkrieg*. Essen: Klartext Verlag, 2007.

'Thirrje e Ismail Qemali Be Vlores Mi Shqiptaret Kur Iku Nga Stambolli'. *Albania e Vogël* 2, no. 19 (15 October 1900).

Thorhallsson, Baldur. 'European Integration: Genuine or False Shelter?' In *Small States and Shelter Theory: Iceland's External Affairs*, edited by Baldur Thorhallsson, 128–68. Abingdon, OX: Routledge, 2019.

Thorhallsson, Baldur. 'The Icelandic Economic Collapse: How to Overcome Constraints Associated with Smallness?' *European Political Science* 12 (2013): 320–32.

Thorhallsson, Baldur. *Iceland's Shelter-Seeking Behaviour: From Settlement to Republic (NY, Cornell University Library Forthcoming)*. Ithaca, NY: Cornell University Press, 2021.

Thorhallsson, Baldur. 'Nordicness as a Shelter: The Case of Iceland'. *Global Affairs* 4, no. 4–5 (2018): 377–90.

Thorhallsson, Baldur. 'Small State Foreign Policy'. *Oxford Research Encyclopedia of Politics*, n.d., 2017. https://doi.org/DOI:10.1093/acrefore/9780190228637.013.48.

Thorhallsson, Baldur, ed. *Small States and Shelter Theory: Iceland's External Affairs*. Abingdon, OX: Routledge, 2019.

Thorhallsson, Baldur. 'Small States in the UN Security Council: Means of Influence?' *Hague Journal of Diplomacy* 7, no. 2 (2012): 135–60.

Thorhallsson, Baldur. 'Studying Small States: A Review'. *Small States & Territories* 1, no. 1 (2018): 17–34.

Thorhallsson, Baldur and Alyson J.K. Bailes. '"Small States": A Theme in Icelandic Political Science and Politics'. *Nordiques* 27 (2014): 118–31.

Thorhallsson, Baldur and Sverrir Steinsson. 'Iceland's Shelter Option in the New Millennium'. In *Small States and Shelter Theory: Iceland's External Affairs*, edited by Baldur Thorhallsson, 171–204. Abingdon, OX: Routledge, 2019.

Thorhallsson, Baldur, Sverrir Steinsson, Thornsteinn Kristinsson and Daniel J. Devine. 'Shelter during the American Period: Icelandic Relations with the US and International Organizations'. In *Small States and Shelter Theory: Iceland's External Affairs*, edited by Baldur Thorhallsson, 61–92. Abingdon, OX: Routledge, 2019.

Thorhallsson, Baldur and Anders Wivel. 'Small States in the European Union: What Do We Know and What Would We Like to Know?' *Cambridge Review of International Affairs* 19, no. 4 (2006): 651–68.

Tipei, Alex. 'How to Make Friends and Influence People: Elementary Education, French "Influence," and the Balkans, 1815–1830s'. *Modern Intellectual History* 15, no. 3 (2018): 621–49.

Tocqueville, Alexis de. *Democracy in America: And Two Essays on America*. Edited by Gerald E. Bevan and Isaac Kramnick. London: Penguin, 2003.

Todorova, Maria. *Imagining the Balkans*. New York: Oxford University Press, 1997.

Todorova, Maria. 'Is There Weak Nationalism and Is It a Useful Category?' *Nations and Nationalism* 21, no. 4 (2015): 681–99.

Todorova, Maria. 'The Trap of Backwardness: Modernity, Temporality, and the Study of Eastern European Nationalism'. *Slavic Review* 64, no. 1 (2005): 140–64.

Tollebeek, Jo. 'Enthousiasme en Evidentie. De negentiende-eeuwse Belgisch-nationale geschiedschrijving'. In *De Ijkmeesters. Opstellen over de geschiedschrijving in Nederland En België*, edited by Jo Tollebeek, 57–74. Amsterdam: Bert Bakker, 1994.

Tollebeek, Jo. 'Het gevoelige punt van Europa. Huizinga, Pirenne en de plaats van het vaderland'. In *De ekster en de kooi: Nieuwe opstellen over de geschiedschrijving*, edited by Jo Tollebeek, 225–47. Amsterdam: Bert Bakker, 1996.

Torre del Río, Rosario de la. 'La Prensa Madrileña y El Discurso de Lord Salisbury Sobre "Las Naciones Moribundas" (Londres, Albert Hall, 4 Mayo 1898), VI, (1985) 163–180'. *Cuadernos de Hstoria Moderna y Contemporánea* IV (1985): 163–80.

Torrecilla, Jesús. *España Exótica. La Formación de La Imagen Española Moderna*. Boulder: Society of Spanish and Spanish-American Studies, 2004.
Towns, Anne E. *Women and States: Norms and Hierarchies in International Society*. Cambridge [etc.]: Cambridge University Press, 2012.
Treitschke, Heinrich von. *Die Zukunft Der Norddeutschen Mittelstaaten*. Berlin: Druck und Verlag von Georg Reimer, 1866.
Trommler, Frank. 'The Lusitania Effect: America's Mobilization against Germany in World War I'. *German Studies Review* 32, no. 2 (2009): 241–66.
Tsinovoi, Alexei. 'The Sacred, the Secular, and the Profane: Introducing Agamben's "Profane Philosophy" to Security Studies and the Case of Israel's Natural Gas Discoveries'. *Journal of International Relations and Development* 22, no. 1 (2019): 215–42.
Tucker, Robert W. *The Inequality of Nations*. New York: Basic Books, 1977.
Tucović, Dimitrije. *Srbija i Arbanija: Jedan Prilog Kritici Zavojevačke Politike Srpske Buržoazije*. Zemun: Mostart, 2011.
Tudeer, Alf Emil. 'Några Synspunkter Angående Konjunkturstatistiken'. In *Förhandlingar Vid Nordiska Statistiskermötet i Stockholm, Den 27 Och 28 September 1927*, 32–41. Stockholm: Det Nordiske statistiskerforbund, 1927.
Tworek, Heidi. *News from Germany. The Competition to Control World Communications, 1900-1945*. Cambridge, MA: Harvard University Press, 2019.
Tworek, Heidi. 'The Creation of European News. News Agency Cooperation in Interwar Europe'. *Journalism Studies* 14, no. 5 (2013): 730–42.
Van Bosstraeten, Truus. *Bezet maar beschermd: België en de markies van Villalobar tijdens de Eerste Wereldoorlog*. Leuven/Voorburg: Acco, 2008.
Van der Essen, Professeur. 'L'Opinion Publique Américaine et Les Souffrances de La Belgique'. In *A Book of Belgium's Gratitude. Comprising Literary Articles by Representative Belgians, Together with Their Translations by Various Hands, and Illustrated throughout in Colour and Black and White by Belgian Artists*, 121–30. London/New York/Toronto: John Lange, 1916.
Vélez Sainz, Julio. 'La Hispanofobia En El Hispanismo: Ticknor, de Gayangos y De Vedia Entre La Leyenda Negra y El Siglo de Oro'. In *La Leyenda Negra En El Crisol de La Comedia: El Teatro Del Siglo de Oro Frente a Los Estereotipos Antihispánicos*, edited by Yolanda Rodríguez Pérez and Antonio Sánchez Jiménez, 205–18. Madrid/Frankfurt am Main: Iberoamericana/Vervuert, 2016.
Verdery, Katherine. *National Identity under Socialism: Identity and Cultural Politics in Ceaușescu's Romania*. Berkely, CA: University of California Press, 1991.
Verdery, Katherine. *The Political Lives of Dead Bodies: Reburial and Postsocialist Change*. New York: Columbia University Press, 1999.
Vickers, Elizabeth Dwyer. 'Frances Elisabeth Crowell: An Evaluation of a European Nursing Experience'. MA Thesis, The University of West Florida, 1996.
Villanueva, Jesús. *Leyenda Negra. Una Polémica Nacionalista En La España Del Siglo XX*. Madrid: La Catarata, 2011.
Vlad, Laurențiu. 'À La Recherche de La „Belgique Orientale". La Roumanie et l'Exposition Universelle et Internationale de Liège, 1905'. *Studia Politica. Romanian Political Science Review* 2, no. 4 (2002): 981–94.
Vlad, Laurențiu. 'Quelques Moments d'une Histoire de La Propagande: La Roumanie Aux Expositions Universelles Ou Internationals d'Anvers, Bruxelles, Liège et Gand, 1894-1935'. *Studia Politica. Romanian Political Science Review* 8, no. 1 (2008): 75–90.

Vladisavljević, Nebojša. *Serbia's Antibureaucratic Revolution: Milošević, the Fall of Communism and Nationalist Mobilization*. Houndsmills: Palgrave Macmillan, 2008.

Vos, Luc De. *Het effectief van de Belgische Krijgsmacht en de militiewetgeving, 1830–1914*. Brussels: Koninklijk Legermuseum/Musee Royal de l'Armee, 1985.

Vries, Jeronimo De. *Proeve eener geschiedenis der Nederduitsche dichtkunde*. Amsterdam: Johannes Allart, 1810.

Vujačić, Veljko. 'Institutional Origins of Contemporary Serbian Nationalism'. *East European Constitutional Review* 5, no. 4 (1996): 51–61.

Wæver, Ole. 'Identity, Communities and Foreign Policy: Discourse Analysis as Foreign Policy Theory'. In *European Integration and National Identity: The Challenge of the Nordic States*, edited by Lene Hansen and Ole Wæver, 20–49. London/New York: Routledge, 2002.

Wagner, Margaret E. *America and the Great War: A Library of Congress Illustrated History*. New York: Bloomsbury Press, 2017.

Walzer, Michael. 'The State of Israel and the Negation of the Exile'. In *Israel in the World. Legitimacy and Exceptionalism*, edited by Emanuel Adler, 24–31. London: Routledge, 2013.

Waxman, Dov. *The Pursuit of Peace and the Crisis of Israeli Identity. Defending / Defining the Nation*. Basingstoke: Palgrave Macmillan, 2006.

Weber, Eugen. *Peasants into Frenchmen: The Modernization of Rural France, 1870–1914*. London: Chatto & Windus, 1976.

Weiss, Tomáš. *Promoting National Priorities in EU Foreign Policies: The Czech Republic's Foreign Policy in the EU*. Abingdon: Routledge, 2017.

Weizman, Eyal. *Hollow Land. Israel's Architecture of Occupation*. London: Verso, 2017.

Welch Larson, Deborah, T.V. Paul and William C. Wohlforth. 'Status and World Order'. In *Status in World Politics*, edited by Deborah Welch Larson, T.V. Paul and William C. Wohlforth, 3–29. Cambridge: Cambridge University Press, 2014.

Wendt, Alexander. 'Anarchy Is What States Make of It: The Social Construction of Power Politics'. *International Organization* 46, no. 2 (1992): 391–425.

Westerman, Thomas D. 'Rough and Ready Relief. American Identity, Humanitarian Experience, and the Commission for Relief in Belgium, 1914–1917'. PhD, University of Connecticut, 2014.

White, Hayden. *Metahistory. The Historical Imagination in Nineteenth-Century Europe*. Baltimore, MD: Johns Hopkins University Press, 1973.

Willequet, M.J. 'Belgique et Allemagne 1914–1945'. In *Sentiment National En Allemagne et En Belgique, XIXe-XXe Siècles. Colloque Des 25 et 26 Avril 1963*, 59–75. Bruxelles: Editions de l'Institut de sociologie de l'Université libre de Bruxelles, 1964.

Wilson, Woodrow. 'An Address to a Joint Session of Congress, 8 January 1918'. In *The Papers of Woodrow Wilson, Volume 45*, edited by Arthur S. Link, 534–8. Princeton, NJ: Princeton University Press, 1994.

Winklerová, Martina. *Karel Kramář (1860–1937)*. Prague: Argo, 2011.

Withington, Robert. *That These May Eat*. Bloomington, IN: Commission for Relief in Belgium, 1917.

Witte, Els. '1828–1847. De Constructie van België'. In *Nieuwe Geschiedenis van België. Dl. 1: 1830–1905*, edited by Els Witte, Jean-Pierre Nandrin, Eliane Gubin and Gita Deneckere, 27–235. Tielt: Lannoo, 2005.

Wittke, Carl Frederick. *German-Americans and the World War*. Columbus: Ohio State Archaeological and Historical Society, 1936.

Wright, Quincy. 'The Equality of States'. *Cornell International Law Review* 3, no. 1 (1970): 1–7.
Ya'ar, Ephraim. 'Continuity and Change in Israeli Society: The Test of the Melting Pot'. *Israel Studies* 10, no. 2 (2005): 91–128.
Žalud, Aug. 'Das Sozialinstitut der Čechoslovakischen Republik'. In *Die Sozialpolitik in der Čechoslovakischen Republik*, edited by Jos Gruber, 129–37. Prague: Orbis-Verlag, 1924.
Zaorolavá, Růžena and Roman Zaoral. 'Masarykova Státní Škola Zdravotní a Socialní Péče v Meziválečném Obdobi'. *Acta Universitatis Carolinae-Historia Universitatis Carolinae Pragensis* 58 (2018): 191–207.
Zarakol, Ayşe. 'Theorising Hierarchies. An Introduction'. In *Hierarchies in World Politics*, edited by Ayşe Zarakol, 1–14. Cambridge [etc.]: Cambridge University Press, 2017.
Zarakolu, Ayşe Nur. *After Defeat. How the East Learned to Live with the West*. Cambridge/New York: Cambridge University Press, 2010.
Zhordania, Noe. *Chemi Tsarsuli*. Tbilisi: Sarangi, 1990.
Zhordania, Noe. 'Dghevandeli Sakhitkhebi'. *Kvali* 1 (1898): 1–3.
Zhordania, Noe. *Erovnuli Kitkha*. Tblisi: s.l., 1922.

Index

Abdülhamid II 42–3
Agences Alliés 122, 127
Albania 10, 35, 36, 42–6, 50, 51, 52 n.7, 135, 138, 146, 207
Albanian uprisings of 1911 44
Alliance Européene des Agences de Presse 127–8
Allied powers 4, 50, 73, 74–7, 83, 85, 86, 87, 88, 91, 97, 99, 102, 104, 118, 124, 126, 207
anti-Hispanism 16, 18–21
Arabs 188, 190–1, 192, 193, 197
Austria 118; Nazi annexation 108
Austria-Hungary 2, 36, 37, 38, 39, 40, 42, 43, 44, 45, 46, 48, 49, 51, 57, 58, 59, 83, 97, 98, 99, 101, 102, 105, 108, 110, 111 n.6, 135, 137, 138, 145, 207, 208
Axis powers 4, 139, 207

Balkan Wars of 1912–13 133, 137–8
Balkans 35, 38, 41, 44, 46, 51, 133, 134, 136, 141, 145, 147
Beaumont and Fletcher 26
Beck, James M. 85
Begin, Menachem 194, 196
Belga press agency 115
Belgian Congo 65–6
Belgium 2, 11, 48, 56, 57–67, 73–91, 115, 118, 123, 206; aid given 73, 77, 84–90; as exemplary nation 57–8, 59, 61; compared to United States 78–80; model for Romania 60, 61–3, 209; neutrality 60, 62, 66, 68, 91; passive recipients of wartime largesse 82–3, 91; relations with Romania 60–1, 64–5; victim of German aggression 67, 73–91
Beneš, Edvard 101, 102
Ben-Gurion, David 186, 188, 193, 202
Beretty, Dominique Willem 119–20
Big Three press agencies 115, 117, 120, 122, 123, 125, 126, 127, 128, 129
Bismarck, Otto von 42, 62, 65

Bohemia 10, 35, 37–42, 46, 50, 98, 101, 110, 111 n.4, 207
Bohr, Niels 103, 104, 105–6, 109
Bosnia and Herzegovina 133, 135, 136, 137, 138, 140, 142, 143, 144, 145
Brandes, Georg 154, 157
Brazil 8
Brexit 12, 163, 167, 168, 169, 206, 208, 209
Brialmont, Henri-Alexis 60
Britain 2, 12, 16, 17, 19, 42, 48, 50, 51, 57, 74, 83, 111, 117, 153, 155, 158, 163, 206, 207, 208, 210; devolution in 180–1; literary historiography and Spanish Golden Age 24–7; relations with Ireland 167–82
British-Ireland Parliamentary Assembly 12, 167, 168, 169–82
Bryce Report 76, 87
Bulgaria 42, 53 n.42, 108, 137, 139
Business cycle research 99, 100, 107–8, 109, 110

Calderón de la Barca, Pedro 22, 26, 27, 28–9
Camp David negotiations (2000) 186, 196
Canada 161
Central Powers 51, 73, 74, 76, 83, 84, 90, 118
Cervantes, Miguel de 22, 24, 25
Charles V 20
Chavchavadze, Ilia 35, 46–8
China 8, 151, 153, 162, 210
Cold War 4, 5, 6, 12, 36, 56, 158, 159, 210
Comenius, John Amos 98
Comité National de Secours et d'Alimentation 81
Commission for the Relief of Belgium 11, 73, 74, 77–91
Committee on Public Information 88
Congress of Berlin 42, 43, 63, 136
Congress of Paris 59
Congress of Vienna 2

Convention of Paris 1859 59
Corneille, Pierre 28
Ćorović, Vladimir 139
Ćosić, Dobrica 141
Coudert, Frederic R. 86
Crimean War 59
Croatia 135, 136, 139, 140, 142, 143, 144, 145
Crowell, Elisabeth 105
Cuza, Prince Alexandru Ioan 59–60, 62
Czartoryski, Adam 135–6
Czechia (formerly Czech Republic) 36, 52 n.7
Czechoslovak Red Cross 99, 101, 102, 108
Czechoslovakia 4, 11, 36, 97, 98, 99, 100–8, 110, 206, 207; admiration for Denmark 98, 104, 207, 210

Dagmar of Bohemia 98
Danish-Icelandic Act of Union 156, 157
Danish Institute for Economics and History 98
Danish West Indies 104
De Clercq, William 24, 28–9
Denmark 8, 11, 17, 48, 97, 103–6, 107–11, 123, 152, 153, 156, 161, 206, 207, 209, 210; admiration for Czechoslovakia 98, 104; Nazi occupation of 9, 106, 125, 158; relations with Iceland after Iceland's independence 157–8; rule of Iceland 152, 153, 156
Didbin, Charles 24, 25–6
Đinđić, Zoran 145
discourse analysis 8–9
Dual Monarchy 39, 49, 50, 111 n.6
Dutch East Indies 117, 121, 128; uprisings 119–20
Dutch National Information Service 120

Edgar, William C. 80
Eighty Years' War 19
Entente Powers 51
European Central Bank 161
European Common Market 159
European Studies 35, 36
European Union 12, 36, 52 n.7, 206, 208; and Brexit 167–82; and Iceland 153, 160, 161, 162; and Serbia 133, 144–6

federalism 39, 41, 44
financial crisis of 2008 5, 12, 151, 159, 160, 163, 173
Finland 123, 124, 125, 161
Fourteen Points speech 4, 90
France 2, 22, 23, 42, 48, 50, 57, 58, 59, 60, 65, 68, 73, 74, 75, 78, 83, 88, 115, 118, 122, 127, 128, 134, 161, 171
Franqui, Émile 81, 82
Frashëri, Abdyl 43
Frashëri, Sami 35, 42, 43

Garašanin, Ilija 135–6
Gaza Strip 186, 187, 190, 195, 196, 197, 198
General Dutch Press Agency (ANP) 115–16, 120–9
General News and Telegraphy Agency (ANTEA) 119–20
Georgia 10, 35, 36, 46–50, 51, 52 n.7, 207
German News Office 122, 124
Germany 3, 4, 11, 23, 37, 38, 42, 48, 51, 57, 65, 73–6, 77, 85, 98, 102, 106, 108, 109, 111, 115, 116, 117, 121, 123, 124, 125, 126, 127, 128, 134, 137, 139, 154, 161, 171, 207, 208, 209; reported atrocities during World War I 87–91
Goebbels, Joseph 122
Grand Duchy of Luxemburg 67
Great Britain. *See* Britain
Great Depression 103, 107
Great Powers 2, 4, 6, 10, 42–3, 44–6, 47, 48, 51, 59, 61, 62, 63, 67, 99, 109, 115, 116, 135, 147, 205, 211
Greece 44, 134, 136, 137
group 39, 116, 117, 126, 127–8
Gunn, Selskar 100, 104, 105, 108

Habsburg Empire. *See* Austria-Hungary
Havas press agency 115, 117, 123, 124, 125
Hay, John 15
Hell Community 123–6, 128–9
Hemphill, Alexander 78, 80, 86, 87
Herder, Johann Gottfried 28, 154
Higgins, Michael D. 178
Hitchens, Robert 75
Hitler, Adolf 98, 106, 108, 122
Honnold, William L. 86

Hoover, Herbert 73, 80, 81, 82, 83, 84, 87, 88, 92
Hope, Anthony 81
Houžvicová, Amálie 105
Hroch, Miroslav 36
Hungary 4, 102, 135, 139
Hunt, Edward Eyre 81, 82, 86, 87
Huygens, Constantijn 28

Iceland 12, 151–64, 206; anticolonial narrative 155–6; application initiative for EU membership 160–1; relations with US 152, 158–9, 163, 164; reluctance to acknowledge smallness 151–2, 164, 206, 208
Imagology 9–10, 29
Institute for Economics and History 100, 104, 109–10
Institute for Public Health 100, 105, 111
Institute for Theoretical Physics 99, 109
International Criminal Tribunal for the Former Yugoslavia 145
International Health Board 99, 100, 106, 108
International Monetary Fund 152, 153, 159, 160, 162
international relations (IR) 36, 109, 185, 186, 197, 211–12; hierarchy studies within 211
Intifada, First and Second 185, 186, 190, 196, 199
Ireland, Republic of 12, 200, 210; relations with Britain 167–82
Irwin, Will 79, 86, 88, 90
Israel 12, 185–200, 210; alleged misrepresentation of 185, 199–200; as 'David' vs 'Goliath' 185, 187, 188–90, 197, 198, 199, 208; as Western state 190–1; 'Greater Israel' idea 194; Jewishness 187–90, 196, 200
Israel Defense Forces 193
Israeli-Palestinian conflict 12, 185–200, 208
Italian-Turkish War 42
Italy 37, 42, 44, 45, 48, 51, 128, 136, 139

Janina 44
Juncker, Jean-Claude 146

Karađorđe (Đorđe Petrović) 134
Karađorđević, Aleksandar 138
Karadžić, Vuk Stefanović 135
Kellogg, Charlotte 80, 82, 87, 88, 90
Kellogg, Vernon 80, 90
Kernahan, Coulson 75
Kingdom of Serbs, Croats and Slovenes (later Kingdom of Yugoslavia) 138
Kogălniceanu, Mihail 62
Kohn, Hans 56
Kollár, Ján 40
Konica, Faik 44
Kosovo 44, 133, 135, 138, 140, 141, 142, 143, 144, 146, 147; battle of 134, 142; war 144
Koselleck, Reinhart 57, 65
Koštunica, Vojislav 145
Kramář, Karel 35, 37, 38, 39, 40, 41, 44
Krogh, August 103
Kumanovo Peace Treaty 144

League of Nations 4, 110, 118, 121, 122
League of Prizren 42
Lebanon wars 186, 190, 197
Leopold II 62, 65–7
Lewes, George Henry 24, 25, 26
Liechtenstein 8
Liège 75, 85
Lope de Vega, Félix 22, 25, 26, 27, 28
López Madera, Gregorio 21
Louvain 75
Lusitania sinking 87
Luxembourg 2, 17, 130 n.38

Macedonia 135, 137, 138
Machiavelli, Niccolò 3
Maiorescu, Titu 64
Marković, Svetozar 137, 138, 145, 146
Marshall Plan 158
Masaryk, Thomas 35, 37, 38, 39, 40, 41, 42, 44, 50–1, 98–9, 101, 102, 112 n.22, 207
Masaryk State School of Public Health and Social Work 105
Masaryková, Alice 99, 100, 101, 102, 103, 105, 106, 108, 112 n.6
Maurice, Arthur B. 90
McDowell, Mary 101

Mexico 88
Mill, John Stuart 153–4
Milošević, Slobodan 141–4, 145, 147
Milton, John 3
Moldova 58, 59, 61
Moljević, Stevan 139
Monastir 44
Montenegro 42, 43, 133, 135, 137, 142, 143, 144
Montesquieu 3, 8
Moravia 39, 111 n.6
Morvilliers, Nicholas Masson de 22
Muller, Joseph Herbert 27
Munch, Peter 103–4, 109, 110

Napoleonic Wars 2
nationalism 11, 36, 55, 58, 64, 67–8, 106, 134, 155, 159, 169, 177, 196; cultural nationalism in Iceland 153; relation to internationalism 106; in Serbia 136, 139–40, 141–7; 'Western' vs 'Eastern' 55–7, 67
Nazism 100, 106, 121, 122, 123
Netenyahu, Benjamin 191, 193, 196
Netherlands 2, 4, 7–8, 16, 17, 48, 57, 59, 67, 115, 116, 117–29, 207; anti-Spanish rhetoric 19, 22; auto-image as neutral nation 121, 207; difficulties during World War I 117–18, 128; Golden Age 14 n.40, 27; post office (PTT) 119, 121, 124, 130; telecommunications network 117–29; literary historiography and Spanish Golden Age 24, 27–9; question of national theatre 27; relations with Spain 19, 27, 28, 57
Nikezić, Marko 140–6
Nikoladze, Niko 35, 48–50
Noli, Fan 35, 42, 44, 51
Non-Aligned Movement 5
Nordic Council 153
North Atlantic Treaty Organization 36, 52 n.7, 144, 145, 152, 158, 161–2, 208
Northern Ireland 12, 167–82, 210
Norway 48, 123, 125, 161

Obrenović, Miloš 135
Ohlin, Bertil 110

Organization for European Economic Co-operation 159
Orientalism 58, 190
Oslo Group 116, 123
Ottoman Empire 35, 36, 42, 44, 46, 49, 51, 58, 59, 134, 135, 207

Palacký, František 39
pan-Germanism 40, 99, 145
pan-Slavism 40, 41
Pardo Bazán, Emilia 18
Paris Peace Conference 4, 46, 47, 67
partisans 139, 140
Pašić, Nikola 138
Pelt, Adriaan 121, 122
Peres, Shimon 191, 199
peripherality 9, 11, 55, 57, 58, 62, 64, 67, 209
Perjevec, Dušan 141
Peace of Westphalia 1
Philip II 20, 21
Philip of Flanders 62
Plemp van Duiveland, I.J. 118
Poland 108, 122
Portugal 48
Prescott, William Hickling 23
propaganda 11, 18, 19, 116, 117, 118, 128, 197; in World War I 73–91; Nazi Germany's use 122, 126
Prussia 2, 74, 85, 111 n.6, 137

Qemali, Ismail 35, 42–6, 51

Rabin, Yitzhak 197
Racine, Jean 28
Rădulescu, Andrei 63
Rama, Edi 36
Ranković, Aleksandar 140
Rask-Ørsted Foundation 104, 109
Ratzel, Friedrich 3
Realist Party (Czech) 37, 39, 41
Reuters 115, 117, 118, 120, 123, 126, 128
Ritzau press agency 125
Rochau, Ludwig August von 3
Rockefeller Foundation 11, 97, 99–111
Romania 10, 42, 43, 55, 56, 58, 135, 137, 207, 209; anti-Jewish legislation 63; 'Belgium of the East' 61–3, 64, 65, 67,

68, 206; bulwark of Christianity 58, 67; claims of Latin heritage 58, 62; peasant revolt of 1907 66; relations with Belgium 60–1, 64–5
Roosevelt, Theodore 84
Rose, Wickliffe 99, 104
Rosetti, Constantin Alexandru 60
Rousseau, Jean-Jacques 3, 154
Russia 2, 36, 41, 42, 43, 48, 49, 51, 59, 63, 135, 137, 145, 146, 160, 210
Russo-Georgian War 145
Russo-Japanese War 49
Russo-Turkish War 42, 63, 137
Ryelandt, Daniël 115, 127

Sandžak 145
Saroléa, Charles 75
Scavenius, Erik 154
Schiller, Friedrich 28
Schlegel brothers 24, 25
scientific internationalism 11, 98, 103–4, 106–11
Scotland 167, 168, 169, 170, 171, 172, 173, 174, 175, 177, 179, 180, 181, 182
Scutari 44
Serbia 11–12, 42, 43, 133–44; Candlemas and 'Turkish' constitutions 135; expansion after Balkan Wars 138; 'Great Serbia' idea 136, 138, 139, 141–4; hostility to perceptions of smallness 133, 136, 147, 209; irredentism 133, 135, 136, 143; Kosovo Albanians 141, 147; 'Ottoman yoke' in Serbian historiography 134; shrinkage 133, 143
Serbian Radical Party 137, 143, 146
Šešelj, Vojislav 143
Seven Years' War 2
Shaw, George Bernard 86
Sinclair, May 85, 86
Six Day War 193
Silesia 39
Sismondi, Sismonde de 25, 28
Slovenia 139, 142, 144
small state studies 2, 4–6, 151, 211–12
small states: belittling characterization 8, 10, 15–29, 176–7, 206; definitional criteria 6–7; dependence on larger states 152; impartiality 4; inferiority 3; moralization 37, 106; neutrality 9, 128, 157, 206; security concerns 5, 162, 192, 193; superiority 3; wielders of 'soft power' 6; weak or obsolete 15, 16, 36, 38, 43, 51, 209; within size and status hierarchies 7, 208, 211
Smallness: and ethnic particularism 191–2; and foreign policy 157–63, 185, 186, 195, 200, 210; and interdependence, 175 and neutrality 128, 157, 158; constructed through language 186, 192; counter to East-West binaries 55; driver of Irish integration 171–2; taboo subject 9, 151, 164, 206, 208; relative term 8–9, 169, 210–11; to be compensated for 158, 161, 163, 164
Social Darwinism 3, 15
Social Science Research Institute 100, 103, 107–8, 109
South African War 117
Soviet Union 35, 36, 46, 100, 124
Spain 4, 10, 15–29, 59, 207, 209; 'disaster' year of, 1898 15; regarded as 'Oriental' culture 23, 28; Black Legend myth 16, 18–19, 22, 23–6, 207; 'golden age' 18, 22; hostility of Enlightenment intellectuals toward 22; foreign writers' perception of theatre 24–9
Spanish-American War 15, 16, 18, 29
Staël, Madame de 25, 26, 28
State Press Service 120–1
Sudetenland crisis 106, 108, 123
Sweden 4, 115, 123, 125, 161, 210
Switzerland 4, 8–9, 48, 124, 130 n.38

Tito, Josip 140, 141
Transylvania 59
Treaty of Adrianople 58
Treaty of London 74
Treaty of Vienna 10
Treitschke, Heinrich von 3, 4, 8
Triple Alliance 37
Tudman, Franjo 142
Turkey 4, 44

United Kingdom. *See* Britain
United Nations 7, 151
United Nations Charter 1
United Nations Security Council 161

United States 8, 11, 13 n.16, 15, 16, 50, 73; Czech and Slovak immigrants 101; views of Belgium 73, 76–91, 207; relations with Iceland 152, 158–9, 163, 164; hetero-images of Germany during World War I 87–90, 91, 207
University of Chicago Settlement 101, 105

Valdemar II 98
Van de Pol, Herman 115, 116, 123–7, 128, 129
Van de Vyvere, Aloys 73
Van der Essen, Leon 74
Van Karnebeek, H.A. 118
Van Limburg Brouwer, Petrus 24, 27–8
Van Sickle, John 108
Vaz Diaz press agency 120
Vojvodina 135, 140, 141, 142, 143, 144, 145
Vučić, Aleksandar 146, 147

Wardwell, Florence 88
Walcott, Frederick C. 78
Wales 168, 169, 170, 171, 173, 174, 177, 179, 180, 181, 182

Wallachia 58, 59, 61
West Bank 185, 186, 187, 190, 193, 194, 195, 196
William II 76
William of Orange 19
Wilson, Woodrow 4, 76, 88, 90, 157
Withington, Robert 78, 83
Wolff press agency 115, 117, 123
World Bank 152, 159
World War I 3–4, 11, 51, 58, 67, 73–91, 98, 102, 110, 115, 117–18, 120, 137, 139, 153, 154, 206, 207, 210; propaganda in 73–91
World War II 4, 9, 11, 115, 122, 129, 153, 210

Yom Kippur War 194
Young Turks 43, 44
Yugoslav's People's Army 142
Yugoslavia 5, 56, 108, 128, 133–44, 145

Zach, Františzek 135–6
Zahle, Carl Theodor 154
Zhordania, Noe 35, 46, 49–50, 51
Zionism 186, 187, 190, 194, 195

www.ingramcontent.com/pod-product-compliance
Lightning Source LLC
Chambersburg PA
CBHW062135300426
44115CB00012BA/1927